McGRAW-HILL READING

Contributing Authors

Barbara Coulter, Frankie Dungan, Joseph B. Rubin, Carl B. Smith, Shirley Wright

Contributors

The Princeton Review, Time Magazine

McGraw-Hill School Division

A Division of The ***McGraw-Hill*** *Companies*

McGraw-Hill School Division
Two Penn Plaza
New York, New York 10121

Printed in the United States of America

ISBN 0-02-184740-1/6
3 4 5 6 7 8 9 [027/043] 04 03 02 01 00

Macmillan/McGraw-Hill Edition

McGRAW-HILL READING

Authors

James Flood
Jan E. Hasbrouck
James V. Hoffman
Diane Lapp
Angela Shelf Medearis
Scott Paris
Steven Stahl
Josefina Villamil Tinajero
Karen D. Wood

McGraw-Hill School Division
New York Farmington

UNIT 1

PATHWAYS

UNIT 2

A Common Thread

UNIT 3

With Flying Colors

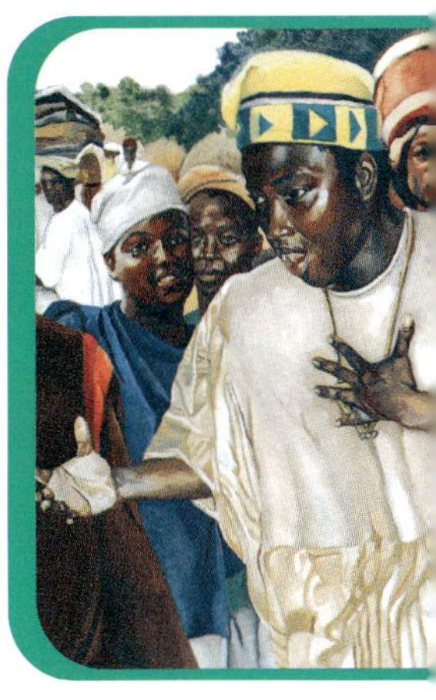

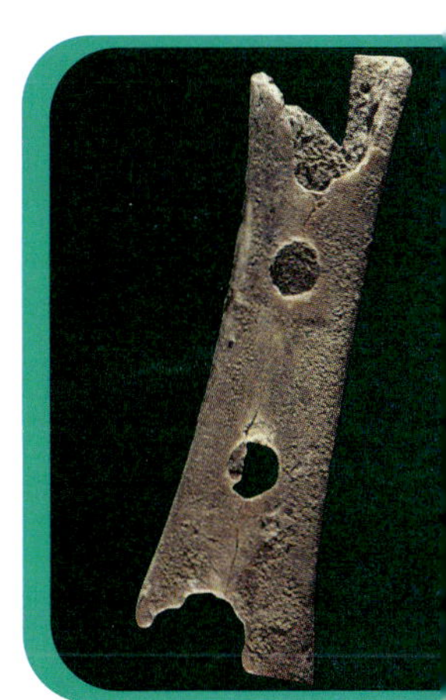

UNIT 4

Seek and Discover

UNIT 5

BRAINSTORMS

UNIT 6

All Things Considered

PATHWAYS

UNIT 1

Come, let us go a-roaming!
        The world is all our own,
And half its paths are still untrod,
        And half its joys unknown.

The way that leads to winter
        Will lead to summer too,
For all roads end in other roads
        Where we may start anew.

by Arthur St. John Adcock

Stories in Art

Fans at sports events are often quick to predict who is going to win. Sometimes their predictions are right. Other times, they have not guessed the outcome.

Look at the painting. What can you tell about the fans and the swimmers at the swim meet? Are the fans watching an exciting race in the pool? How can you tell? What about the swimmers who are sitting? What feelings do most of them show?

Imagine that you are one of the swimmers in the painting. Do you think your team will win? Why or why not? How important is winning to you?

Swim Meet
by Dale Kennington

TAC
TAC
ICE

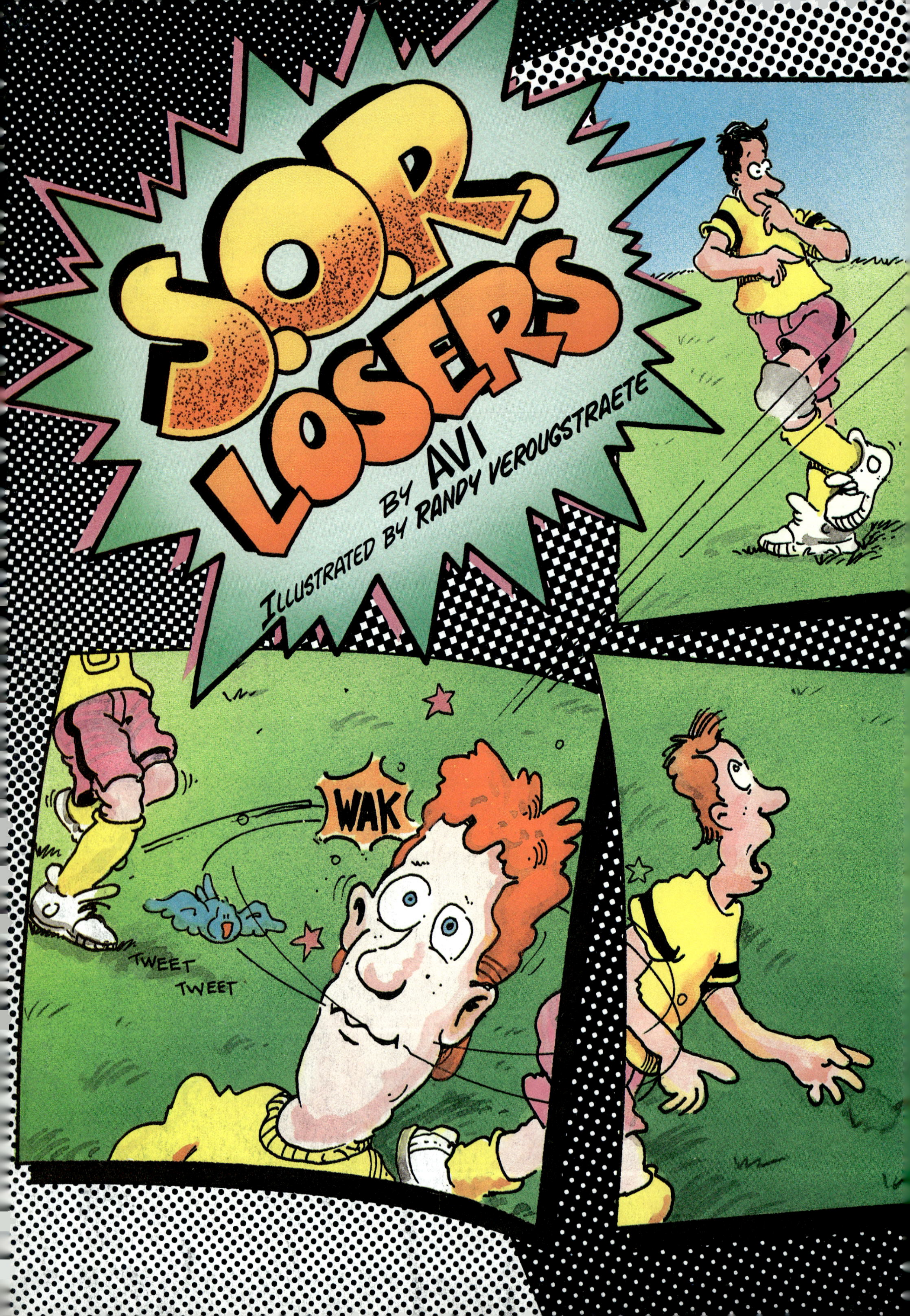
S.O.R. LOSERS
BY AVI
ILLUSTRATED BY RANDY VEROUGSTRAETE
WAK
TWEET
TWEET

ZZZZZ
EACH STUDENT AT SOUTH ORANGE RIVER MIDDLE SCHOOL IS REQUIRED TO PLAY ONE SPORT A YEAR. AFTER ALL, THE SCHOOL IS FAMOUS FOR ITS WINNING TEAMS. BUT ED SITROW AND HIS FRIENDS HAVE MANAGED TO SLIP THROUGH SIXTH GRADE WITHOUT PLAYING A SPORT, SO A SPECIAL SEVENTH GRADE SOCCER TEAM IS CREATED JUST FOR THEM. DESPITE ENCOURAGEMENT FROM EVERYONE, INCLUDING THE COACH, MR. LESTER, AND THE SCHOOL COUNSELOR, MR. TILLMAN, THE TEAM HAS LOST EVERY GAME SO FAR. THE PRESSURE IS ON FOR THEM TO WIN THEIR LAST GAME!

The Tension Builds...

I should have guessed what was going to happen next when this kid from the school newspaper interviewed me. It went this way.

NEWSPAPER: How does it feel to lose every game?

ME: I never played on a team that won, so I can't compare. But it's . . . interesting.

NEWSPAPER: How many teams have you been on?

ME: Just this one.

NEWSPAPER: Do you want to win?

ME: Wouldn't mind knowing what it feels like. For the novelty.

NEWSPAPER: Have you figured out why you lose all the time?

ME: They score more goals.

NEWSPAPER: Have you seen any improvement?

ME: I've been too busy.

NEWSPAPER: Busy with what?

ME: Trying to stop their goals. Ha-ha.

NEWSPAPER: From the scores, it doesn't seem like you've been too successful with that.

ME: You can imagine what the scores would have been if I wasn't there. Actually, I'm the tallest.

NEWSPAPER: What's that have to do with it?

ME: Ask Mr. Lester.

NEWSPAPER: No S.O.R. team has ever lost all its games in one season. How do you feel about that record?

ME: I read somewhere that records are made to be broken.

NEWSPAPER: But how will you feel?

ME: Same as I do now.

NEWSPAPER: How's that?

ME: Fine.

NEWSPAPER: Give us a prediction. Will you win or lose your last game?

ME: As captain, I can promise only one thing.

NEWSPAPER: What's that?

ME: I don't want to be there to see what happens.

Naturally, they printed all that. Next thing I knew some kids decided to hold a pep rally.

"What for?" asked Radosh.

"To fill us full of pep, I suppose."

"What's pep?"

Hays looked it up. "Dash," he read.

Saltz shook his head.

"What's dash?" asked Porter.

"Sounds like a deodorant soap," said Eliscue.

And then Ms. Appleton called me aside. "Ed," she said, sort of whispering (I guess she was embarrassed to be seen talking to any of us), "people are asking, 'Do they *want* to lose?'"

"Who's asking?"

"It came up at the last teachers' meeting. Mr. Tillman thinks you might be encouraging a defeatist attitude in the school. And Mr. Lester . . ."

"What about him?"

"He doesn't know."

It figured. "Ms. Appleton," I said, "why do people care so much if we win or lose?"

"It's your . . . attitude," she said. "It's so unusual. We're not used to . . . well . . . not winning sometimes. Or . . . or not caring if you lose."

"Think there's something the matter with us?" I wanted to know.

"No," she said, but when you say "no" the way she did, slowly, there's lots of

time to sneak in a good hint of "yes." "I don't think you *mean* to lose."

"That's not what I asked."

"It's important to win," she said.

"Why? We're good at other things. Why can't we stick with that?"

But all she said was, "Try harder."

I went back to my seat. "I'm getting nervous," I mumbled.

"About time," said Saltz.

"Maybe we should defect."

"Where to?"

"There must be some country that doesn't have sports."

Then, of course, when my family sat down for dinner that night it went on.

"In two days you'll have your last game, won't you," my ma said. It was false cheerful, as if I had a terminal illness and she wanted to pretend it was only a head cold.

"Yeah," I said.

"You're going to win," my father announced.

"How do you know?" I snapped.

"I sense it."

"Didn't know you could tell the future."

"Don't be so smart," he returned. "I'm trying to be supportive."

"I'm sick of support!" I yelled and left the room.

Twenty minutes later I got a call. Saltz.

"Guess what?" he said.

"I give up."

"Two things. My father offered me a bribe."

"To lose the game?"

"No, to win it. A new bike."

"Wow. What did you say?"

"I told him I was too honest to win a game."

"What was the second thing?"

"I found out that at lunch tomorrow they are doing that pep rally, and worse. They're going to call up the whole team."

I sighed. "Why are they doing all this?" I asked.

"Nobody loves a loser," said Saltz.

"Why?" I asked him, just as I had asked everybody else.

"Beats me. Like everybody else does." He hung up.

I went into my room and flung myself on my bed and stared up at the ceiling. A short time later my father came into the room. "Come on, kid," he said. "I was just trying to be a pal."

"Why can't people let us lose in peace?"

"People think you feel bad."

"We feel *fine!*"

"Come on. We won't talk about it any more. Eat your dinner."

I went.

Next day, when I walked into the school eating area for lunch there was the usual madhouse. But there was also a big banner across the front part of the room:

I wanted to start a food fight right then and there.

I'm not going through the whole bit. But halfway through the lunch period, the president of the School Council, of all people, went to a microphone and called for attention. Then she made a speech.

"We just want to say to the Special Seventh-Grade Soccer Team that we're all behind you."

"It's in front of us where we need people," whispered Saltz. "Blocking."

The president went on. "Would you come up and take a bow." One by one she called our names. Each time one of us went up, looking like cringing but grinning worms, there was some general craziness, hooting, foot stomping, and an occasional milk carton shooting through the air.

The president said: "I'd like the team captain, Ed Sitrow, to say a few words."

What could I do? Trapped, I cleared my throat. Four times. "Ah, well . . . we . . . ah . . . sure . . . hope to get there . . . and . . . you know . . . I suppose . . . play and . . . you know!"

The whole room stood up to cheer. They even began the school chant.

"Give me an S! Give me an O . . . "

After that we went back to our seats. I was madder than ever. And as I sat there, maybe two hundred and fifty kids filed by, thumping me hard on the back, shoulder, neck and head, yelling, "Good luck! Good luck!" They couldn't fool me. I knew what they were doing: beating me.

"Saltz," I said when they were gone and I was merely numb, "I'm calling an emergency meeting of the team."

TEAM
GO
TEAM!
GO!

Secret Meeting...

Like thieves, we met behind the school, out of sight. I looked around. I could see everybody was feeling rotten.

"I'm sick and tired of people telling me we have to win," said Root.

"I think my folks are getting ready to disown me," said Hays. "My brother and sister too."

"Why can't they just let us lose?" asked Macht.

"Yeah," said Barish, "because we're not going to win."

"We might," Lifsom offered. "Parkville is supposed to be the pits too."

"Yeah," said Radosh, "but we're beneath the pits."

"Right," agreed Porter.

For a moment it looked like everyone was going to start to cry.

"I'd just like to do my math," said Macht. "I like that."

There it was. Something clicked. "Hays," I said, "you're good at music, right."

"Yeah, well, sure—rock 'n' roll."

"Okay. And Macht, what's the lowest score you've pulled in math so far?"

"A-plus."

"Last year?"

"Same."

"Lifsom," I went on, getting excited, "how's your painting coming?"

"I just finished something real neat and . . ."

"That's it," I cut in, because that kid can go on forever about his painting. "Every one of us is good at something. Right? Maybe more than one thing. The point is, *other* things."

"Sure," said Barish.

"Except," put in Saltz, "sports."

We were quiet for a moment. Then I saw what had been coming to me: "That's *their* problem. I mean, we are good, good at *lots* of things. Why can't we just plain stink in some places? That's got to be normal."

"Let's hear it for normal," chanted Dorman.

"Doesn't bother me to lose at sports," I said. "At least, it didn't bother me until I let other people make me bothered."

"What about the school record?" asked Porter. "You know, no team ever losing for a whole season. Want to be famous for that?"

"Listen," I said, "did we want to be on this team?"

"No!" they all shouted.

"I can see some of it," I said. "You know, doing something different. But I don't like sports. I'm not good at it. I don't enjoy it. So I say, so what? I mean if Saltz here writes a stinko poem—and he does all the time—do they yell at him? When was the last time Mr. Tillman came around and said, 'Saltz, I *believe* in your being a poet!'"

"Never," said Saltz.

"Yeah," said Radosh. "How come sports is so important?"

"You know," said Dorman, "maybe a loser makes people think of things *they* lost. Like Mr. Tillman not getting into pro football. Us losing makes him remember that."

"Us winning, he forgets," cut in Eliscue.

"Right," I agreed. "He needs us to win for *him,* not for us. Maybe it's the same for others."

"Yeah, but how are you going to convince them of that?" said Barish.

"By not caring if we lose," I said.

"Only one thing," put in Saltz. "They say this Parkville team is pretty bad too. What happens if we, you know, by mistake, win?"

That set us back for a moment.

"I think," suggested Hays after a moment, "that if we

just go on out there, relax, and do our best, and not worry so much, we'll lose."

There was general agreement on that point.

"Do you know what I heard?" said Eliscue.

"What?"

"I didn't want to say it before, but since the game's a home game, they're talking about letting the whole school out to cheer us on to a win."

"You're kidding."

He shook his head.

There was a long, deep silence.

"Probably think," said Saltz, "that we'd be ashamed to lose in front of everybody."

I took a quick count. "You afraid to lose?" I asked Saltz.

"No way."

"Hays?"

"No."

"Porter?"

"Nope."

And so on. I felt encouraged. It was a complete vote of no confidence.

"Well," I said, "they just might see us lose again. With Parkville so bad I'm not saying it's automatic. But I'm not going to care if we do."

"Right," said Radosh. "It's not like we're committing treason or something. People have a right to be losers."

We considered that for a moment. It was then I had my most brilliant idea. "Who has money?"

"What for?"

"I'm your tall captain, right? Trust me. And bring your soccer T-shirts to me in the morning, early."

I collected about four bucks and we split up. I held Saltz back.

"What's the money all about?" he wanted to know. "And the T-shirts."

"Come on," I told him. "Maybe we can show them we really mean it."

When I woke the next morning, I have to admit, I was excited. It wasn't going to be an ordinary day. I looked outside and saw the sun was shining. I thought, "Good."

For the first time I *wanted* a game to happen.

I got to breakfast a little early, actually feeling happy.

"Today's the day," Dad announced.

"Right."

"Today you'll really win," chipped in my ma.

"Could be."

My father leaned across the table and gave me a tap. "Winning the last game is what matters. Go out with your head high, Ed."

"And my backside up if I lose?" I wanted to know.

"Ed," said my ma, "don't be so hard on yourself. Your father and I are coming to watch."

"Suit yourselves," I said, and beat it to the bus.

As soon as I got to class Saltz and I collected the T-shirts. "What are you going to do with them?" the others kept asking.

"You picked me as captain, didn't you?"

"Mr. Lester did."

S.O.R. LOSERS
S.O.R. LOSERS
S.O.R. LOSERS
S.O.R.
S.O.R.

"Well, this time, trust *me.*"

When we got all the shirts, Saltz and I sneaked into the home ec room and did what needed to be done. Putting them into a bag so no one would see, we went back to class.

"Just about over," I said.

"I'm almost sorry," confessed Saltz.

"Me too," I said. "And I can't figure out why."

"Maybe it's—the team that loses together, really stays together."

"Right. Not one fathead on the whole team. Do you think we should have gotten a farewell present for Mr. Lester?"

"Like what?"

"A begging cup."

It was hard getting through the day. And it's impossible to know how many people wished me luck. From all I got it was clear they considered me the unluckiest guy in the whole world. I kept wishing I could have banked it for something important.

But the day got done.

It was down in the locker room, when we got ready, that I passed out the T-shirts.

Barish held his up. It was the regular shirt with "S.O.R." on the back. But under it Saltz and I had ironed on press letters. Now they all read:

S.O.R.
LOSERS

Barish's reaction was just to stare. That was my only nervous moment. Then he cracked up, laughing like crazy. And the rest, once they saw, joined in. When Mr. Lester came down he brought Mr. Tillman. We all stood up and turned our backs to them.

"Oh, my goodness," moaned Mr. Lester.

"That's sick," said Mr. Tillman. "Sick!" His happy beads shook furiously.

"It's honest," I said.

"It's defeatist," he yelled.

"Mr. Tillman," I asked, "is that true, about your trying out for pro football?"

He started to say something, then stopped, his mouth open. "Yeah. I tried to make it with the pros, but couldn't."

"So you lost too, right?"

"Yeah," chimed in Radosh, "everyone loses sometime."

"Listen here, you guys," said Mr. Tillman, "it's no fun being rejected."

"Can't it be okay to lose sometimes? You did. Lots do. You're still alive. And we don't dislike you because of that."

"Right. We got other reasons," I heard a voice say. I think it was Saltz.

Mr. Tillman started to say something, but turned and fled.

Mr. Lester tried to give us a few final pointers, like don't touch the ball with our hands, only use feet, things that we didn't always remember to do.

"Well," he said finally, "I enjoyed this."

"You did?" said Porter, surprised.

"Well, not much," he admitted. "I never coached anything before. To tell the truth, I don't know anything about soccer."

"Now you tell us," said Eliscue. But he was kidding. We sort of guessed that before.

Just as we started out onto the field, Saltz whispered to me, "What if we win?"

"With our luck, we will," I said.

And on we went.

Meet... Avi

Avi and the characters he created for *S.O.R. Losers* know something about failure and losing, and they share the experience of turning defeat into victory.

It may come as quite a surprise to learn that this successful author once had problems with writing and needed a summer tutor to keep from failing high school English. That summer, as he learned how to write, Avi also learned something else—that he really wanted to write. He recalls, "It was the one thing everybody said I could not do."

It was not until Avi had his own children that he thought about writing books for a young audience. He quickly discovered just how much he enjoyed trying to communicate with young people.

Avi gets reactions about early manuscript drafts from some very tough critics—his children, his wife, and local school students. He reworks his stories, over and over, until they are just right, for he believes in giving his readers his very best.

The care he takes in his writing shows. His novel *The True Confessions of Charlotte Doyle* was a Newbery Honor Book in 1991. Other award winners include *The Fighting Ground, Encounter at Easton,* and *Man from the Sky.*

1. How did Ed and his teammates get to be on the soccer team?
2. Why do the S.O.R. teammates not mind losing games?
3. Why is it so important to everyone else that the soccer team win?
4. Do you think the S.O.R. Losers will win the last game of the season? Explain your prediction.
5. Imagine that the S.O.R. Losers stepped into the painting on pages 18–19. What do you think they would say to the students on the swimming team?

Write a Personal Narrative

To nearly everyone at school, winning is important. Yet to the S.O.R. Losers, it's okay to lose. How do you feel about winning and losing? Use your own experience to write a personal narrative about a time you won or lost. How did it make you feel?

Create a Mural

Each student at South Orange River Middle School is required to play one sport a year. What about your school? Does every student play a sport? Plan a mural of sports played at your school. Use a long sheet of paper, markers or paints, and photographs or magazine clippings to create your sports mural.

Design a Logo

Ed makes up special T-shirts for his team that say "S.O.R. Losers." Now it's your turn. Create a T-shirt logo or design for a team or a group that is important to you. Then explain to a partner why you chose this design.

Find Out More

The S.O.R. Losers had a coach who had never coached anything before. Suppose you were asked to coach a soccer team. Would you know what to do? What are the rules of the game? Start by looking in an encyclopedia or in a book about soccer. Use what you learn to compare soccer with a sport that is popular at your school.

Conduct an Interview

In this story, a reporter from the school newspaper interviews Ed Sitrow about the losing soccer team. No sooner is the interview printed than some students decide to hold a pep rally for the team. What is an interview? What makes it a powerful tool?

Like a conversation, an **interview** follows a pattern of questions and answers. To prepare for an interview, first find out about the person you will be interviewing. Then decide the questions you will ask. A good way to make an interview flow smoothly is to make a note card of questions you will ask. Here is also a list of speaking and listening guidelines that will make your interview more effective.

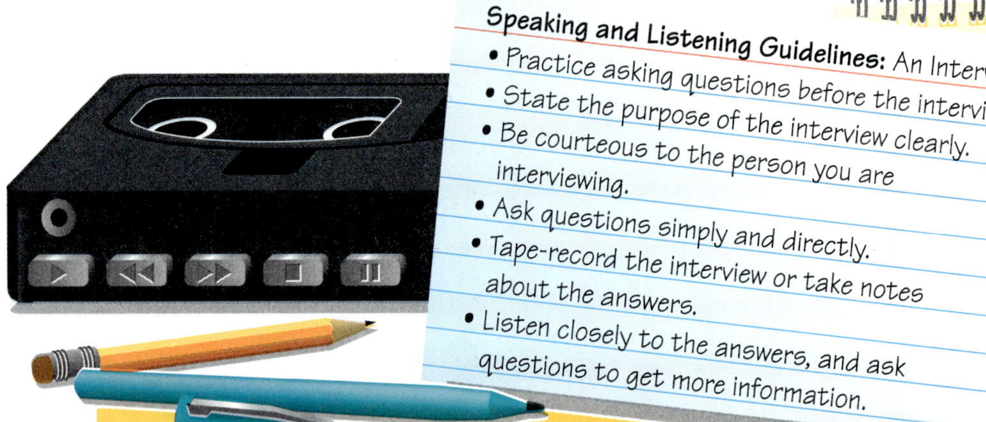
Speaking and Listening Guidelines: An Interview

- Practice asking questions before the interview.
- State the purpose of the interview clearly.
- Be courteous to the person you are interviewing.
- Ask questions simply and directly.
- Tape-record the interview or take notes about the answers.
- Listen closely to the answers, and ask questions to get more information.

Use the guidelines for an interview to answer these questions.

1. Why should you practice asking questions before the interview?
2. Why is it important to state the purpose of the interview?
3. Why is tape-recording the interview a good idea?
4. How can good speaking and listening skills help make your interview more effective?
5. What makes an interview an important source of information?

TEST POWER

Test Tip

Make sure you read each question slowly and carefully.

DIRECTIONS

Read the sample story. Then read each question about the story.

SAMPLE

How to Make Your Own Paper

You might not realize it, but making your own paper is a simple and environmentally friendly project. (Make sure that you have parental supervision for this craft.)

In a food processor, mix a handful of shredded newspaper and some water. Add more paper until you have a large, gray clump.

Put a small, flat screen at the bottom of a basin that contains 12 cups water and 2 tablespoons glue mixed together. Add the processed clump of paper to the basin. Mix the paper clump into the water/glue mixture thoroughly. Flatten the mixture onto the screen. Slowly lift the screen up, catching the paper mixture in it. Let the water drain from the screen until the paper is dry.

1 You can tell from the passage that —

- **A** this project takes many days to complete
- **B** you will need glue for this project
- **C** this project will require use of an oven
- **D** paper clips are needed to make the paper

2 After the paper is dry, what will probably happen next?

- **F** It will be put into the food processor.
- **G** It will be torn up.
- **H** It will be removed from the screen.
- **J** It will be thrown away.

Why are these answers correct? Explain.

Stories in Art

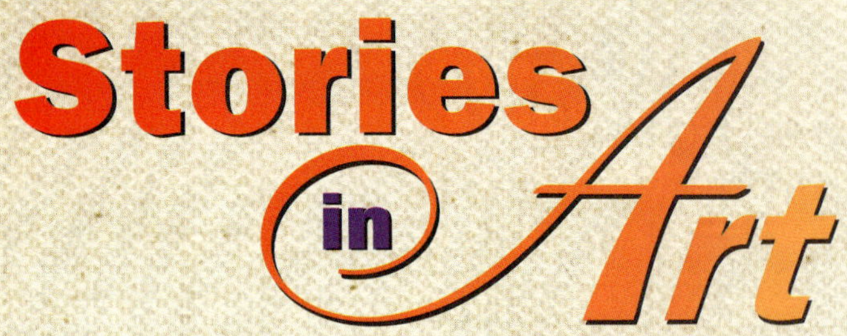

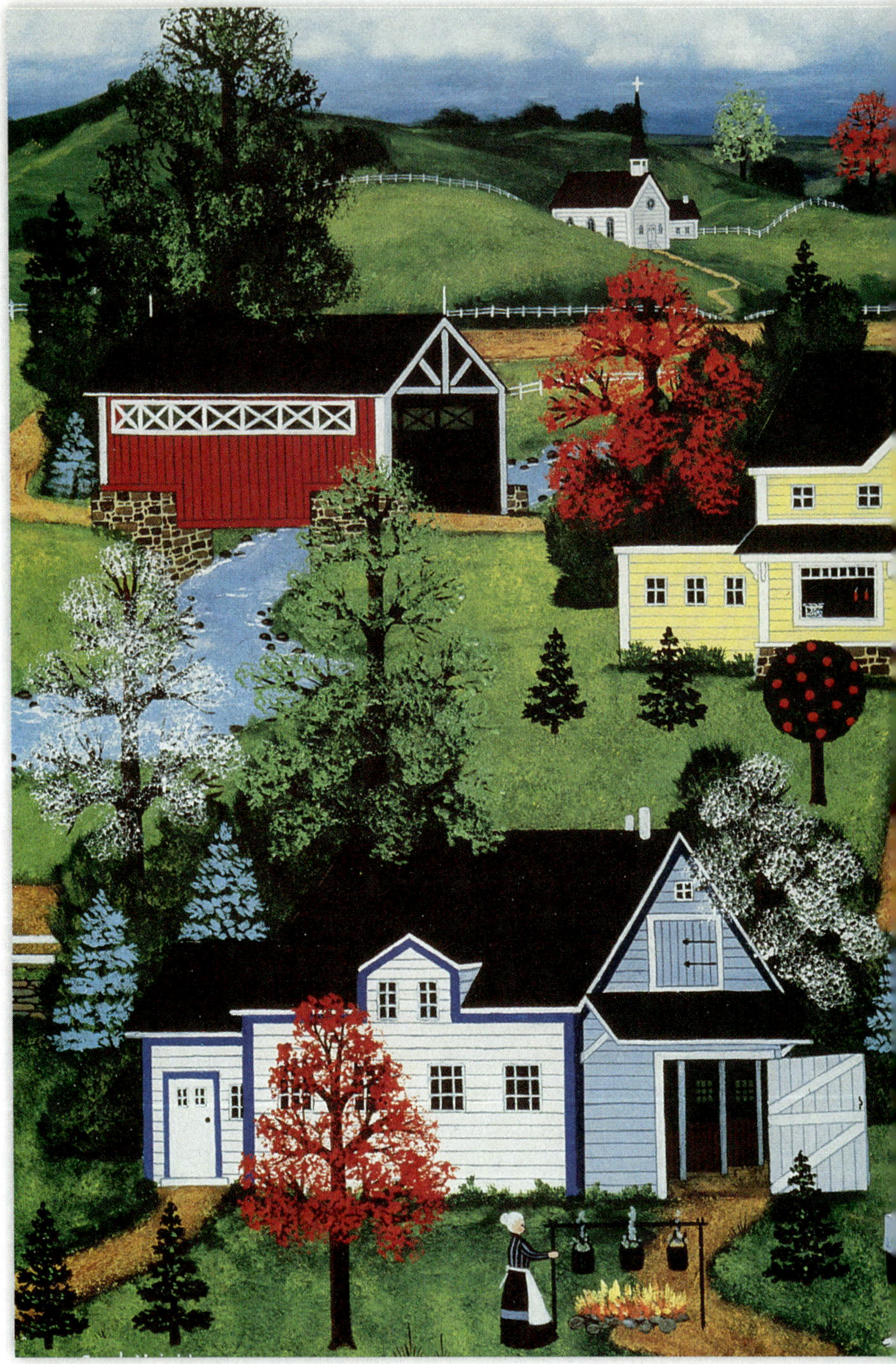

Few American paintings show events in rural America as well as this one. What makes this so? Would the scene be different today? How?

Look at the painting. What is the center of interest? How does the artist focus your eye on the event? What are most of the people doing in the picture? What did they do first to build the house? What will they do after they put on the roof? What will they do last?

Notice the title of the painting. What makes these people "good neighbors"? What about you? Are you a good neighbor? Explain.

Good Neighbors
by Jane Wooster Scott

MEET LENSEY NAMIOKA

For Lensey Namioka, writing about different cultures is second nature. Born in China in 1929, Namioka went to college in the United States. There, she met her husband Isaac Namioka, a Japanese American. Since she is a member of three cultures—Chinese, Japanese, and American, it is easy to imagine that many of the events in *The All-American Slurp* might have happened to Lensey Namioka and her family.

Namioka has also written a play, travel books about China and Japan, and novels such as *Den of the White Fox.* "The more important the author's message," Namioka says, "the more fun her books should be."

MEET YOSHI MIYAKE

Yoshi Miyake was born and raised in Tokyo, Japan. Both her uncle and great uncle were painters, and Miyake always loved drawing and painting. Although she began her college studies in chemistry, she still had a very strong desire to become an artist. Thus, after she finished college, she came to Chicago to study art and illustration.

Miyake began her art career in advertising, but soon began working as a children's book illustrator. "My real love is illustration and my favorite subjects are children and animals," she says. Illustrating children's books is the perfect job for Miyake. "I think it is the best when your hobby is your work," she claims. "Because of this, I am a very lucky person."

As someone who grew up in Japan and then moved to the United States, Miyake can appreciate the changes in customs required for a family like the Lins in *The All-American Slurp.* Miyake has always enjoyed the challenges of adjusting to life in a new country. She has a great interest in other cultures and languages. Besides her knowledge of Japanese and English, she has also studied Dutch and German. She has spent time learning the language and customs of the Native American Sioux and Blackfoot peoples, as well.

Today, Miyake lives in Chicago. She has received numerous awards and honors for her work. Besides illustration and her many pets, Miyake enjoys skiing and hiking.

THE ALL-AMERICAN
Slurp
ILLUSTRATED BY YOSHI MIYAKE
WRITTEN BY LENSEY NAMIOKA

The first time our family was invited out to dinner in America, we disgraced ourselves while eating celery. We had emigrated to this country from China, and during our early days here we had a hard time with American table manners.

In China we never ate celery raw, or any other kind of vegetable raw. We always had to disinfect the vegetables in boiling water first. When we were presented with our first relish tray, the raw celery caught us unprepared.

We had been invited to dinner by our neighbors, the Gleasons. After arriving at the house, we shook hands with our hosts and packed ourselves into a sofa. As our family of four sat stiffly in a row, my younger brother and I stole glances at our parents for a clue as to what to do next.

Mrs. Gleason offered the relish tray to Mother. The tray looked pretty, with its tiny red radishes, curly sticks of carrots, and long, slender stalks of pale green celery. "Do try some of the celery, Mrs. Lin," she said. "It's from a local farmer, and it's sweet."

Mother picked up one of the green stalks, and Father followed suit. Then I picked up a stalk, and my brother did too. So there we sat, each with a stalk of celery in our right hand.

Mrs. Gleason kept smiling. "Would you like to try some of the dip, Mrs. Lin? It's my own recipe: sour cream and onion flakes, with a dash of Tabasco sauce."

Most Chinese don't care for dairy products, and in those days I wasn't even ready to drink fresh milk. Sour cream sounded perfectly revolting. Our family shook our heads in unison.

Mrs. Gleason went off with the relish tray to the other guests, and we carefully watched to see what they did. Everyone seemed to eat the raw vegetables quite happily.

Mother took a bite of her celery. *Crunch.* "It's not bad!" she whispered.

Father took a bite of his celery. *Crunch.* "Yes, it *is* good," he said, looking surprised.

I took a bite, and then my brother. *Crunch, crunch.* It was more than good; it was delicious. Raw celery has a slight sparkle, a zingy taste that you don't get in cooked celery. When Mrs. Gleason came around with the relish tray, we each took another stalk of celery, except my brother. He took two.

There was only one problem: long strings ran through the length of the stalk, and they got caught in my teeth. When I help my mother in the kitchen, I always pull the strings out before slicing celery.

I pulled the strings out of my stalk. *Z-z-zip, z-z-zip.* My brother followed suit. *Z-z-zip, z-z-zip.* To my left, my parents were taking care of their own stalks. *Z-z-zip, z-z-zip, z-z-zip.*

Suddenly I realized that there was dead silence except for our zipping. Looking up, I saw that the eyes of everyone in the room were on our family. Mr. and Mrs. Gleason, their daughter Meg, who was my friend, and their neighbors the Badels—they were all staring at us as we busily pulled the strings of our celery.

That wasn't the end of it. Mrs. Gleason announced that dinner was served and invited us to the dining table. It was lavishly covered with platters of food, but we couldn't see any chairs around the table. So we helpfully carried over some dining chairs and sat down. All the other guests just stood there.

Mrs. Gleason bent down and whispered to us, "This is a buffet dinner. You help yourselves to some food and eat it in the living room."

Our family beat a retreat back to the sofa as if chased by enemy soldiers. For the rest of the evening, too mortified to go back to the dining table, I nursed a bit of potato salad on my plate.

Next day Meg and I got on the school bus together. I wasn't sure how she would feel about me after the spectacle our family made at the party. But she was just the same as usual, and the only reference she made to the party was, "Hope you and your folks got enough to eat last night. You certainly didn't take very much. Mom never tries to figure out how much food to prepare. She just puts everything on the table and hopes for the best."

I began to relax. The Gleasons' dinner party wasn't so different from a Chinese meal after all. My mother also puts everything on the table and hopes for the best.

Meg was the first friend I had made after we came to America. I eventually got acquainted with a few other kids in school, but Meg was still the only real friend I had.

My brother didn't have any problems making friends. He spent all his time with some boys who were teaching him baseball, and in no time he could speak English much faster than I could—not better, but faster.

I worried more about making mistakes, and I spoke carefully, making sure I could say everything right before opening my mouth. At least I had a better accent than my parents, who never really got rid of their Chinese accent, even years later. My parents had both studied English in school before coming to America, but what they had studied was mostly written English, not spoken.

Father's approach to English was a scientific one. Since Chinese verbs have no tense, he was fascinated by the way English verbs changed form according to whether they were in the present, past imperfect, perfect, pluperfect, future, or future perfect tense. He was always making diagrams of verbs and their inflections, and he looked for opportunities to show off his mastery of the pluperfect and future perfect tenses, his two favorites. "I shall have finished my project by Monday," he would say smugly.

Mother's approach was to memorize lists of polite phrases that would cover all possible social situations. She was constantly muttering things like, "I'm fine, thank you. And you?" Once she accidentally stepped on someone's foot and hurriedly blurted, "Oh, that's quite all right!" Embarrassed by her slip, she resolved to do better next time. So when someone stepped on *her* foot, she cried, "You're welcome!"

In our own different ways, we made progress in learning English. But I had another worry, and that was my appearance. My brother didn't have to worry, since Mother bought him blue jeans for school, and he dressed like all the other boys. But she insisted that girls had to wear skirts. By the time she saw that Meg and the other girls were wearing jeans, it was too late. My school clothes were bought already, and we didn't have money left to buy new outfits for me. We had too many other things to buy first, like furniture, pots, and pans.

The first time I visited Meg's house, she took me upstairs to her room, and I wound up trying on her clothes. We were pretty much the same size, since Meg was shorter and thinner than average. Maybe that's how we became friends in the first place. Wearing Meg's jeans and T-shirt, I looked at myself in the mirror. I could almost pass for an

American—from the back, anyway. At least the kids in school wouldn't stop and stare at me in the hallways, which was what they did when they saw me in my white blouse and navy blue skirt that went a couple of inches below the knees.

When Meg came to my house, I invited her to try on my Chinese dresses, the ones with a high collar and slits up the sides. Meg's eyes were bright as she looked at herself in the mirror. She struck several sultry poses, and we nearly fell over laughing.

The dinner party at the Gleasons' didn't stop my growing friendship with Meg. Things were getting better for me in other ways too. Mother finally bought me some jeans at the end of the month, when Father got his paycheck. She wasn't in any hurry about buying them at first, until I worked on her. This is what I did. Since we didn't have a car in those days, I often ran down to the neighborhood store to pick up things for her. The groceries cost less at a big supermarket, but the closest one was many blocks away. One day, when she ran out of flour, I offered to borrow a bike from our neighbor's son and buy a ten-pound bag of flour at the big supermarket. I mounted the boy's bike and waved to Mother. "I'll be back in five minutes!"

Before I started pedaling, I heard her voice behind me. "You can't go out in public like that! People can see all the way up to your thighs!"

"I'm sorry," I said innocently. "I thought you were in a hurry to get the flour." For dinner we were going to have pot-stickers (fried Chinese dumplings), and we needed a lot of flour.

"Couldn't you borrow a girl's bicycle?" complained Mother. "That way your skirt won't be pushed up."

"There aren't too many of those around," I said. "Almost all the girls wear jeans while riding a bike, so they don't see any point buying a girl's bike."

We didn't eat pot-stickers that evening, and Mother was thoughtful. Next day we took the bus downtown and she bought me a pair of jeans. In the same week, my brother made the baseball team of his junior high school, Father started taking driving lessons, and Mother discovered rummage sales. We soon got all the furniture we needed, plus a dart board and a 1,000-piece jigsaw puzzle (fourteen hours later, we discovered that it was a 999-piece jigsaw puzzle). There was hope that the Lins might become a normal American family after all.

Then came our dinner at the Lakeview restaurant.

The Lakeview was an expensive restaurant, one of those places where a headwaiter dressed in tails conducted you to your seat, and the only light came from candles and flaming desserts. In one corner of the room a lady harpist played tinkling melodies.

Father wanted to celebrate, because he had just been promoted. He worked for an electronics company, and after his English started improving, his superiors decided to appoint him to a position more suited to his training. The promotion not only brought a higher salary but was also a tremendous boost to his pride.

Up to then we had eaten only in Chinese restaurants. Although my brother and I were becoming fond of hamburgers, my parents didn't care much for western food, other than chow mein.

Menu

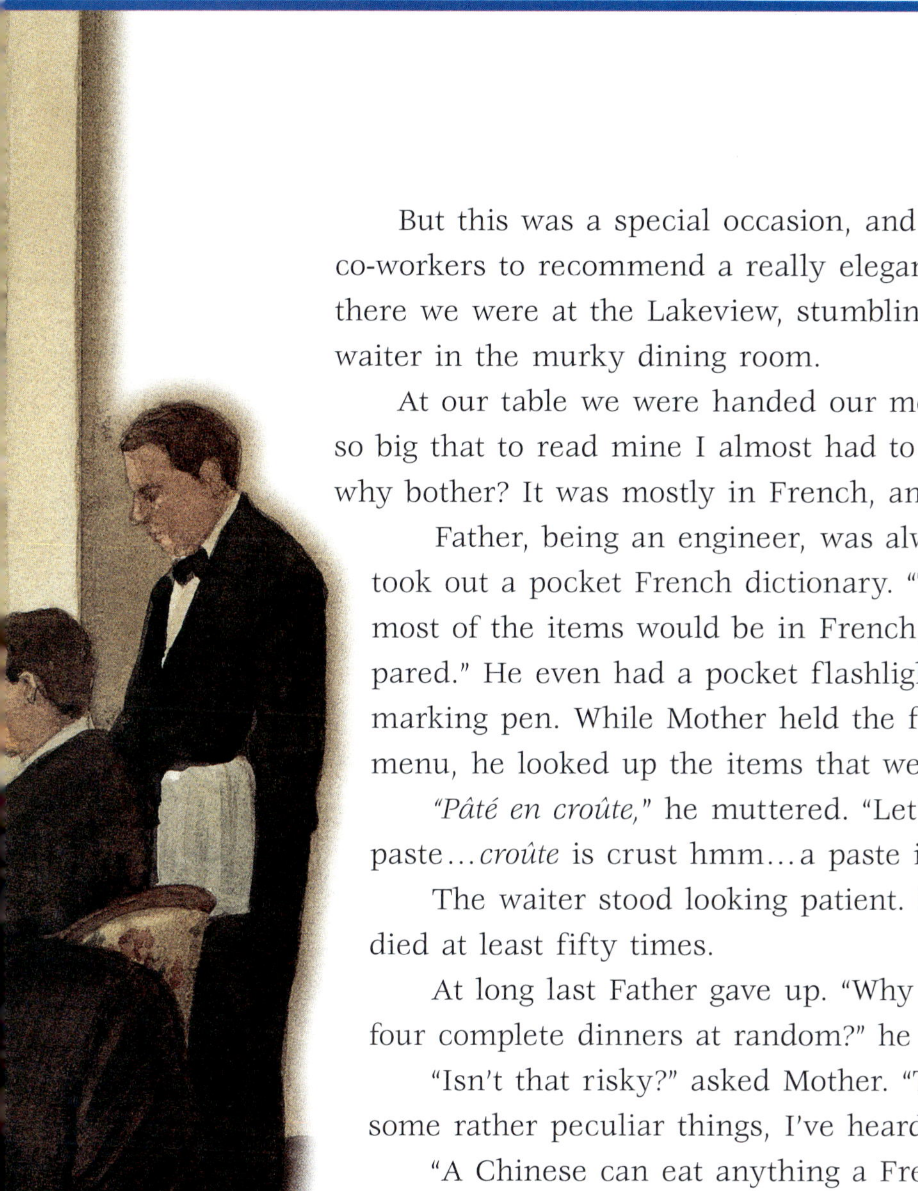

But this was a special occasion, and Father asked his co-workers to recommend a really elegant restaurant. So there we were at the Lakeview, stumbling after the head-waiter in the murky dining room.

At our table we were handed our menus, and they were so big that to read mine I almost had to stand up again. But why bother? It was mostly in French, anyway.

Father, being an engineer, was always systematic. He took out a pocket French dictionary. "They told me that most of the items would be in French, so I came prepared." He even had a pocket flashlight, the size of a marking pen. While Mother held the flashlight over the menu, he looked up the items that were in French.

"Pâté en croûte," he muttered. "Let's see...*pâté* is paste...*croûte* is crust hmm...a paste in crust."

The waiter stood looking patient. I squirmed and died at least fifty times.

At long last Father gave up. "Why don't we just order four complete dinners at random?" he suggested.

"Isn't that risky?" asked Mother. "The French eat some rather peculiar things, I've heard."

"A Chinese can eat anything a Frenchman can eat," Father declared.

The soup arrived in a plate. How do you get soup up from a plate? I glanced at the other diners, but the ones at the nearby tables were not on their soup course, while the more distant ones were invisible in the darkness.

Fortunately my parents had studied books on western etiquette before they came to America. "Tilt your plate," whispered my mother. "It's easier to spoon the soup up that way."

She was right. Tilting the plate did the trick. But the etiquette book didn't say anything about what you did after the soup reached your lips. As any respectable Chinese knows, the correct way to eat your soup is to slurp. This helps to cool the liquid and prevent you from burning your lips. It also shows your appreciation.

We showed our appreciation. *Shloop,* went my father. *Shloop,* went my mother. *Shloop, shloop,* went my brother, who was the hungriest.

The lady harpist stopped playing to take a rest. And in the silence, our family's consumption of soup suddenly seemed unnaturally loud. You know how it sounds on a rocky beach when the tide goes out and the water drains from all those little pools? They go *shloop, shloop, shloop.* That was the Lin family, eating soup.

At the next table a waiter was pouring wine. When a large *shloop* reached him, he froze. The bottle continued to pour, and red wine flooded the tabletop and into the lap of a customer. Even the customer didn't notice anything at first, being also hypnotized by the *shloop, shloop, shloop.*

It was too much. "I need to go to the toilet," I mumbled, jumping to my feet. A waiter, sensing my urgency, quickly directed me to the ladies' room.

I splashed cold water on my burning face, and as I dried myself with a paper towel, I stared into the mirror. In this perfumed ladies' room, with its pink-and-silver wall paper and marbled sinks, I looked completely out of place. What was I doing here? What was our family doing in the Lakeview restaurant? In America?

The door to the ladies' room opened. A woman came in and glanced curiously at me. I retreated into one of the toilet cubicles and latched the door.

Time passed—maybe half an hour, maybe an hour. Then I heard the door open again, and my mother's voice. "Are you in there? You're not sick, are you?"

There was real concern in her voice. A girl can't leave her family just because they slurp their soup. Besides, the toilet cubicle had a few drawbacks as a permanent residence. "I'm all right," I said, undoing the latch.

Mother didn't tell me how the rest of the dinner went, and I didn't want to know. In the weeks following, I managed to push the whole thing into the back of my mind, where it jumped out at me only a few times a day. Even now, I turn hot all over when I think of the Lakeview restaurant.

But by the time we had been in this country for three months, our family was definitely making progress toward becoming Americanized. I remember my parents' first PTA meeting. Father wore a neat suit and tie, and Mother put on her first pair of high heels. She stumbled only once. They met my homeroom teacher and beamed as she told them that I would make honor roll soon at the rate I was going. Of course Chinese etiquette forced Father to say that I was a very stupid girl and Mother to protest that the teacher was showing favoritism toward me. But I could tell they were both very proud.

The day came when my parents announced that they wanted to give a dinner party. We had invited Chinese friends to eat with us before, but this dinner was going to be different. In addition to a Chinese-American family, we were going to invite the Gleasons.

"Gee, I can hardly wait to have dinner at your house," Meg said to me. "I just *love* Chinese food."

That was a relief. Mother was a good cook, but I wasn't sure if people who ate sour cream could also eat chicken gizzards stewed in soy sauce.

Mother decided not to take a chance with chicken gizzards. Since we had western guests, she set the table with large dinner plates, which we never used in Chinese meals. In fact we didn't use individual plates at all, but picked up food from the platters in the middle of the table and brought it directly to our rice bowls. Following the practice of Chinese-American restaurants, Mother also placed large serving spoons on the platters.

The dinner started well. Mrs. Gleason exclaimed at the beautifully arranged dishes of food: the colorful candied fruit in the sweet-and-sour pork dish, the noodle-thin shreds of chicken meat stir-fried with tiny peas, and the glistening pink prawns in a ginger sauce.

At first I was too busy enjoying my food to notice how the guests were doing. But soon I remembered my duties. Sometimes guests were too polite to help themselves and you had to serve them with more food.

I glanced at Meg, to see if she needed more food, and my eyes nearly popped out at the sight of her plate. It was piled with food: the sweet-and-sour meat pushed right against the chicken shreds, and the chicken sauce ran into the prawns. She had been taking food from a second dish before she finished eating her helping from the first!

Horrified, I turned to look at Mrs. Gleason. She was dumping rice out of her bowl and putting it on her dinner plate. Then she ladled prawns and gravy on top of the rice and mixed everything together, the way you mix sand, gravel, and cement to make concrete.

I couldn't bear to look any longer, and I turned to Mr. Gleason. He was chasing a pea around his plate. Several times he got it to the edge, but when he tried to pick it up with his chopsticks, it rolled back toward the center of the plate again. Finally he put down his chopsticks and picked up the pea with his fingers. He really did! A grown man!

All of us, our family and the Chinese guests, stopped eating to watch the activities of the Gleasons. I wanted to giggle. Then I caught my mother's eyes on me. She frowned and shook her head slightly, and I understood the message: the Gleasons were not used to Chinese ways, and they were just coping the best they could. For some reason I thought of celery strings.

When the main courses were finished, Mother brought out a platter of fruit. "I hope you weren't expecting a sweet

dessert," she said. "Since the Chinese don't eat dessert, I didn't think to prepare any."

"Oh, I couldn't possibly eat dessert!" cried Mrs. Gleason. "I'm simply stuffed!"

Meg had different ideas. When the table was cleared, she announced that she and I were going for a walk. "I don't know about you, but I feel like dessert," she told me, when we were outside. "Come on, there's a Dairy Queen down the street. I could use a big chocolate milkshake!"

Although I didn't really want anything more to eat, I insisted on paying for the milkshakes. After all, I was still hostess.

Meg got her large chocolate milkshake and I had a small one. Even so, she was finishing hers while I was only half done. Toward the end she pulled hard on her straws and went *shloop, shloop.*

"Do you always slurp when you eat a milkshake?" I asked, before I could stop myself.

Meg grinned. "Sure. All Americans slurp."

1. What happens at the first dinner party the Lin family attends?
2. Why does the narrator want her mother to buy her some jeans? Give two reasons.
3. Why is it hard for the Lin family to adapt to a new culture? Explain.
4. What are the important events in this story? Give them in the order in which they happened.
5. How do you think the narrator in this story would feel about the S.O.R. Losers?

Write a Diary Entry

How did you feel when you had to adjust to something new? One way to make sense of your experiences is by keeping a diary.

Write a diary entry about how you adjusted to something new. Begin with a chart of two columns, labeled What Happened and Feelings. Put facts and events in the first column and your feelings about them in the second. Then use your chart to write your diary entry.

Create a Chinese Cookbook

In the story, the Lins prepared and ate Chinese food. Find a book on Chinese cooking in the library. Choose three recipes you think the Lin family would enjoy. Copy the recipes and use them to design a small Chinese cookbook. Then add facts about the ingredients, the method of cooking, and some Chinese customs and traditions.

Make a Multimedia Display

The Lins' Chinese customs and culture are different from those of their new American friends. Choose someone you know from another country who has come to live in the United States. Interview the person on audio- or videocassette. Use the tape as the basis for a multimedia display about the person's country and culture.

Find Out More

The Lins are from China. China is the third largest country in the world in square miles, and it has more people than any other country. Read about China in an encyclopedia or another book. Discover five interesting facts about China's history, culture, or people. Draw a map, a picture, or a diagram to illustrate one of your interesting facts.

Use a Dictionary

In the restaurant, Mr. Lin looks up the French word *pâté* in a dictionary. A French-English dictionary gives the English translations of French words and the French translations of English words. Most English dictionaries, however, have some foreign words and phrases, so you may not need a special dictionary to look up these words. If Mr. Lin had been using an ordinary English dictionary, he might have found the homographs below. **Homographs** are words that are spelled the same but have different meanings and often different pronunciations.

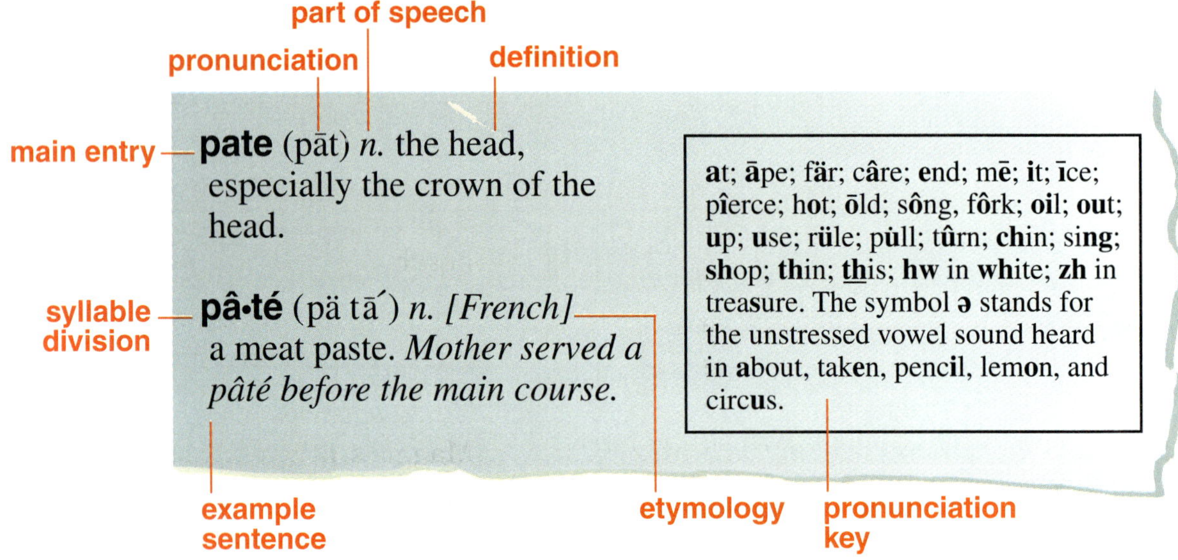

Use the dictionary entries above to answer these questions.

1. Which entry would be more helpful in a restaurant?
2. Which part of speech are these homographs?
3. Which word is pronounced with two syllables? How can you tell?
4. When two words are spelled the same, how can you tell which word you want?
5. Why do you think it is important to know how to use a dictionary?

TEST POWER

Test Tip

Always answer all questions.

DIRECTIONS

Read the sample story. Then read each question about the story.

SAMPLE

The Seashell Lady

Maggie Burke loved to look for seashells. Every weekend, she walked along the shore and gathered seashells. Maggie was lucky; she lived on the coast of England, where beautiful seashells were plentiful. She often walked along the bottoms of high cliffs in search of the perfect shell. She had to be watchful, though. If the tide came up, she would have to walk through the water to get back home.

Maggie often found perfect seashells. She found several seashells that were so extraordinary that local collectors offered her money for them. It didn't take long for people to realize that Maggie was not only lucky, but she also had an eye for beauty. As she grew older, she made many remarkable seashell discoveries and became famous in England as the "Seashell Lady."

1 How did people feel about Maggie at the end of the story?

A They were angry that she was taking shells off the beach.

B They felt afraid that the tide might rise too quickly.

C They were respectful of Maggie's talents.

D They felt disappointed that so many of the shells Maggie found were perfect.

2 In this passage, the word plentiful means —

F many

G few

H not enough

J only one kind

Stories in Art

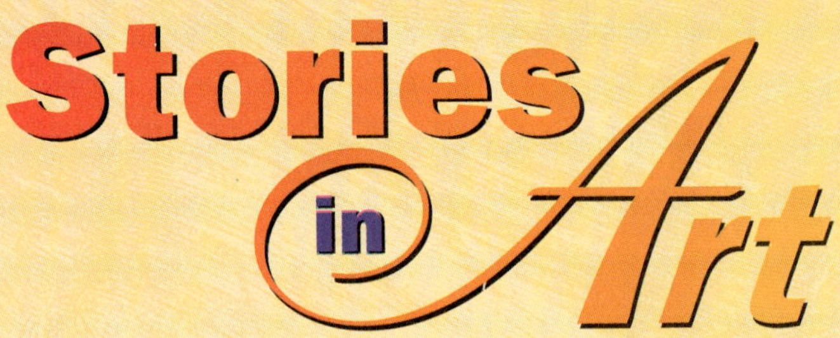

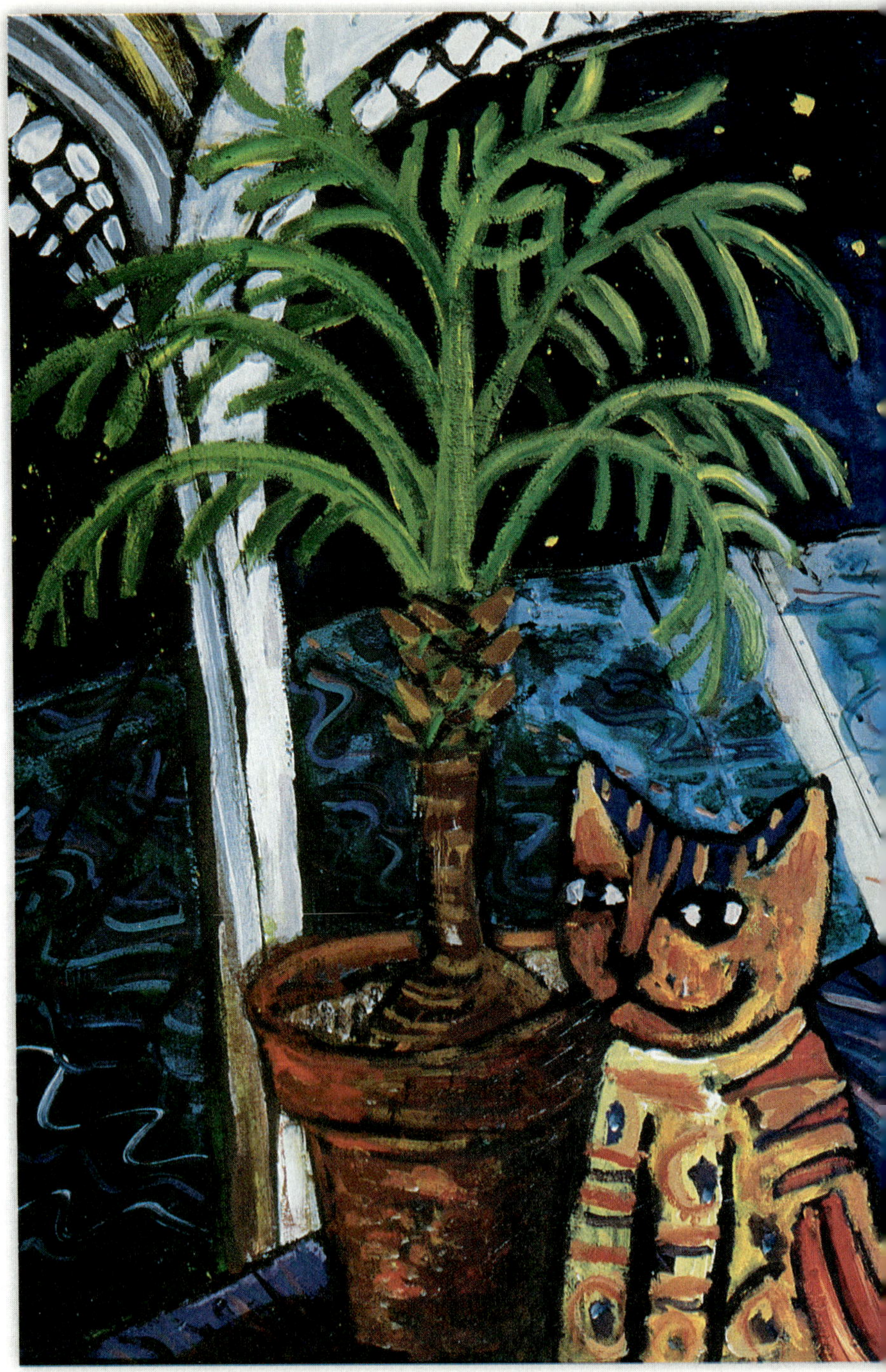

Like words in a book, a painting can tell you a story. Some parts of the plot you get right away. Others you have to discover.

Look at this painting. Who are the main characters? What can you tell about them? How does the artist show you the setting? Why does he paint a day and night sky?

Study the painting. If you were using it to write a story, what would be the events of your plot? What adventures might you show between the main characters? How would the setting enter into the plot?

El Gibarito **by Christian Pierre, 1962**
Private Collection

MEET

GLORIA GONZALEZ

Gloria Gonzalez was born in New York City in 1940. Before her recent move to Las Vegas, Nevada, she lived for many years in West New York, New Jersey—where this story takes place.

Gonzalez has written three young-adult novels, including *Gaucho,* which was made into a TV movie. Today she devotes herself full-time to the kind of writing she loves the most—writing plays. Her first success came at age 25, when she won a national playwriting contest with her play *Curtains*. Since then, her plays have been produced all over the country.

Gonzalez says she likes the immediate feedback she gets from the people who see her plays. With novels, she has to wait "months, even a year after the book is written," to read reviews. In the theater, she can tell right away how much audiences like her work.

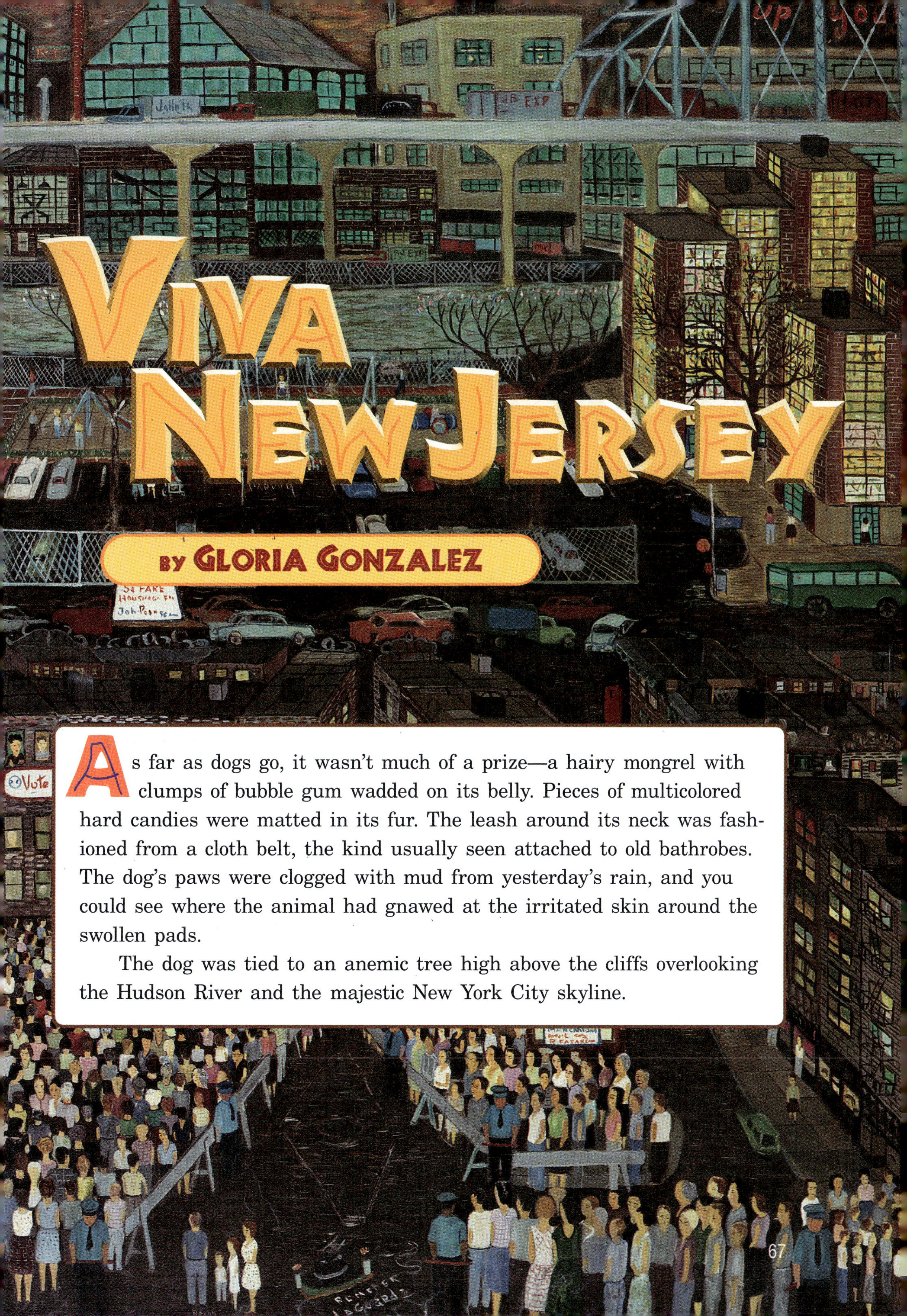

Viva New Jersey

by Gloria Gonzalez

As far as dogs go, it wasn't much of a prize—a hairy mongrel with clumps of bubble gum wadded on its belly. Pieces of multicolored hard candies were matted in its fur. The leash around its neck was fashioned from a cloth belt, the kind usually seen attached to old bathrobes. The dog's paws were clogged with mud from yesterday's rain, and you could see where the animal had gnawed at the irritated skin around the swollen pads.

The dog was tied to an anemic tree high above the cliffs overlooking the Hudson River and the majestic New York City skyline.

Lucinda traveled the route each day on her way to the high school, along the New Jersey side of the river. The short walk saddened her, despite its panoramic vista of bridges and skyscrapers, for the river reminded her of the perilous journey six months earlier, when she and her family had escaped from Cuba in a makeshift boat with seven others.

They had spent two freezing nights adrift in the ocean, uncertain of their destination, till a U. S. Coast Guard cutter towed them to the shores of Key West.

From there they wound their way north, staying temporarily with friends in Miami and finally settling in West New York, New Jersey, the most densely populated town in the United States. Barely a square mile, high above the Palisades, the town boasted a population of 85,000. Most of the community was housed in mammoth apartment buildings that seemed to reach into the clouds. The few private homes had cement lawns and paved driveways where there should have been backyards.

Lucinda longed for the spacious front porch where she'd sat at night with her friends while her grandmother bustled about the house, humming her Spanish songs. Lucinda would ride her bike to school and sometimes not see a soul for miles, just wild flowers amid a forest of greenery.

Now it was cement and cars and trucks and motorcycles and clanging fire engines that seemed to be in constant motion, shattering the air with their menacing roar.

Lucinda longed painfully for her grandmother. The old woman had refused to leave her house in Cuba, despite the family's pleas, so she had remained behind, promising to see them again one day.

The teenager, tall and slight of build with long dark hair that reached down her spine, was uncomfortable among her new classmates, most of whom she towered over. Even though the majority of them spoke Spanish and came from Cuba, Argentina, and Costa Rica, they were not like any of her friends back home. These "American" girls wore heavy makeup to school, dressed in jeans and high heels, and talked about rock singers and TV stars that she knew nothing of. They all seemed to be busy, rushing through the school corridors, huddling in laughing groups, mingling freely with boys, and chatting openly with teachers as if they were personal friends.

It was all too confusing.

Things weren't much better at home. Her parents had found jobs almost immediately and were often away from the tiny, cramped apartment. Her brother quickly made friends and was picked for the school baseball team, traveling to nearby towns to compete.

All Lucinda had were her memories—and now this dog, whom she untied from the tree. The animal was frightened and growled at her when she approached, but she spoke softly and offered a soothing hand, which he tried to attack. Lucinda persisted, and the dog, perhaps grateful to be freed from the mud puddles, allowed her to lead him away.

She didn't know what she was going to do with him now that she had him. Pets were not allowed in her building, and her family could be evicted. She couldn't worry about that now. Her main concern was to get him out of the cold.

Even though it was April and supposedly spring, the weather had yet to top fifty degrees.

Sunday Afternoon *1953 Ralph Fasanella*

At night she slept under two blankets, wearing warm socks over her cold feet. Another night outdoors, and the dog could freeze to death.

Lucinda reached her building and comforted the dog. "I'm not going to hurt you." She took off her jacket and wrapped it quickly around the animal, hoping to disguise it as a bundle under her arm. "Don't make any noise," she begged.

She waited till a woman with a baby stroller exited the building and quickly dashed inside, unseen. She opted not to take the elevator, fearful of running into someone, and instead lugged the dog and her schoolbag up the eight flights of stairs.

Lucinda quickly unlocked the apartment door and plopped the dog on her bed. The animal instantly shook its hair free and ran in circles atop her blanket.

"Don't get too comfortable," Lucinda cautioned. "You can't stay."

She dashed to the kitchen and returned moments later with a bowl of water and a plate of leftover chicken and yellow rice.

The dog bolted from the bed and began attacking the food before she even placed it on the floor. The girl sat on the edge of the bed and watched contentedly as he devoured the meal.

"How long has it been since you've eaten?"

The dog swallowed the food hungrily, not bothering to chew, and quickly lapped up the water.

It was then, with the dog's head lowered to the bowl, that Lucinda spotted the small piece of paper wedged beneath the belt around its neck. She slid it out carefully and saw the word that someone had scrawled with a pencil.

"Chauncey. Is that your name?"

The dog leaped to her side and nuzzled its nose against her arm.

"It's a crazy name, but I think I like it." She smiled. Outside the window, eight stories below, two fire engines pierced the afternoon with wailing sirens. Lucinda didn't seem to notice as she stroked the animal gently.

Working quickly, before her parents were due to arrive, she filled the bathtub with water and soap detergent and scrubbed the animal clean. The dog didn't enjoy it—he kept trying to jump out—so Lucinda began humming a Spanish song her grandmother used to sing to her when she was little. It didn't work. Chauncey still fought to get free.

Once the animal was bathed, Lucinda attacked the clumps of hair with a scissor and picked out the sticky globs of candy.

"My God, you're white!" Lucinda discovered. While using her brother's hair blower, she ran a quick comb through the fur, which now was silvery and tan with faint traces of black. "You're beautiful." The girl beamed.

The dog seemed to agree. It picked up its head proudly and flicked its long ears with pride.

Lucinda hugged him close, "I'll find you a good home. I promise," she told the animal.

Knowing that her parents would arrive any moment, Lucinda gathered up the dog, covering him with her coat, and carried him down nine flights to the basement. She crept quietly past the superintendent's apartment and deposited the animal in a tiny room behind the bank of washing machines.

The room, the size of a small closet, contained all the electrical levers that supplied power to the apartments and the elevator.

Chauncey looked about, confused. He jumped up as if he knew he was about to be abandoned again. His white hairy paw came dangerously close to hitting the protruding, red master switch near the door.

Lucinda knelt to the animal. "I'll be back. Promise."

She closed the door behind her, praying the dog wouldn't bark, and hurried away. An outline of a plan was taking shape in her mind.

Ashley.

The girl sat in front of her in English and always went out of her way to say hi. She didn't seem to hang out with the other kids, and whenever they passed in the corridor, she was alone. But what really made her even more appealing was that she lived in a real house. Just a block away. Lucinda had seen her once going in. Maybe Ashley would take Chauncey.

Lucinda's parents arrived from work, and she quickly helped her mother prepare the scrumptious fried bananas. Her father had stopped at a restaurant on his way home and brought a *cantina* of food—white rice, black beans, avocado salad, and meat stew. Each food was placed in its own metal container and clipped together like a small pyramid. The local restaurant would have delivered the food to the house each day, if the family desired, but Lucinda's father always liked to stop by and check the menu. The restaurant also made fried bananas, but Lucinda's mother didn't think they were as tasty as her own. One of the nice surprises of moving to New Jersey was discovering that the Latin restaurants supplied *cantina* service.

"How was school today?" her mother asked.

"Okay," Lucinda replied.

The dinner conversation drifted, as it

always did, to Mama's problems at work with the supervisor and Papa's frustration with his job. Every day he had to ride two buses and a subway to get to work, which he saw as wasted hours.

"You get an education, go to college," Lucinda's father sermonized for the thousandth time, "and you can work anywhere you like—even in your own house, if you want. Like a doctor! And if it is far away, you hire someone like me, with no education, to drive you."

Lucinda had grown up hearing the lecture. Perhaps she would have been a good student anyway, for she certainly took to it with enthusiasm. She had discovered books at a young age. School only heightened her love of reading, for its library supplied her with an endless source of material. She excelled in her studies and won top honors in English class. She was so proficient at learning the English language that she served as a tutor to kids in lower grades.

Despite her father's wishes, Lucinda had no intention of becoming a doctor or lawyer. She wasn't sure what she would do—the future seemed far too distant to address it—but she knew somehow it would involve music and dance and magnificent costumes and glittering shoes and plumes in her hair.

They were talking about her brother's upcoming basketball game when suddenly all the lights in the apartment went out.

"*¿Qué pasó?*" her father exclaimed.

Agitated voices could be heard from the outside hallway. A neighbor banged on the door, shouting, "Call the fire department! Someone's trapped in the elevator!"

Groups of tenants mingled outside their apartments, some carrying candles and flashlights. The building had been pitched into darkness.

"We'll get you out!" someone shouted to the woman caught between floors.

Lucinda cried: "Chauncey!"

He must've hit the master switch. She could hear the distant wail of the fire engines and knew it was only a matter of minutes before they checked the room where the dog was hidden.

"I'll be right back!" Lucinda yelled to her mother as she raced out the door. Groping onto the banister, she felt her way down the flights of steps as people with candles hurried to escape.

The rescuers reached the basement before she did. Two firemen were huddled in the doorway checking the power supply. Lucinda looked frantically for the dog, but he was gone.

She raced out into the nippy night, through the throng of people crowded on the sidewalk, and searched for the dog. She was afraid to look in the street, expecting to see his lifeless body, the victim of a car.

Lucinda looked up at the sound of her name. Her mother was calling to her from the window.

"Come home! What are you doing?"

The girl shouted, "In a minute!" The crowd swelled about her as she quickly darted away.

Lucinda didn't plan it, but she found herself in front of Ashley's house minutes later. She was on the sidewalk, with the rest of her neighbors, gazing up the block at the commotion in front of Lucinda's building.

"Hi," Lucinda stammered.

Ashley took a moment to place the face and then returned the smile. "Hi."

Lucinda looked about nervously, wondering if any of the adults belonged to Ashley's family. She didn't have a moment to waste.

Across the River to the Country *1969 Ralph Fasanella*

"What happens," she blurted out, "when a dog runs away? Do the police catch it?"

The blond, chubby teenager, with light green eyes and glasses with pink frames, shrugged. "Probably. If they do, they only take it to the pound."

"What's that?" It sounded bad, whatever it was.

"A shelter. Where they keep animals. If nobody claims 'em, they kill 'em."

Lucinda started to cry. She couldn't help it. It came upon her suddenly. Greatly embarrassed, she turned quickly and hurried away.

"Wait up!" The blonde hurried after her. "Hey!"

Lucinda stopped, too ashamed to meet her eyes.

"Did you lose your dog?" Ashley's voice sounded concerned.

Lucinda nodded.

"Well, let's go find him," Ashley prodded.

They searched the surrounding neighborhood and checked underneath all the cars parked in the area in case he was hiding. They searched basements and rooftops. When all else failed, they walked to the park along the river, where Lucinda pointed out the tree where she had found him.

The girls decided to sit on a nearby bench in case Chauncey reappeared, though they realized there was little hope.

Lucinda knew her mother would be frantically worried.

"She probably has the police looking for me," she told Ashley.

"You've only been gone an hour."

"It's the first time I've left the house, except to go to school, since we moved here," she revealed.

It was a beautiful night, despite the cold tingling breeze that swept up from the river.

The New York skyline was ablaze with golden windows silhouetted against dark, boxlike steel structures. You could make out the red traffic lights along the narrow streets. A long, thin barge sailed down the river like a rubbery snake.

Lucinda learned that Ashley's mother was a lawyer, often away from home for long periods, and her father operated a small business in New York's Chinatown, which kept him busy seven days a week. An only child, she spent her time studying and writing letters.

"Who do you write to?" Lucinda asked.

"My grandmother, mostly. She lives in Nevada. I spend the summers with her."

Lucinda told her how lucky she was to be able to see her grandmother. She felt dangerously close to tears again and quickly changed the subject. "I never see you with any friends in school. Why?"

Ashley shrugged. "Guess I'm not the friendly type. Most of the girls are only interested in boys and dates. I intend to be a famous writer one day, so there's a lot of books I have to read. Just so I know what's been done."

It made sense.

"What are you going to be?"

Lucinda admitted she had no ambition. No particular desire. But maybe, if she had her choice, if she could be anything she wanted, it would probably be a dancer.

"My grandmother used to take me to her friend's house who used to be a famous ballerina in Cuba. She'd let me try on her costumes, and she'd play the records and teach me the steps. It hurt my feet something awful. Hers used to bleed when she first started, but she said it got easier after the first year."

Ashley told her, "You have the body for it. I bet you'd make a wonderful dancer."

When it became apparent that Chauncey would never return, the girls walked home together.

Despite all that happened, Lucinda found herself sad to have the evening end. For the first time since leaving her homeland, she felt somewhat at peace with herself. She now had someone to talk to. Someone who understood. Someone who carried her own pain.

"Wanna have lunch tomorrow?" Ashley asked her. "I usually run home and eat in front of the television. I'm a great cook. My first book is going to be filled with exotic recipes of all the countries I plan to visit. And if you want," she gushed excitedly, "after school we can go to the library. You can get out a book on how to be a ballerina."

Lucinda agreed immediately, "That would be wonderful!"

The girls parted on the sidewalk, and Lucinda raced home where her irate father and weeping mother confronted her angrily.

"Where have you been! I was only going to wait five more minutes and then I was calling the police! Where were you?"

Before she could stammer a reply, the lights went out.

"Not again!" her mother shrieked.

Lucinda's heart throbbed with excitement.

Chauncey was back!

She ran out of the apartment, unmindful of the darkness, with her mother's screams in the air: "Come back here!"

This time Lucinda made it to the basement before the firemen, and she led her pal safely out the building. She reached Ashley's doorstep just as the first fire engine turned the corner.

Story Questions & Activities

1. How did Lucinda and her family get from Cuba to New Jersey?
2. How does Lucinda feel about her new home? Why does she feel this way?
3. Why is Chauncey important to the story?
4. What are the most important events in the story?
5. Suppose that the daughter of the Lin family and Lucinda were to meet. What do you think they would find they had in common?

Write an Autobiographical Sketch

In "Viva New Jersey" we learn a lot about Lucinda. We know that she is from Cuba and that she wants to be a dancer. More importantly, we know how she feels about herself and her life. Now it's your turn. Write an autobiographical sketch that describes you. Before you write, jot down some notes. Include what you are like and what your personal goals and achievements are. Begin with an interesting anecdote. Finish by summarizing the main points about you.

Make a Comparison Chart

Cuba and West New York, New Jersey, are very different places. Use information from the story and from an encyclopedia or another source to make a chart comparing the two places. Illustrate your chart with drawings that highlight the differences.

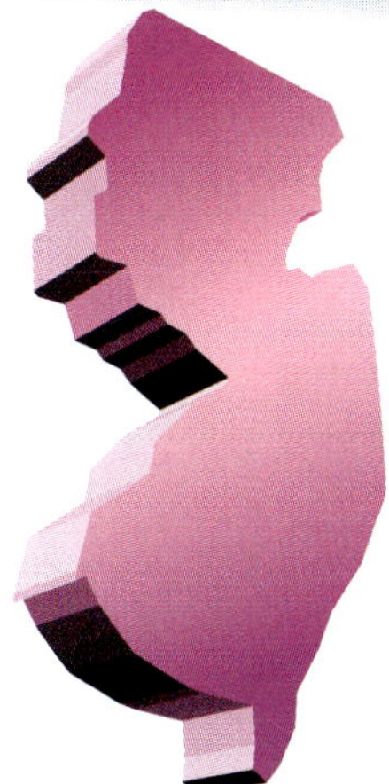

Draw a Map

The part of New Jersey that Lucinda lives in is a city. Is all of New Jersey the way she sees it? Use an atlas *and* an encyclopedia to find out about New Jersey. Draw a map that shows the state. Indicate New Jersey's major products and industries. How is the state different from what you expected?

Find Out More

Cuba, the country Lucinda comes from, is the largest island in the West Indies. It is approximately 90 miles south of Florida. Check an encyclopedia or a book about Cuba to find five facts about what life on the island is like. Write down the five facts and share them with classmates.

Use a Thesaurus

A **thesaurus** is a book that lists common words and groups of synonyms for those words. Synonyms are words that have the same or almost the same meaning. Some thesauruses also give **antonyms**, or words that have the opposite meaning. A thesaurus is usually arranged like a dictionary, with **entry words** in alphabetical order.

Many word processing programs for computers have a thesaurus feature. It suggests synonyms for a word you select. On the screen below, the thesaurus was found under Tools.

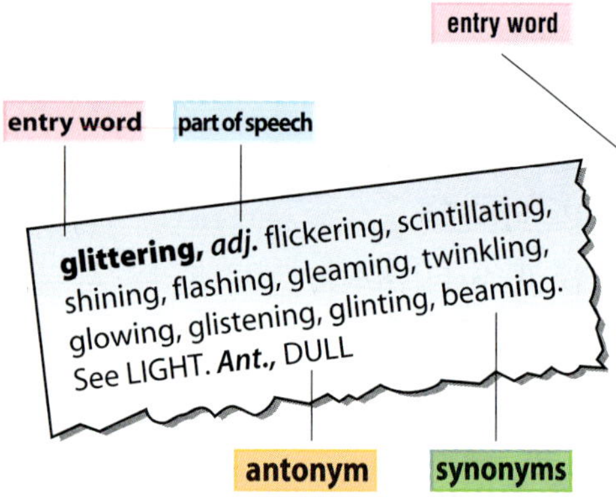

entry word | part of speech

glittering, ***adj.*** flickering, scintillating, shining, flashing, gleaming, twinkling, glowing, glistening, glinting, beaming. See LIGHT. ***Ant.,*** DULL

antonym | synonyms

entry word

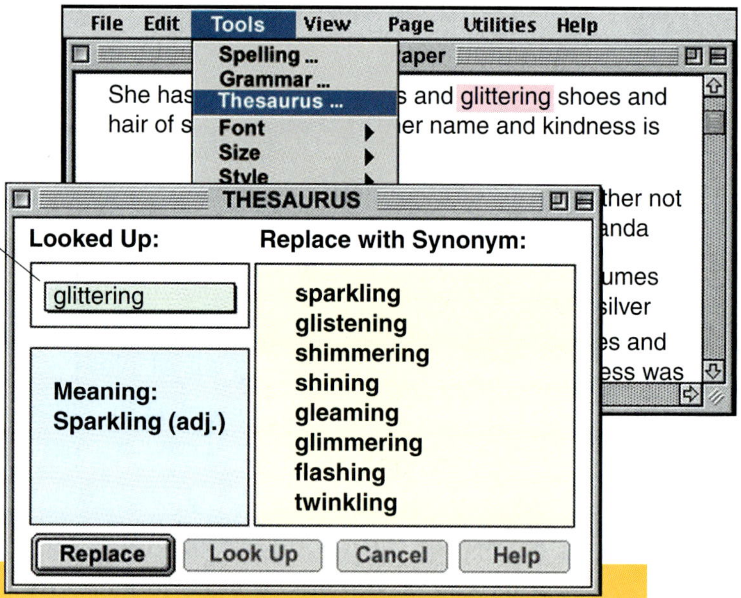

File Edit Tools View Page Utilities Help

Spelling ...
Grammar ...
Thesaurus ...
Font
Size
Style

She has ... and glittering shoes and hair of s... her name and kindness is

THESAURUS

Looked Up: glittering

Meaning: Sparkling (adj.)

Replace with Synonym: sparkling, glistening, shimmering, shining, gleaming, glimmering, flashing, twinkling

Replace | Look Up | Cancel | Help

Use the thesaurus to answer these questions.

1. What is the antonym for the word *glittering*?
2. What are three synonyms for the word *glittering*?
3. Is *glittering* an adjective or a noun? How do you know?
4. How would you look up a word in a thesaurus arranged like a dictionary? In a thesaurus found on a computer?
5. Is a thesaurus more helpful for reading or writing? Explain.

TEST POWER

Test Tip

Rule out wrong answer choices.

DIRECTIONS

Read the sample story. Then read each question about the story.

SAMPLE

In-Line Skates

Jesse had wanted new in-line skates for months. His old pair, which he had outgrown by several sizes, now sat in his closet. He and his father were going shopping that weekend, but his father had said that he would like Jesse to contribute to the purchase. At the moment, Jesse had no money. On the way home from school, Jesse saw this billboard. He was certain that he could win the contest. Since he only had three days before the contest would end, he began designing his poster as soon as he got home.

ATTENTION: SKATERS
Sports-R-Us is having a ***poster competition*** that needs your entry! We're looking for a poster with five reasons why sports are good for kids. Three winners will receive ***$50*** gift certificates to ***Sports-R-Us***. ***Enter today—contest ends May 16.***

1 The billboard for Sports-R-Us tries to make you think that —

A kids should not be involved in sports

B they sell many in-line skates

C sports are good for kids

D posters are easy to make

2 The billboard uses different kinds of lettering to —

F show that Sports-R-Us is expensive

G catch the reader's attention

H emphasize the deadline

J show different poster entries

Did you rule out wrong answers? Tell how.

Stories in Art

When you first look at this painting, you might see raindrops. If you look again, you will notice that these raindrops are really businessmen in bowler hats.

What can you tell about this painting? What makes it strange? How does the artist mix things from real life with those that could never happen?

Look at the painting again. What do you think will happen when all these men hit the street? What might the artist be saying about crowded cities? About business? If it is raining men today, what might it rain tomorrow? Cats and dogs?

Golconde, Golconda
by René Magritte
Menil Foundation, Houston, Texas

Magritte

Meet Isaac Asimov

Once called "the human writing machine," Isaac Asimov (1920–1992) was the author of more than 470 books. "I must write," the prolific Asimov explained. "I look upon everything but writing as an interruption."

He became perhaps the most widely known science-fiction writer in the world. Among his honors were five Hugo Awards from the World Science Fiction Conventions, including best all-time science-fiction series (for his *Foundation* series); best novel, 1973 (for *The Gods Themselves*); and best short story, 1983 (for "*The Bicentennial Man*"). The Science Fiction Writers of America voted his work "*Nightfall*" the best all-time science-fiction story.

Asimov also wrote dozens of popular nonfiction books and articles about science, math, and other topics.

Rain, Rain, Go Away

Written by Isaac Asimov
Illustrated by Bruno Paciulli

There she is again," said Lillian Wright as she adjusted the venetian blinds carefully. "There she is, George."

"There who is?" asked her husband, trying to get satisfactory contrast on the TV so that he might settle down to the ball game.

"Mrs. Sakkaro," she said, and then, to forestall her husband's inevitable "Who's that?" added hastily, "The new neighbors, for goodness sake."

"Oh."

"Sunbathing. Always sunbathing. I wonder where her boy is. He's usually out on a nice day like this, standing in that tremendous yard of theirs and throwing the ball against the house. Did you ever see him, George?"

"I've heard him. It's a version of the Chinese water torture. Bang on the wall, biff on the ground, smack in the hand. Bang, biff, smack, bang, biff—"

"He's a *nice* boy, quiet and well-behaved. I wish Tommie would make friends with him. He's the right age, too, just about ten, I should say."

"I didn't know Tommie was backward about making friends."

"Well, it's hard with the Sakkaros. They keep so to themselves. I don't even know what Mr. Sakkaro does."

"Why should you? It's not really anyone's business what he does."

"It's odd that I never see him go to work."

"No one ever sees me go to work."

"You stay home and write. What does *he* do?"

"I dare say Mrs. Sakkaro knows what Mr. Sakkaro does and is all upset because she doesn't know what *I* do."

"Oh, George." Lillian retreated from the window and glanced with distaste at the television. (Schoendienst was at bat.) "I think we should make an effort; the neighborhood should."

"What kind of an effort?" George was comfortable on the couch now, with a king-size coke in his hand, freshly opened and frosted with moisture.

"To get to know them."

"Well, didn't you, when she first moved in? You said you called."

"I said hello but, well, she'd just moved in and the house was still upset, so that's all it could be, just hello. It's been two months now and it's still nothing more than hello, sometimes. —She's so odd."

"Is she?"

"She's always looking at the sky; I've seen her do it a hundred times and she's never been out when it's the least bit cloudy. Once, when the boy was out playing, she called to him to come in, shouting that it was going to rain. I happened to hear her and I thought, Good Lord, wouldn't you know and me with a wash on the line, so I hurried out and, you know, it was broad sunlight. Oh, there were some clouds, but nothing, really."

"Did it rain, eventually?"

"Of course not. I just had to run out in the yard for nothing."

George was lost amid a couple of base hits and a most embarrassing bobble that meant a run. When the excitement was over and the pitcher was trying to regain his composure, George called out after Lillian, who was vanishing into the kitchen, "Well, since they're from Arizona, I dare say they don't know rainclouds from any other kind."

Lillian came back into the living room with a patter of high heels. "From where?"

"From Arizona, according to Tommie."

"How did Tommie know?"

"He talked to their boy, in between ball chucks, I guess, and he told Tommie they came from Arizona and then the boy was called in. At least, Tommie says it might have been Arizona, or maybe Alabama or some place like that. You know Tommie and his nontotal recall. But if they're that nervous about the weather, I guess it's Arizona and they don't know what to make of a good rainy climate like ours."

"But why didn't you ever tell me?"

"Because Tommie only told me this morning and because I

thought he must have told you already and, to tell the absolute truth, because I thought you could just manage to drag out a normal existence even if you never found out. Wow—"

The ball went sailing into the right field stands and that was that for the pitcher.

Lillian went back to the venetian blinds and said, "I'll simply just have to make her acquaintance. She looks *very* nice.—Oh, Lord, look at that, George."

George was looking at nothing but the TV.

Lillian said, "I know she's staring at that cloud. And now she'll be going in. Honestly."

George was out two days later on a reference search in the library and came home with a load of books. Lillian greeted him jubilantly.

She said, "Now, you're not doing anything tomorrow."

"That sounds like a statement, not a question."

"It is a statement. We're going out with the Sakkaros to Murphy's Park."

"With—"

"With the next-door neighbors, George. *How* can you never remember the name?"

"I'm gifted. How did it happen?"

"I just went up to their house this morning and rang the bell."

"That easy?"

"It wasn't easy. It was hard. I stood there, jittering, with my finger on the doorbell, till I thought that ringing the bell would be easier than having the door open and being caught standing there like a fool."

"And she didn't kick you out?"

"No. She was sweet as she could be. Invited me in, knew who I was, said she was so glad I had come to visit. *You* know."

"And you suggested we go to Murphy's Park."

"Yes. I thought if I suggested something that would let the children have fun, it would be easier for her to go along with it. She wouldn't want to spoil a chance for her boy."

"A mother's psychology."

"But you should see her home."

"Ah. You had a reason for all this. It comes out. You wanted the Cook's tour. But, please, spare me the color-scheme details. I'm not interested in the bedspreads, and the size of the closets is a topic with which I can dispense."

It was the secret of their happy marriage that Lillian paid no attention to George. She went into the color-scheme details, was most meticulous about the bedspreads, and gave him an inch-by-inch description of closet-size.

"And *clean*? I have never seen any place so spotless."

"If you get to know her, then, she'll be setting you impossible standards and you'll have to drop her in self-defense."

"Her kitchen," said Lillian, ignoring him, "was so spanking clean you just couldn't believe she ever used it. I asked for a drink of water and she held the glass underneath the tap and poured slowly so that not one drop fell in the sink itself. It wasn't affectation. She did it so casually that I just knew she always did it that way. And when she gave me the glass she held it with a clean napkin. Just hospital-sanitary."

"She must be a lot of trouble to herself. Did she agree to come with us right off?"

"Well—not right off. She called to her husband about what the weather forecast was, and he said that the newspapers all said it would be fair tomorrow but that he was waiting for the latest report on the radio."

"*All* the newspapers said so, eh?"

"Of course, they all just print the official weather forecast, so they would all agree. But I think they do subscribe to all the newspapers. At least I've watched the bundle the newsboy leaves—"

"There isn't much you miss, is there?"

"Anyway," said Lillian severely, "she called up the weather bureau and had them tell her the latest and she called it out to her husband and they said they'd go, except they said they'd phone us if there were any unexpected changes in the weather."

"All right. Then we'll go."

The Sakkaros were young and pleasant, dark and handsome. In fact, as they came down the long walk from their home to where the Wright automobile was parked, George leaned toward his wife and breathed into her ear, "So *he's* the reason."

"I wish he were," said Lillian. "Is that a handbag he's carrying?"

"Pocket-radio. To listen to weather forecasts, I bet."

The Sakkaro boy came running after them, waving something which turned out to be an aneroid barometer, and all three got into the back seat. Conversation was turned on and lasted, with neat give-and-take on impersonal subjects, to Murphy's Park.

The Sakkaro boy was so polite and reasonable that even Tommie Wright, wedged between his parents in the front seat, was subdued by example into a semblance of civilization. Lillian couldn't recall when she had spent so serenely pleasant a drive.

She was not the least disturbed by the fact that, barely to be heard under the flow of the conversation, Mr. Sakkaro's small radio was on, and she never actually saw him put it occasionally to his ear.

It was a beautiful day at Murphy's Park; hot and dry without being too hot; and with a cheerfully bright sun in a blue, blue sky. Even Mr. Sakkaro, though he inspected every quarter of the heavens with a careful eye and then stared piercingly at the barometer, seemed to have no fault to find.

Lillian ushered the two boys to the amusement section and bought enough tickets to allow one ride on each variety of centrifugal thrill that the park offered.

"Please," she had said to a protesting Mrs. Sakkaro, "let this be my treat. I'll let you have your turn next time."

When she returned, George was alone. "Where—" she began.

"Just down there at the refreshment stand. I told them I would wait here for you and we would join them." He sounded gloomy.

"Anything wrong?"

"No, not really, except that I think he must be independently wealthy."

"What?"

"I don't know what he does for a living. I hinted—"

"Now who's curious?"

"I was doing it for you. He said he's just a student of human nature."

"How philosophical. That would explain all those newspapers."

"Yes, but with a handsome, wealthy man next door, it looks as though I'll have impossible standards set for me, too."

"Don't be silly."

"And he doesn't come from Arizona."

"He doesn't?"

"I said I heard he was from Arizona. He looked so surprised, it was obvious he didn't. Then he laughed and asked if he had an Arizona accent."

Lillian said thoughtfully, "He has some kind of accent, you know. There are lots of Spanish-ancestry people in the Southwest, so he could still be from Arizona. Sakkaro could be a Spanish name."

"Sounds Japanese to me.—Come on, they're waving. Oh, good Lord, look what they've bought."

The Sakkaros were each holding three sticks of cotton candy, huge swirls of pink foam consisting of threads of sugar dried out of frothy syrup that had been whipped about in a warm vessel. It melted sweetly in the mouth and left one feeling sticky.

The Sakkaros held one out to each Wright, and out of politeness the Wrights accepted.

They went down the midway, tried their hand at darts, at the kind of poker game where balls were rolled into holes, at knocking wooden cylinders off pedestals. They took pictures of themselves and recorded their voices and tested the strength of their handgrips.

Eventually they collected the youngsters, who had been reduced to a satisfactorily breathless state of roiled-up insides, and the Sakkaros ushered theirs off instantly to the refreshment stand. Tommie hinted the extent of his pleasure at the possible purchase of a hot-dog and George tossed him a quarter. He ran off, too.

"Frankly," said George, "I prefer to stay here. If I see them biting away at another cotton candy stick I'll turn green and sicken on the spot. If they haven't had a dozen apiece, I'll eat a dozen myself."

"I know, and they're buying a handful for the child now."

"I offered to stand Sakkaro a hamburger and he just looked grim and shook his head. Not that a hamburger's much, but after enough cotton candy, it ought to be a feast."

"I know. I offered her an orange drink and the way she jumped when she said no, you'd think I'd thrown it in her face.—Still, I suppose they've never been to a place like this before and they'll need time to adjust to the novelty. They'll fill up on cotton candy and then never eat it again for ten years."

"Well, maybe." They strolled toward the Sakkaros.

"You know, Lil, it's clouding up."

Mr. Sakkaro had the radio to his ear and was looking anxiously toward the west.

"Uh-oh," said George, "he's seen it. One gets you fifty, he'll want to go home."

All three Sakkaros were upon him, polite but insistent. They were sorry, they had had a wonderful time, a marvelous time, the Wrights would have to be their guests as soon as it could be managed, but now, really, they had to go home. It looked stormy. Mrs. Sakkaro wailed that all the forecasts had been for fair weather.

George tried to console them. "It's hard to predict a local thunderstorm, but even if it were to come, and it mightn't, it wouldn't last more than half an hour on the outside."

At which comment, the Sakkaro youngster seemed on the verge of tears, and Mrs. Sakkaro's hand, holding a handkerchief, trembled visibly.

"Let's go home," said George in resignation.

The drive back seemed to stretch interminably. There was no conversation to speak of. Mr. Sakkaro's radio was quite loud now as he switched from station to station, catching a weather report every time. They were mentioning "local thundershowers" now.

The Sakkaro youngster piped up that the barometer was falling, and Mrs. Sakkaro, chin in the palm of her hand, stared dolefully at the sky and asked if George could not drive faster, please.

"It does look rather threatening, doesn't it?" said Lillian in a polite attempt to share their guests' attitude. But then George heard her mutter, "Honestly!" under her breath.

A wind had sprung up, driving the dust of the weeks-dry road before it, when they entered the street on which they lived, and the leaves rustled ominously. Lightning flickered.

George said, "You'll be indoors in two minutes, friends. We'll make it."

He pulled up at the gate that opened onto the Sakkaros' spacious front yard and got out of the car to open the back door. He thought he felt a drop. They were *just* in time.

The Sakkaros tumbled out, faces drawn with tension, muttering thanks, and started off toward their long front walk at a dead run.

"Honestly," began Lillian, "you would think they were—"

The heavens opened and the rain came down in giant drops as though some celestial dam had suddenly burst. The top of their car was pounded with a hundred drum sticks, and halfway to their front door the Sakkaros stopped and looked despairingly upward.

Their faces blurred as the rain hit; blurred and shrank and ran together. All three shriveled, collapsing within their clothes, which sank down into three sticky-wet heaps.

And while the Wrights sat there, transfixed with horror, Lillian found herself unable to stop the completion of her remark: "—made of sugar and afraid they would melt."

Story Questions & Activities

1. What unusual habit has Mrs. Wright noticed about her new neighbor, Mrs. Sakkaro?

2. What clues at the beginning of the story suggest that there is something unusual about the Sakkaros?

3. What do you think Mr. Sakkaro meant when he said he was "a student of human nature"?

4. Summarize this story. Did it end as you expected? Why or why not?

5. Imagine that the Sakkaros stepped into the picture on pages 84–85. What do you think would happen to them?

Write a Letter

Have you ever been to an amusement park or fair? What did you do while you were there? Who came along with you? What did you have to eat?

Write a letter to a friend describing a visit you made to an amusement park, fair, or another memorable place. Include details about what you did and how you felt.

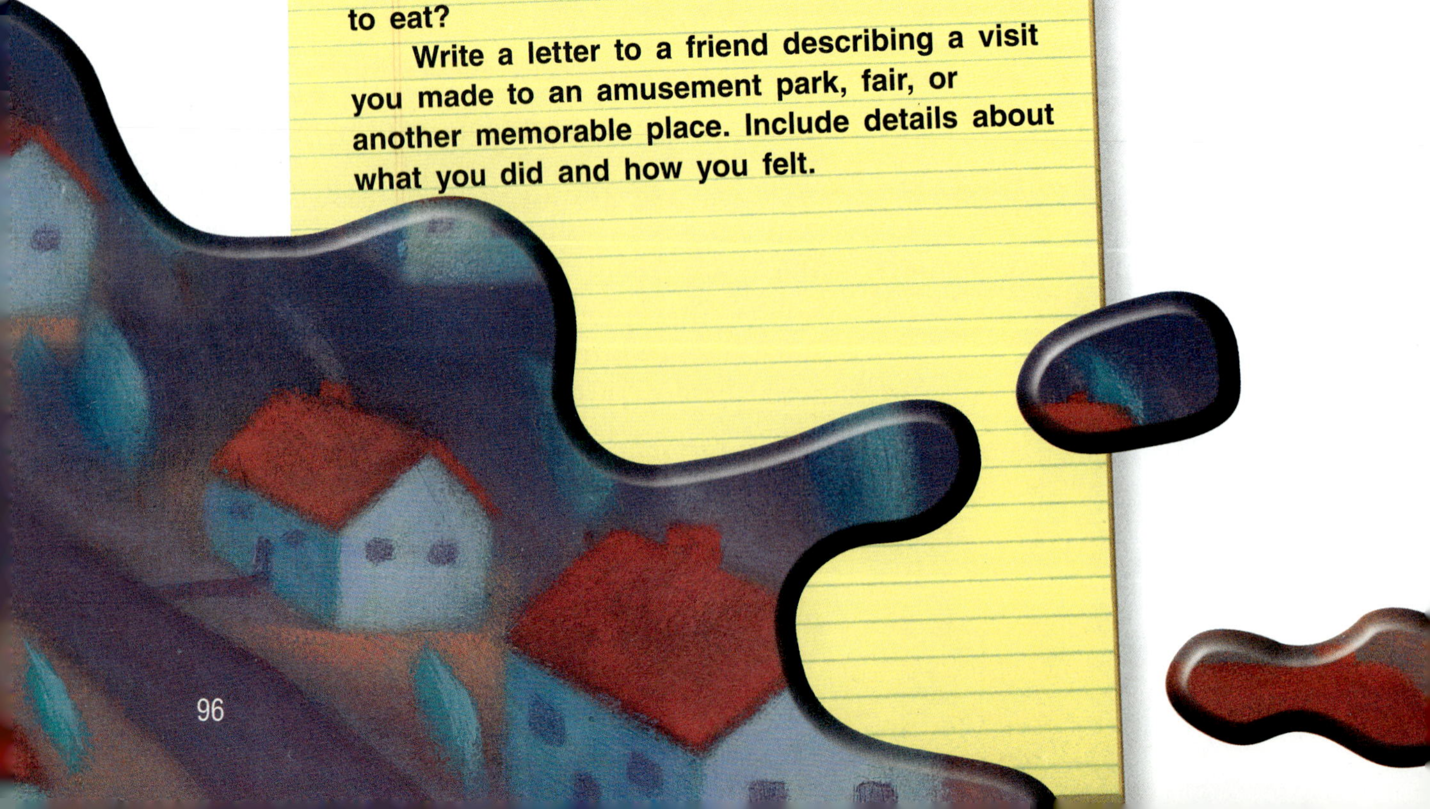

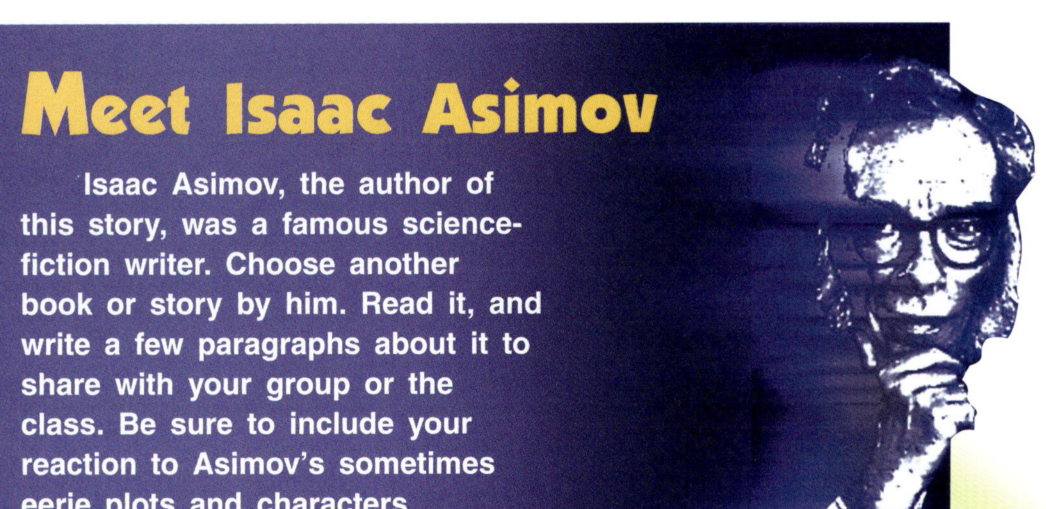

Meet Isaac Asimov

Isaac Asimov, the author of this story, was a famous science-fiction writer. Choose another book or story by him. Read it, and write a few paragraphs about it to share with your group or the class. Be sure to include your reaction to Asimov's sometimes eerie plots and characters.

Spin with Centrifugal Force

In the story, the boys experience the amusement park's "centrifugal thrills" on rides that rely on centrifugal force. *Centrifugal* means "moving or directed away from the center." Draw a picture of an amusement park ride that involves centrifugal force. Under your drawing, explain what the ride does and why it might give its riders a "centrifugal thrill."

Find Out More

The Sakkaro boy carried around an *aneroid barometer*, an instrument used for weather forecasting. Find out more about this instrument and others used by weather forecasters. Look in an encyclopedia or in books about weather. Share what you learn with the class.

Use the Library

Did you know that most libraries organize their books the same way? **Fiction books** are in alphabetical order by author, **biographies** and **autobiographies** are in alphabetical order by the name of the person they are about, and other **nonfiction books** are in order by subject. Reference books—such as dictionaries, thesauruses, encyclopedias, and atlases—are in their own section.

To find nonfiction books that are in subject order, you need to know their **call numbers.** Usually, the call numbers follow the Dewey Decimal System. You can learn a book's call number by checking the library's online catalog or card catalog.

Use the information about the library to answer these questions.

1. Both *Little Women* and *The Call of the Wild* are novels. Which would come first on a library's shelves?
2. How many of the books shown would be in the library's reference section?
3. Would a biography of Isaac Asimov be in order by his name, the author's name, or the subject?
4. If you knew who wrote a book about thunderstorms, could you find it without looking up the call number? Explain
5. Why is it important to know how to use the library?

TEST POWER

Test Tip

The summary tells what the passage is mostly about.

DIRECTIONS

Read the sample story. Then read each question about the story.

SAMPLE

Speech Club

Saraya was so excited that she could barely sit still. Ten minutes more and the bell would ring. After that, Saraya would go to the first weekly meeting of the Speech Club. Her favorite teacher, Ms. Malone, was the club's advisor and had shown an interest in Saraya's writing ability. She had also commented on Saraya's calmness during an oral presentation that Saraya had made last year.

As she had been asked to do, Saraya had prepared an introduction to present to the group. She had taken time to include some humor in her speech. Saraya knew that a little laughter always went a long way to make people feel more relaxed. She had often used her sense of humor to ease her classmates' tension when faced with a big test.

As Saraya walked into Ms. Malone's room, she felt confident that her speech would go just fine.

1 Which is the best summary of this passage?

- **A** Saraya is anxious about giving her speech in front of her classmates.
- **B** Ms. Malone is the advisor for the Speech Club.
- **C** Saraya looks forward to being a part of the Speech Club.
- **D** The Speech Club begins after school ends.

2 Ms. Malone had shown an interest in Saraya because —

- **F** Ms. Malone needed some writing samples for the school paper.
- **G** Saraya wrote well and was calm when speaking to an audience.
- **H** The Speech Club needed new people to join it.
- **J** Saraya's sense of humor is just what the Speech Club needs.

This painting is filled with movement. Notice how the artist uses curved lines to make the waves, the sails, and the flags blowing in the wind. This helps to give the feeling of tall ships in motion.

What can you tell about this painting? Are the ships waging war? Are they setting out to explore foreign lands? What makes you think so? What do you think will happen next?

Study the painting. Notice the dark storm clouds. Are the boats and the rowers sailing into the sun? What might that mean? Do you think the voyage has been exciting? Explain.

Tall Ships, Full Sail
by Unknown French Artist
David David Gallery, Philadelphia, Pennsylvania

TIME FOR KIDS

SPECIAL REPORT

A Viking Voyage

A Viking Ship Sets Sail

Modern sailors repeat Leif Ericson's historic journey to the Western Hemisphere

On June 28, 1998, people on the western shore of Greenland may have thought they were dreaming when they saw a Viking ship sail by. But what they were seeing wasn't a dream, it was a dream come true. Aboard the ship, named *Snorri*, were 10 men, including writer, explorer, and bigtime dreamer W. Hodding Carter.

When he was 10, Carter read about the Viking Age, A.D. 800 to 1050. That's when Vikings sailed from Norway, Denmark, and Sweden for distant lands. "As a kid, I was always reading history books and imagining I was a Viking," says Carter. As an adult, Carter decided to let his imagination take charge.

Carter asked Maine boatbuilder Robert Stevens to build a *knarr*, a Viking merchant ship powered by oars and a square sail. Stevens used plans from a museum in Denmark.

The modern-day crew first tried in July 1997 to re-create the journey of Viking explorer Leif Ericson. But the trip came to an end when the rudder, which steers the boat, broke. The next summer, the crew tried again to sail the seas much as Leif Ericson had done.

Ericson came to North America, which he called Vinland, 1,000 years ago, about 500 years before Columbus. He left from Greenland and went at least as far as L'Anse aux Meadows, Newfoundland, the site of the only known Viking settlement in North America.

ILLUSTRATION FOR TIME FOR KIDS BY RITA LASCARO; ALL PHOTOS: RUSSELL KAYE

Vikings came from Norway, Sweden, and Denmark in Scandinavia. The big map shows Leif Ericson's route. He sailed close to shore so he could spot landmarks.

THE SHIP SAILS

On the 1998 voyage, the crew left from Nuuk, a small port in Greenland. This time they carried an extra rudder, in case the first one broke.

Like a giant canoe, a *knarr* is completely open. The sailors have no shelter from wind, rain, or waves. So the crew wore heavy sweaters, rain gear, caps, jeans, and sneakers.

The 1,500-mile journey took 12 weeks to complete. Crew members sometimes rowed ashore to gather plants and berries to eat. They fished for some of their food, though they didn't have much luck catching their dinner. They also brought food aboard, including pasta, peanut butter, honey, cereals, dried fruits, and nuts.

The *knarr* was built from old plans of a Viking ship.

Carter at the rudder of the *Snorri*.

Unlike the real Vikings, the *Snorri's* crew didn't feast on wild seals or walruses.

Since the summer sun sets late near the Arctic Circle, the sailors had between 14 and 20 hours of daylight. The average temperature was about 50°F (10°C), and the water was a very chilly 40°F (5°C). Though most of the voyage was fairly smooth, the *Snorri* sometimes sailed through 15-foot-high waves and gale-force winds. "She was an absolute beauty," notes John Abbott, a crew member.

Carter and crew wanted to stay true to Viking technology, but they

When Carter and crew arrived at L'Anse aux Meadows, they swam ashore.

No wind to fill the sail? No problem! The crew rows the 25-ton ship with wooden oars to keep things moving.

had modern backup systems to keep them safe. A radio, compasses, a lifeboat, wet suits, and a medical kit were on board. Satellites gave a precise reading of the boat's location.

THE REAL VIKINGS HAD IT ROUGH

Vikings relied on nature and luck to guide their journeys. They tracked their progress by spotting landmarks. On the open seas, they watched for birds as a sign that land was near. At night they steered by the North Star. Like most people of the time, Vikings believed the Earth was flat. Still, they bravely sailed into the unknown.

Did Carter and his crew feel as fearless as the Vikings? "I'm afraid of everything," Carter says, laughing. "It all scares me or challenges me, both at the same time. That's what makes me go out and do it."

Carter met the challenge of the second voyage head on. And on September 22, the crew arrived at L'Anse aux Meadows, Newfoundland. At last, they had successfully re-created Leif Ericson's 1,000-year-old journey.

FIND OUT MORE

Visit our website:

www.mhschool.com/reading

Based on an article in *TIME FOR KIDS*.

Story Questions & Activities

1. What is *a knarr*? Describe it.
2. What happened when the modern-day crew re-created a Viking journey?
3. Why may the crew have wanted to re-create Leif Ericson's voyage?
4. What happened on the 1998 trip? Give the events in time order.
5. Suppose that Carter and his crew could re-create the voyage shown in the painting on pages 100–101. Where do you think they would be going? What do you think would happen on the trip?

Write a Photo Essay

Think of a day when you had the best time ever. Were you on a family vacation? Were you attending a special event with your friends? How did you get there?

Write an essay describing the day. Collect one or two photos or, if you cannot find any, make drawings. Write a caption for each photo or drawing. Be sure to describe events from your point of view, using *I* or *We* in your writing.

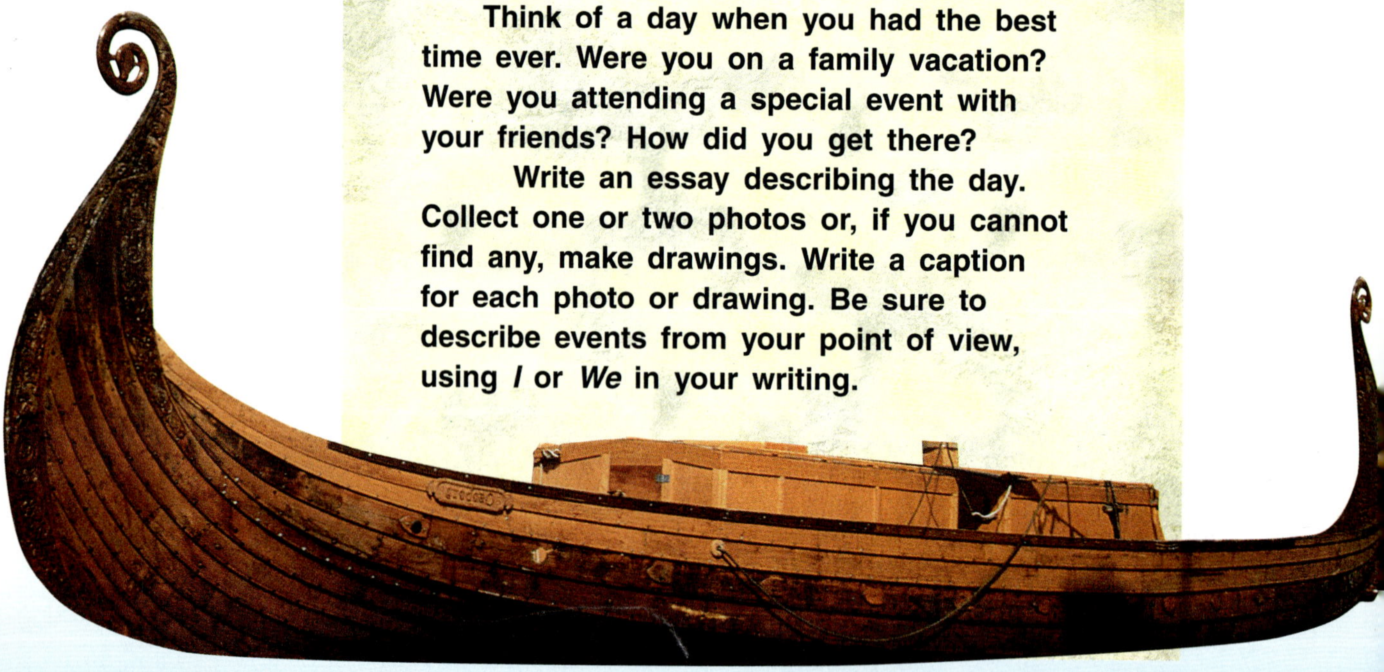

Make a Comparison Chart

W. Hodding Carter wanted his voyage to be like Leif Ericson's, but in some ways that was impossible. Make a two-column chart that compares and contrasts the two voyages. Some things you might compare are the ship, food, clothing, navigational tools, and safety measures.

Trace a Viking Voyage

The Vikings reached almost every part of the world that was known in their time. They ranged up and down the coasts of Scandinavia and Europe and built permanent settlements in the British Isles and Europe. They also settled Iceland, Greenland, and the tip of what is now Newfoundland, Canada. On a map of Europe and the Atlantic coast, trace the areas that the Vikings explored and settled.

Find Out More

Who were the Vikings? Use an encyclopedia and books on the Vikings to find out more about them. Some areas you might explore are armor and weapons, Viking treasures, Viking settlements, clothing, jewelry, and utensils. Share your findings with the class.

Choose Reference Sources

If you wanted to write a report about Viking voyages, where would you begin your research? By choosing reference sources wisely, you can find the information you need quickly and easily. For example, you could look in an encyclopedia for general information and in an atlas for maps. For the most recent information on a topic, you could check the *Readers' Guide to Periodical Literature*, which is an index of magazine articles, or search on the Internet.

Use the descriptions to answer these questions.

1. Where would you look to find the meaning of *fiord*?
2. In which reference source would you find several maps of northern Europe?
3. How could you find recent magazine articles about the discovery of Viking artifacts?
4. What reference source would give you the most information about the Viking Age?
5. Why is it important to know how to choose a reference source when writing a research report?

TEST POWER

Test Tip

Read all answer choices for each question.

DIRECTIONS

Read the sample story. Then read each question about the story.

SAMPLE

Will Jan win the contest?

Jan had only three more weeks to practice her free throws until the big contest would be held. Every year at the middle school, contestants tried their best to make as many baskets as they could during the five-minute intermission of an exhibition game.

"Do you think that you'll win this year?" asked Jan's friend Robyn. Robyn had been helping Jan practice every day after school.

"I don't know. I feel that I have a good shot, but I think more practice would help me become consistent," Jan responded as she took aim for another shot.

SWISH, the basketball slid evenly through the hoop. Jan turned to Robyn and grinned. "If I can shoot the ball like that, there's no doubt that I'll be victorious."

Robyn agreed as she tossed another basketball to Jan. "I'm sure that you'll be great!" Robyn said.

1 How does Robyn feel about Jan's ability to win the contest?

- **A** She is uncertain about who will win.
- **B** She doesn't want Jan to compete.
- **C** Robyn wants to win the contest herself.
- **D** She thinks that Jan will win.

2 What is the main idea of this story?

- **F** Jan believes that practicing will help her win the big contest.
- **G** Practicing for the contest isn't very important to Jan.
- **H** Robyn and Jan wish that they were in the contest together.
- **J** Jan has practiced every day after school for the contest.

Daydreamers

Daydreamers...

holding their bodies still
for a time
letting the world turn around them

while their dreams hopscotch,
doubledutch, dance,

thoughts rollerskate,
crisscross,
bump into hopes and wishes.

Dreamers
thinking up new ways,
looking toward new days,

planning new tries,
asking new whys.
Before long,
hands will start to move again,
eyes turn outward,
bodies shift for action,
but for this moment they are still,

they are
the daydreamers
letting the world dizzy itself
without them.

Scenes passing through their minds
make no sound
glide from hiding places
promenade and return
silently
the children watch their memories
with spirit-eyes
seeing more than they saw before

feeling more
or maybe less
than they felt the time before
reaching with spirit-hands
to touch the dreams
drawn from their yesterdays.

They will not be the same
after this growing time,
this dreaming.
In their stillness they have moved
forward

toward womanhood
toward manhood.
This dreaming has made them
new.

by Eloise Greenfield

A Common Thread

UNIT 2

PEOPLE

Some people talk and talk
and never say a thing.
Some people look at you
and birds begin to sing.

Some people laugh and laugh
and yet you want to cry.
Some people touch your hand
and music fills the sky.

by Charlotte Zolotow

Stories in Art

Every picture tells a story. This painting of mothers walking their children home from school was painted more than 60 years ago.

Look at the painting. What story does it tell? What details do you notice? Compare the scene in the painting with a school scene of today. What are the differences? What has remained the same?

Look at the painting again. What colors did the artist use? Why do you think he used primary colors—red, blue, and yellow? What do these colors make you think of? Explain.

School's Out
by Allan Rohan Crite, 1936
The National Museum of American Art, Washington, D.C.

LAST SUMMER WITH MAIZON

BY JACQUELINE WOODSON

ILLUSTRATED BY CORNELIUS VAN WRIGHT

IT WAS THE SUMMER MARGARET TORY'S FATHER DIED. WHILE TRYING TO COME TO TERMS WITH THIS LOSS, MARGARET ALSO HAS TO FACE BEING SEPARATED FROM HER BEST FRIEND, MAIZON, WHO IS GOING AWAY TO BOARDING SCHOOL. AS MARGARET AND HER MOTHER ACCOMPANY MAIZON AND HER GRANDMOTHER TO THE TRAIN STATION IN NEW YORK CITY, BOTH GIRLS WONDER HOW THEY WILL GET ALONG WITHOUT EACH OTHER.

"Sure wish you weren't going away," Margaret said, choking back tears for what seemed like the millionth time. They were sitting on the M train, crossing the Williamsburg Bridge, and Margaret shivered as the train passed over the water. The L train would have made the trip easier but the L didn't go over the bridge and Maizon had wanted to ride over it once more before she left.

Maizon sat nervously drumming her fingers against the windowpane. "Me too," she said absently.

Margaret looked over at Mama and Grandma. Grandma stared out of her window. She looked old and out of place on the train.

"Maizon?" Margaret said, turning back toward her.

"Hmm?" Maizon frowned. She seemed to be concentrating on something in the water. It rippled and danced below them.

"Even though I wrote you those two letters, you only have to write me one back if you don't have a lot of time or something." Margaret looked down at her fingers. She had begun biting the cuticles, and now the skin surrounding her nails was red and ragged.

8
B-10 WIN

"I'll write you back," Maizon promised.

"Maizon . . ."

"What, Margaret!"

Margaret jumped and looked at Maizon. There was an uneasiness in her eyes she had never seen before.

"Forget it," she said.

Ms. Tory leaned over. "We'll be getting off in a few stops."

They rode the rest of the way in silence. At Delancey Street they changed for another train and a half hour later they were at Penn Station.

"I guess now we'll have to call each other to plan the same outfits," Maizon said as they waited for her train. Her voice sounded forced and fake, Margaret thought, like a grown-up trying to make a kid smile.

"I guess," Margaret said. The conductor called Maizon's train.

"I guess I gotta go," Maizon said softly, and Margaret felt a lump rise in her throat.

"I'll write you back, Margaret. Promise. Thanks for letting me keep the double-dutch trophy even if it is only second place." They hugged for a long time. Maizon sniffed loudly. "I'm scared, Margaret," she whispered.

Margaret didn't know what to say. "Don't be."

"Bye, Ms. Tory."

Margaret's mother bent down and hugged Maizon. "Be good," she said as Maizon and her grandmother made their way toward the train.

"Mama," Margaret said as they watched Maizon and her grandmother disappear into the tunnel.

"What, dear?"

"What's the difference between a best friend and an old friend?"

"I guess . . ." Her mother thought for a moment. "I guess an old friend is a friend you once had and a best friend is a friend you'll always have."

"Then maybe me and Maizon aren't best friends anymore."

"Don't be silly, Margaret. What else would you two be? Some people can barely tell you apart. I feel like I've lost a daughter."

"Maybe . . . I don't know . . . Maybe we're old friends now. Maybe this was our last summer as best friends. I feel like something's going to change now and I'm not going to be able to change it back."

Ms. Tory's heels made a clicking sound through the terminal. She stopped to buy tokens and turned to Margaret.

"Like when Daddy died?" she asked, looking worried.

Margaret swallowed. "No. I just feel empty instead of sad, Mama," she said.

Her mother squeezed her hand as they waited for the train. When it came, they took seats by the window.

Ms. Tory held on to Margaret's hand. "Sometimes it just takes a while for the pain of loss to set in."

"I feel like sometimes Maizon kept me from doing things, but now she's not here. Now I don't have any"—Margaret thought for a moment, but couldn't find the right words—"now I don't have any excuse not to do things."

When the train emerged from its tunnel, the late afternoon sun had turned a bright orange. Margaret watched it for a moment. She looked at her hands again and discovered a cuticle she had missed.

Margaret pressed her pencil to her lips and stared out the classroom window. The school yard was desolate and gray. But everything seemed that way since Maizon left. Especially since a whole week had passed now without even a letter from her. Margaret sighed and chewed her eraser.

"Margaret, are you working on this assignment?"

Margaret jumped and turned toward Ms. Peazle. Maizon had been right—Ms. Peazle was the crabbiest teacher in the school. Margaret wondered why she had been picked to teach the smartest class. If students were so smart, she thought, the least the school could do was reward them with a nice teacher.

"I'm trying to think about what to write, Ms. Peazle."

"Well, you won't find an essay on your summer vacation outside that window, I'm sure. Or is that where you spent it?"

The class snickered and Margaret looked down, embarrassed. "No, ma'am."

"I'm glad to hear that," Ms. Peazle continued, looking at Margaret over granny glasses. "And I'm sure in the next ten minutes you'll be able to read your essay to the class and prove to us all that you weren't just daydreaming. Am I right?"

"I hope so, ma'am," Margaret mumbled. She looked around the room. It seemed everyone in 6-1 knew each other from the previous year. On the first day, a lot of kids asked her about Maizon, but after that no one said much to her. Things had changed since Maizon left. Without her, a lot of the fun had gone out of sitting on the stoop with Ms. Dell, Hattie, and Li'l Jay. Maybe she could write about that. No, Margaret thought, looking down at the blank piece of paper in front of her. It was too much to tell. She'd never get finished and Ms. Peazle would scold her—making her feel too dumb to be in 6-1. Margaret chewed her eraser and stared out the window again. There had to be something she could write about quickly.

"Margaret Tory!" Ms. Peazle warned. "Am I going to have to change your seat?"

"Ma'am? I was just . . ."

"I think I'm going to have to move you away from that window unless you can prove to me that you can sit there without being distracted."

"I can, Ms. Peazle. It helps me write," she lied.

"Then I take it you should be ready to read your essay in"—Ms. Peazle looked at her watch—"the next seven minutes."

Margaret started writing frantically. When Ms. Peazle called her to the front of the room, her sheet of notebook paper shook in her hand. She pulled nervously at the hem of the maroon dress she and Maizon had picked out for school and tried not to look out at the twenty-six pairs of eyes she knew were on her.

"Last summer was the worst summer of my life. First my father died and then my best friend went away to a private boarding school. I didn't go anywhere except Manhattan. But that wasn't any fun because I was taking Maizon to the train. I hope next summer is a lot better."

She finished reading and walked silently back to her desk and tried to concentrate on not looking out the window. Instead, she rested her eyes on the half-written page. Margaret knew she could write better than that, but Ms. Peazle had rushed her. Anyway, she thought, that is what happened last summer.

"I'd like to see you after class, Margaret."

"Yes, ma'am," Margaret said softly. *This is the end,* she thought. One week in the smartest class and it's over. Maizon was smart enough to go to a better *school* and I can't even keep up in this class. Margaret sighed and tried not to stare out the window for the rest of the day.

When the three o'clock bell rang, she waited uneasily in her seat while Ms. Peazle led the rest of the class out to the school yard. Margaret heard the excited screams and laughter as everyone poured outside.

The empty classroom was quiet. She looked around at the desks. Many had words carved into them. They reminded her of the names she and Maizon had carved into the tar last summer. They were faded and illegible now.

Ms. Peazle came in and sat at the desk next to Margaret's. "Margaret," she said slowly, pausing for a moment to remove her glasses and rub her eyes tiredly. "I'm sorry to hear about your father . . ."

"That's okay." Margaret fidgeted.

"No, Margaret, it's not okay," Ms. Peazle continued, "not if it's going to affect your schoolwork."

"I can do better, Ms. Peazle, I really can!" Margaret looked up pleadingly. She was surprised at herself for wanting so badly to stay in Ms. Peazle's class.

"I know you can, Margaret. That's why I'm going to ask you to do this. For homework tonight . . ."

Margaret started to say that none of the other students had been assigned homework. She decided not to, though.

"I want you to write about your summer," Ms. Peazle continued. "I want it to express all of your feelings about your friend Maizon going away. Or it could be about your father's death and how you felt then. It doesn't matter what you write, a poem, an essay, a short story. Just so long as it expresses how you felt this summer. Is that understood?"

"Yes, ma'am." Margaret looked up at Ms. Peazle. "It's understood."

Ms. Peazle smiled. Without her glasses, Margaret thought, she wasn't that mean-looking.

"Good, then I'll see you bright and early tomorrow with something wonderful to read to the class."

Margaret slid out of the chair and walked toward the door.

"That's a very pretty dress, Margaret," Ms. Peazle said.

Margaret turned and started to tell her that Maizon was wearing the same one in Connecticut, but changed her mind. What did Ms. Peazle know about best friends who were almost cousins, anyway?

"Thanks, ma'am," she said instead, and ducked out of the classroom. All of a sudden, she had a wonderful idea!

The next morning Ms. Peazle tapped her ruler against the desk to quiet the class. "Margaret," she asked when the room was silent. "Do you have something you want to share with us today?"

Margaret nodded and Ms. Peazle beckoned her to the front of the room.

"This," Margaret said, handing Ms. Peazle the sheet of looseleaf paper. It had taken her most of the evening to finish the assignment.

Ms. Peazle looked it over and handed it back to her.

"We're ready to listen," she said, smiling.

Margaret looked out over the class and felt her stomach slide up to her throat. She swallowed and counted to ten. Though the day was cool, she found herself sweating. Margaret couldn't remember when she had been this afraid.

"My pen doesn't write anymore," she began reading.

"I can't hear," someone called out.

"My pen doesn't write anymore," Margaret repeated. In the back of the room, someone exaggerated a sigh. The class chuckled. Margaret ignored them and continued to read.

"It stumbles and trembles in my hand.
If my dad were here—he would understand.
Best of all—It'd be last summer again.

But they've turned off the fire hydrants
Locked green leaves away.
Sprinkled ashes on you
and sent you on your way.

I wouldn't mind the early autumn
if you came home today
I'd tell you how much I miss you
and know I'd be okay.

Mama isn't laughing now
She works hard and she cries
she wonders when true laughter
will relieve her of her sighs
And even when she's smiling
Her eyes don't smile along
her face is growing older
She doesn't seem as strong.
I worry cause I love her
Ms. Dell says, 'where there is love,
there is a way.'

It's funny how we never know
exactly how our life will go
It's funny how a dream can fade
With the break of day.

I'm not sure where you are now
though I see you in my dreams
Ms. Dell says the things we see
are not always as they seem.

So often I'm uncertain
if you have found a new home
and when I am uncertain
I usually write a poem.

Time can't erase the memory
and time can't bring you home
Last summer was a part of me
and now a part is gone."

It's funny how we never
exactly how our life
It's funny how a dream
the break of day

The class stared at her blankly, silent. Margaret lowered her head and made her way back to her seat.

"Could you leave that assignment on my desk, Margaret?" Ms. Peazle asked. There was a small smile playing at the corners of her mouth.

"Yes, ma'am," Margaret said. Why didn't anyone say anything?

"Now, if everyone will open their history books to page two seventy-five, we'll continue with our lesson on the Civil War."

Margaret wondered what she had expected the class to do. Applaud? She missed Maizon more than she had in a long time. *She would know what I'm feeling,* Margaret thought. And if she didn't, she'd make believe she did.

Margaret snuck a look out the window. The day looked cold and still. *She'd tell me it's only a feeling poets get and that Nikki Giovanni feels this way all of the time.* When she turned back, there was a small piece of paper on her desk.

"I liked your poem, Margaret," the note read. There was no name.

Margaret looked around but no one looked as though they had slipped a note on her desk. She smiled to herself and tucked the piece of paper into her notebook.

The final bell rang. As the class rushed out, Margaret was bumped against Ms. Peazle's desk.

"Did you get my note?" Ms. Peazle whispered. Margaret nodded and floated home.

Ms. Dell, Hattie, and Li'l Jay were sitting on the stoop when she got home.

"If it weren't so cold," she said, squeezing in beside Hattie's spreading hips, "it would be like old times."

"Except for Maizon," Hattie said, cutting her eyes toward her mother.

"Hush, Hattie," Ms. Dell said. She shivered and pulled Li'l Jay closer to her. For a moment, Margaret thought she looked old.

"It's just this cold spell we're having," Ms. Dell said. "Ages a person. Makes them look older than they are."

Margaret smiled. "Reading minds is worse than eavesdropping, Ms. Dell."

"Try being her daughter for nineteen years," Hattie said.

"Hattie," Margaret said, moving closer to her for warmth. "How come you never liked Maizon?"

"No one said I never liked her."

"No one had to," Ms. Dell butted in.

"She was just too much ahead of everyone. At least she thought she was."

"But she was, Hattie. She was the smartest person at P.S. 102. Imagine being the smartest person."

"But she didn't have any common sense, Margaret. And when God gives a person that much brain, he's bound to leave out something else."

"Like what?"

Ms. Dell leaned over Li'l Jay's head and whispered loudly, "Like the truth."

She and Hattie laughed but Margaret couldn't see the humor. It wasn't like either of them to say something wrong about a person.

"She told the truth . . ." Margaret said weakly.

Ms. Dell and Hattie exchanged looks.

"How was school?" Hattie asked too brightly.

"Boring," Margaret said. She would tuck what they said away until she could figure it out.

"That's the only word you know since Maizon left. Seems there's gotta be somethin' else going on that's not so *boring* all the time," Ms. Dell said.

"Well, it's sure not school. I read a poem to that stupid class and no one but Ms. Peazle liked it." She sighed and rested her chin on her hand.

"That's the chance you gotta take with poetry," Ms. Dell said. "Either everybody likes it or everybody hates it, but you hardly ever know 'cause nobody says a word. Too afraid to

offend you or, worse yet, make you feel good."

Margaret looked from Ms. Dell to Hattie then back to Ms. Dell again.

"How come you know so much about poetry?"

"You're not the first li'l black girl who wanted to be a poet."

"And you can bet your dress you won't be the last," Hattie concluded.

"You wanted to be a poet, Hattie??!!"

"Still do. Still make up poems in my head. Never write them down, though. The paper just yellows and clutters useful places. So this is where I keep it all now," she said, pointing to her head.

"A poem can't exist inside your head. You forget it," Margaret said doubtfully.

"Poems don't exist, Miss Know-It-All. Poems live! In your head is where a poem is born, isn't it?"

Margaret nodded and Hattie continued. "Well, my poetry chooses to live there!"

"Then recite one for me, please." Margaret folded her arms across her chest the way she had seen Ms. Dell do so many times.

"Some poems aren't meant to be heard, smarty-pants."

"Aw, Hattie," Ms. Dell interrupted, "let Margaret be the judge of that."

"All right. All right." Hattie's voice

dropped to a whisper. "Brooklyn-bound robin redbreast followed me from down home / Brooklyn-bound robin, you're a long way from your own / So fly among the pigeons and circle the sky with your song."

They were quiet. Ms. Dell rocked Li'l Jay to sleep in her arms. Hattie looked somberly over the block in silence and Margaret thought of how much Hattie's poem made her think of Maizon. What was she doing now that the sun was almost down? she wondered. Had she found a new best friend?

"Maybe," she said after a long time. "Maybe it wasn't that the class didn't like my poem. Maybe it was like your poem, Hattie. You just have to sit quietly and think about all the things it makes you think about after you hear it. You have to let . . . let it sink in!"

"You have to feel it, Margaret," Hattie said softly, draping her arm over Margaret's shoulder.

"Yeah. Just like I felt when I wrote my poem, or you felt when you found a place for that one in your head!"

"Margaret," Ms. Dell said, "you gettin' too smart for us ol' ladies."

Margaret leaned against Hattie and listened to the fading sounds of construction. Soon the building on Palmetto Street would be finished. She closed her eyes and visions of last summer came into her head. She saw herself running down Madison Street arm in arm with Maizon. They were laughing. Then the picture faded into a new one. She and Maizon were sitting by the tree watching Li'l Jay take his first steps. He stumbled and fell into Maizon's arms. Now it all seemed like such a long time ago.

When she opened her eyes again, the moon was inching out from behind a cloud. It was barely visible in the late afternoon. The sky had turned a wintry blue and the streetlights flickered on. Margaret yawned, her head heavy all of a sudden from the long day.

"Looks like your mother's workin' late again. Bless that woman's heart. Seems she's workin' nonstop since your daddy passed."

"She's taking drawing classes. She wants to be an architect. Maybe she'll make a lot of money."

"Architects don't make a lot of money," Hattie said. "And anyway, you shouldn't be worrying your head over money."

"She has a gift," Ms. Dell said. "All of you Torys have gifts. You with your writing, your mama with her drawings, and remember the things your daddy did with wood. Oh, that man was something else!"

"What's Li'l Jay's going to be?"

Ms. Dell stood up and pressed Li'l Jay's face to her cheek.

"Time's gonna tell us, Margaret. Now, come inside and do your homework while I fix you something to eat. No use sitting out in the cold."

Margaret rose and followed them inside.

"You hear anything from Maizon yet?" Hattie asked.

Margaret shook her head. If only Maizon were running up the block!

"I wrote her two letters and she hasn't written me one. Maybe she knows we're not really best friends anymore." Margaret sighed. She had been right in thinking she and Maizon were only old friends now, not the friends they used to be. "Still, I wish I knew how she was doing," she said, turning away so Hattie wouldn't see the tears in her eyes.

"We all do, honey," Hattie said, taking Margaret's hand. "We all do."

MEET JACQUELINE WOODSON

A seven-year-old Jacqueline Woodson refused to give up her dream of becoming a writer—not even when her older sister told her that no one would publish her book of poems.

Years later, Woodson's determination to be a writer finally paid off. Her first published novel, *Last Summer with Maizon,* a book about friends and change, takes place on the Brooklyn street where Woodson once lived. It is based partly on her childhood friendship with a girl named Maria. "I wanted to write a book about friendship so that people could remember how important friends are." She explains further, "You can't write a book without putting a little bit of yourself into it. You mix that bit of yourself up with your imagination. That's how you create fiction. Well, that's how *I* create fiction."

Story Questions & Activities

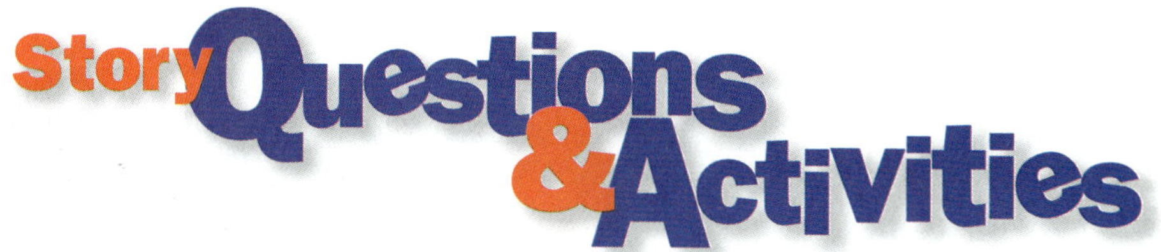

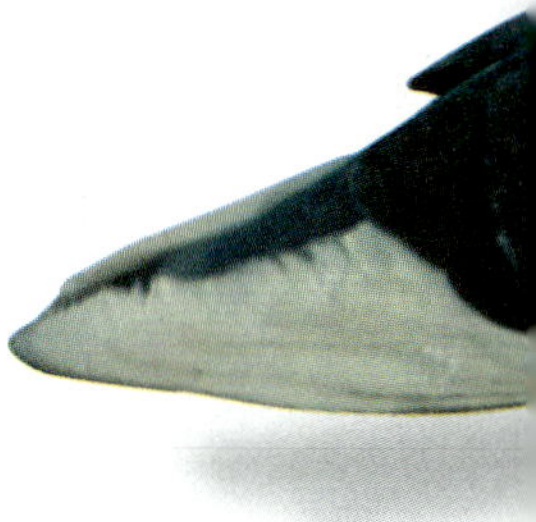

1. Where is Maizon going?
2. Compare how Margaret felt this past summer with the way she felt the summer before. How was this summer different?
3. How does writing a poem help Margaret express her feelings?
4. What is this story mostly about?
5. Suppose that Margaret and Maizon stepped into the painting on pages 114–115. What do you think the girls would be doing? How do you think they would be feeling?

Write an Essay

Margaret's poem expresses her thoughts and feelings about last summer. Now it's your turn. Write an essay about how you have changed in the past year. Include the ways you have grown, the goals you have achieved, and the new dreams you have made. Try to create images that will help readers understand how you have changed.

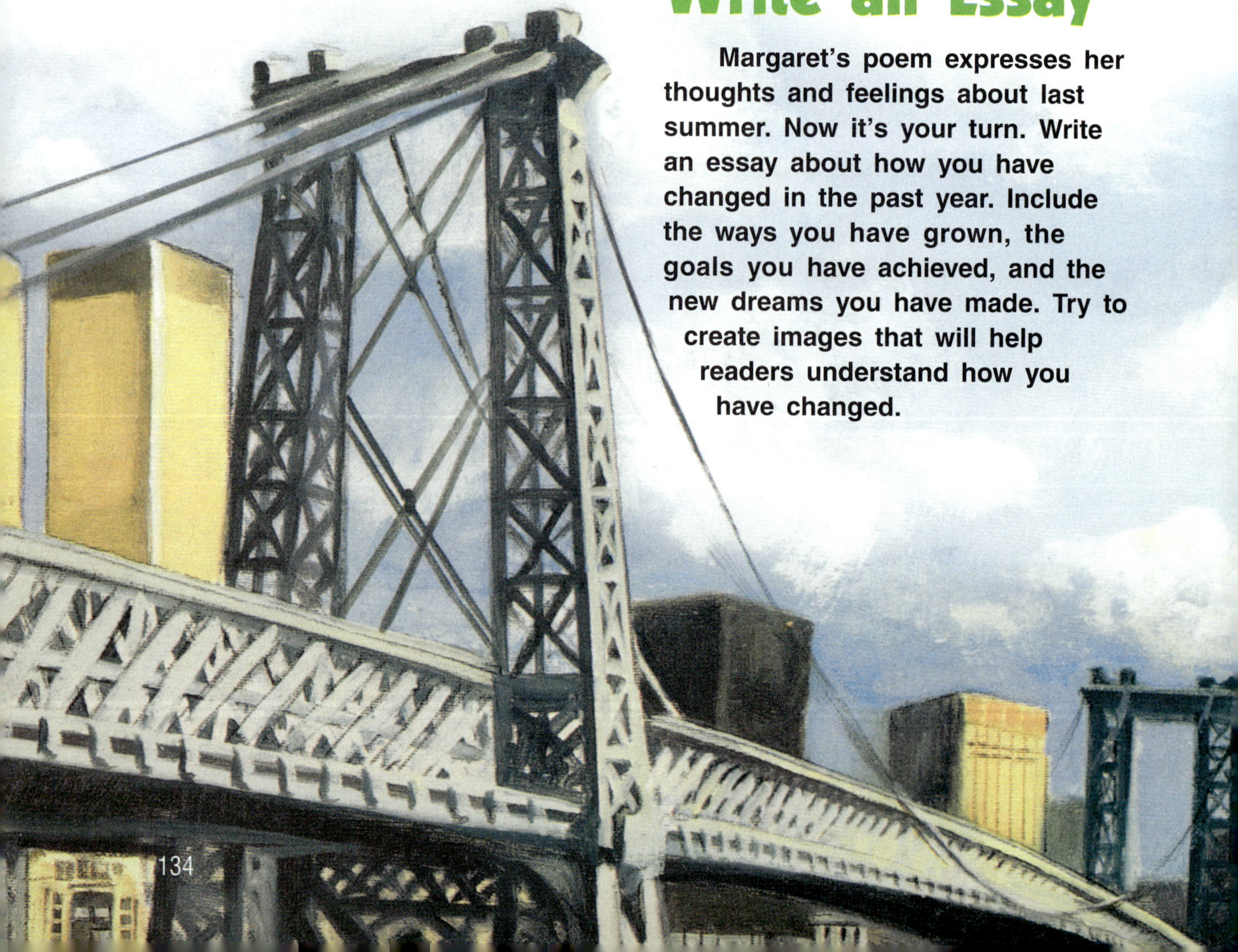

Observe Nature

Hattie's poem tells of a robin that flies with the pigeons in a city. Although pigeons are the most common city birds, city parks may be home to robins and other wildlife. With a partner or a family member, observe the wildlife found in your city or town. Keep a journal of what you see. Share your journal with your classmates or family.

Create a Careers Box

CAREERS BOX

Margaret's mother is studying to be an architect. What does an architect do? Interview an architect, or invite one to speak to your class. Find out about the special training that architects receive, the kinds of plans they draw, and the buildings they design. Write a job description of an architect on an index card, and place it in a careers box. Add to the box as you learn about other careers.

Find Out More

Maizon and Margaret took the subway to the railroad station. With a partner, record questions you have about subways. For example: When and where was the world's first subway opened? Use an encyclopedia or the internet to learn more about subways. Create an "Amazing Subway Facts" booklet based on your research. Illustrate your booklet with maps and pictures.

Read a Form

Now that Maizon has moved to a new town, she will have to fill out an application for a new library card. An **application** is a type of form that is completed to make a request. Some libraries post library card applications on their Internet Web sites. Here is a sample, which has been partially filled in. Clicking on the SUBMIT icon will send the completed application to the library.

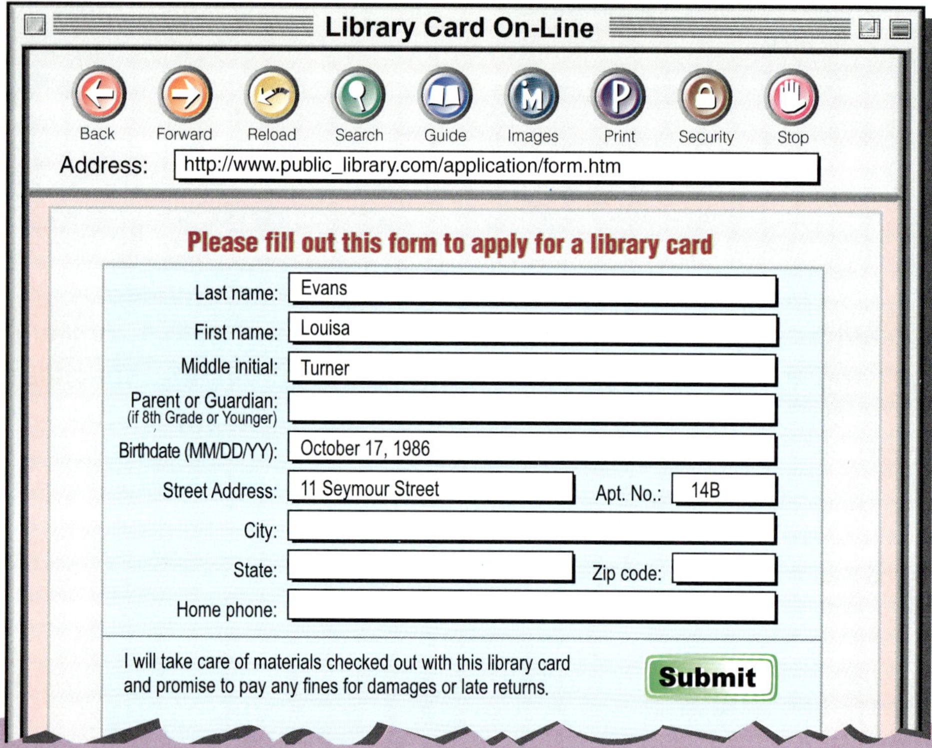
Library Card On-Line

Back Forward Reload Search Guide Images Print Security Stop

Address: http://www.public_library.com/application/form.htm

Please fill out this form to apply for a library card

Last name:	Evans
First name:	Louisa
Middle initial:	Turner
Parent or Guardian: (if 8th Grade or Younger)	
Birthdate (MM/DD/YY):	October 17, 1986
Street Address:	11 Seymour Street — Apt. No.: 14B
City:	
State:	Zip code:
Home phone:	

I will take care of materials checked out with this library card and promise to pay any fines for damages or late returns.

Submit

Use the application to answer these questions.

1. What is the first name of the person who is filling out this application?
2. What is incorrect about her birthdate information?
3. Which line can a high school student skip?
4. Why might a middle name be good to include?
5. Why is it important to fill out applications carefully and completely?

TEST POWER

Test Tip

If you are not sure how to answer these questions, now is the time to ask your teacher.

DIRECTIONS

Read the sample story. Then read each question about the story.

SAMPLE

Babe Didrikson Zaharias

Mildred "Babe" Didrikson Zaharias was the greatest woman athlete of all time. Nobody won more medals or awards than she did. Babe played basketball, baseball, and professional golf, and she was a master at swimming, tennis, and track and field.

Babe started by playing basketball, and because she ran so fast and could jump so far, she began to compete in track and field events. She soon held the world record in the long jump and the high jump. In 1932, she won 8 of the 10 events in the Women's Track and Field National Championships and won two gold medals at the Olympics.

1 This passage provides evidence that Babe —

A was best at basketball

B excelled at many sports

C hit many home runs

D was friendly

2 Which is an OPINION in the story?

F Babe won two gold medals.

G Babe played professional golf.

H Babe was the greatest woman athlete of all time.

J Babe could not run fast.

How do you know which choices are facts, and which are opinions?

Artists often tell their stories in materials they know well. Look at this *winter count.* It is a calendar record of events. Year after year, tribal leaders chose the most important event of that year and had it painted on this animal hide.

Look at this winter count. What can you tell about it? Where do you think it begins? Which buffalo hunt might have been the most dangerous? Why?

Study this winter count. How does it give you the history of a group of Plains Indians? What problems did they face? How did they solve them? Do you think their lives are much different today?

Painted Hide
by Kadzie Cody, 1900

Meet Mary Whitebird

Native American themes are central to the stories that Mary Whitebird creates. As a Native American, she writes about her culture and the Native American experience. Her stories help her share with younger generations her pride in her Native American heritage. They also show her young readers the challenges faced by Native Americans living in today's modern world.

First published in a magazine for students, "Ta-Na-E-Ka" has appeared in many student anthologies. Today, it remains one of the most popular coming-of-age stories for students.

Meet Shonto Begay

Shonto Begay was born on a Native American reservation five miles from the town of Shonto, Arizona. Begay was raised and educated on Native American reservations, and what he learned of his own culture remains the most important part of his life and work. "The teachings of my elders make it very clear that this land is sacred," he says. "We belong to it; it does not belong to us."

As an artist, Begay shows his paintings in galleries and museums across the country. He is also the author of many books and poems for young people. In addition, Begay travels to many schools, speaking of his life as an artist and as a traditional Navajo. His work remains deeply connected to his heritage and to what he has become through its teachings. "My works are personal visions shared," he says. "My art is created from my heart and from the earth. It is my truth."

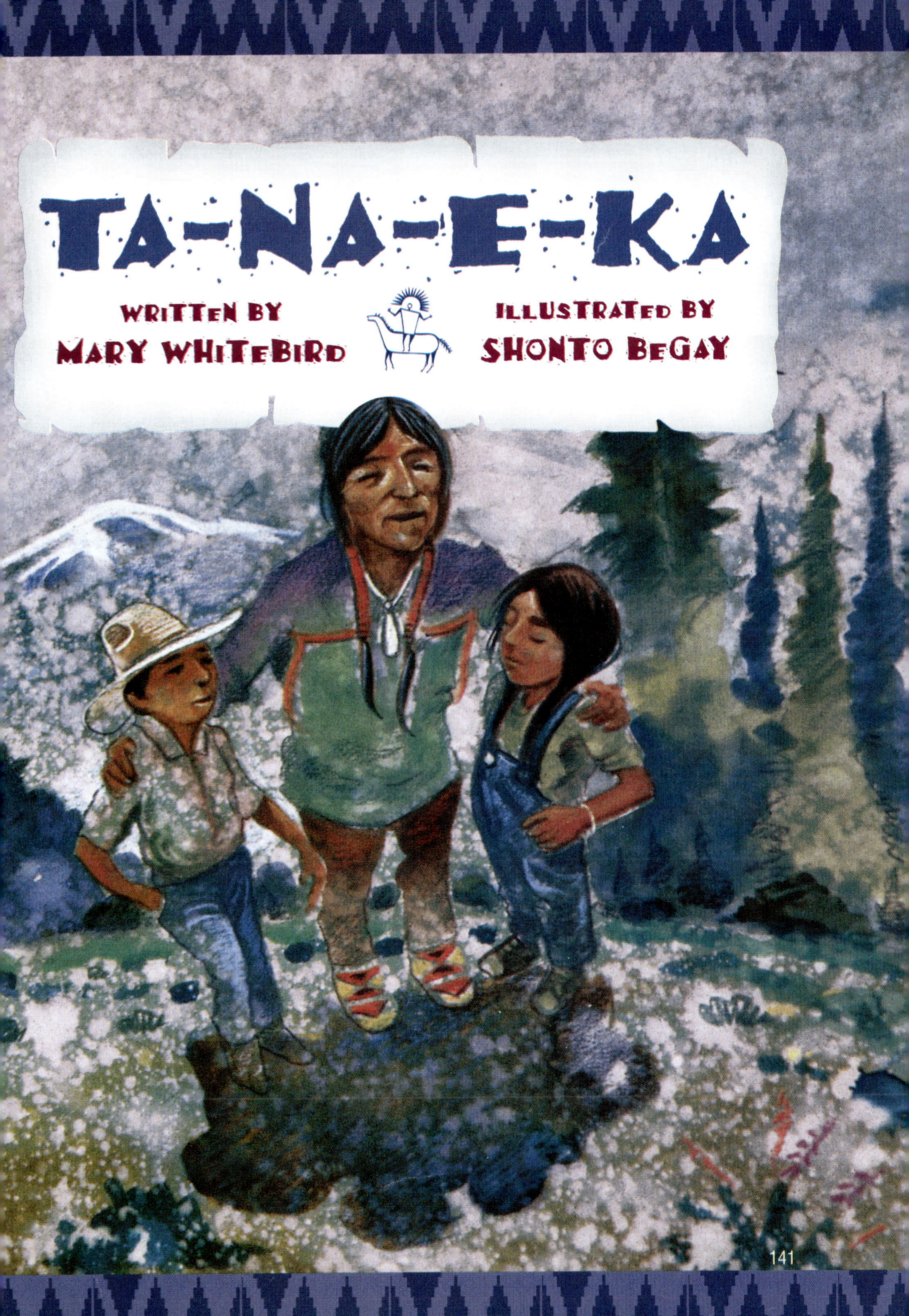

TA-NA-E-KA

WRITTEN BY MARY WHITEBIRD

ILLUSTRATED BY SHONTO BEGAY

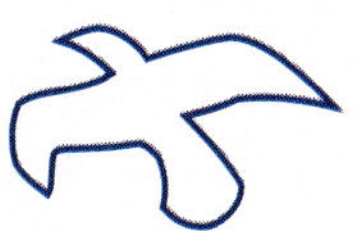

As my birthday drew closer, I had awful nightmares about it. I was reaching the age at which all Kaw Indians had to participate in Ta-Na-E-Ka. Well, not all Kaws. Many of the younger families on the reservation were beginning to give up the old customs. But my grandfather, Amos Deer Leg, was devoted to tradition. He still wore handmade beaded moccasins instead of shoes, and kept his iron-gray hair in tight braids. He could speak English, but he spoke it only with white men. With his family he used a Sioux dialect.

Grandfather was one of the last living Indians (he died in 1953 when he was 81) who actually fought against the U.S. Cavalry. Not only did he fight, he was wounded in a skirmish at Rose Creek—a famous encounter in which the celebrated Kaw chief Flat Nose lost his life. At the time, my grandfather was only eleven years old.

Eleven was a magic word among the Kaws. It was the time of Ta-Na-E-Ka, the "flowering of adulthood." It was the age, my grandfather informed us hundreds of times, "when a boy could prove himself to be a warrior and a girl took the steps to womanhood."

"I don't want to be a warrior," my cousin, Roger Deer Leg, confided to me. "I'm going to become an accountant."

"None of the other tribes make girls go through the endurance ritual," I complained to my mother.

"It won't be as bad as you think, Mary," my mother said, ignoring my protests. "Once you've gone through it, you'll certainly never forget it. You'll be proud."

I even complained to my teacher, Mrs. Richardson, feeling that, as a white woman, she would side with me.

She didn't. "All of us have rituals of one kind or another," Mrs. Richardson said. "And look at it this way: How many girls have the opportunity to compete on equal terms with boys? Don't look down on your heritage."

Heritage, indeed! I had no intention of living on a reservation for the rest of my life. I was a good student. I loved school. My fantasies were about knights in armor and fair ladies in flowing gowns, being saved from dragons. It never once occurred to me that being an Indian was exciting.

But I've always thought that the Kaw were the originators of the women's liberation movement. No other Indian tribe—and I've spent half a lifetime researching the subject—treated women more "equally" than the Kaw. Unlike most of the sub-tribes of the Sioux Nation, the Kaw allowed men and women to eat together. And hundreds of years before we were "acculturated," a Kaw woman had the right to refuse a prospective husband even if her father arranged the match.

The wisest women (generally wisdom was equated with age) often sat in tribal councils. Furthermore, most Kaw legends revolve around "Good Woman," a kind of super-squaw, a Joan of Arc of the high plains. Good Woman led Kaw warriors into battle after battle from which they always seemed to emerge victorious.

And girls as well as boys were required to undergo Ta-Na-E-Ka.

The actual ceremony varied from tribe to tribe, but since the Indians' life on the plains was dedicated to survival, Ta-Na-E-Ka was a test of survival.

"Endurance is the loftiest virtue of the Indian," my grandfather explained. "To survive, we must endure. When I was a boy, Ta-Na-E-Ka was more than the mere symbol it is now. We were painted white with the juice of a sacred herb and sent naked into the wilderness without so much as a knife. We couldn't return until the white had worn off. It wouldn't wash off. It took almost eighteen days, and during that time we had to stay alive, trapping food, eating insects and roots and berries, and watching out for enemies. And we did have enemies—both the white soldiers and the Omaha warriors, who were always trying to capture Kaw boys and girls undergoing their endurance test. It was an exciting time."

"What happened if you couldn't make it?" Roger asked. He was born only three days after I was, and we were being trained for Ta-Na-E-Ka together. I was happy to know he was frightened, too.

"Many didn't return," Grandfather said. "Only the strongest and shrewdest. Mothers were not allowed to weep over those who didn't return. If a Kaw couldn't survive, he or she wasn't worth weeping over. It was our way."

"What a lot of hooey," Roger whispered. "I'd give anything to get out of it."

"I don't see how we have any choice," I replied.

Roger gave my arm a little squeeze. "Well, it's only five days."

Five days! Maybe it was better than being painted white and sent out naked for eighteen days. But not much better.

We were to be sent, barefoot and in bathing suits, into the woods. Even our very traditional parents put their foot down when Grandfather suggested we go naked. For five days we'd have to live off the land, keeping warm as best we could, getting food where we could. It was May, but on the northernmost reaches of the Missouri River the days were still chilly and the nights were fiercely cold.

Grandfather was in charge of the month's training for Ta-Na-E-Ka. One day he caught a grasshopper and demonstrated how to pull its legs and wings off in one flick of the fingers and how to swallow it.

I felt sick, and Roger turned green. "It's a darn good thing it's 1947," I told Roger teasingly. "You'd make a terrible warrior." Roger just grimaced.

I knew one thing. This particular Kaw Indian girl wasn't going to swallow a grasshopper no matter how hungry she got. And then I had an idea. Why hadn't I thought of it before? It would have saved nights of bad dreams about squooshy grasshoppers.

I headed straight for my teacher's house. "Mrs. Richardson," I said, "would you lend me five dollars?"

"Five dollars!" she exclaimed. "What for?"

"You remember the ceremony I talked about?"

"Ta-Na-E-Ka. Of course. Your parents have written me and asked me to excuse you from school so you can participate in it."

"Well, I need some things for the ceremony," I replied, in a half-truth. "I don't want to ask my parents for the money."

"It's not a crime to borrow money, Mary. But how can you pay it back?"

"I'll babysit for you ten times."

"That's more than fair," she said, going to her purse and handing me a crisp, new, five-dollar bill. I'd never had that much money at once.

"I'm happy to know the money's going to be put to a good use," Mrs. Richardson said.

A few days later, the ritual began with a long speech from my grandfather about how we had reached the age of decision, how we now had to fend for ourselves and prove that we could survive the most horrendous of ordeals. All the friends and relatives who had gathered at our house for dinner made jokes about their own Ta-Na-E-Ka experiences. They all advised us to fill up now, since for the next five days we'd be gorging ourselves on crickets. Neither Roger nor I was very hungry. "I'll probably laugh about this when I'm an accountant," Roger said, trembling.

"Are you trembling?" I asked.

"What do you think?"

"I'm happy to know boys tremble, too," I said.

At six the next morning, we kissed our parents and went off to the woods. "Which side do you want?" Roger asked. According to the rules, Roger and I would stake out "territories" in separate areas of the woods and we weren't to communicate during the entire ordeal.

"I'll go toward the river, if it's OK with you," I said.

"Sure," Roger answered. "What difference does it make?"

To me, it made a lot of difference. There was a marina a few miles up the river and there were boats moored there. At least, I hoped so. I figured that a boat was a better place to sleep than under a pile of leaves.

"Why do you keep holding your head?" Roger asked.

"Oh, nothing. Just nervous," I told him. Actually, I was afraid I'd lose the five-dollar bill, which I had tucked into my hair with a bobby pin. As we came to a fork in the trail, Roger shook my hand. "Good luck, Mary."

"N'ko-n'ta," I said. It was the Kaw word for *courage.*

The sun was shining and it was warm, but my bare feet began to hurt immediately. I spied one of the berry bushes Grandfather had told us about. "You're lucky," he had said. "The berries are ripe in the spring, and they are delicious and nourishing." They were orange and fat and I popped one into my mouth.

Argh! I spat it out. It was awful and bitter, and even grasshoppers were probably better tasting, although I never intended to find out.

I sat down to rest my feet. A rabbit hopped out from under the berry bush. He nuzzled the berry I'd spat out and ate it. He picked another one and ate that, too. He liked them. He looked at me, twitching his nose. I watched a red-headed woodpecker bore into an elm tree, and I caught a glimpse of a civet cat waddling through some twigs. All of a sudden I realized I was no longer frightened. Ta-Na-E-Ka might be more fun than I'd anticipated. I got up and headed toward the marina.

"Not one boat," I said to myself dejectedly. But the restaurant on the shore, "Ernie's Riverside," was open. I walked in, feeling silly in my bathing suit. The man at the counter was big and tough-looking. He wore a sweatshirt with the words "Fort Sheridan, 1944," and he had only three fingers on one of his hands. He asked me what I wanted.

"A hamburger and a milk shake," I said, holding the five-dollar bill in my hand so he'd know I had money.

"That's a pretty heavy breakfast, honey," he murmured.

"That's what I always have for breakfast," I lied.

"Forty-five cents," he said, bringing me the food. (Back in 1947, hamburgers were twenty-five cents and milk shakes were twenty cents.)

"Delicious," I thought. "Better 'n grasshoppers—and Grandfather never once mentioned that I couldn't eat hamburgers."

While I was eating, I had a grand idea. Why not sleep in the restaurant? I went to the ladies' room and made sure the window was unlocked. Then I went back outside and played along the riverbank, watching the water birds and trying to identify each one. I planned to look for a beaver dam the next day.

The restaurant closed at sunset, and I watched the three-fingered man drive away. Then I climbed in the unlocked window. There was a night-light on, so I didn't turn on any lights. But there was a radio on the counter. I turned it on to a music program. It was warm in the restaurant, and I was hungry. I helped myself to a glass of milk and a piece of pie, intending to keep a list of what I'd eaten so I could

leave money. I also planned to get up early, sneak out through the window, and head for the woods before the three-fingered man returned. I turned off the radio, wrapped myself in the man's apron, and in spite of the hardness of the floor, fell asleep.

"What the heck are you doing here, kid?"

It was the man's voice.

It was morning. I'd overslept. I was scared.

"Hold it, kid. I just wanna know what you're doing here. You lost? You must be from the reservation. Your folks must be worried sick about you. Do they have a phone?"

"Yes, yes," I answered. "But don't call them."

I was shivering. The man, who told me his name was Ernie, made me a cup of hot chocolate while I explained about Ta-Na-E-Ka.

"Darnedest thing I ever heard," he said, when I was through. "Lived next to the reservation all my life and this is the first I've heard of Ta-Na whatever-you-call-it." He looked at me, all goosebumps in my bathing suit. "Pretty silly thing to do to a kid," he muttered.

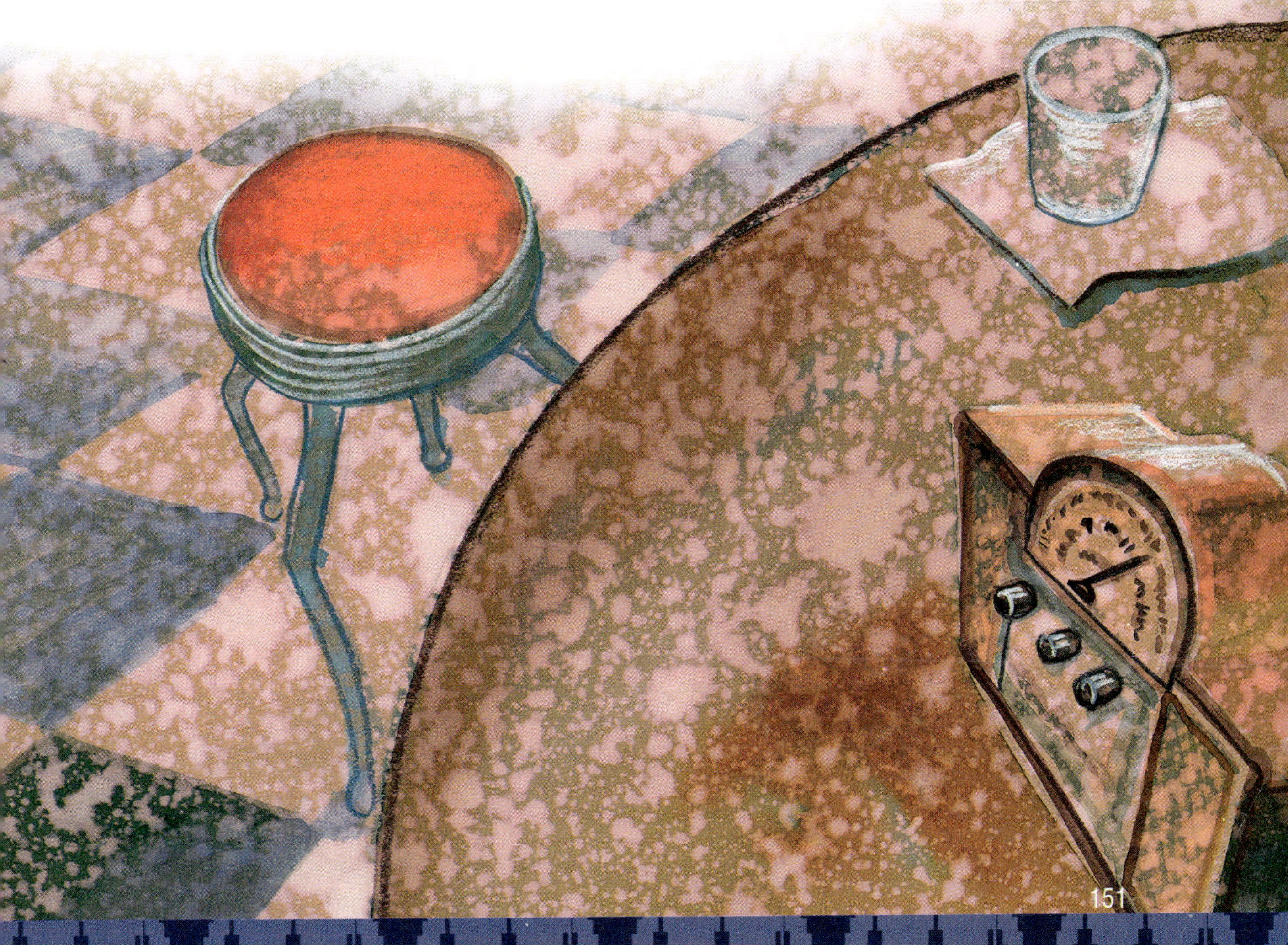

That was just what I'd been thinking for months, but when Ernie said it, I became angry. "No, it isn't silly. It's a custom of the Kaw. We've been doing this for hundreds of years. My mother and my grandfather and everybody in my family went through this ceremony. It's why the Kaw are great warriors."

"Okay, great warrior," Ernie chuckled, "suit yourself. And, if you want to stick around, it's okay with me." Ernie went to the broom closet and tossed me a bundle. "That's the lost-and-found closet," he said. "Stuff people left on boats. Maybe there's something to keep you warm."

The sweater fitted loosely, but it felt good. I felt good. And I'd found a new friend. Most important, I was surviving Ta-Na-E-Ka.

My grandfather had said the experience would be filled with adventure, and I was having my fill. And Grandfather had never said we couldn't accept hospitality.

I stayed at Ernie's Riverside for the entire period. In the mornings

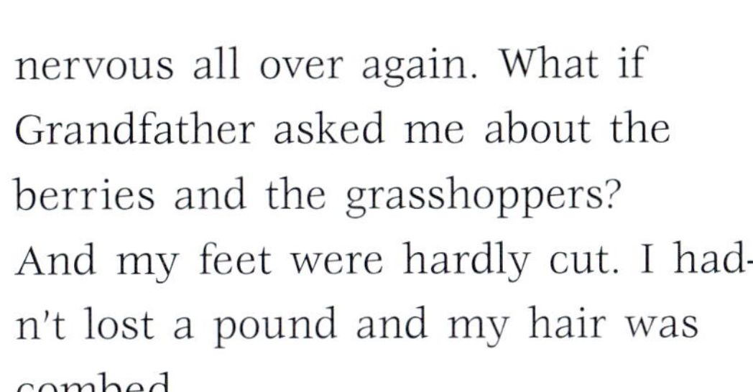

I went into the woods and watched the animals and picked flowers for each of the tables in Ernie's. I had never felt better. I was up early enough to watch the sun rise on the Missouri, and I went to bed after it set. I ate everything I wanted—insisting that Ernie take all my money for the food. "I'll keep this in trust for you, Mary," Ernie promised, "in case you are ever desperate for five dollars." (He did, too, but that's another story.)

I was sorry when the five days were over. I'd enjoyed every minute with Ernie. He taught me how to make western omelets and to make Chili Ernie Style (still one of my favorite dishes). And I told Ernie all about the legends of the Kaw. I hadn't realized I knew so much about my people.

But Ta-Na-E-Ka was over, and as I approached my house, at about nine-thirty in the evening, I became nervous all over again. What if Grandfather asked me about the berries and the grasshoppers? And my feet were hardly cut. I hadn't lost a pound and my hair was combed.

"They'll be so happy to see me," I told myself hopefully, "that they won't ask too many questions."

I opened the door. My grandfather was in the front room. He was wearing the ceremonial beaded deerskin shirt which had belonged to his grandfather. "N'g'da'ma," he said. "Welcome back."

I embraced my parents warmly, letting go only when I saw my cousin Roger sprawled on the couch. His eyes were red and swollen. He'd lost weight. His feet were an unsightly mass of blood and blisters, and he was moaning: "I made it, see. I made it. I'm a warrior. A warrior."

My grandfather looked at me strangely. I was clean, obviously well-fed, and radiantly healthy. My parents got the message. My uncle and aunt gazed at me with hostility.

Finally my grandfather asked, "What did you eat to keep you so well?"

I sucked in my breath and blurted out the truth: "Hamburgers and milk shakes."

"Hamburgers!" my grandfather growled.

"Milk shakes!" Roger moaned.

"You didn't say we had to eat grasshoppers," I said sheepishly.

"Tell us all about your Ta-Na-E-Ka," my grandfather commanded.

I told them everything, from borrowing the five dollars, to Ernie's kindness, to observing the beaver.

"That's not what I trained you for," my grandfather said sadly.

I stood up. "Grandfather, I learned that Ta-Na-E-Ka is important. I didn't think so during training. I was scared stiff of it. I handled it my way. And I learned I had nothing to be afraid of. There's no reason in 1947 to eat grasshoppers when you can eat a hamburger."

I was inwardly shocked at my own audacity. But I liked it. "Grandfather, I'll bet you never ate one of those rotten berries yourself."

Grandfather laughed!

He laughed aloud! My mother and father and aunt and uncle were all dumbfounded. Grandfather never laughed. Never.

"Those berries—they are terrible," Grandfather admitted. "I could never swallow them. I found a dead deer on the first day of my Ta-Na-E-Ka—shot by a soldier, probably—and he kept my belly full for the entire period of the test!"

Grandfather stopped laughing. "We should send you out again," he said.

I looked at Roger. "You're pretty smart, Mary," Roger groaned. "I'd never have thought of what you did."

"Accountants just have to be good at arithmetic," I said comfortingly. "I'm terrible at arithmetic."

Roger tried to smile but couldn't. My grandfather called me to him. "You should have done what your cousin did. But I think you are more alert to what is happening to our people today than we are. I think you would have passed the test under any circumstances, in any time. Somehow, you know how to exist in a world that wasn't made for Indians. I don't think you're going to have any trouble surviving."

Grandfather wasn't entirely right. But I'll tell about that another time.

Story Questions & Activities

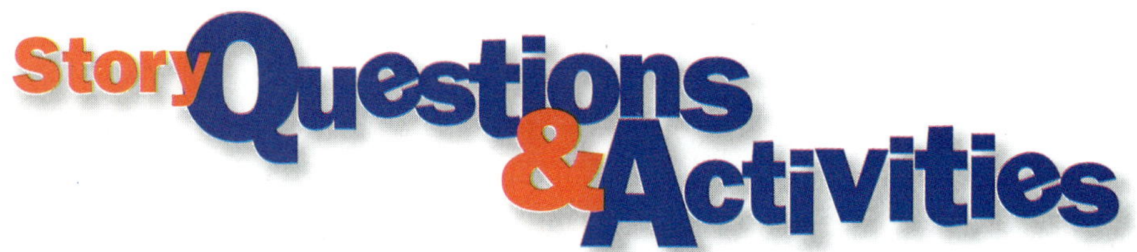

1. What is Ta-Na-E-Ka?
2. Why doesn't Mary want to participate in Ta-Na-E-Ka?
3. Mary and Roger make different choices about Ta-Na-E-Ka. Who do you think got more from the experience? Explain.
4. What is Mary's problem in the story? How does she solve it?
5. Suppose that Ed Sitrow in "S.O.R. Losers" had been faced with the problem of "Ta-Na-E-Ka." What do you think he would have done? Defend your answer.

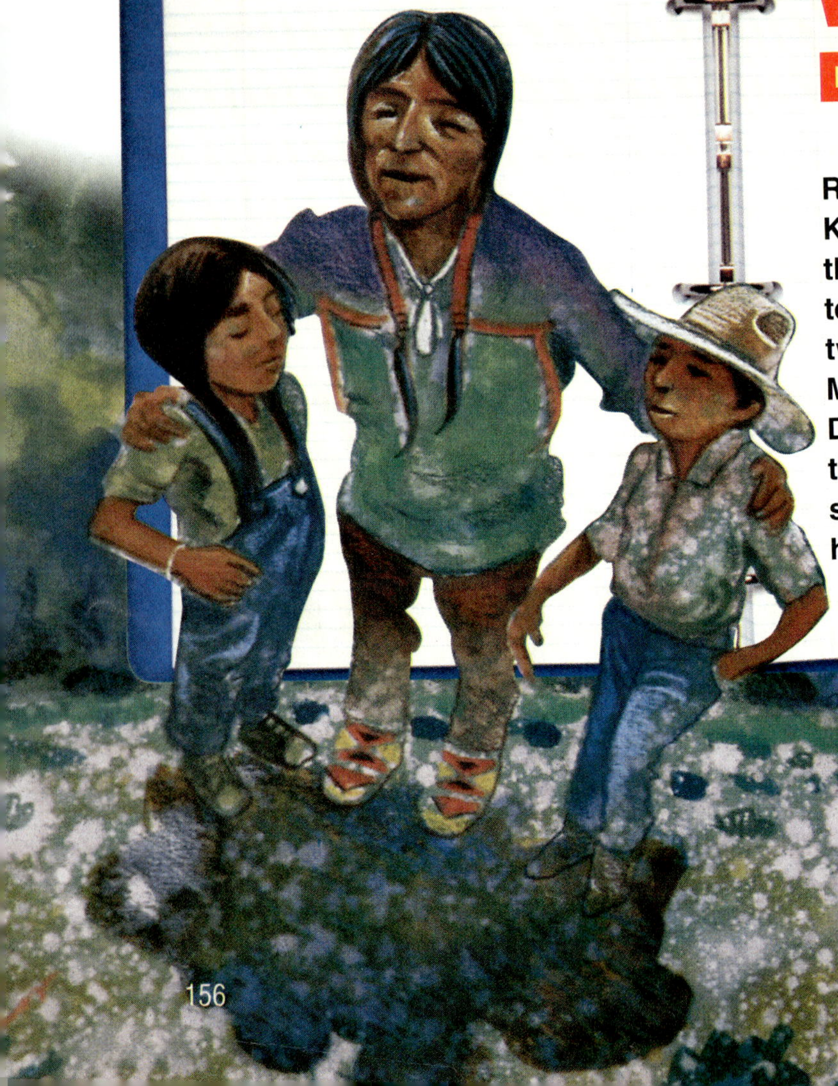

Write Paired Diary Entries

Mary and her cousin Roger go through Ta-Na-E-Ka at the same time. Yet their experiences during the test are quite different. Write two diary entries, one for Mary, the other for Roger. Describe one day during their Ta-Na-E-Ka. Show the similar experiences they may have had. Also include the differences.

Learn About Traditions

Ta-Na-E-Ka is just one ceremony celebrating a young person's coming of age. Interview friends, classmates, and people in your community to find out what their young people do. Do they go through special religious ceremonies or get new responsibilities at a certain age? Make a chart of coming-of-age traditions. In one column, tell what the tradition is. In the other, tell why it is important.

Plan Money Needs

Mary takes $5 with her on her Ta-Na-E-Ka. She spends 45 cents on a hamburger and a milkshake. Today, the cost of a hamburger and a milkshake is about 10 times greater than when the story took place. Figure out how much money Mary would have had to take with her today if she planned to eat breakfast, lunch, and dinner every day for five days.

Find Out More

In the story, Mary says that she always thought that the Kaw started "the women's liberation movement." More than any other group, the Kaw "treated women more 'equally.'" Choose a Native American group, such as the Kaw or the Iroquois. Find out the important role that women played. Look in an encyclopedia or a book about Native Americans. Then compare your findings with those of your classmates.

Use a Field Guide

During Ta-Na-E-Ka, Mary and Roger are expected to "live off the land" for five days. Grandfather has taught them which berries and other plants are safe to eat, and which are not. You can learn more about a plant, an animal, or a flower by using a field guide. **Field guides** describe plants or animals and their features so that you can identify them. They also provide special facts. These facts about plants and animals can be useful to you while hiking or camping.

Here is a page from a field guide about plants.

Common Name: Spanish Iris
Scientific Name: Iris xiphium
Family: Iridaceae
Origin: Spain and Portugal; first brought to Great Britain in 1596
Description: May be white, yellow, sky-blue, or purple; narrow leaves, grown from bulb. Flowers in late spring or early summer.
Type of soil: No special soil needed.
Type of light: Full sun

Use the field guide to answer these questions:

1. What are common colors of the Spanish iris?
2. If you wanted to grow Spanish iris, would you start with seeds? Why or why not?
3. Why do you think this kind of iris is called a Spanish iris?
4. Would London gardens of the 1400s include Spanish iris? Why or why not?
5. How would a field guide help you during a nature walk?

TEST POWER

Test Tip

Restate the questions to make sure you understand them.

DIRECTIONS

Read the sample story. Then read each question about the story.

SAMPLE

Summer on the Farm

One summer many years ago, Mikhail went to live with his Uncle Ivan on a farm. Mikhail had never been out of the city before. As he watched the countryside from the window of the train, he was surprised by the beauty of the Russian plains. To Mikhail, the huge open spaces were just as <u>impressive</u> as the churches of St. Petersburg.

When Mikhail finally arrived at his uncle's farm, he told his uncle how beautiful he thought the countryside was.

Uncle Ivan smiled. "Mikhail, thank you for giving me new eyes. I have lived here so long that I had forgotten that it was beautiful."

1 The word <u>impressive</u> in this story means —

A grand

B peaceful

C ordinary

D endangered

2 At the end of the passage, Mikhail's uncle said that he had new eyes because —

F Mikhail's uncle had gotten new glasses

G Mikhail had helped his uncle see something that he had forgotten about

H Uncle Ivan's eyes were full of tears

J Mikhail had to squint because it was so sunny

Mountain rescue teams like this one in France are kept busy by stranded skiers, hikers, and mountain climbers. How do you think their work is like the rescue work done by fire fighters? How does it differ?

Look at the photograph. What is happening in this picture? How can you tell? What do you think may have happened to the dog to bring out the rescue team? How does this photographer make the rescue exciting? How did he take the picture? Explain.

Close your eyes. Think about the rescue. How would it feel to be saved? To what other experience could you compare it?

The Gamma Liaison Network, French Mountain Rescue Squad
by Georges Merillon, 1998

Number the Stars

It is 1943 and the Nazis have occupied Denmark. As the German soldiers begin their campaign to "relocate" all the Jews in Denmark, the Johansen family takes in Annemarie Johansen's best friend, Ellen Rosen.

Illustrations by Larry Winborg

Alone in the apartment while Mama was out shopping with Kirsti, Annemarie and Ellen were sprawled on the living room floor playing with paper dolls. They had cut the dolls from Mama's magazines, old ones she had saved from past years. The paper ladies had old-fashioned hair styles and clothes, and the girls had given them names from Mama's very favorite book. Mama had told Annemarie and Ellen the entire story of *Gone With the Wind,* and the girls thought it much more interesting and romantic than the king-and-queen tales that Kirsti loved.

"Come, Melanie," Annemarie said, walking her doll across the edge of the rug. "Let's dress for the ball."

"All right, Scarlett, I'm coming," Ellen replied in a sophisticated voice. She was a talented performer; she often played the leading roles in school dramatics. Games of the imagination were always fun when Ellen played.

The door opened and Kirsti stomped in, her face tear-stained and glowering. Mama followed her with an exasperated look and set a package down on the table.

"I won't!" Kirsti sputtered. "I won't ever, *ever* wear them! Not if you chain me in a prison and beat me with sticks!"

Annemarie giggled and looked questioningly at her mother. Mrs. Johansen sighed. "I bought Kirsti some new shoes," she explained. "She's outgrown her old ones."

"Goodness, Kirsti," Ellen said, "I wish my mother would get *me* some new shoes. I love new things, and it's so hard to find them in the stores."

"Not if you go to a *fish* store!" Kirsti bellowed. "But most mothers wouldn't make their daughters wear ugly *fish* shoes!"

"Kirsten," Mama said soothingly, "you know it wasn't a fish store. And we were lucky to find shoes at all."

Kirsti sniffed. "Show them," she commanded. "Show Annemarie and Ellen how ugly they are."

Mama opened the package and took out a pair of little girl's shoes. She held them up, and Kirsti looked away in disgust.

"You know there's no leather anymore," Mama explained. "But they've found a way to make shoes out of fish skin. I don't think these are too ugly."

Annemarie and Ellen looked at the fish skin shoes. Annemarie took one in her hand and examined it. It was odd-looking; the fish scales were visible. But it was a shoe, and her sister needed shoes.

"It's not so bad, Kirsti," she said, lying a little.

Ellen turned the other one over in her hand. "You know," she said, "it's only the color that's ugly."

"Green!" Kirsti wailed. "I will never, *ever* wear green shoes!"

"In our apartment," Ellen told her, "my father has a jar of black, black ink. Would you like these shoes better if they were black?"

Kirsti frowned. "Maybe I would," she said, finally.

"Well, then," Ellen told her, "tonight, if your mama doesn't mind, I'll take the shoes home and ask my father to make them black for you, with his ink."

Mama laughed. "I think that would be a fine improvement. What do you think, Kirsti?"

Kirsti pondered. "Could he make them shiny?" she asked. "I want them shiny."

Ellen nodded. "I think he could. I think they'll be quite pretty, black and shiny."

Kirsti nodded. "All right, then," she said. "But you mustn't tell anyone that they're *fish.* I don't want anyone to know." She took her new shoes, holding them disdainfully, and put them on a chair. Then she looked with interest at the paper dolls.

"Can I play, too?" Kirsti asked. "Can I have a doll?" She squatted beside Annemarie and Ellen on the floor.

Sometimes, Annemarie thought, Kirsti was such a pest, always butting in. But the apartment was small. There was no other place for Kirsti to play. And if they told her to go away, Mama would scold.

"Here," Annemarie said, and handed her sister a cut-out little girl doll. "We're playing *Gone With the Wind.* Melanie and Scarlett are going to a ball. You can be Bonnie. She's Scarlett's daughter."

Kirsti danced her doll up and down happily. "I'm going to the ball!" she announced in a high, pretend voice.

Ellen giggled. "A little girl wouldn't go to a ball. Let's make them go someplace else. Let's make them go to Tivoli!"

"Tivoli!" Annemarie began to laugh. "That's in Copenhagen! *Gone With the Wind* is in America!"

"Tivoli, Tivoli, Tivoli," little Kirsti sang, twirling her doll in a circle.

"It doesn't matter, because it's only a game anyway," Ellen pointed out. "Tivoli can be over there, by that chair. 'Come, Scarlett,'" she said, using her doll voice, "'we shall go to Tivoli to dance and watch the fireworks, and maybe there will be some handsome men there! Bring your silly daughter Bonnie, and she can ride on the carousel.'"

Annemarie grinned and walked her Scarlett toward the chair that Ellen had designated as Tivoli. She loved Tivoli Gardens, in the heart of Copenhagen; her parents had taken her there, often, when she was a little girl. She remembered the music and the brightly colored lights, the carousel and ice cream and especially the magnificent fireworks in the evenings: the huge colored splashes and bursts of lights in the evening sky.

"I remember the fireworks best of all," she commented to Ellen.

"Me too," Kirsti said. "I remember the fireworks."

"Silly," Annemarie scoffed. "You never saw the fireworks." Tivoli Gardens was closed now. The German occupation forces had burned part of it, perhaps as a way of punishing the fun-loving Danes for their lighthearted pleasures.

Kirsti drew herself up, her small shoulders stiff. "I did too," she said belligerently. "It was my birthday. I woke up in the night and I could hear the booms. And there were lights in the sky. Mama said it was fireworks for my birthday!"

Then Annemarie remembered. Kirsti's birthday was late in August. And that night, only a month before, she, too, had been awakened and frightened by the sound of explosions. Kirsti was right—the sky in the southeast had been ablaze, and Mama had comforted her by calling it a birthday celebration. "Imagine, such fireworks for a little girl five years old!" Mama had said, sitting on their bed, holding the dark curtain aside to look through the window at the lighted sky.

The next evening's newspaper had told the sad truth. The Danes had destroyed their own naval fleet, blowing up the vessels one by one, as the Germans approached to take over the ships for their own use.

"How sad the king must be," Annemarie had heard Mama say to Papa when they read the news.

"How proud," Papa had replied.

It had made Annemarie feel sad and proud, too, to picture the tall, aging king, perhaps with tears in his blue eyes, as he looked at the remains of his small navy, which now lay submerged and broken in the harbor.

"I don't want to play anymore, Ellen," she said suddenly, and put her paper doll on the table.

"I have to go home, anyway," Ellen said. "I have to help Mama with the housecleaning. Thursday is our New Year. Did you know that?"

"Why is it yours?" asked Kirsti. "Isn't it our New Year, too?"

"No. It's the Jewish New Year. That's just for us. But if you want, Kirsti, you can come that night and watch Mama light the candles."

Annemarie and Kirsti had often been invited to watch

Mrs. Rosen light the Sabbath candles on Friday evenings. She covered her head with a cloth and said a special prayer in Hebrew as she did so. Annemarie always stood very quietly, awed, to watch; even Kirsti, usually such a chatterbox, was always still at that time. They didn't understand the words or the meaning, but they could feel what a special time it was for the Rosens.

"Yes," Kirsti agreed happily. "I'll come and watch your mama light the candles, and I'll wear my new black shoes."

But this time was to be different. Leaving for school on Thursday with her sister, Annemarie saw the Rosens walking to the synagogue early in the morning, dressed in their best clothes. She waved to Ellen, who waved happily back.

"Lucky Ellen," Annemarie said to Kirsti. "She doesn't have to go to school today."

"But she probably has to sit very, very still, like we do in church," Kirsti pointed out. "*That's* no fun."

That afternoon, Mrs. Rosen knocked at their door but didn't come inside. Instead, she spoke for a long time in a hurried, tense voice to Annemarie's mother in the hall. When Mama returned, her face was worried, but her voice was cheerful.

"Girls," she said, "we have a nice surprise. Tonight Ellen will be coming to stay overnight and to be our guest for a few days! It isn't often we have a visitor."

Kirsti clapped her hands in delight.

"But, Mama," Annemarie said, in dismay, "it's their New Year. They were going to have a celebration at home! Ellen told me that her mother managed to get a chicken someplace, and she was going to roast it—their first roast chicken in a year or more!"

"Their plans have changed," Mama said briskly. "Mr. and Mrs. Rosen have been called away to visit some relatives. So Ellen will stay with us. Now, let's get busy and put clean sheets on your bed. Kirsti, you may sleep with Mama and Papa tonight, and we'll let the big girls giggle together by themselves."

Kirsti pouted, and it was clear that she was about to argue. "Mama will tell you a special story tonight," her mother said. "One just for you."

"About a king?" Kirsti asked dubiously.

"About a king, if you wish," Mama replied.

"All right, then. But there must be a queen, too," Kirsti said.

Though Mrs. Rosen had sent her chicken to the Johansens, and Mama made a lovely dinner large enough for second helpings all around, it was not an evening of laughter and talk. Ellen was silent at dinner. She looked frightened. Mama and Papa tried to speak of cheerful things, but it was clear that they were worried, and it made Annemarie worry, too. Only Kirsti was unaware of the quiet tension in the room. Swinging her feet in their newly blackened and shiny shoes, she chattered and giggled during dinner.

"Early bedtime tonight, little one," Mama announced after the dishes were washed. "We need extra time for the long story I promised, about the king and queen." She disappeared with Kirsti into the bedroom.

"What's happening?" Annemarie asked when she and Ellen were alone with Papa in the living room. "Something's wrong. What is it?"

Papa's face was troubled. "I wish that I could protect you children from this knowledge," he said quietly. "Ellen, you already know. Now we must tell Annemarie."

He turned to her and stroked her hair with his gentle hand. "This morning, at the synagogue, the rabbi told his congregation that the Nazis have taken the synagogue lists of all the Jews. Where they live, what their names are. Of course the Rosens were on that list, along with many others."

"Why? Why did they want those names?"

"They plan to arrest all the Danish Jews. They plan to take them away. And we have been told that they may come tonight."

"I don't understand! Take them where?"

Her father shook his head. "We don't know where, and we don't really know why. They call it 'relocation.' We don't even know what that means. We only know that it is wrong, and it is dangerous, and we must help."

Annemarie was stunned. She looked at Ellen and saw that her best friend was crying silently.

"Where are Ellen's parents? We must help them, too!"

"We couldn't take all three of them. If the Germans came to search our apartment, it would be clear that the Rosens were here. One person we can hide. Not three. So Peter has helped Ellen's parents to go elsewhere. We don't know where. Ellen doesn't know either. But they are safe."

Ellen sobbed aloud, and put her face in her hands. Papa put his arm around her. "They are safe, Ellen. I promise you that. You will see them again quite soon. Can you try hard to believe my promise?"

Ellen hesitated, nodded, and wiped her eyes with her hand.

"But, Papa," Annemarie said, looking around the small apartment, with its few pieces of furniture: the fat stuffed sofa, the table and chairs, the small bookcase against the wall. "You said that we would hide her. How can we do that? Where can she hide?"

Papa smiled. "That part is easy. It will be as your mama said: you two will sleep together in your bed, and you may giggle and talk and tell secrets to each other. And if anyone comes—"

Ellen interrupted him. "Who might come? Will it be soldiers? Like the ones on the corners?" Annemarie remembered how terrified Ellen had looked the day when the soldier had questioned them on the corner.

"I really don't think anyone will. But it never hurts to be prepared. If anyone should come, even soldiers, you two will be sisters. You are together so much, it will be easy for you to pretend that you are sisters."

He rose and walked to the window. He pulled the lace curtain aside and looked down into the street. Outside, it was beginning to grow dark. Soon they would have to draw the black curtains that all Danes had on their windows; the entire city had to be completely darkened at night. In a nearby tree, a bird was singing; otherwise it was quiet. It was the last night of September.

"Go, now, and get into your nightgowns. It will be a long night."

Annemarie and Ellen got to their feet. Papa suddenly crossed the room and put his arms around them both. He kissed the top of each head: Annemarie's blond one, which reached to his shoulder, and Ellen's dark hair, the thick curls braided as always into pigtails.

"Don't be frightened," he said to them softly. "Once I had three daughters. Tonight I am proud to have three daughters again."

"Do you really think anyone will come?" Ellen asked nervously, turning to Annemarie in the bedroom. "Your father doesn't think so."

"Of course not. They're always threatening stuff. They just like to scare people." Annemarie took her nightgown from a hook in the closet.

"Anyway, if they did, it would give me a chance to practice acting. I'd just pretend to be Lise. I wish I were taller, though." Ellen stood on tiptoe, trying to make herself tall. She laughed at herself, and her voice was more relaxed.

"You were great as the Dark Queen in the school play last year," Annemarie told her. "You should be an actress when you grow up."

"My father wants me to be a teacher. He wants *everyone* to be a teacher, like him. But maybe I could convince him that I should go to acting school." Ellen stood on tiptoe again, and made an imperious gesture with her arm. "I am the Dark Queen," she intoned dramatically. "I have come to command the night!"

"You should try saying, 'I am Lise Johansen!'" Annemarie said, grinning. "If you told the Nazis that you were the Dark Queen, they'd haul you off to a mental institution."

Ellen dropped her actress pose and sat down, with her legs curled under her, on the bed. "They won't really come here, do you think?" she asked again.

Annemarie shook her head. "Not in a million years." She picked up her hairbrush.

The girls found themselves whispering as they got ready for bed. There was no need, really, to whisper; they were, after all, supposed to be normal sisters, and Papa had said they could giggle and talk. The bedroom door was closed.

But the night did seem, somehow, different from a normal night. And so they whispered.

"How did your sister die, Annemarie?" Ellen asked suddenly. "I remember when it happened. And I remember the funeral—it was the only time I have ever been in a Lutheran church. But I never knew just what happened."

"I don't know *exactly*," Annemarie confessed. "She and Peter were out somewhere together, and then there was a telephone call, that there had been an accident. Mama and Papa rushed to the hospital—remember, your mother came and stayed with me and Kirsti? Kirsti was already asleep and she slept right through everything, she was so little then. But I stayed up, and I was with your mother in the living room when my parents came home in the middle of the night. And they told me Lise had died."

"I remember it was raining," Ellen said sadly. "It was still raining the next morning when Mama told me. Mama was crying, and the rain made it seem as if the whole *world* was crying."

Annemarie finished brushing her long hair and handed her hairbrush to her best friend. Ellen undid her braids, lifted her dark hair away from the thin gold chain she wore around her neck—the chain that held the Star of David—and began to brush her thick curls.

"I think it was partly because of the rain. They said she was hit by a car. I suppose the streets were slippery, and it was getting dark, and maybe the driver just couldn't see," Annemarie went on, remembering. "Papa looked so angry. He made one hand into a fist, and he kept pounding it into the other hand. I remember the noise of it: slam, slam, slam."

Together they got into the wide bed and pulled up the covers. Annemarie blew out the candle and drew the dark curtains aside so that the open window near the bed let in some air. "See that blue trunk in the corner?" she said, pointing through the darkness. "Lots of Lise's things are in there. Even her wedding dress. Mama and Papa have never looked at those things, not since the day they packed them away."

Ellen sighed. "She would have looked so beautiful in her wedding dress. She had such a pretty smile. I used to pretend that she was *my* sister, too."

"She would have liked that," Annemarie told her. "She loved you."

"That's the worst thing in the world," Ellen whispered. "To be dead so young. I wouldn't want the Germans to take my family away—to make us live someplace else. But still, it wouldn't be as bad as being dead."

Annemarie leaned over and hugged her. "They won't take you away," she said. "Not your parents, either. Papa promised that they were safe, and he always keeps his promises. And you are quite safe, here with us."

For a while they continued to murmur in the dark, but the murmurs were interrupted by yawns. Then Ellen's voice stopped, she turned over, and in a minute her breathing was quiet and slow.

Annemarie stared at the window where the sky was outlined and a tree branch moved slightly in the breeze. Everything seemed very familiar, very comforting. Dangers were no more than odd imaginings, like ghost stories that children made up to frighten one another: things that couldn't possibly happen. Annemarie felt completely safe here in her own home, with her parents in the next room and her best friend asleep beside her. She yawned contentedly and closed her eyes.

It was hours later, but still dark, when she was awakened abruptly by the pounding on the apartment door.

Annemarie eased the bedroom door open quietly, only a crack, and peeked out. Behind her, Ellen was sitting up, her eyes wide.

She could see Mama and Papa in their nightclothes, moving about. Mama held a lighted candle, but as Annemarie watched, she went to a lamp and switched it on. It was so long a time since they had dared to use the strictly rationed electricity after dark that the light in the room seemed startling to Annemarie, watching through the slightly opened bedroom door. She saw her mother look automatically to the blackout curtains, making certain that they were tightly drawn.

Papa opened the front door to the soldiers.

"This is the Johansen apartment?" A deep voice asked the question loudly, in the terribly accented Danish.

"Our name is on the door, and I see you have a flashlight," Papa answered. "What do you want? Is something wrong?"

"I understand you are a friend of your neighbors the Rosens, Mrs. Johansen," the soldier said angrily.

"Sophy Rosen is my friend, that is true," Mama said quietly. "Please, could you speak more softly? My children are asleep."

"Then you will be so kind as to tell me where the Rosens are." He made no effort to lower his voice.

"I assume they are at home, sleeping. It is four in the morning, after all," Mama said.

Annemarie heard the soldier stalk across the living room toward the kitchen. From her hiding place in the narrow sliver of open doorway, she could see the heavy uniformed man, a holstered pistol at his waist, in the entrance to the kitchen, peering in toward the sink.

Another German voice said, "The Rosens' apartment is empty. We are wondering if they might be visiting their good friends the Johansens."

"Well," said Papa, moving slightly so that he was standing in front of Annemarie's bedroom door, and she could see nothing except the dark blur of his back, "as you see, you are mistaken. There is no one here but my family."

"You will not object if we look around." The voice was harsh, and it was not a question.

"It seems we have no choice," Papa replied.

"Please don't wake my children," Mama requested again. "There is no need to frighten little ones."

The heavy, booted feet moved across the floor again and into the other bedroom. A closet door opened and closed with a bang.

Annemarie eased her bedroom door closed silently. She stumbled through the darkness to the bed.

"Ellen," she whispered urgently, "take your necklace off!"

Ellen's hands flew to her neck. Desperately she began trying to unhook the tiny clasp. Outside the bedroom door, the harsh voices and heavy footsteps continued.

"I can't get it open!" Ellen said frantically. "I never take it off—I can't even remember how to open it!"

Annemarie heard a voice just outside the door. "What is here?"

"Shhh," her mother replied. "My daughters' bedroom. They are sound asleep."

"Hold still," Annemarie commanded. "This will hurt." She grabbed the little gold chain, yanked with all her strength, and broke it. As the door opened and light flooded into the bedroom, she crumpled it into her hand and closed her fingers tightly.

Terrified, both girls looked up at the three Nazi officers who entered the room.

One of the men aimed a flashlight around the bedroom. He went to the closet and looked inside. Then with a sweep of his gloved hand he pushed to the floor several coats and a bathrobe that hung from pegs on the wall.

There was nothing else in the room except a chest of drawers, the blue decorated trunk in the corner, and a heap of Kirsti's dolls piled in a small rocking chair. The flashlight beam touched each thing in turn. Angrily the officer turned toward the bed.

"Get up!" he ordered. "Come out here!"

Trembling, the two girls rose from the bed and followed him, brushing past the two remaining officers in the doorway, to the living room.

Annemarie looked around. These three uniformed men were different from the ones on the street corners. The street soldiers were often young, sometimes ill at ease, and Annemarie remembered how the Giraffe had, for a moment, let his harsh pose slip and had smiled at Kirsti.

But these men were older and their faces were set with anger.

Her parents were standing beside each other, their faces tense, but Kirsti was nowhere in sight. Thank goodness that Kirsti slept through almost everything. If they had wakened her, she would be wailing—or worse, she would be angry, and her fists would fly.

"Your names?" the officer barked.

"Annemarie Johansen. And this is my sister—"

"Quiet! Let her speak for herself. Your name?" He was glaring at Ellen.

Ellen swallowed. "Lise," she said, and cleared her throat. "Lise Johansen."

The officer stared at them grimly.

"Now," Mama said in a strong voice, "you have seen that we are not hiding anything. May my children go back to bed?"

The officer ignored her. Suddenly he grabbed a handful of Ellen's hair. Ellen winced.

He laughed scornfully. "You have a blond child sleeping in the other room. And you have this blond daughter—" He gestured toward Annemarie with his head. "Where did you get the dark-haired one?" He twisted the lock of Ellen's hair. "From a different father? From the milkman?"

Papa stepped forward. "Don't speak to my wife in such a way. Let go of my daughter or I will report you for such treatment."

"Or maybe you got her someplace else?" the officer continued with a sneer. "From the Rosens?"

For a moment no one spoke. Then Annemarie, watching in panic, saw her father move swiftly to the small bookcase and take out a book. She saw that he was holding the family photograph album. Very quickly he searched through its pages, found what he was looking for, and tore out three pictures from three separate pages.

He handed them to the German officer, who released Ellen's hair.

"You will see each of my daughters, each with her name written on the photograph," Papa said.

Annemarie knew instantly which photographs he had chosen. The album had many snapshots—all the poorly focused pictures of school events and birthday parties. But it also contained a portrait, taken by a photographer, of each girl as a tiny infant. Mama had written, in her delicate handwriting, the name of each baby daughter across the bottom of those photographs.

She realized too, with an icy feeling, why Papa had torn them from the book. At the bottom of each page, below the photograph itself, was written the date. And the real Lise Johansen had been born twenty-one years earlier.

"Kirsten Elisabeth," the officer read, looking at Kirsti's baby picture. He let the photograph fall to the floor.

"Annemarie," he read next, glanced at her, and dropped the second photograph.

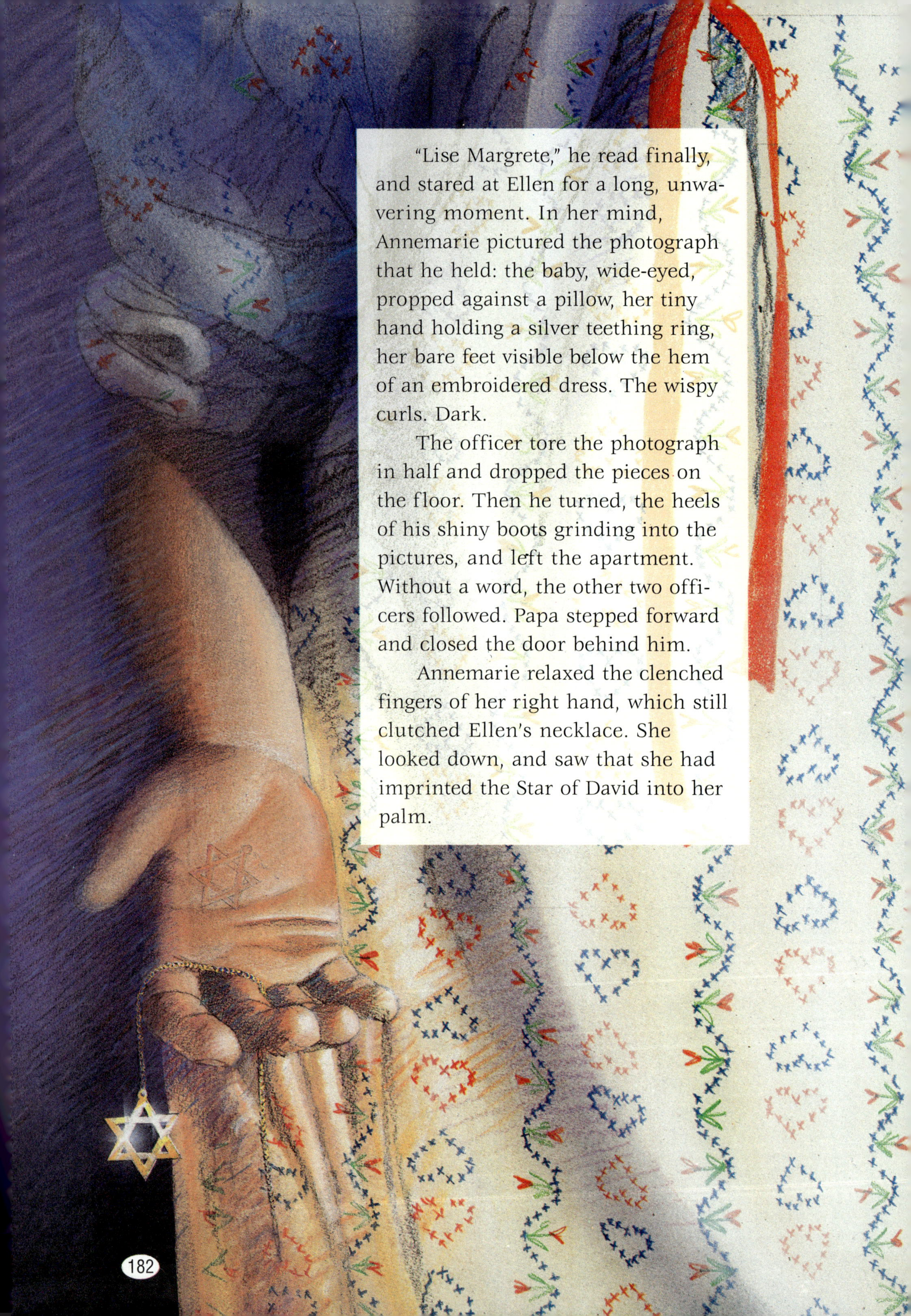

"Lise Margrete," he read finally, and stared at Ellen for a long, unwavering moment. In her mind, Annemarie pictured the photograph that he held: the baby, wide-eyed, propped against a pillow, her tiny hand holding a silver teething ring, her bare feet visible below the hem of an embroidered dress. The wispy curls. Dark.

The officer tore the photograph in half and dropped the pieces on the floor. Then he turned, the heels of his shiny boots grinding into the pictures, and left the apartment. Without a word, the other two officers followed. Papa stepped forward and closed the door behind him.

Annemarie relaxed the clenched fingers of her right hand, which still clutched Ellen's necklace. She looked down, and saw that she had imprinted the Star of David into her palm.

MEET *Lois Lowry*

Well known for her lighthearted books about Anastasia Krupnik, Lois Lowry selected a more serious topic when she wrote Number the Stars. *Experiences of her close friend Annelise, who lived through the Nazi occupation of Denmark during World War II, inspired Lowry to write this Newbery Medal-winning book.*

In the course of writing Number the Stars, *Lowry traveled to Denmark, where she listened to others describe their experiences. She also observed the places she was writing about. As she puts it, "I came home and rewrote the entire book. Same characters; same plot. But now it had the real Denmark in it."*

Story Questions & Activities

1. Why does Ellen have to hide in the Johansens' apartment?
2. Compare life in Denmark before the Nazis came and after. How did life change for the Danes? What dangers did the Danish Jews face?
3. By hiding Ellen in their apartment, the Johansens acted bravely. What does their act show you about the way the Danes felt toward the Jews during the Nazi occupation?
4. How would you summarize the events in this story?
5. In "Last Summer With Maizon," Margaret's mother says that "an old friend is a friend you once had and a best friend is a friend you'll always have." Compare the friendship between Margaret and Maizon with that of Annemarie and Ellen. Do you think that the girls in each story will always be friends? Why or why not?

Write a Comparison-Contrast Essay

Annemarie and Ellen are best friends. Like best friends, they share much in common. Yet they also differ in a number of ways. Make a comparison chart that lists their likenesses and differences. Then use the details on the chart to write a brief essay comparing and contrasting the two girls. In your conclusion, sum up whether Annemarie and Ellen are best friends despite, or because of, their differences.

Plan a New Year's Celebration

In the story, Ellen Rosen and her family are preparing to celebrate the Jewish New Year. Other cultures also celebrate the New Year in a special way. With a group of classmates, choose one of these cultures, such as the Chinese or the Vietnamese, and plan a New Year's celebration for your class. Decide what kind of food, music, and decorations to bring. Ask people from other cultures to share their New Year's traditions.

Make a Family Album

What happens when Mr. Johansen shows the Nazi officers the family photograph album? How does the picture of his daughter, Lise, probably save Ellen's life? Now create your own family album. Include photographs or illustrations of your family, and label each picture. Start with a picture of yourself, as if you were inviting others to "read" your life story.

Find Out More

What happened to the Danish people during World War II? How did they protect their Jewish citizens? How did they finally become free of the Nazi occupation? Look for information in an encyclopedia, in a book about Denmark's role in World War II, or on the Internet. Share your information with the class.

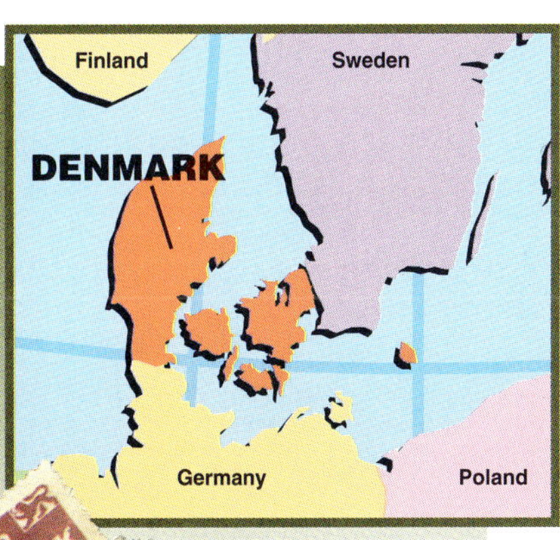

Use Parts of a Book

Would you like to know more about Denmark? You could find information in a book like this. Knowing which parts of a book to use will help you find what you're looking for. A **title page** gives a book's name, author, publisher, and place of publication. A **table of contents** lists a book's chapters and the pages where they begin. The back of a book may contain an **index.** An index tells where to find names and topics mentioned in a book.

Title Page

A History of Modern Denmark 1800–2000

by Anne-Margrethe Ansgar

Overview Press New York

Table of Contents

Chapter	Page
1 The Napoleonic Wars	3
2 A New Constitution	27
3 The Schleswig Wars	49
4 An Age of Reform	73
5 The Early 20th Century	110
6 World War II	134

Index

N

Napoleonic alliance	6, 21–24
Nazi occupation	136, 138, 144–150
Neutrality	
in Napoleonic Wars	4–5
in World War I	112–114, 123
in World War II	134–135
Nordic Council	177–178
Norway	3, 7, 26, 65, 77, 185–186

Use the sample parts of a book to answer these questions.

1. On which pages can you find information on the Nordic Council?
2. Which chapter is about World War II?
3. What company published Ms. Ansgar's book?
4. Queen Margrete ruled Denmark from 1389–1396. Would you learn about her in this book? Why or why not?
5. How is knowing the parts of the book helpful?

TEST POWER

Test Tip

Check your understanding as you read the story.

DIRECTIONS

Read the sample story. Then read each question about the story.

SAMPLE

Who was Mickey Mantle?

Baseball fans revere Mickey Mantle. Mantle is known as the greatest switch-hitter in the game. He batted easily from both his left and right sides.

During his career, Mickey Mantle hit 536 home runs. He won the Triple Crown Award and was a three-time American League Most Valuable Player. He was one of two players in baseball history to win a batting title with 50 home runs.

Mickey Mantle was famous for his home runs. He hit more World Series home runs than any other player. But his most memorable home run occurred in the '64 World Series. Mantle broke Babe Ruth's World Series record and helped the Yankees win game three against the St. Louis Cardinals.

For all his accomplishments, Mantle was elected to the Baseball Hall of Fame in 1974.

1 According to this passage, which event happened last?

- **A** Mickey Mantle broke Babe Ruth's record.
- **B** The Yankees won game three of the 1964 World Series.
- **C** Mickey Mantle was elected to the Baseball Hall of Fame.
- **D** Mickey Mantle hit his first home run.

2 The main idea of the third paragraph of the passage is that —

- **F** Mickey Mantle hit 536 home runs
- **G** Mickey Mantle broke records and helped his team win a World Series game
- **H** Mickey Mantle was a talented switch-hitter
- **J** Mickey Mantle won the Triple Crown Award and was a three-time Most Valuable Player

Like a still life, a family portrait freezes a moment in time. It also presents one main idea.

Look at the family in this painting. What can you tell about them? How many generations are shown? Notice the curves and soft lines. What is the dominant color? How do line, form, and color help you to see how the family feel toward one another? How would you state this feeling in one main idea?

Look at this painting again. How is it more interesting than a family photograph? If you could write a caption for it, what would you say?

The Family
by Romare Bearden, 1988
National Museum of American Art, Washington, D.C.

OPERA, KARATE & BANDITS

from THE LAND I LOST

Adventures of a Boy in Vietnam

by Huynh Quang Nhuong

illustrated by Robert Roth

I was born on the central highlands of Vietnam in a small hamlet on a riverbank that had a deep jungle on one side and a chain of high mountains on the other. Across the river, rice fields stretched to the slopes of another chain of mountains.

There were fifty houses in our hamlet, scattered along the river or propped against the mountainsides.

The houses were made of bamboo and covered with coconut leaves, and each was surrounded by a deep trench to protect it from wild animals or thieves. The only way to enter a house was to walk across a "monkey bridge"—a single bamboo stick that spanned the trench. At night we pulled the bridges into our houses and were safe.

There were no shops or marketplaces in our hamlet. If we needed supplies—medicine, cloth, soaps, or candles—we had to cross over the mountains and travel to a town nearby. We used the river mainly for traveling to distant hamlets, but it also provided us with plenty of fish.

During the six-month rainy season, nearly all of us helped plant and cultivate fields of rice, sweet potatoes, Indian mustard, eggplant, tomatoes, hot peppers, and corn. But during the dry season, we became hunters and turned to the jungle.

Wild animals played a very large part in our lives. There were four animals we feared the most: the tiger, the lone wild hog, the crocodile, and the horse snake. Tigers were always trying to steal cattle. Sometimes, however, when a tiger became old and slow it became a maneater. But a lone wild hog was even more dangerous than a tiger. It attacked every creature in sight, even when it had no need for food. Or it did crazy things, such as charging into the hamlet in broad daylight, ready to kill or to be killed.

The river had different dangers: crocodiles. But of all the animals, the most hated and feared was the huge horse snake. It was sneaky and attacked people and cattle just for the joy of killing. It would either crush its victim to death or poison it with a bite.

Like all farmers' children in the hamlet, I started working at the age of six. My seven sisters helped by

working in the kitchen, weeding the garden, gathering eggs, or taking water to the cattle. I looked after the family herd of water buffaloes. Someone always had to be with the herd because no matter how carefully a water buffalo was trained, it always was ready to nibble young rice plants when no one was looking. Sometimes, too, I fished for the family while I guarded the herd, for there were plenty of fish in the flooded rice fields during the rainy season.

I was twelve years old when I made my first trip to the jungle with my father. I learned how to track game, how to recognize useful roots, how to distinguish edible mushrooms from poisonous ones. I learned that if birds, raccoons, squirrels, or monkeys had eaten the fruits of certain trees, then those fruits were not poisonous. Often they were not delicious, but they could calm a man's hunger and thirst.

My father, like most of the villagers, was a farmer and a hunter, depending upon the season. But he also had a college education, so in the evenings he helped to teach other children in our hamlet, for it was too small to afford a professional schoolteacher.

My mother managed the house, but during the harvest season she could be found in the fields, helping my father get the crops home; and as the wife of a hunter, she knew how to dress and nurse a wound and took good care of her husband and his hunting dogs.

I went to the lowlands to study for a while because I wanted to follow my father as a teacher when I grew up. I always planned to return to my hamlet to live the rest of my life there. But war disrupted my dreams. The land I love was lost to me forever.

These stories are my memories. . . .

—H.Q.N.

When she was eighty years old my grandmother was still quite strong. She could use her own teeth to eat corn on the cob or to chew on sugar plants to extract juice from them. Every two days she walked for more than an hour to reach the marketplace, carrying a heavy load of food with her, and then spent another hour walking back home. And even though she was quite old, traces of her beauty still lingered on: Her hands, her feet, her face revealed that she had been an attractive young woman. Nor did time do much damage to the youthful spirit of my grandmother.

One of her great passions was theater, and this passion never diminished with age. No matter how busy she was, she never missed a show when there was a group of actors in town. If no actors visited our hamlet for several months, she would organize her own show in which she was the manager, the producer, and the young leading lady, all at the same time.

My grandmother's own plays were always melodramas inspired by books she had read and by what she had seen on the stage. She always chose her favorite grandson to play the role of the hero, who would, without fail, marry the heroine at the end and live happily ever after. And when my sisters would tell her that she was getting too old to play the role of the young heroine anymore, my grandmother merely replied: "Anybody can play this role if she's young at heart."

When I was a little boy my grandmother often took me to see the opera. She knew Chinese mythology by heart, and the opera was often a dramatization of this mythology. On one special occasion, during the Lunar New Year celebrations—my favorite holiday, because children could do anything they wanted and by

tradition no one could scold them—I accompanied my grandmother to the opera.

When we reached the theater I wanted to go in immediately. But my grandmother wanted to linger at the entrance and talk to her friends. She chatted for more than an hour. Finally we entered the theater, and at that moment the "Faithful One" was onstage, singing sadly. The "Faithful One" is a common character in Chinese opera. He could be a good minister, or a valiant general, or someone who loved and served his king faithfully. But in the end he is unjustly persecuted by the king, whose opinion of him has been changed by the lies of the "Flatterer," another standard character.

When my grandmother saw the "Faithful One" onstage she looked upset and gave a great sigh. I was too interested in what was happening to ask her the reason, and we spent the next five hours watching the rest of the opera. Sometimes I cried because my grandmother cried at the pitiful situation of the "Faithful One." Sometimes I became as angry as my grandmother did at the wickedness of the "Flatterer."

When we went home that night my grandmother was quite sad. She told my mother that she would have bad luck in the following year because when we entered the theater, the "Faithful One" was onstage. I was puzzled. I told my grandmother that she was confused. It would be a good year for us because we saw the good guy first. But my mother said, "No, son. The 'Faithful One' always is in trouble and it takes him many years to vindicate himself. Our next year is going to be like one of his bad years."

So, according to my mother's and grandmother's logic, we would have been much better off in the new year if we had been lucky enough to see the villain first!

My grandmother had married a man whom she loved with all her heart, but who was totally different from her. My grandfather was very shy, never laughed loudly, and always spoke very softly. And physically he was not as strong as my grandmother. But he excused his lack of physical strength by saying that he was a "scholar."

About three months after their marriage, my grandparents were in a restaurant and a rascal began to insult my grandfather because he looked weak and had a pretty wife. At first he just made insulting remarks, such as, "Hey! Wet chicken! This is no place for a weakling!"

My grandfather wanted to leave the restaurant even though he and my grandmother had not yet finished their meal. But my grandmother pulled his shirt sleeve and signaled him to remain seated. She continued to eat and looked as if nothing had happened.

Tired of yelling insults without any result, the rascal got up from his table, moved over to my grandparents' table, and grabbed my grandfather's chopsticks. My grandmother immediately wrested the chopsticks from him and struck the rascal on his cheekbone with her elbow. The blow was so quick and powerful that he lost his balance and fell on the floor. Instead of finishing him off, as any street fighter would do, my grandmother let the rascal recover from the blow. But as soon as he got up again, he kicked over the table between him and my grandmother, making food and drink fly all over the place. Before he could do anything else, my grandmother kicked him on the chin. The kick was so swift that my grandfather didn't even see it. He only heard a heavy thud, and then saw the rascal tumble backward and collapse on the ground.

All the onlookers were surprised and delighted, especially the owner of the restaurant. Apparently the rascal, one of the best karate fighters of our area, came to his restaurant every day and left without paying for his food or drink, but the owner was too afraid to confront him.

While the rascal's friends tried to revive him, everyone else surrounded my grandmother and asked her who had taught her karate. She said, "Who else? My husband!"

After the fight at the restaurant people assumed that my grandfather knew karate very well but refused to use it for fear of killing someone. In reality, my grandmother had received special training in karate from my great-great uncle from the time she was eight years old.

Anyway, after that incident, my grandfather never had to worry again. Anytime he had some business downtown, people treated him very well. And whenever anyone happened to bump into him on the street, they bowed to my grandfather in a very respectful way.

When my father was about ten years old a group of bandits attacked our house. There had been a very poor harvest that year, and bandits had already attacked several homes in other hamlets. My grandmother had a premonition this would also happen to them, so she devised a plan. In case of danger, she would carry the children to safety, and my grandfather would carry the bow and arrows, a bottle of poison, and the box containing the family jewels.

It was night when the bandits came. My grandfather became scared to death and forgot his part of the plan, but my grandmother remained very calm. She led her husband and children to safety through a secret back door that opened into a double hedge of cactus

that allowed a person to walk inside, undetected, to the banana grove. When they were safely inside the banana grove, my grandfather realized that he had forgotten the bow and arrows and the bottle of poison. So my grandmother stole back into the house and retrieved the weapons.

The bandits were still trying to smash through our very solid front door when she sneaked out of the house for the second time. She dipped one arrow in poison and crawled around to the front of the house near the bandits. But, upon second thought, she put the poisoned arrow aside and took another arrow and carefully aimed at the leg of the bandit leader. When the arrow hit his thigh the bandit let out a loud cry and fell backward.

The night was so dark that none of the bandits knew where the arrow had come from. And moments later, friends started arriving and began to attack them from the road in front of our house. The bandits panicked and left in a hurry. But my grandmother spent the rest of the night with her family in the banana grove, just in case the bandits came back.

When my grandmother became older she felt sick once in a while. Before the arrival of the doctor, she would order everybody in the house to look sad. And during the consultation with the doctor she acted as if she were much sicker than she really was. My grandmother felt that she had to make herself look really sick so that the doctor would give her good medicine. She told the doctor that she had a pain in the head, in the shoulders, in the chest, in the back, in the limbs—pain everywhere. Finally the doctor would become confused and wouldn't know what could be wrong with her.

Whenever the doctor left, my mother would sneak out of the house, meet him at the other side of the garden, and tell him exactly where my grandmother hurt.

Two or three days later my grandmother usually felt much better. But before the doctor arrived for another visit she ordered us to look sad again—not as sad as the first time, but quite sad. She would tell the doctor that her situation had improved a little bit but that she still felt quite sick. My grandmother thought that if she told the doctor she had been feeling much better he would stop giving her good medicine. When the doctor left my mother sneaked out of the house again and informed him of the real condition of my grandmother.

I don't think my grandmother ever guessed it was my mother's reports to the doctor, and not her acting, that helped her get well.

One morning my grandmother wanted me to go outside with her. We climbed a little hill that looked over the whole area, and when we got to the top she looked at the rice field below, the mountain on the horizon, and especially at the river. As a young girl she had often brought her herd of water buffaloes to the river to drink while she swam with the other children of the village. Then we visited the graveyard where her husband and some of her children were buried. She touched her husband's tombstone and said, "Dear, I will join you soon." And then we walked back to the garden and she gazed at the fruit trees her husband had planted, a new one for each time she had given birth to a child. Finally, before we left the garden my sister joined us, and the two of them fed a few ducks swimming in the pond.

That evening my grandmother did not eat much of her dinner. After dinner she combed her hair and put on her best dress. We thought that she was going to go out again, but instead she went to her bedroom and told us that she didn't want to be disturbed.

The family dog seemed to sense something was amiss, for he kept looking anxiously at everybody and whined from time to time. At midnight my mother went to my grandmother's room and found that she had died, with her eyes shut, as if she were sleeping normally.

It took me a long time to get used to the reality that my grandmother had passed away. Wherever I was, in the house, in the garden, out on the fields, her face always appeared so clearly to me. And even now, many years later, I still have the feeling that my last conversation with her has happened only a few days before.

Meet HUYNH QUANG NHUONG

Many people might have given up in despair if they had lost their homeland and had been disabled in a war. But not Huynh Quang Nhuong. After leaving Vietnam for medical treatment, he made a new home in the United States and went on to earn two college degrees as well as to become a prizewinning author and playwright.

Nhuong's first book, *The Land I Lost: Adventures of a Boy in Vietnam,* has won many awards. His plays have been produced in several cities, including his new hometown of Columbia, Missouri. In 1990, he received a grant from the National Endowment for the Arts to encourage his creative writing.

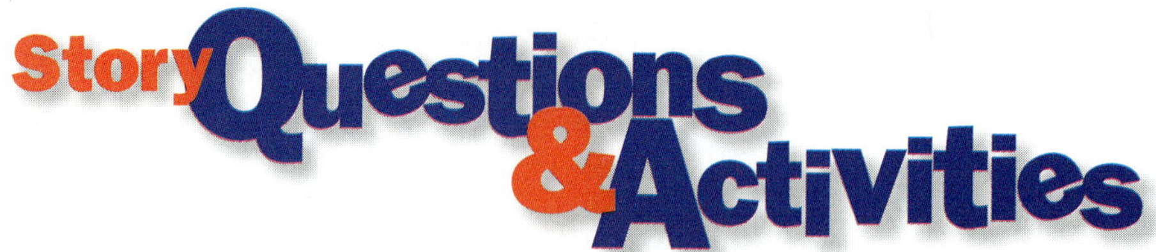

Story Questions & Activities

1. What is the author's grandmother like?
2. Why is this selection called "Opera, Karate, and Bandits"?
3. How are these stories the author's "memories" of his life in Vietnam? Explain.
4. What is the main idea of this selection?
5. Compare the author's grandmother with Mary's grandfather in "Ta-Na-E-Ka." What are the similarities? What are the differences?

Write an Anecdote

Do you remember how the author's grandmother used karate in the restaurant? The author uses this anecdote, or amusing story, to show how different his grandmother and grandfather were. Yet in spite of their differences, they loved each other. Write an anecdote about two people who are different but who like each other very much. Make your story humorous by choosing details that will amuse your readers.

Create a Storyboard

Draw a storyboard for one of the three "memories" in "Opera, Karate, and Bandits." Show the events in the order in which they happened.

Draw a Memory

In the story, the author shares a special relationship with his grandmother. Now choose a grandparent, another relative, or an older friend, neighbor, or teacher who is important to you. Recall a special time you have shared with that person. Draw a picture of that vivid memory. Then write a caption for your illustration.

Find Out More

The author expected to return to Vietnam, but war made that impossible. What do you know about Vietnam? Find out more about the country by using a social studies textbook, another book, an atlas, an encyclopedia, a video source, or the Internet. Include information about the Vietnam War. Compare life in that country before and after the war.

Read a Bibliography

Suppose that you have been asked to write a research report about the Vietnam War. You can find the information you need in books and other reference sources. To let your readers know where you have found your information, you will need to include a bibliography. A **bibliography** is a list of all the sources you have used to prepare your report. This list includes the name of the author, the title of the book, the place where the book was published, the publisher, and the date of the book. Note that in a bibliography most of the sources are arranged in alphabetical order by the author's last name. You may also need to refer to a bibliography when preparing your own report.

BIBLIOGRAPHY

Atlas of the World. New York: Oxon University Press, 1992.

Bainbridge, Barry. *Words from Vietnam.* New York: Angora Press, 1999.

Weston, David K. *A Portrait of the War in Vietnam.* Chicago: Learner Books, 1998.

Use the sample bibliography to answer these questions.

1. What is a bibliography?
2. Who is the author of *Words from Vietnam*?
3. Why do you think a bibliography must include the date of the book?
4. Which book was probably used to find quotations by people who served in the war?
5. Why is it important to include a bibliography at the end of a research report?

TEST POWER

Test Tip

Look for clues to the meaning of the underlined word.

DIRECTIONS

Read the sample story. Then read each question about the story.

SAMPLE

At the Cabin

Ngoc and her family had just arrived at the cabin. The dense woods that surrounded it <u>shrouded</u> the cabin in a canopy of green, feathery branches. Ngoc had never been in such a pristine place. It was so quiet that she felt like a clumsy intruder as she stepped lightly on the soft path.

Ngoc's father had built this cabin many years ago when he moved north to work in the timber industry. After he had started a family, he returned to the city. The cabin had been vacant for many years now, but Ngoc's father had wanted Ngoc to see it now that she was old enough to appreciate its natural beauty.

The cabin was simple, with its rough-hewn siding and plain wooden front door. Ngoc was surprised when the door opened to reveal a sparsely furnished but tidy cabin. The cozy feel of the rustic room thrilled Ngoc. She was thankful that her father had wanted to share this special place with her.

1 What happened after the cabin door opened?

- **A** Ngoc was frightened by a mouse.
- **B** Ngoc's father tidied up the cabin.
- **C** Ngoc saw a sparse but clean room.
- **D** Ngoc entered the cabin.

2 In this passage, the word <u>shrouded</u> means —

- **F** opened
- **G** cleaned
- **H** helped
- **J** covered

Stories in Art

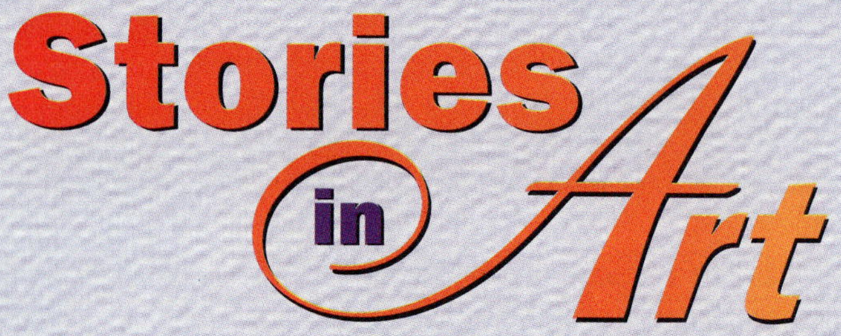

When you first look at this painting, you might think that the towers on the left match the towers on the right. But do they?

Study the painting again. Do you reach a different conclusion? How are the right and left towers different? What might this say about the American Republic?

If you could, would you like to explore this monument? Why? What might you discover? How is uncovering history like finding a treasure from the past?

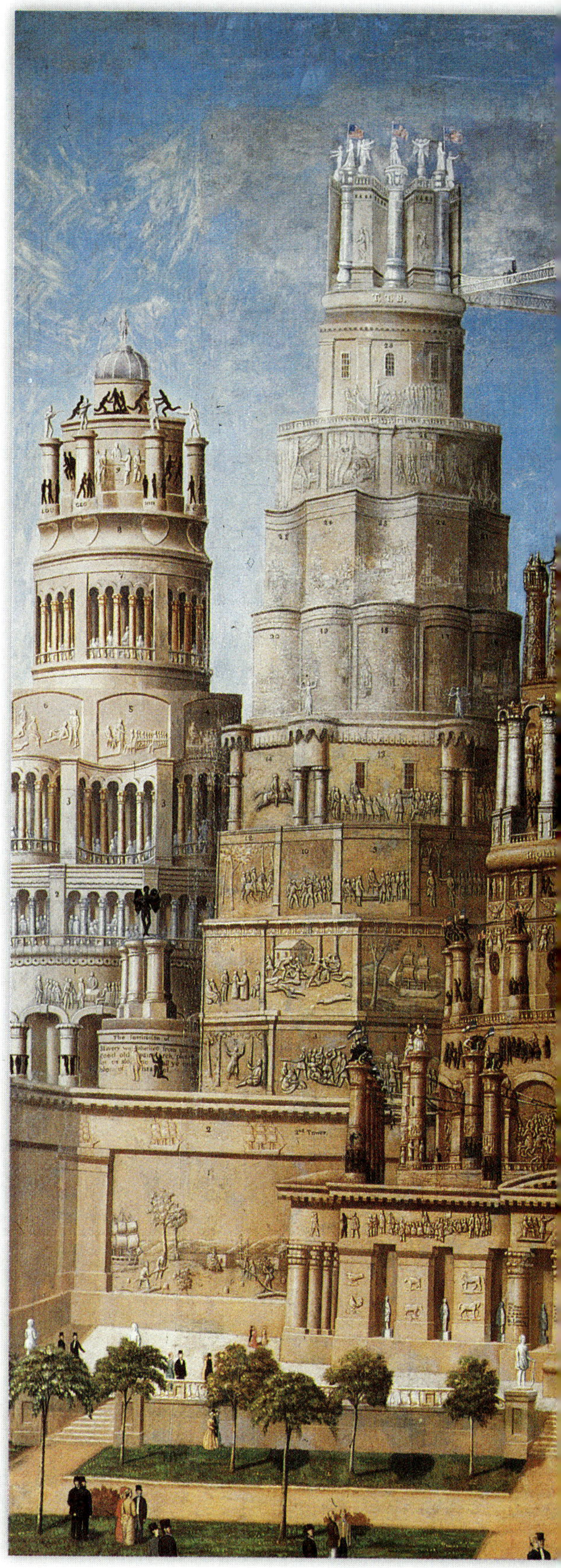

Historical Monument of the American Republic
by Erastus Salisbury Field, c. 1876
Museum of Fine Arts, Springfield, Massachusetts

Cleopatra's Lost Palace

The home of ancient Egypt's last queen has been found after 1,600 years under water.

Raising Royal Treasures

Bit by bit, divers are recovering pieces of Cleopatra's lost palace

Ancient Alexandria was once a busy center of trade. In 332 B.C., Alexander the Great was so enchanted with the Egyptian harbor that he ordered a city to be built there and named after him. Temples, gardens, and fountains decorated the sparkling city. Many years later, within a palace there, a romance took place between the Roman general Mark Antony and Cleopatra, the last Pharaoh of Egypt.

What exactly did Alexandria's splendors and royal palace look like? For years, historians could not say. Ancient Egyptian writings and drawings indicate that Cleopatra owned a palace on an island named Antirhodos. The island was near Alexandria, which became the capital city of Egypt during Cleopatra's rule in the first century B.C.

COVER: CORBIS-BETTMANN; RIGHT: LEILA GROCHEV-AP; FAR RIGHT: WERNER FROMAN/CORBIS

Explorers lift an ancient sphinx from the water near modern Alexandria.

A deep-sea staring contest? No. Explorer Franck Goddio meets a sunken sphinx. The statue's face is that of Cleopatra's father.

But no one was certain exactly where the palace had stood or what it contained. Although the city of Alexandria still exists, floods and earthquakes buried Antirhodos under water more than 1,600 years ago.

In 1996, undersea explorer Franck Goddio found the site beneath just 18 feet of water, off the shore of Alexandria. The ruins of what appears to be Cleopatra's palace lay buried in layers of mud, seaweed, and garbage.

Underwater Mission

Goddio and his team of divers spent two years uncovering statues, columns, and pottery that may have belonged to the young queen.

Among the most sensational finds are two statues of sphinxes, imaginary creatures with the head of a human and the body of a lion. The faces of the sphinxes are in surprisingly good shape—so good that experts have been able to identify one face as that of King Ptolemy XII, Cleopatra's father.

How does it feel to come face to face underwater with an ancient sphinx? "It's fascinating!" Goddio told

FIND OUT MORE

Visit our website:

www.mhschool.com/reading

TFK. "You see the sphinx, and it's looking at you! You know that it's the father of Cleopatra and that Cleopatra once saw it." Adds Goddio: "We were touching stones and columns and thinking Cleopatra had touched them."

An Ancient Romance

The fallen pillars and cobblestone pavements the team discovered may mark the spot where Cleopatra ruled between 51 B.C. and 30 B.C. and fell in love with Mark Antony. Their romance angered Roman leaders and eventually led to both Antony's and Cleopatra's death. Soon after her death at the age of 39, the Romans took control of Egypt.

Goddio hopes to set up an underwater museum at the palace site. Visitors would be able to explore and experience Cleopatra's world up close. "To be there, underwater where she reigned and died," says Goddio, "is unbelievable."

OPPOSITE PAGE: J. DELAFOSSE-HILTI FOUNDATION/FRANCK GODDIO/DCI; BELOW LEFT: CHRISTOPH GERIGK-HILTI FOUNDATION/FRANCK GODDIO/DCI; BELOW RIGHT: LEILA GROCHEV-AP

DID YOU KNOW?
ANCIENT EGYPTIAN FACTS

◆ **Egypt began as two kingdoms, Upper and Lower Egypt. They were united in 3100 B.C.**

◆ **Egypt's kings were called pharaohs.**

◆ **Ancient Egyptians loved games! Kids played leapfrog and tug-of-war. Grown-ups played a board game called senet. Players threw sticks to determine which way to move on the board.**

◆ **Egyptians worshipped hundreds of gods and goddesses. Ra, the sun god, was the most important, but there was even a cat goddess, named Bastet!**

Far left: A statue of the Egyptian goddess Isis rested under water for 1,600 years.

Near left: Isis finally comes up for air. Isis stands for the human cycle of birth and death.

Based on an article in *TIME FOR KIDS.*

Story Questions & Activities

1. Where did explorer Franck Goddio find Cleopatra's palace?
2. How is the discovery of the sphinxes an important find?
3. What makes Goddio's discovery of Cleopatra's lost palace so exciting? Explain.
4. What is the main idea of this selection?
5. Explorer Franck Goddio's discovery has been made into a television program. How do you think the television show differs from the magazine article you have just read? What do you think they have in common?

Write Two Paragraphs

According to ancient Egyptian myth, a sphinx was an imaginary creature with the head of a human and the body of a lion. Think of another imaginary creature. It might be a creature you have seen in a movie or on television, or have read about in a book. In two paragraphs, compare this imaginary creature with the Egyptian sphinx. Present the two creatures' similarities in the first paragraph. Then present all their differences in the next.

Create a Sphinx

In "Cleopatra's Lost Palace," divers uncovered two statues of sphinxes. Now design a sphinx of your own out of clay. Choose the face of a famous person from history. Model the face, and use clay to create the body of a lion. Be sure that your sphinx appears strong and wise.

Invent a Game

The Egyptians loved games and were always inventing new ones! Think of a simple game such as hopscotch or tag. Make up a variation of it. Teach the new game to several friends and then play it. If you can, research and report on a game played in Egypt.

Find Out More

Franck Goddio explored an ancient underwater palace near Alexandria, Egypt. Now it's your turn. Start by checking in an encyclopedia or in your social studies textbook. Gather facts about Alexandria. How did this city get its name? What happened to its famous library? Choose a topic, and share your findings in a report to the class.

Read a Newspaper

The discovery that Franck Goddio and his team of explorers made near Alexandria, Egypt, caused worldwide attention. In fact, newspaper reporters came from around the world to write about the find.

Look at this news article. A **news article** describes an important event that has recently taken place. News articles tell the facts about local, state, national, or international events. They also answer the questions *Who? What? When?* and *Where?* Notice the **headline** printed in large type at the top of the article. How does it summarize the story and also catch the reader's attention? Now read the **dateline.** How does it tell when and where the news article was written?

The Village Crier

New York, New York | Monday, October 28, 1996 | 65 PAGES • 50 CENTS

Cleopatra's Palace Found

ALEXANDRIA, Egypt, Oct. 28, 1996—Divers working in the waters near Alexandria, Egypt, believe they have uncovered the ruins of Cleopatra's palace. Led by Frenchman Franck Goddio, the team of undersea explorers has been excavating Antirhodus, the underwater island where they discovered the foundations of the ancient palace.

Two statues were lifted out of the water today. One is of a priest of the goddess Isis. The other is a sphinx with the face of King Ptolemy XII, Cleopatra's father.

Use the news article to answer these questions.

1. What is the name of the newspaper?
2. How does the headline grab your attention?
3. When and where was the news article written? How do you know?
4. How does the first sentence answer the questions *Who?* and *What?*
5. Compare the news article and the selection. How are they alike? How are they different?

TEST POWER

Test Tip

Read the directions first.

DIRECTIONS

Read the sample story. Then read each question about the story.

SAMPLE

Jeannie Longo

Champions don't succeed just because they are naturally good at something. A champion is someone who doesn't give up.

Jeannie Longo is a champion bicycle racer. She trains hard because she has always loved sports. As a child she loved hiking, swimming, skiing, and riding her bicycle. Her parents encouraged her to wrestle and box.

In 1980, when Jeannie was 21 years old, the French Cycling Championships took place near her home town in France. She entered the race, and won! Winning that race was just the first step in becoming a champion, however. While competing in the 1984 Olympics, Jeannie had a small collision, but she did not become discouraged. Instead, she took sixth place by walking her broken bicycle across the finish line!

1 After Jeannie Longo's bicycle broke, she —

A felt sad

B took up boxing

C bought a new one

D continued the race

2 The author gives you reason to believe that Jeannie —

F is a gifted athlete

G is afraid of a challenge

H gave advice to other cyclists

J was critical of her competitors

Did you reread the story to find the best answer? Tell why.

A Song of Greatness

CHIPPEWA TRADITIONAL

When I hear the old men
Telling of heroes,
Telling of great deeds
Of ancient days—
When I hear that telling,
Then I think within me
I, too, am one of these.

When I hear the people
Praising great ones,
Then I know that I too—
Shall be esteemed:
I, too, when my time comes
Shall do mightily.

transcribed by Mary Austin

UNIT 3

With Flying Colors

To You

To sit and dream, to sit and read,
To sit and learn about the world
Outside our world of here and now—
        Our problem world—
To dream of vast horizons of the soul
Through dreams made whole,
Unfettered, free—help me!
All you who are dreamers too,
        Help me to make
        Our world anew.
I reach out my dreams to you.

by Langston Hughes

Like poets who create word pictures, artists use their work to show something just as it appears to them. Sometimes their vision is unusual. But always it is a unique point of view.

Look at the painting by Pablo Picasso. What do you notice about the woman's face? How does the artist organize his shapes, lines, and colors into two halves? What is his point of view? What is his purpose in painting this woman? How does he feel about her? What does he want you to feel? Why?

Look at the painting again. How would you describe it to someone who had never seen it? What would you say about the artist's vision? Is it unusual? How?

Head of a Woman
by Pablo Picasso, 1924
Tate Gallery, London

Photos by David Harp, courtesy of the Baltimore Sun

A Boy of Unusual Vision

by Alice Steinbach

First, the eyes: They are large and blue, a light, opaque blue, the color of a robin's egg. And if, on a sunny spring day, you look straight into these eyes—eyes that cannot look back at you—the sharp, April light turns them pale, like the thin blue of a high, cloudless sky.

Ten-year-old Calvin Stanley, the owner of these eyes and a boy who has been blind since birth, likes this description and asks to hear it twice. He listens as only he can listen, then: "Orange used to be my favorite color but now it's blue," he announces. Pause. The

♦ ♦ ♦ ♦ ♦

eyes flutter between the short, thick lashes. "I know there's light blue and there's dark blue, but what does sky-blue look like?" he wants to know. And if you watch his face as he listens to your description, you get a sense of a picture being clicked firmly into place behind the pale eyes.

He is a boy who has a lot of pictures stored in his head, retrievable images which have been fashioned for him by the people who love him—by family and friends and teachers who have painstakingly and patiently gone about creating a special world for Calvin's inner eye to inhabit.

Picture of a rainbow: "It's a lot of beautiful colors, one next to the other. Shaped like a bow. In the sky. Right across."

Picture of lightning, which frightens Calvin: "My mother says lightning looks like a Christmas tree—the way it blinks on and off across the sky," he says, offering a comforting description that would make a poet proud.

"Child," his mother once told him, "one day I won't be here and I won't be around to pick you up when you fall—nobody will be around all the time to pick you up—so you have to try to be something on your own. You have to learn how to deal with this. And to do that, you have to learn how to think."

There was never a moment when Ethel Stanley said to herself, "My son is blind and this is how I'm going to handle it."

Calvin's mother: "When Calvin was little, he was so inquisitive. He wanted to see everything, he wanted to touch everything. I had to show him every little thing there is. A spoon, a fork. I let him play with them, just hold them. The pots, the pans. *Everything.* I showed him the sharp edges of the table. 'You cannot touch this; it will hurt you.' And I showed him what would hurt. He still bumped into it anyway, but he knew what he wasn't supposed to do and what he could do. And he knew that nothing in his room—*nothing*—could hurt him.

"And when he started walking and we went out together—I guess he was about two—I never said anything to him about what to do. When we got to the curbs, Calvin knew that when I stopped, he should step down, and when I stopped again, he should step up. I never

♦ ♦ ♦ ♦ ♦

said anything, that's just the way we did it. And it became a pattern."

Calvin remembers when he began to realize that something about him was "different": "I just figured it out myself. I think I was about four. I would pick things up and I couldn't see them. Other people would say they could see things and I couldn't."

And his mother remembers the day her son asked her why he was blind and other people weren't.

"He must have been about four or five. I explained to him what happened, that he was born that way and that it was nobody's fault and he didn't have to blame himself. He asked, 'Why me?' And I said, 'I don't know why, Calvin. Maybe there's a special plan for you in your life and there's a reason for this. But this is the way you're going to be and you can deal with it.' "

Then she sat her son down and told him this: "You're *seeing*, Calvin. You're just using your hands instead of your eyes. But you're seeing. And, remember, there is *nothing* you can't do."

It's spring vacation and Calvin is out in the alley behind his house riding his bike, a serious-looking, black and silver two-wheeler. "Stay behind me," he shouts to his friend Kellie Bass, who's furiously pedaling her bike down the one-block stretch of alley where Calvin is allowed to bicycle.

Now: Try to imagine riding a bike without being able to see where you're going. Without even knowing what an "alley" looks like. Try to imagine how you navigate a space that has no visual boundaries, that exists only in your head. And then try to imagine what Calvin is feeling as he pedals his bike in that space, whooping for joy as the air rushes past him on either side.

And although Calvin can't see the signs of spring sprouting all around him in the neighboring backyards—the porch furniture and barbecue equipment being brought out of storage, the grass growing emerald green from the April rains, the forsythia exploding yellow over the fences—still, there are signs of another sort which guide him along his route:

Past the German shepherd who always barks at him, telling Calvin that he's three houses away from his home; then past the purple hyacinths, five gardens away, throwing out their fragrance (later it will

♦ ♦ ♦ ♦ ♦

be the scent of the lilacs which guides him); past the large diagonal crack which lifts the front wheel of his bike up and then down, telling him he's reached his boundary and should turn back—past all these familiar signs Calvin rides his bike on a warm spring day.

Ethel Stanley: "At six, one of his cousins got a new bike and Calvin said, 'I want to learn how to ride a two-wheeler bike.' So we got him one. His father let him help put it together. You know, whatever Calvin gets he's going to go all over it with those hands and he knows every part of that bike and what it's called. He learned to ride it the first day, but I couldn't watch. His father stayed outside with him."

Calvin: "I just got mad. I got tired of riding a little bike. At first I used to zig-zag, go all over. My cousin would hold onto the bike and then let me go. I fell a lot in the beginning. But a lot of people fall when they first start."

♦ ♦ ♦ ♦ ♦

There's a baseball game about to start in Calvin's backyard and Mrs. Stanley is pitching to her son. Nine-year-old Kellie, on first base, has taken off her fake fur coat so she can get a little more steam into her game and the other team member, Monet Clark, six, is catching. It is also Monet's job to alert Calvin, who's at bat, when to swing. "Hit it, Calvin," she yells. "Swing!"

He does and the sound of the ball making solid contact with the bat sends Calvin running off to first base, his hands groping in front of his body. His mother walks over to stand next to him at first base and unconsciously her hands go to his head, stroking his hair in a soft, protective movement.

"Remember," the mother had said to her son six years earlier, "there's *nothing* you can't do."

Calvin's father, 37-year-old Calvin Stanley, Jr., a Baltimore city policeman, has taught his son how to ride a bike and how to shift gears in the family's Volkswagen and how to put toys together. They go to the movies together and they tell each other they're handsome.

The father: "You know, there's nothing much I've missed with him. Because he does everything. Except see. He goes swimming out in the pool in the backyard. Some of the other kids are afraid of the water, but he jumps right in, puts his head under. If it were me I wouldn't be as brave as he is. I probably wouldn't go anywhere. If it were me I'd probably stay in this house most of the time. But he's always ready to go, always on the telephone, ready to do something.

"But he gets sad, too. You can just look at him sometimes and tell he's real sad."

The son: "You know what makes me sad? *Charlotte's Web.* It's my favorite story. I listen to the record at night. I like Charlotte, the spider. The way she talks. And, you know, she really loved Wilbur, the pig. He was her best friend." Calvin's voice is full of warmth and wonder as he talks about E. B. White's tale of the spider who befriended a pig and later sacrificed herself for him.

"It's a story about friendship. It's telling us how good friends are supposed to be. Like Charlotte and Wilbur," he says, turning away from you suddenly to wipe his eyes. "And when Charlotte dies, it makes me real sad. I always feel like I've lost a friend. That's why I try not to listen to that part. I just move the needle forward."

♦ ♦ ♦ ♦ ♦

Something else makes Calvin sad: "I'd like to see what my mother looks like," he says, looking up quickly and swallowing hard. "What does she look like? People tell me she's pretty."

The mother: "One day Calvin wanted me to tell him how I looked. He was about six. They were doing something in school for Mother's Day and the kids were drawing pictures of their mothers. He wanted to know what I looked like and that upset me because I didn't know how to tell him. I thought, 'How am I going to explain this to him so he will really know what I look like?' So I tried to explain to him about facial features, noses, and I just used touch. I took his hand and I tried to explain about skin, let him touch his, and then mine.

"And I think that was the moment when Calvin really *knew* he was blind, because he said, 'I won't ever be able to see your face . . . or Daddy's face,'" she says softly, covering her eyes with her hands, but not in time to stop the tears. "That's the only time I've ever let it bother me that much."

But Mrs. Stanley knew what to tell her only child: "I said, 'Calvin, you *can* see my face. You can see it with your hands and by listening to my voice and you can tell more about me that way than somebody who can use his eyes.'"

Thirty-three-year-old Ethel Stanley, a handsome, strong-looking woman with a radiant smile, is the oldest of seven children and grew up looking after her younger brothers and sisters while her mother worked. "She was a wonderful mother," Mrs. Stanley recalls. "Yes, she had to work, but when she was there, she was with you every minute and those minutes were worth a whole day. She always had time to listen to you."

Somewhere—perhaps from her own childhood experiences—Mrs.

◆ ◆ ◆ ◆ ◆

Stanley, who has not worked since Calvin was born, acquired the ability to nurture and teach and poured her mothering love into Calvin. And it shows. He moves in the sighted world with trust and faith and the unshakable confidence of a child whose mother has always been there for him. "If you don't understand something, ask," she tells Calvin again and again, in her open, forthright way. "Just ask."

"When he was little he wanted to be Stevie Wonder," says Calvin's father, laughing. "He started playing the piano and he got pretty good at it. Now he wants to be a computer programmer and design programs for the blind."

Calvin's neatly ordered bedroom is outfitted with all the comforts you would find in the room of many ten-year-old, middle-class boys: a television set (black and white, he tells you), an Atari game with a box of cartridges (his favorite is "Phoenix"), a braille Monopoly set, records, tapes, and programmed talking robots. "I watch wrestling on TV every Saturday," he says. "I wrestle with my friends. It's fun."

He moves around his room confidently and easily. "I know this house like a book." Still, some things are hard for him to remember since, in his case, much of what he remembers has to be imagined visually first. Like the size and color of his room. "I think it's kind of big," he says of the small room. "And it's green," he says of the deep rose-colored walls.

And while Calvin doesn't need to turn the light on in his room, he does like to have some kind of sound going constantly. *Loud* sound.

"It's three o'clock," he says, as the theme music from a TV show blares out into his room.

"Turn that TV down," says his mother, evenly. "You're not *deaf*, you know."

Two P.M., Vivian Jackson's class, Room 207.

What Calvin can't see: He can't see the small, pretty girl sitting opposite him, the one who is wearing little rows of red, yellow, and blue barrettes shaped like airplanes in her braided hair. He can't see the line of small, green plants growing in yellow pots all along the sunny window sill. And he can't see Mrs. Jackson in her rose-pink suit and pink enameled earrings shaped like little swans.

("Were they really shaped like little swans?" he will ask later.)

♦ ♦ ♦ ♦ ♦

But Calvin can feel the warm spring breeze—invisible to *everyone's* eyes, not just his—blowing in through the window, and he can hear the tapping of a young oak tree's branches against the window. He can hear Mrs. Jackson's pleasant, musical voice and, later, if you ask him what she looks like, he will say, "She's nice."

But best of all, Calvin can read and spell and do fractions and follow the classroom work in his specially prepared braille books. He is smart and he can do everything the rest of his class can do. Except see.

"What's the next word, Calvin?" Mrs. Jackson asks.

"Eleven," he says, reading from his braille textbook.

"Now tell us how to spell it—without looking back at the book!" she says quickly, causing Calvin's fingers to fly away from the forbidden word.

"E-l-e-v-e-n," he spells out easily.

It all seems so simple, the ease with which Calvin follows along, the manner in which his blindness has been accommodated. But it's deceptively simple. The amount of work that has gone into getting Calvin to this point—the number of teachers, vision specialists and mobility instructors, and the array of special equipment—is staggering.

Patience and empathy from his teachers have played a large role, too.

For instance, there's Dorothy Lloyd, the specialist who is teaching Calvin the slow and very difficult method of using an Optacon, a device which allows a blind person to read a printed page by touch by converting printed letters into a tactile representation.

And there's Charleye Dyer, who's teaching Calvin things like "mobility" and "independent travel skills," which includes such tasks as using a cane and getting on and off buses. Of course, what Miss Dyer is really teaching Calvin is freedom; the ability to move about independently and without fear in the larger world.

There's also Lois Sivits who, among other things, teaches Calvin braille and is his favorite teacher. And, to add to a list which is endless, there's the music teacher who comes in 30 minutes early each Tuesday to give him a piano lesson, and his home room teacher, Mrs. Jackson, who is as finely tuned to Calvin's cues as a player in a musical duet would be to her partner.

♦ ♦ ♦ ♦ ♦

An important part of Calvin's school experience has been his contact with sighted children.

"When he first started school," his mother recalls, "some of the kids would tease him about his eyes. 'Oh, they're so big and you can't see.' But I just told him, 'Not any time in your life will everybody around you like you—whether you can see or not. They're just children and they don't know they're being cruel. And I'm sure it's not the last time someone will be cruel to you. But it's all up to you because you have to go to school and you'll have to deal with it.' "

Calvin's teachers say he's well liked, and watching him on the playground and in class you get the impression that the only thing that singles him out from the other kids is that someone in his class is always there to take his hand if he needs help.

"I'd say he's really well accepted," says his mobility teacher, Miss Dyer, "and that he's got a couple of very special friends."

Eight-year-old Brian Butler is one of these special friends. "My *best* friend," says Calvin proudly,

♦ ♦ ♦ ♦ ♦

introducing you to a studious-looking boy whose eyes are alert and serious behind his glasses. The two boys are not in the same class, but they ride home together on the bus every day.

Here's Brian explaining why he likes Calvin so much: "He's funny and he makes me laugh. And I like him because he always makes me feel better when I don't feel good." And, he says, his friendship with Calvin is no different from any other good friendship. Except for one thing: "If Calvin's going to bump into a wall or something, I tell him, 'Look out,'" says Brian, sounding as though it were the most natural thing in the world to do when walking with a friend.

"Charlotte would have done it for Wilbur," is the way Calvin sizes up Brian's help, evoking once more that story about "how friendship ought to be."

A certain moment: Calvin is working one-on-one with Lois Sivits, a teacher who is responsible for the braille skills which the four blind children at Cross Country must have in order to do all the work necessary in their regular classes. He is very relaxed with Miss Sivits, who is gentle, patient, smart, and, like Calvin, blind. Unlike Calvin, she was not able to go to public school but was sent away at age six, after many operations on her eyes, to a residential school—the Western Pennsylvania School for the Blind.

And although it was 48 years ago that Lois Sivits was sent away from her family to attend the school for the blind, she remembers—as though it were 48 minutes ago—how that blind, six-year-old girl felt about the experience: "Oh, I was so *very* homesick. I had a very hard time being separated from my family. It took me three years before I began getting used to it. But I knew I had to stay there. I would have given anything to stay at home and go to a public school like Calvin," says the small, kind-looking woman with very still hands.

Now, the moment: Calvin is standing in front of the window, the light pouring in from behind him. He is listening to a talking clock which tells him, "It's 11:52 A.M." Miss Sivits stands about three feet away from him, also in front of the window, holding a huge braille dictionary in her hands, fingers flying across the page as she silently reads from it. And for a few moments, there they are, as if frozen in a tableau, the two of them

♦ ♦ ♦ ♦ ♦

standing in darkness against the light, each lost for a moment in a private world that is composed only of sound and touch.

There was another moment, years ago, when Calvin's mother and father knew that the operations had not helped, that their son was probably never going to see. "Well," said the father, trying to comfort the mother, "we'll do what we have to do and Calvin will be fine."

He is. And so are they.

by Alice Steinbach

Alice Steinbach came to writing through art. A Baltimore native, she was writing articles about artists when she realized she could apply what she had learned to writing about other kinds of people, too.

Her articles led to a job writing for the *Baltimore Sun*. One day she realized that she didn't know much about children who are blind. After deciding to write about Calvin Stanley, Steinbach spent three weeks interviewing Calvin and his family and observing his daily life. "A Boy of Unusual Vision" won a 1985 Pulitzer Prize and has been reprinted more than 50 times.

Her secret for success? "Observe the world in *your* way: through scientific facts, through art, or through words. Then think about what you observed."

Story Questions & Activities

1. How does Calvin "see" with his hands?
2. Why does the author describe Calvin as "a boy of unusual vision"?
3. What was the author's purpose in writing this newspaper article? Explain.
4. What is the main idea of this selection?
5. Friendship plays an important part in many stories in this book. Choose one of these stories, such as "Last Summer with Maizon" or "Number the Stars." Compare the friendship described in that selection with the friendship shared by Calvin and Brian.

Write Instructions

Even though Calvin can't see, he is still able to play baseball. Besides listening for the sound of the ball, he has his friend's instructions to help him. Think of a game or a sport you feel Calvin would be able to play. Write a set of instructions that will tell Calvin how to play the game by using his sense of hearing and touch.

Visualize Your Classroom

Calvin knows his house like a book. Yet "much of what he remembers has to be imagined visually first." Close your eyes. Visualize the size and color of your classroom. "See" the objects and their arrangement in the room. Then draw a picture of your classroom, keeping your eyes tightly closed. When you have completed your drawing, open your eyes. Compare what you remember seeing with your actual classroom.

Make a Book Cover

The book *Charlotte's Web* is very important to Calvin. Make a book cover to protect your favorite book. Use a brown paper bag, a piece of oilcloth, or a large sheet of paper. Draw a scene from the book on the front cover. On the inside flap, write a paragraph that explains why this is your favorite book.

Find Out More

Calvin has a special teacher who helps him practice reading the braille alphabet. Investigate the braille system further. Discover who developed it, and why. Find out how this system of reading works. Start by checking in an encyclopedia or another reference source. Share your information with the class.

Read a Braille Chart

In the story, you discovered that Calvin reads from specially prepared braille books. Almost 200 years ago in France, a 15-year-old blind student named Louis Braille developed a special alphabet that could be read by the blind. Braille's alphabet had a series of raised dots, with one group of dots standing for each letter. This meant that the blind could read by running their fingertips over the dots.

Look at the braille chart below. Notice that each letter is three dots high and two dots wide.

BRAILLE ALPHABET

a 1, b 2, c 3, d 4, e 5, f 6, g 7, h 8, i 9, j 0

k, l, m, n, o, p, q, r, s, t

u, v, w, x, y, z

Capital Sign

Numeral Sign

Use the braille chart to answer these questions.

1. Which letter does this series of dots represent: ?
2. What is the difference between the letter *b* and the letter *k?*
3. The braille system has been called "The Six Magic Dots." How do you think it got that name?
4. How do the blind read the braille alphabet?
5. Why do you think it is important for you to know about the braille alphabet?

TEST POWER

Test Tip

Take a moment to think about what the whole passage was about. Put it in your own words.

DIRECTIONS

Read the sample story. Then read each question about the story.

SAMPLE

Ada Byron

Ada Byron was born in December 1815. She was the daughter of Lord Byron, one of the most famous poets in England, and she became an expert in mathematics. Five weeks after Ada was born, her mother took her away from Lord Byron. The Byrons' marriage had not been happy.

When Ada was 18 years old, she met a fellow mathematician named Charles Babbage. Mr. Babbage had invented a machine that could count, add, and subtract. Ada admired Mr. Babbage and his machine. In 1843, she helped Mr. Babbage write an article about the workings of the machine.

Ada expected that machines like the one Babbage made would be used to compose music and make pictures in the future. Of course, Ada was correct. Today, we call Babbage's machines "computers."

1 After reading this passage, one can conclude that Ada Byron —

A was a famous poet

B was willing to write stories for her mother

C should not have helped Charles Babbage

D was interested in technology

2 What is the main idea of the passage?

F Ada Byron was a talented woman who predicted the future of computers.

G Ada Byron married Charles Babbage and together they invented the computer.

H Ada Byron used the computer to compose music.

J Ada Byron moved away from Lord Byron when she was five weeks old.

Stories in Art

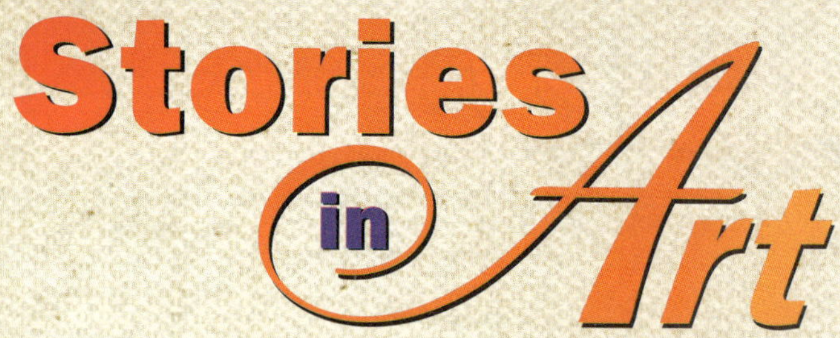

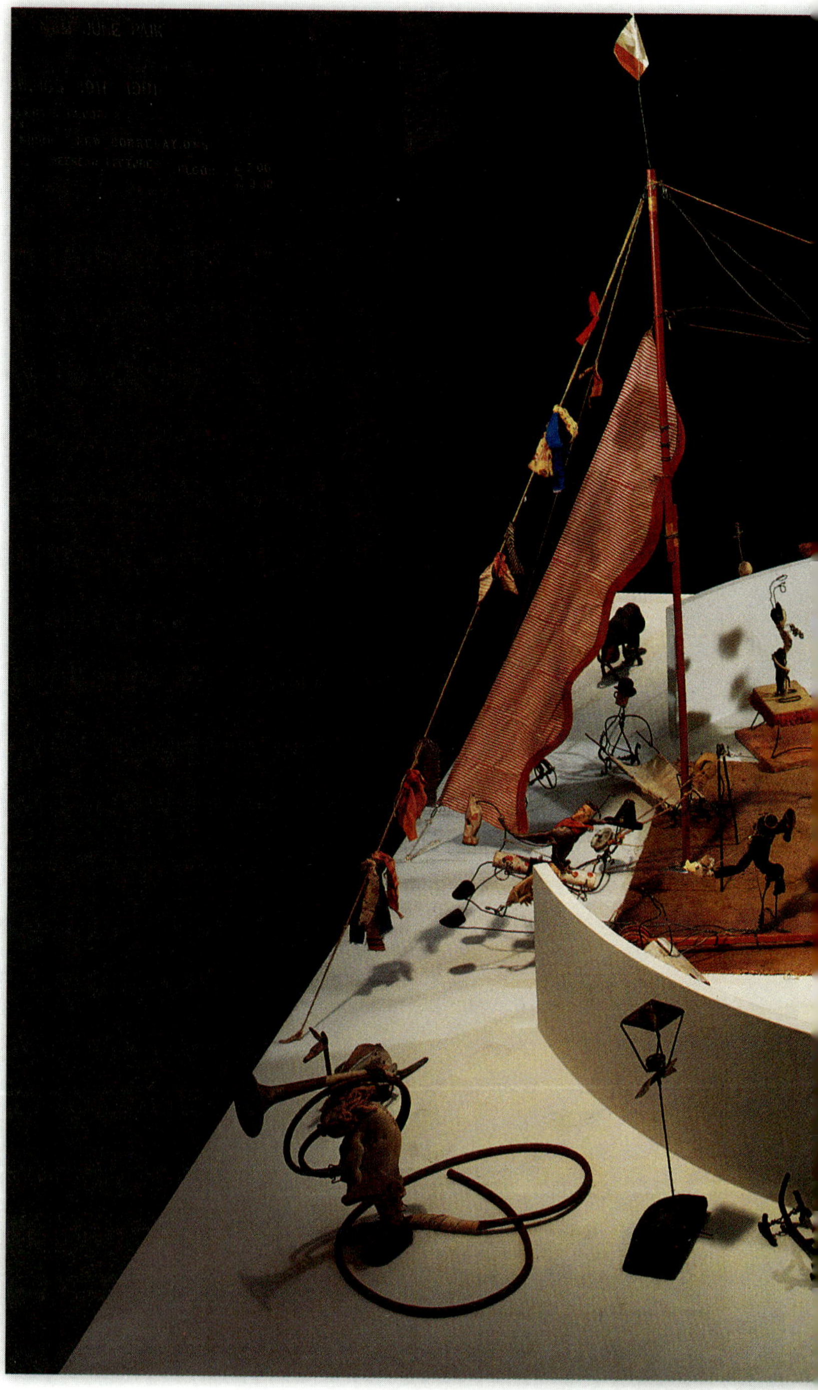

What do you see when you first look at this sculpture? How did the artist put all of these pieces together to make a work of art?

Look at this sculpture. What kinds of things are the circus characters made of? Look at the buttons, bottle caps, and strings. What do you think the artist did first after collecting these items? What steps did he take to turn them into art?

Look at this sculpture again. Why do you think the artist used things that people usually throw away? What could you make from old buttons, toys, clothing, and other objects? How does it feel to create a work of art?

Calder's Circus **by Alexander Calder, 1926-1931**
Whitney Museum of American Art, New York

Meet Gary Soto

Gary Soto grew up in a Mexican-American community in Fresno, California. "Even as a child I felt like a writer," Soto admits. "I'd read a book and it was such a powerful experience." Soto's first book of poetry, called the *Elements of San Joaquin*, won an important award. In addition, many of his stories are award winners. "People tell me my stories are funny," Soto says, but they "have pain and sorrow of life, too."

Today, Soto teaches English and Chicano studies at the University of California at Berkeley. He is also a volunteer English teacher. He encourages his students to read. "Everyone has to live beyond the years they're in," he says. To young people, he also gives this advice: Share your writing. Give your poems as a gift to your family or friends—or leave them "on a picnic bench or in the park" for someone to find.

Meet Jack E. Davis

As a child, Jack E. Davis loved best the time he spent drawing in art class, playing baseball, and performing in the school band. His dream was to become a professional in one of these fields. And for much of his adult life, Davis did earn his living as a musician in a blues band. In fact, his career as an artist of young people's books did not begin until his own children were nearly grown.

THE School Play
Written by Gary Soto
Illustrated by Jack E. Davis

In the school play at the end of his sixth-grade year, all Robert Suarez had to remember to say was, "Nothing's wrong, I can see," to a pioneer woman who was really Belinda Lopez. Belinda was one of the toughest girls since the beginning of the world. She was known to slap boys and grind their faces into the grass until they bit into chunks of wormy earth. More than once Robert had witnessed Belinda staring down the janitor's pit bull, a dog that licked his frothing chops but didn't dare mess with her.

The class rehearsed the play for three weeks, at first without costumes. Early one morning Mrs. Bunnin wobbled into the classroom carrying a large cardboard box. She wiped her brow and said, "Thanks for the help, Robert."

Robert was at his desk etching a ballpoint tattoo—D-U-D-E—on the mountaintops of his knuckles. He looked up and stared at his teacher. "Oh, did you need some help?" he asked.

She rolled her eyes at him and told him to stop writing on his skin. "You'll look like a criminal," she scolded.

Robert stuffed his hands into his pockets as he rose from his seat. "What's in the box?" he asked.

She popped open the Scotch-taped top and brought out skirts, hats, snowshoes, scarves, and vests. She tossed Robert a red beard, which he held up to his face thinking it made him look handsome.

"I like it," Robert said. He sneezed and ran one hand across his moist nose.

His classmates looked at Robert in awe. "That's *bad*," Alfredo said. "What do I get?"

Mrs. Bunnin threw him a wrinkled shirt. Alfredo raised it to his chest and said, "My dad could wear this. Can I give it to him after the play is done?"

Mrs. Bunnin turned away in silence.

Most of the actors didn't have speaking parts. They were given cut-out crepe-paper snowflakes to pin to their shirts or crepe-paper leaves to wear.

During the blizzard scene in which Robert delivered his line, Belinda asked, "Is there something wrong with your eyes?" Robert looked at the "audience," which for rehearsal was all the things that filled the classroom: empty chairs, a dented world globe that had been dropped by almost everyone, one limp flag, one wastebasket, and a picture of George Washington, whose eyes seemed to follow you around the room when you got up to sharpen your pencil. Robert answered, "Nothing's wrong. I can see."

Mrs. Bunnin, biting on the end of her pencil, said, "Louder, both of you."

Belinda stepped forward, her nostrils flaring so that the shadows on her nose quivered, and said louder, "Sucka, is there something wrong with your eyeballs?"

"Nothing's wrong. I can see."

"Louder! Make sure the audience can hear you," Mrs. Bunnin directed. She tapped her pencil hard against the desk. "Robert, I'm not going to tell you again to quit fooling with the beard."

"It's itchy."

"We can't do anything about that. Actors need props. You're an actor. Now try again."

Robert and Belinda stood center stage as they waited for Mrs. Bunnin to call "Action!" When she did Belinda approached Robert slowly. "Sucka face, is there anything wrong with your mug?" Belinda asked. Her eyes were flecked with anger. For a moment Robert saw his head grinding into the playground grass.

"Nothing's wrong. I can see."

Robert giggled behind his red beard. Belinda popped her gum and smirked. She stood with her hands on her hips.

"What? What did you say?" Mrs. Bunnin asked, pulling off her glasses. "Are you chewing gum, Belinda?"

"No, Mrs. Bunnin," Belinda lied. "I just forgot my lines."

The play, *The Last Stand*, was about the Donner party, with the action taking place just before the starving members of the expedition started eating each other. Everyone who scored twelve or more out of fifteen on the spelling tests got to say at least one line. Everyone else had to stand around and be trees or snowflakes.

Mrs. Bunnin wanted the play to be a success. She couldn't risk having kids with bad memories on stage. The nonspeaking trees and snowflakes hummed to create the effects of snow flurries and blistering wind. They produced hail by clacking their teeth.

Robert's mother was proud of him because he was living up to the legend of Robert DeNiro, for whom he was named. During dinner he said, "Nothing's wrong. I can see," when his brother asked him to pass the dish towel, their communal napkin. His sister said, "It's your turn to do dishes," and he said, "Nothing's wrong. I can see." His dog, Queenie, begged him for more than water and a Milkbone. He touched his dog's own hairy beard and said, "Nothing's wrong. I can see."

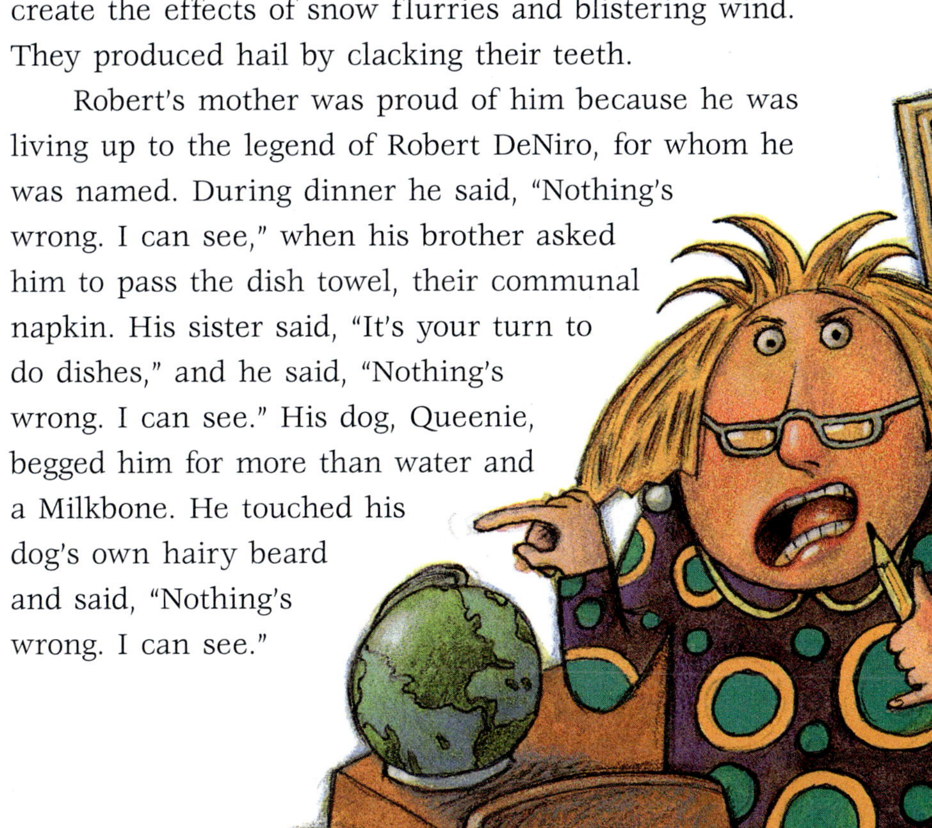

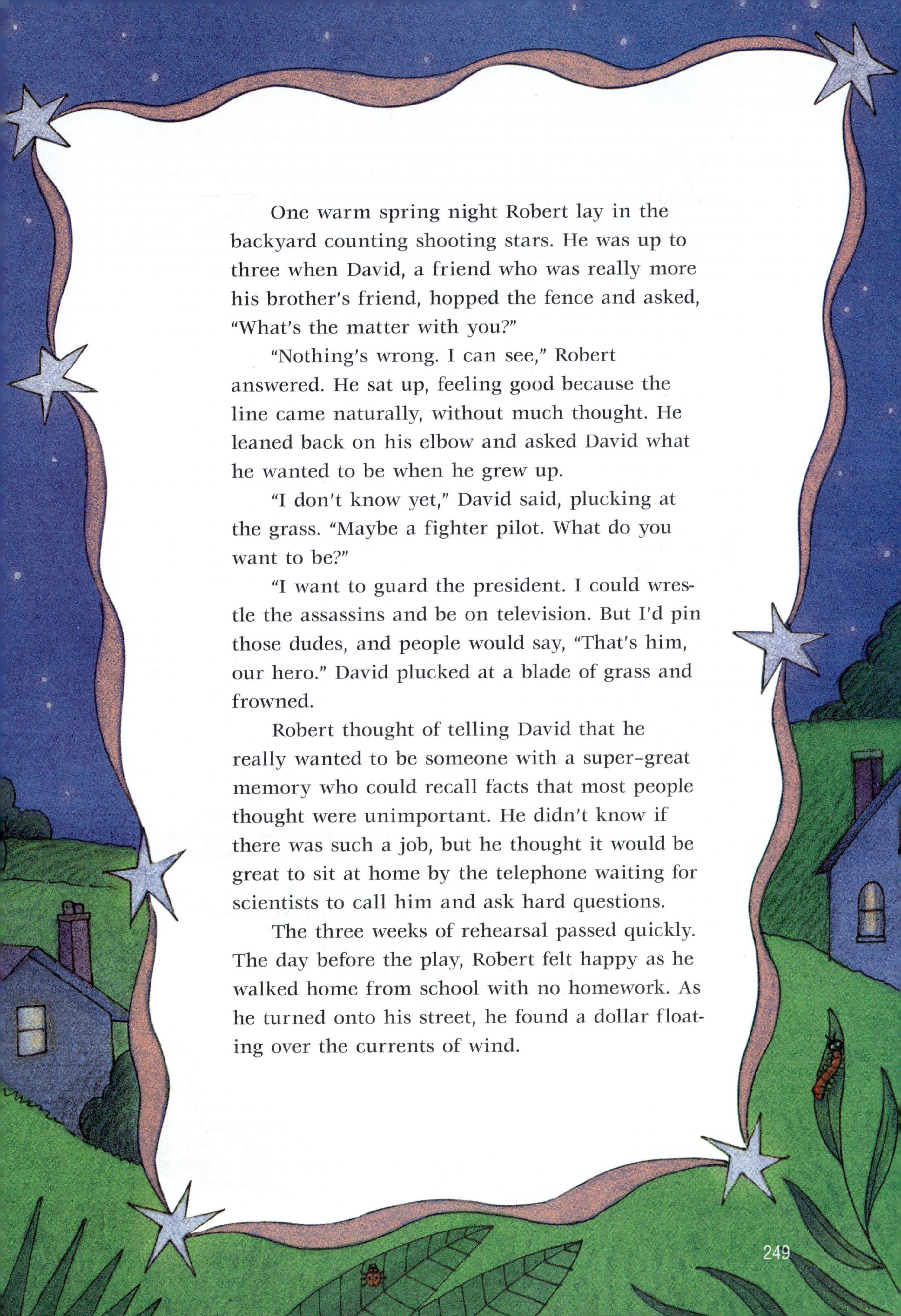

One warm spring night Robert lay in the backyard counting shooting stars. He was up to three when David, a friend who was really more his brother's friend, hopped the fence and asked, "What's the matter with you?"

"Nothing's wrong. I can see," Robert answered. He sat up, feeling good because the line came naturally, without much thought. He leaned back on his elbow and asked David what he wanted to be when he grew up.

"I don't know yet," David said, plucking at the grass. "Maybe a fighter pilot. What do you want to be?"

"I want to guard the president. I could wrestle the assassins and be on television. But I'd pin those dudes, and people would say, "That's him, our hero." David plucked at a blade of grass and frowned.

Robert thought of telling David that he really wanted to be someone with a super-great memory who could recall facts that most people thought were unimportant. He didn't know if there was such a job, but he thought it would be great to sit at home by the telephone waiting for scientists to call him and ask hard questions.

The three weeks of rehearsal passed quickly. The day before the play, Robert felt happy as he walked home from school with no homework. As he turned onto his street, he found a dollar floating over the currents of wind.

"A buck," he screamed to himself. He snapped it up and looked for others. But he didn't find any more. It was his lucky day, though. At recess he had hit a fluke home run on a bunt—a fluke because the catcher had kicked the ball, another player had thrown it into center field, and the pitcher wasn't looking when Robert slowed down at third, then burst home with dust flying behind him.

That night was his sister's turn to do the dishes. They had eaten enchiladas with "the works," so she slaved away in suds up to her elbows. Robert bathed in Mr. Bubble, the suds peaked high like the Donner Pass. He thought about how full he was and how those poor people had had nothing to eat but snow. I can live on nothing, he thought, and whistled like

wind through a mountain pass, flattening the Mr. Bubble suds with his palm.

The next day after lunch he was ready for the play, red beard in hand, his one line trembling on his lips. Classes were herded into the auditorium. As the actors dressed and argued about stepping on each other's feet, Robert stood near a cardboard barrel full of toys, whispering over and over to himself: "Nothing's wrong. I can see." He was hot, itchy, and confused. When he tied on the beard, he sneezed. He said louder: "Nothing's wrong. I can see," but the words seemed to get caught in the beard. "Nothing, no, no. I can see great," he said louder, then under his breath because the words seemed wrong. "Nothing's wrong, can't you see?" "Nothing's wrong. I can see you." Worried, he approached Belinda and asked if she remembered his line. Balling her hand into a fist, Belinda warned, "Sucka, I'm gonna bury your ugly face in the ground if you mess up."

"I won't," Robert said as he walked away. He bit a fingernail and looked into the barrel of toys. A clown's mask stared back at him. He prayed that his line would come back to him. He would hate to disappoint his teacher and didn't like the thought of his face being rubbed into spiky grass.

The curtain parted slightly and the principal stepped out, smiling, onto the stage. She said some words about pioneer history and then, stern-faced, warned the people in the audience not to scrape their chairs on the freshly waxed floor. The principal then introduced Mrs. Bunnin, who told the audience about how they had rehearsed for weeks.

Meanwhile the class stood quietly in place behind the curtain. They were ready. Belinda had swallowed her gum because she knew this was for real. The snowflakes clumped together and began howling.

Robert retied his beard. Belinda, smoothing her skirt, looked at him and said, "If you know what's good for you, you better do it right." Robert felt nervous when the curtain parted, and his classmates—the snow, wind, and hail—broke into song.

Alfonso stepped forward with his narrative about a blot on American history that would live on forever. He looked at the audience, lost for a minute. But he continued, saying that if the Donner party could come back, hungry from not eating for over a hundred years, they would be sorry for what they had done.

The play began with some boys in snowshoes shuffling around the stage, muttering that the blizzard would cut them off from civilization. They looked up, held out their hands, and said in unison, "Snow." One stepped center stage and said, "I wish I had never left the prairie." Another said, "California is just over there." He pointed, and some of the first-graders looked in the direction of the piano.

"What are we going to do?" one kid asked, pretending to brush snow off his vest.

"I'm getting pretty hungry," another said, rubbing her stomach.

The audience seemed to be following the play. A ribbon of sweat ran down Robert's face. When it was time for his scene he staggered to center stage and dropped to the floor, just as Mrs. Bunnin had directed, just as he had seen Robert DeNiro do in that movie about a boxer. Belinda, bending over him with an "Oh, my," yanked him up so hard that something clicked in his elbow. She boomed: "Is there anything wrong with your eyes?"

Robert rubbed his elbow, then his eyes, and said, "I can see nothing wrong. Wrong is nothing, I can see."

"How are we going to get through?" Belinda boomed, wringing her hands together in front of her schoolmates in the audience, some of whom had their mouths taped shut because they were known talkers. "My husband needs a doctor." The drama advanced through snow, wind, and hail that sounded like chattering teeth.

Belinda turned to Robert and muttered, "You mess-up. You're gonna hate life."

But Robert thought he'd done OK. At least, he reasoned to himself, I got the words right. Just not in the right order.

After finishing his scene he joined the snowflakes and trees, chattering his teeth the loudest. He bayed like a hound to suggest the howling wind and snapped his fingers furiously in a snow flurry. He trembled from the cold.

The play ended with Alfonso saying again that if they were to come back to life, the members of the Donner party would be sorry for having eaten each other. "It's just not right," he argued. "You gotta suck it up in bad times."

Robert remembered how one day his sister had locked him in the closet and he didn't eat or drink for five hours. When he got out, he hit his sister, but not so hard it left a bruise. Then he ate three sandwiches and felt a whole lot better. Robert figured that Alfonso was right.

The cast paraded up the aisle through the audience. Belinda pinched Robert hard, but only once because she was thinking that it could have been worse. As he passed a smiling and relieved Mrs. Bunnin, she patted Robert's shoulder and said, "Almost perfect."

Robert was happy. He'd made it through without passing out from fear. Now the first- and second-graders were looking at him and clapping. He was sure everyone wondered who the actor was behind that smooth voice and red, red beard.

Story Questions & Activities

1. What lines does Robert have to say in the play?
2. What steps does he take to prepare for the play?
3. How is Robert's class like your own? What are the differences? Explain.
4. What is this story mostly about?
5. Imagine that Robert has been asked to play a role in a movie or a television series. What role could he play? Explain your choice.

Write a Plan for a Stage Set

Imagine that you have been asked to design the set for Robert's class play, *The Last Stand*. This play is about the Donner Party, a group of pioneers who were snowbound on their way West. Write your plan for the stage set, describing the steps you will take to design it. How will it look when you have finished? Draw sketches of your stage-set design. Attach them to your plan.

Draw a Poster

To advertise their play, Robert and his classmates might have created posters to display around their school and community. Think of an event that is happening in your school or class. It might be a play, a science fair, a concert, a sports event, or an election. Gather information, such as the time, date, and location of the event. Then draw your poster on a large sheet of poster board.

Put on a Play

Robert's class play is a drama about an historical event. Get together with a group of classmates to brainstorm ideas to create a list of important events from history. Choose one of these events, and write a one-act play about it. Assign parts, and learn your lines. Then present your play to the class. Ask your audience what they thought of the performance.

Find Out More

The Donner Party was a group of settlers who met with tragedy while crossing the snowy Sierra Nevada Mountains of California in the winter of 1846–1847. Use an encyclopedia or another reference source to find out more about Donner Pass, where many of these settlers died. Investigate its history and the role it plays today as a national historical landmark.

Read a Diagram

In rehearsal, actors like Robert might want a diagram to show them how to move on stage. A **diagram** of a stage shows the parts of a stage and how the parts work together.

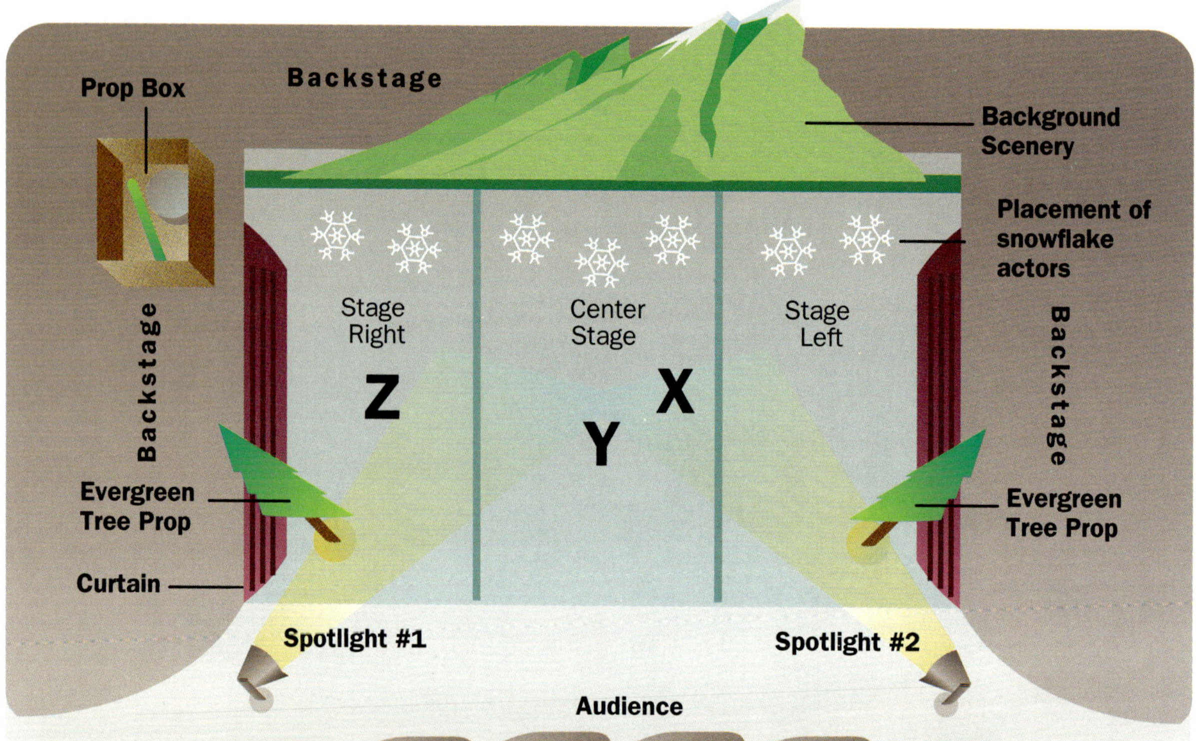

Use the diagram to answer these questions.

1. Where is the prop box located?
2. The letters *X*, *Y*, and *Z* stand for different characters. Which characters stand at center stage?
3. On whom does spotlight 2 shine?
4. If an actor enters from stage right near spotlight 1, which prop would be closest to him or her?
5. Why is it important for actors to know how to move on stage?

TEST POWER

Test Tip

Read all answer choices. Then pick the best one.

DIRECTIONS

Read the sample story. Then read each question about the story.

SAMPLE

Earth Day

Jodi and her father were on their way to the local park to plant trees. Jodi was excited because it was Earth Day, and her father had told her that this was an important event.

"Tell me about Earth Day," she asked her father.

"In 1963, Senator Nelson began to worry that the earth was getting dirty," Jodi's father said. "He worried that many of the earth's plants and animals were dying because of it. He wanted to make sure that we take care of our forests, deserts, and oceans. And he wanted to make sure that we protect endangered animals. Senator Nelson set aside a special day to celebrate the beauty of our environment. On April 22, 1970, the first Earth Day was held."

"This holiday is a great way to educate people about saving the earth," Jodi exclaimed.

1 How did Jodi feel about planting trees for Earth Day?

A Concerned

B Enthusiastic

C Disheartened

D Troubled

2 Senator Nelson started Earth Day to —

F give people a day off

G win an Earth Day contest

H work with endangered animals

J celebrate the environment

Why are these answers the best choices?

Stories in Art

Like music or poetry, a painting can "speak" to you. If you look hard at this painting, you might just be able to hear the kind of music the woman is playing.

What can you tell about this painting? What kind of setting is this? How do the light and shadows create a certain mood? What do you think has caused the woman to start playing her guitar? What effect is the music having on her? On you? Do you think the music is matching the mood of the painting? How?

Some composers like to think of their music as colors. Do the colors in the painting tell you anything about the mood? About the music the woman is playing? Explain.

The Guitar Player
by Clara Klinghoffer, 20th Century German

Meet Angela Shelf Medearis

Angela Shelf Medearis started writing when she was young. "Any child who writes is a writer," she says. "And every one of us has something interesting to say!" As an adult, Medearis has continued writing. Today, she has published many award-winning books of both fiction and poetry.

Medearis' interest in African history can be traced back to her childhood. As a child she used to listen to her father's stories about her ancestors in Africa. *The Singing Man* is such a story. "Praise singers and their songs helped to preserve the wonderful history of the African people," Medearis explains about her story. "Long before African history was written in books, it was sung."

Meet Terea Shaffer

Terea Shaffer and Angela Shelf Medearis share a special relationship. Both are interested in African culture and history, and both have worked on several books together. *The Singing Man,* in fact, is the third book in which the two women have joined their talents and interests. Of her work on this book, Shaffer says, "The colors were inspired by the textiles of West Africa. Through color, texture, and the characters portrayed, I wanted to show the diversity of Nigeria's people and landscapes." For her efforts, Shaffer has received the Coretta Scott King Illustrator Honor Book Award.

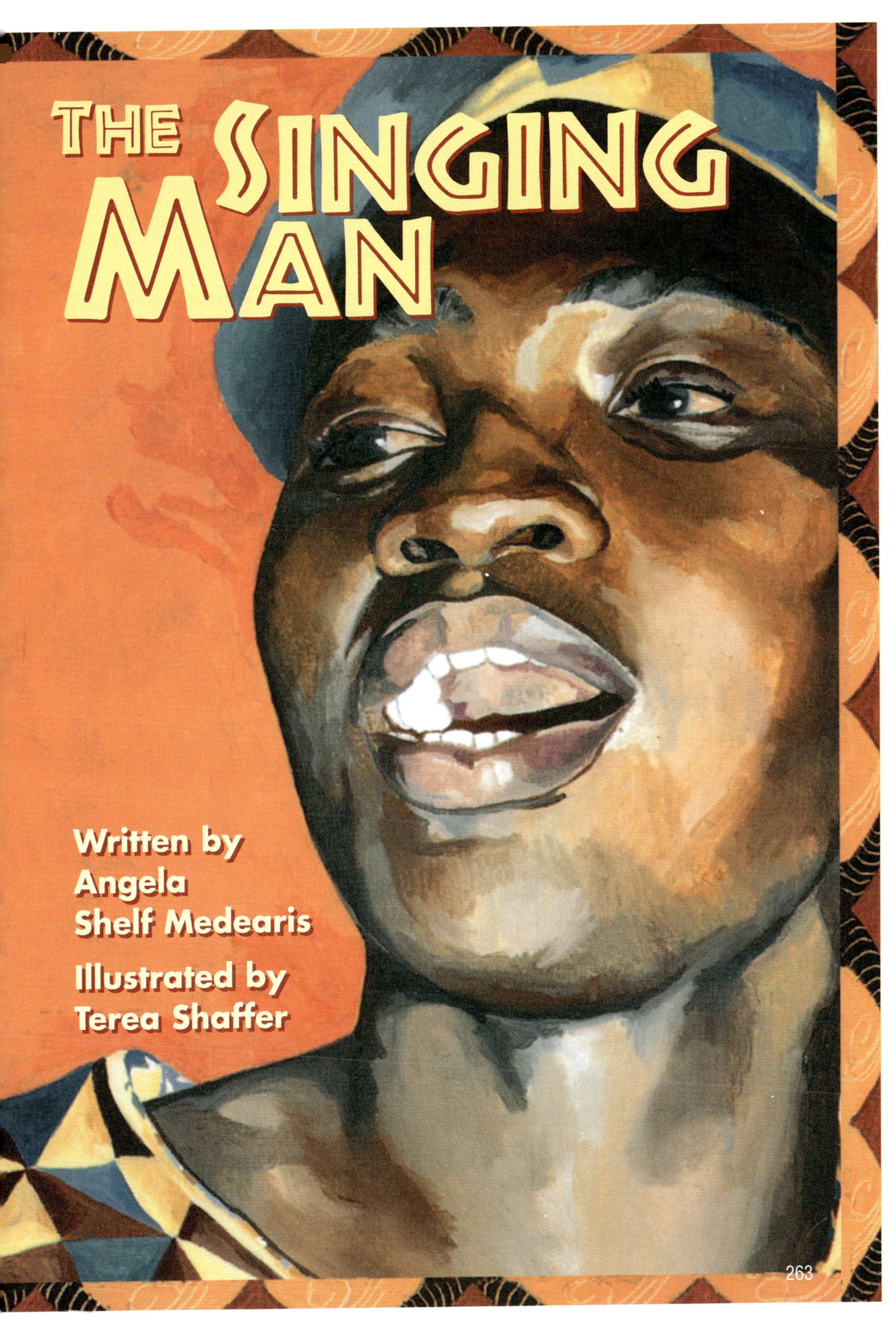

The Singing Man

Written by
Angela
Shelf Medearis

Illustrated by
Terea Shaffer

Long ago in West Africa, the people spoke of the Singing Man. Some tell his story this way . . .

In a small village near the city of Lagos, there lived a man and woman who had three sons: Swanga, Taki, and Banzar.

When the boys of the village reached a certain age, their fathers took them deep into the bush for their manhood ceremony. The elders shared the wisdom of their years, and the young men danced and feasted with the boys. When the manhood ceremonies were over, the boys chose their life's work.

After Swanga was initiated into manhood, he decided to become a farmer and follow his father into the fields. The two men labored under the hot sun to grow acres of beans, grain, and yams.

When Taki was initiated, he decided to become a blacksmith. He fanned the flames of the fire and twisted the hot metal into tools. Then he took his wares to sell at the market.

But Banzar, the third brother, had no interest in these things. He did not want to be a farmer or a blacksmith. And he hated the very thought of selling things all day in the noisy, crowded marketplace.

Banzar loved music and nature. Every day he listened to the songs the birds sang, the tune that the wind whispered to the trees, and the melody the river made as it rushed over the rocks.

Soon it was time for Banzar to be initiated into manhood. After the secret ceremony, the elders of the village called Banzar before them. "What work will you do to help the village?" asked one of the elders.

"I want to be a musician," Banzar said.

"A musician!" said the elders. They whispered among themselves for a moment. Then they spoke quietly to Banzar's father.

"The elders say that music is not an acceptable choice," Banzar's father told his son. "Can music grow yams to fill your stomach? Can music make iron into tools to sell in the marketplace? The elders have declared that you must work for the good of the village or you cannot remain here. Please, son, make another choice. If you don't, you will have to leave. We must abide by the wisdom of the elders."

"I am sorry, Father," Banzar said. "I want only to be a musician, so I will go."

Banzar and his parents were very sad. When it was time for Banzar to leave, his father gave him a few coins. His mother gave him a water jug and a package of food. Banzar took their gifts and his flute. He waved goodbye to his family. Then he set off on the road to the town of Otolo.

Banzar walked for a long time. The birds chirped and a gentle breeze blew through the trees. He took out his flute and began to play. When he finished his song, he felt better and decided to eat. He sat down on a flat rock and unwrapped his food. As he started his meal, a blind man came down the road, swinging a crooked wooden stick in front of him. He wore the necklace of a praise singer and had an omele drum tied to his back. He played the drum when he sang praise songs for the village chiefs. For a few coins, he sang special songs he composed to honor the chiefs and his ancestors. He traveled from village to village, singing about the history of the African people.

"Good day to you, my father," said Banzar politely. "Have you eaten yet?"

"Good day to you, my son," said the old man. "Yes, I have eaten. Thank you very much. Could you tell me if I'm near the town of Otolo?"

"Yes, it is just down the road," said Banzar. "I'm going to Otolo also."

"Then we can travel together," said the old man. "Are you going to the marketplace to buy or to sell?"

"Neither," said Banzar. "I have just a few coins and therefore I cannot buy anything. The only thing I own is my flute, and I would never sell that."

"Ah," said the old man. "You must be a musician. Let me hear you play."

Banzar made the flute trill like a songbird.

"Yes, you have the gift," said the old man. "Why don't you travel with me? My name is Sholo. If you help me, I will teach you the ways of a musician."

"Thank you, Sholo," said Banzar. He finished his meal and together they traveled to Otolo.

"We will go to the chief's house," said Sholo as he placed his hand on Banzar's arm. "I will show you how to make your living as a musician."

Banzar and the old man turned up and down the narrow streets of Otolo and through the busy marketplace until they came to the chief's house.

Sholo squatted in front of the door. He placed the omele drum between his knees and beat out a wild rhythm. **PUM PUM BA LUM BO, PUM PUM BA LUM BO**. The old man sang of the mighty warriors of Otolo and of the chief's bravery in battle. He sang of the chief's goodness to his people and his wisdom as a leader. A crowd gathered around Sholo and Banzar. They clapped and danced to the music of the drum. The chief came out of his house and sat upon his chair. He listened solemnly to the old man's music.

Sholo sang and played for a long time. When he seemed to tire of singing, Banzar played his flute along with the **PUM PUM BA LUM BO** of the omele drum. He played the songs that he had learned from nature.

When the music stopped, the crowd clapped their hands. The chief gave Banzar and Sholo money and food and lodging for the night.

As they prepared their sleeping mats, Sholo told Banzar about the history of the praise singers.

For many years, Banzar traveled with Sholo from town to town. Sholo taught Banzar how to play the omele drum and compose the praise songs that honored the ancestors of the village chiefs. "We are the keepers of the past," Sholo told Banzar. "A people without a past have no future."

As the years went by, Banzar grew taller and stronger. But Sholo grew older and more feeble. It took longer and longer for them to travel from village to village. And then one day, Sholo died.

For a long time, Banzar stopped playing his flute. He sat by the river for hours, gently tapping Sholo's omele drum and thinking about his friend. He remembered Sholo's words.

"I alone know the history of our people," Banzar thought to himself. "I must tell them about the past so they will be strong in the future. I know that is what Sholo would want me to do."

Suddenly Banzar felt better. He lifted his flute to his lips and played song after song. He pounded out the **PUM PUM BA LUM BO** beat on the omele drum. He made up a song about Sholo and his wisdom. Then Banzar, the praise singer, picked up his instruments and traveled to the nearest town.

Banzar became very famous. When he entered a village, the children would clap their hands and shout, "The singing man has come! The singing man has come!" The children would dance before Banzar all the way to the house of the chief.

Now Banzar was the one who squatted down in front of the chief's door. He beat the wild **PUM PUM BA LUM BO, PUM PUM BA LUM BO** sound on the drum in the same way Sholo had for so many years.

Banzar made a very good living as a praise singer. But he was lonely. He missed Sholo. He thought often about his mother and father and his brothers, Swanga and Taki. He wondered if he would ever see his family again.

One day Banzar's travels brought him to the city of Lagos. The Feast of Igodo, the yam festival celebration, had begun. Everyone was rejoicing that the harvest season was over—with music, feasting, and dancing. All the praise singers had been invited to attend. One by one they played the omele drums and sang their songs for the king of Lagos. Each was given a small reward.

Finally it was Banzar's turn. He pounded out the wild **PUM PUM BA LUM BO, PUM PUM BA LUM BO** beat on his drum. He sang the songs of ancient Africa and the new songs he'd written about the king's wisdom, kindness, and bravery.

Then Banzar began to play his flute. He played the beautiful melodies that were taught him by the birds in the jungle. He trilled the secrets the wind whispered to the trees. He ended with the song the river sings on its journey to the sea.

When he finished playing, the king of Lagos beckoned him to come near. "Where did you learn our history, and to sing and play like that?" he asked.

"From Sholo, who is now dead," said Banzar.

"Of all the musicians I have heard, you have the greatest gift," said the king. "If you will remain in Lagos as my personal musician, you will be handsomely rewarded."

"I would be honored," said Banzar.

The king gave Banzar a house, money, and servants. Banzar wore robes made of rich material and a special golden necklace. He became a very respected man in Lagos.

One day, when Banzar was in the marketplace, he saw his brothers, Swanga and Taki. He greeted them, but they did not recognize him.

"How are your crops, friend?" asked Banzar.

"There has been a great famine in our land," said Swanga. "My fields barely yield anything to eat."

"How is your trade?" Banzar asked Taki.

"I have no money to buy iron," said Taki sadly. "Therefore I have nothing to make or to sell."

"Are your parents well?" asked Banzar.

"They live as well as can be expected in these hard times," said Swanga.

"Have you any other brothers?" asked Banzar.

"Our younger brother has been gone these many years," said Taki. "He would not work and desired only to play his flute. Can music make your fortune? So, he was sent away."

"I would like to visit with you at your home," said Banzar. "Tell your parents and your chief that the king's musician is coming."

Swanga and Taki left quickly to spread the news.

Banzar put on his finest robe. He filled his bags with food, gifts, and money, and called his servants. They went before Banzar into the village of his boyhood, beating drums and gongs and calling out, "Make way for the musician of the king of Lagos."

The procession stopped in front of the home of the village chief. The villagers gathered around Banzar. He sang song after song and beat out the wild **PUM PUM BA LUM BO, PUM PUM BA LUM BO** rhythm on his omele drum. The people clapped and clapped.

As the night drew near, Banzar saw his father, mother, and two brothers on the edge of the crowd. He took out his flute and stood before them. Then he played a few sad notes and sang:

A man and woman had three fine sons.
When the first son became a man, his desire was to till the land,
When the second son became a man, his desire was to make things of iron,
When the third son became a man, his desire was to become a musician.
And the first son was honored,
and the second son was praised,
but the third son was cast out from his family to wander for the rest of his days.

"Oh," said Banzar's father, "this song is just like the thing that has happened to us. Our third son wanted to be a musician. He has been gone these many years and by now is probably dead."

"No, my father, he lives," said Banzar. "I am he." Then Banzar and his family rejoiced. Banzar ordered his servants to prepare a feast. For many days, the village celebrated his good fortune. Banzar gave money and gifts to his family and the chief of the village. Then Banzar, the third son who became the king's musician, returned to the city of Lagos. Singing and dancing, his servants led the way.

Now here is a new saying: "Yams fill the belly and trade fills the pockets, but music fills the heart."

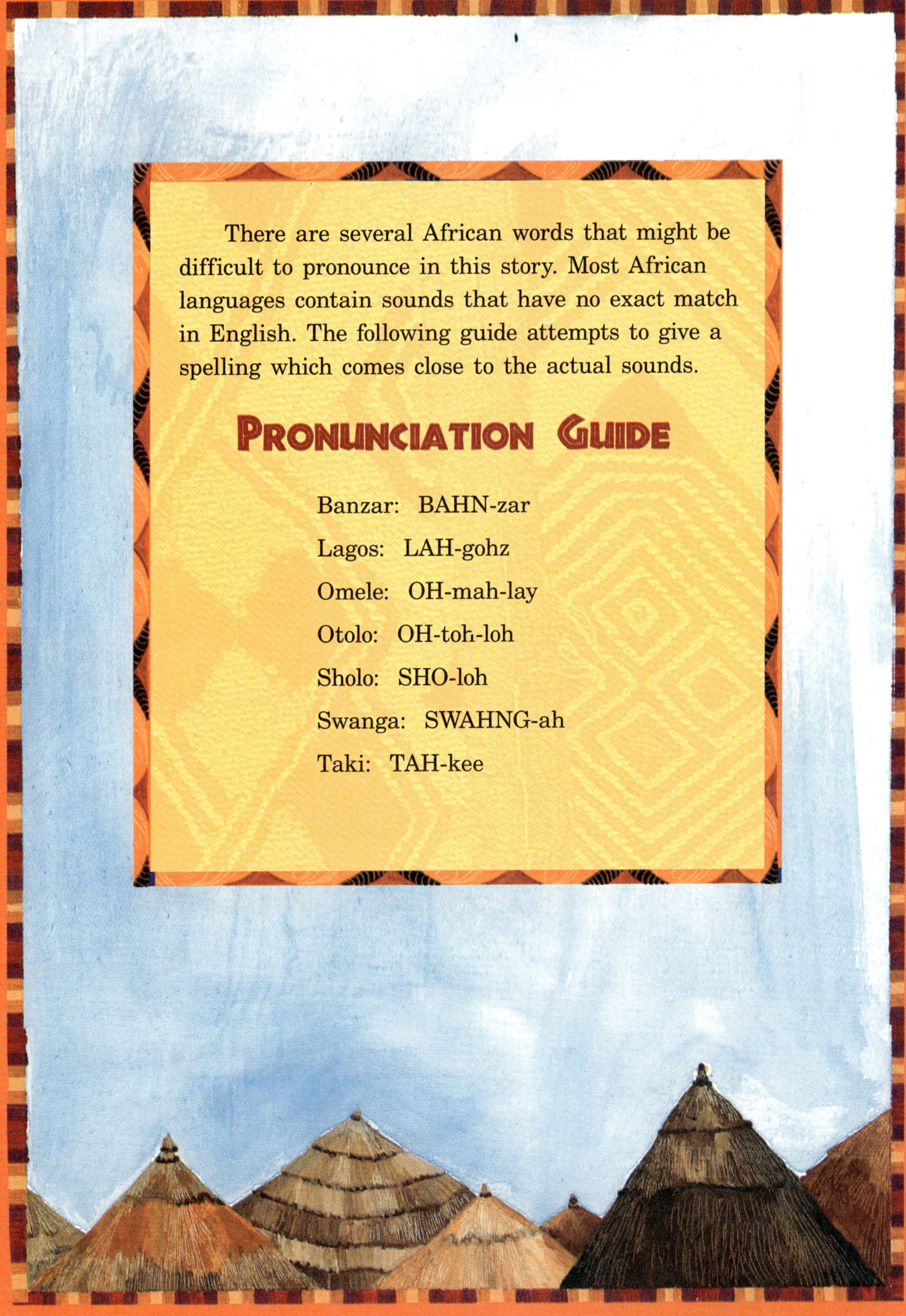

There are several African words that might be difficult to pronounce in this story. Most African languages contain sounds that have no exact match in English. The following guide attempts to give a spelling which comes close to the actual sounds.

PRONUNCIATION GUIDE

Banzar: BAHN-zar

Lagos: LAH-gohz

Omele: OH-mah-lay

Otolo: OH-toh-loh

Sholo: SHO-loh

Swanga: SWAHNG-ah

Taki: TAH-kee

Story Questions & Activities

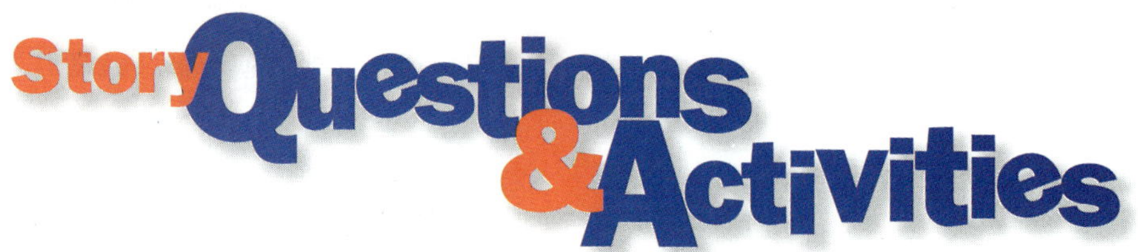

1. What causes Banzar to leave his village?

2. What effect does Banzar's fame have on his family?

3. How is a praise singer like a "walking history book"?

4. The story ends with this saying: "Yams fill the belly and trade fills the pocket, but music fills the heart." How is this the "message" of the story?

5. Sholo, the praise singer, is blind. Yet he "sees" many things. Calvin in "A Boy of Unusual Vision" also "sees without seeing." Suppose that Sholo and Calvin met. What could Sholo teach Calvin? How might they both be described as people of "unusual vision"?

Write a Story Plan

Every story has a plan. Writers follow this plan to help them write a story. Now it's your turn. Write a plan for a story you would like to write. Include the setting (when and where the story takes place), the main characters, the beginning event, the problem (or conflict), and the events that lead one or more characters to solve the problem. Save your story plan. Use it to write your short story.

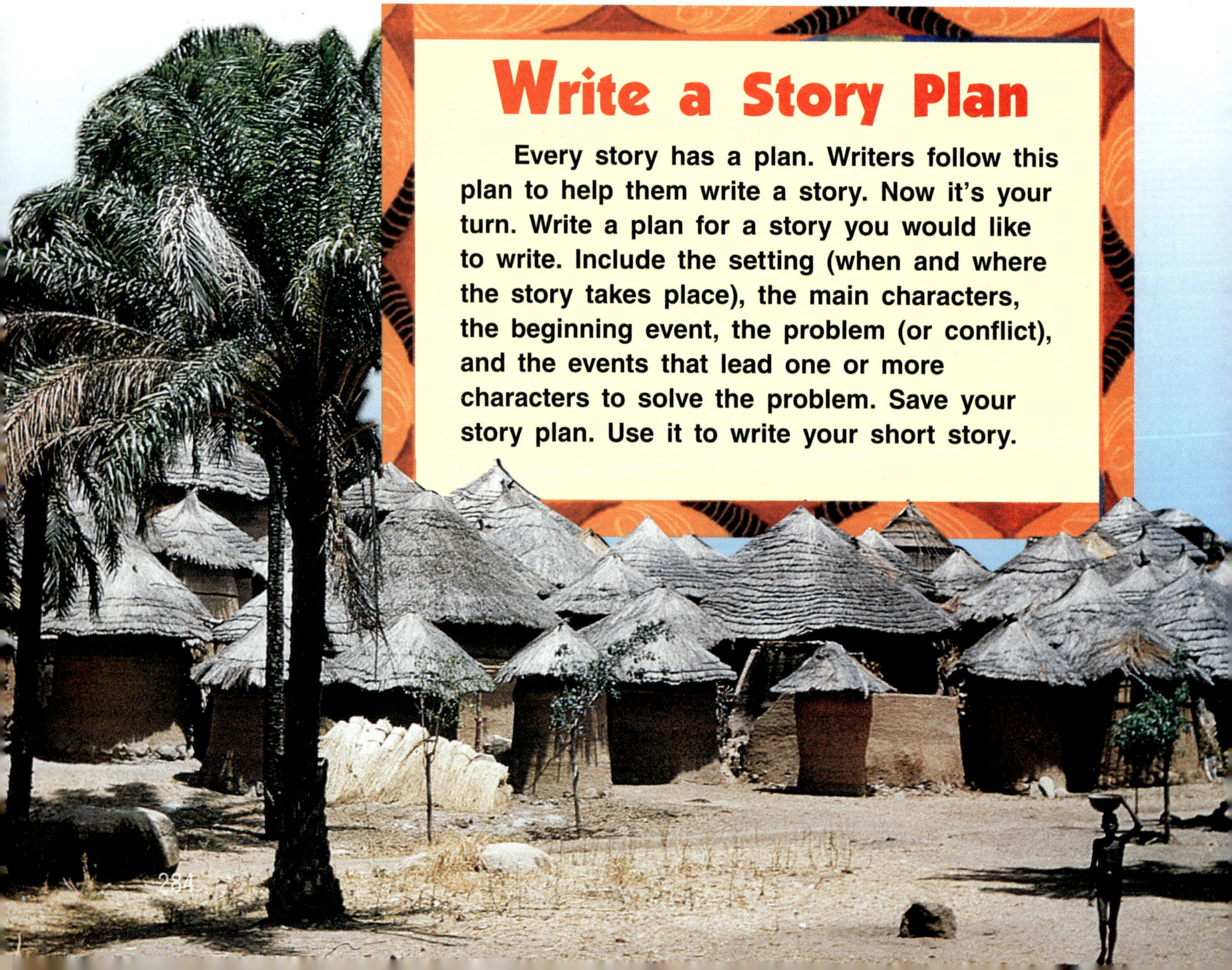

Collect Oral History

The songs Sholo and Banzar sang were a way of passing on oral history. Some of these oral histories teach a lesson. Others are simply amusing. Ask an older family member to tell you a story about something that happened before you were born. Tape-record this oral history. Play back the tape to help you write a poem or a song about what you discover.

Discover How Music Is Made

Banzar played the flute, and Sholo beat the omele drum. Now it's your turn. Borrow some simple musical instruments, such as a drum, a triangle, or a tambourine, from your school music department. What happens when you strike them? Now try the same thing with other instruments. Do they all vibrate? What are vibrations? Check a dictionary or another reference source to find out. Share your findings.

Find Out More

"The Singing Man" is based on a folk tale from the Yoruba people of Nigeria. Find out more about this African country and its people. Start by looking in an encyclopedia, an atlas, or another nonfiction book. Use the information you find to create a travel poster of Nigeria.

Read an Outline

"The Singing Man" is a folk tale from Nigeria. Suppose you wanted to write a report on this West African country. Creating an outline, such as this one, could be a useful way to organize the information before you started to write.

I. General Information
  A. Size 360, 360 sq. mi. (about 15% of Africa)
  B. Population–108.5 million (about 56% of Africa's population)
  C. Location–West Africa, between Benin and Cameroon
  D. Currency–Niara
II. Cultural Information
  A. Languages
    1. English
    2. Hausa
    3. Yoruba
    4 Ibo
  B. Art
    1. Wooden masks
    2. Bronze sculptures
    3. Pottery
III. Tourist Information
  A. Lagos–Old capital
  B. Abuja–New capital
  C. Kano–Oldest city in West Africa
  D. Yankari National Part–Nature preserve

Use the outline to answer these questions.

1. Where is Nigeria located?
2. Where might tourists go if they want to see wildlife?
3. Where in the outline could you add information about painting in Nigeria?
4. In your report, what else could you say in the paragraph that mentions that English is spoken there?
5. How can making an outline help you to write a better report?

TEST POWER

Test Tip

A FACT is something that is true in the passage.

DIRECTIONS

Read the sample story. Then read each question about the story.

SAMPLE

The Lemming

At first glance, you might mistake a lemming for a mouse. While a lemming is a rodent, this particular type lives only in the Arctic. The lemming usually grows to approximately four or six inches long. It has a short tail and a plump, furry body.

Lemmings typically eat twigs in the winter, but prefer berries and leaves. They gather what they can in the summer months and save it in large tunnels they have dug. Often, an entire family of lemmings will live together in a single tunnel.

Lemmings are excellent swimmers. Because they are constantly trying to escape Arctic predators, they will swim across rivers and streams with little thought to their own safety, just to get away. The tiny rodents have been known to swim across bodies of water more than a kilometer wide.

1 The lemming spends most of its time —

- **A** escaping its enemies
- **B** building tunnels
- **C** swimming
- **D** eating berries

2 Which of these is a FACT presented in this passage?

- **F** Lemmings enjoy swimming in Arctic water.
- **G** Lemmings never grow longer than six inches.
- **H** Lemmings store food in tunnels.
- **J** Families of lemmings live in attached tunnels.

Did you reread the story to find the right answer? Explain.

The painting on this Japanese folding screen shows a polo match among Tartars, a group that invaded Asia. However, it also gives a glimpse into Japanese life in the seventeenth century.

Look carefully at the painting. Why has the artist used several panels? When opened, how do these panels show the movement and excitement of the polo match? Who are the people in the background? Summarize their way of life. How is it different from the fierce life and play of the Tartars?

Notice the rich rectangles of gold leaf. Why do you think the artist used gold? What might he be saying about Japanese society of the past? For whom might he have painted this folding screen? Why do you think so?

Tartars Playing Polo **(detail),**
attributed to Kano Jinnojo, 17th century Japan
The Freer Gallery of Art, Washington, D.C.

MEET PATRICIA LAUBER

From prehistoric caves and volcanoes of the Earth to the farthest reaches of the solar system, Patricia Lauber's books span a wide variety of subjects. "My ideas come from everywhere—from things I read, from things people tell me about . . . from things I experience." Lauber believes that "sailing a boat or exploring a forest can often be described as 'doing research.'" It is important to Lauber that her subjects interest her very much, because, then, she says, "I want to share them with other people and so I write about them."

Many of Lauber's books have won awards for their ability to explain complicated topics and for their "top-notch nonfiction writing." Her outstanding books include *Journey to the Planets*, which received an American Book award nomination, and *Volcano: The Eruption and Healing of Mount St. Helens*, which was a Newbery Honor Book. Lauber's book *Flood: Wrestling with the Mississippi* was a School Library Journal Best Book of the Year.

PAINTERS OF THE CAVES

WRITTEN BY PATRICIA LAUBER

INTRODUCTION

Exploring caves can be dangerous work. But it can also be exciting—and more than a little surprising, as three friends found out in southeastern France. Deep in a cave, named Chauvet after one of the three explorers, the friends discovered 300 colorful cave paintings of animals that lived 32,000 years ago. The names of the Stone Age artists are not known. But one thing is certain. Their paintings of bears, horses, wild cattle, lions, mammoths, and other prehistoric animals link these people of the past with us. What is not certain is exactly who these late Stone Age people were. How did they create their art? What do their cave paintings tell about their way of life? No one knows all the answers. But scientists are examining clues to solve the mystery of the painters of the caves.

Caves riddle the limestone cliffs of gorges carved long ago by the Ardèche River.

A GREAT DISCOVERY

One chilly afternoon in December 1994, three old friends met to go exploring. The three—two men and a woman—shared a great enthusiasm: searching for caves in the limestone hills near Avignon, in southeast France.

Limestone is fairly soft rock. Long ago, over many years, the Ardèche River carved deep gorges in these hills, creating cliffs of limestone. The cliffs are honeycombed with caves, some hollowed out by underground rivers, some by rainwater that sank in and dissolved the limestone.

For thousands of years, starting in the Stone Age, people used these caves and left behind traces of themselves. In their exploring, the three friends had found several caves with traces of wall art done by Stone Age painters. They hoped to find more, but what they found that December day was something they had only dreamed about.

They followed an ancient mule path up a cliff and arrived at a narrow ledge. An opening in the cliff led to a pile of rocks where they could feel air coming out—the sign of a cave. Tearing away the rocks, they uncovered a small passageway, just big enough for a person to wriggle through.

Exploring caves is dangerous. It is all too easy to get stuck, to take a bad fall, to become lost. But the three had twenty years of experience and they had come equipped with lights, ropes, and a ladder. They pressed ahead.

One of the three explorers, Jean-Marie Chauvet, examines a panel of horse heads in the cave that was named for him in southeastern France. Chauvet is a source of much new information about the painters of the caves.

The woman went first, lying on her stomach. At the end of the passageway was a 30-foot drop to the cave floor. Their ladder took them down. The cave was so big that darkness swallowed their lights; they could hardly see the walls. Moving with care, they came to a place where the floor of the cave was strewn with bear bones and teeth, where bears had dug hollows to hibernate in.

Moments later they saw a drawing of a little red mammoth on a spur of rock. As they looked around, a 3-foot-high bear loomed before them on a white wall. Discovery followed discovery—a huge red rhinoceros, a big mammoth, a bear or lion, human handprints stenciled on the walls.

They had made a truly great discovery. The cave, named Chauvet after one of the explorers, holds more than 300 paintings of animals that lived some 32,000 years ago, late in the Stone Age: horses, bears, hyenas, woolly rhinos, mammoths, bison, wild cattle, lions, deer, panthers, mountain goats. Drawn in black, red, and yellow, they parade across rock walls, sometimes leaping or running.

Chauvet is far from the only cave with Stone Age wall paintings. Most such caves lie to the west, in southwest France and northern Spain. Some are found elsewhere in Europe and on other continents from Africa to Australia. But Chauvet is one of the biggest and best, and it is the oldest known. Because its original entrance had been blocked by a rockfall, no one else visited the cave for thousands of years.

To the left of the panel of horse heads, cave artists painted aurochs (ancestors of today's cattle) and rhinoceroses.

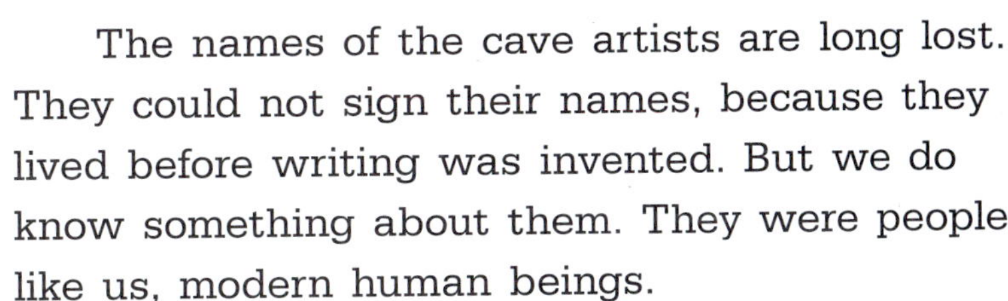

The names of the cave artists are long lost. They could not sign their names, because they lived before writing was invented. But we do know something about them. They were people like us, modern human beings.

Ice Age horses were short and stocky, about the size of today's ponies. The animal at lower left is a rhinoceros.

Their story has been pieced together by scientists who study ancient peoples. Part of the story is told by fossils, which are traces of ancient life. A fossil can be many things. The footprints of Stone Age artists who worked in the caves are fossils, as are the footprints of children who played there. But most fossils are skulls, bones, and teeth—hard parts of the body that were preserved when rock formed around them. Another part of the story is told by stone tools and other objects that people left behind and that, in time, became buried under dust, dirt, and rock.

The first modern humans to live in Europe are sometimes called Cro-Magnons, for the rock-shelter in France where their fossils and stone tools were first found. More often today, they are called early modern humans. They arrived in the Middle East and Europe during the Ice Age.

Realistic human figures and faces are seldom found in Stone Age art. This 5-inch-high ivory head is a rare example.

The carved bison, caught in the act of licking an insect bite, was the head of a spear-thrower and is about 3 1/2 inches long.

Two 4-foot-long bison (above) leap across the walls at Lascaux, captured in action by a Stone Age painter.

Stone Age Artists

No one knows when modern humans first became artists. Good art seems to appear suddenly. If there were earlier works, they have not been found—or have not survived. But the artists used their talents in many ways and made use of many materials.

They made small objects that could be worn or carried around. They pierced and strung seashells and animal teeth to wear as necklaces, earrings, bracelets. They carved animal figures out of mammoth ivory and also used ivory to make beads that decorated clothing. Three bodies found in a grave in Russia each had 3,500 beads of mammoth ivory, arranged in rows. The clothing had rotted away, but the rows suggest that the beads were strung and the strings sewn to the clothing. One scientist found by experimenting that it takes 45 minutes to make a bead. And so each body had 2,625 hours of beadwork buried with it. The people in the grave must have been important.

Scientists think the moderns may have stenciled their handprints on walls by blowing paint through a tube, as shown in this recent drawing.

Using sharp tools, artists engraved bones, antlers, pebbles, and slabs of stone that were used to pave cave floors. The art often showed animals. In time, artists began to engrave weapons and everyday tools as well as art objects. They made small clay figures of animals and women and hardened them in kilns.

When bands of people came together at big campsites, did they exchange art? Was some jewelry a badge of membership in a certain group? Were some pieces lucky charms? There is no way to tell.

The artists who worked in caves often engraved the walls. Some of the engravings are done in fine line and are almost invisible when lighted from the front. They seem to leap out when lighted from the side. Perhaps lighting was used for magic—making animals appear and disappear.

Some of the cave artists worked in clay—engraving the cave floor or sculpting banks of clay.

And some artists drew or painted on the cave walls. Their colors were red, yellow, brown, and black. At times they used charcoal for black, but mostly they took their colors from minerals that could be ground into powder or turned into a kind of crayon. The powder had to be mixed with something to make paint. To find out what that something was, one scientist carried out 205 experiments with cave painting over three years. In the end, he discovered that what worked best was water, especially cave water.

To apply the paint, artists sometimes used their fingers. Sometimes they used a pad of animal fur. But usually they painted with brushes made from animal hair or crushed twigs.

Handprints are common in caves. Some were created by a palm coated with paint. Most were stenciled by blowing paint from a tube or perhaps from the mouth.

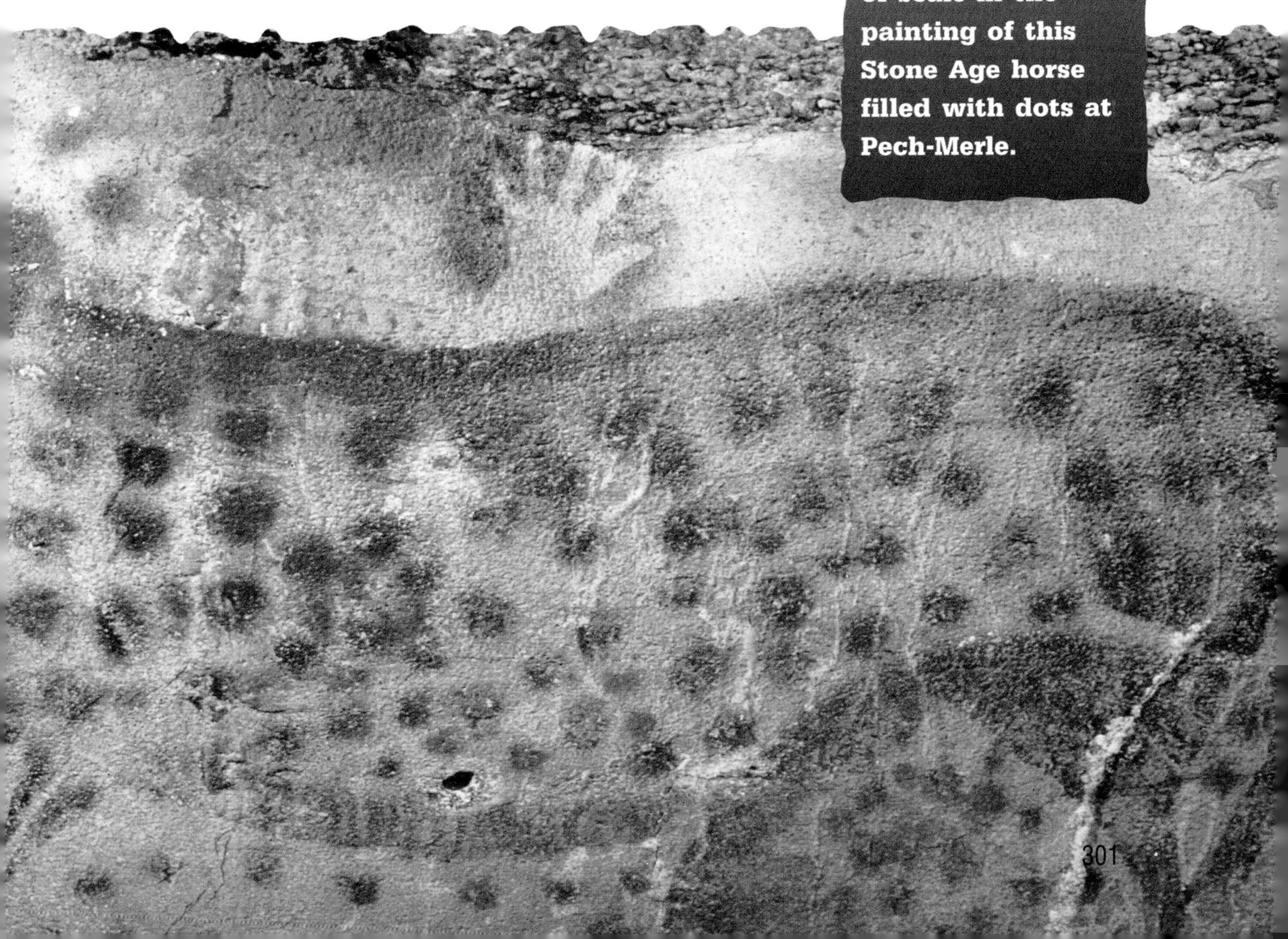

The human handprints give an idea of scale in the painting of this Stone Age horse filled with dots at Pech-Merle.

An artist of today imagines a Stone Age artist standing on a scaffold and painting an aurochs. Light in the caves came from torches and from fat-burning limestone lamps like this one, which is about 8 inches long.

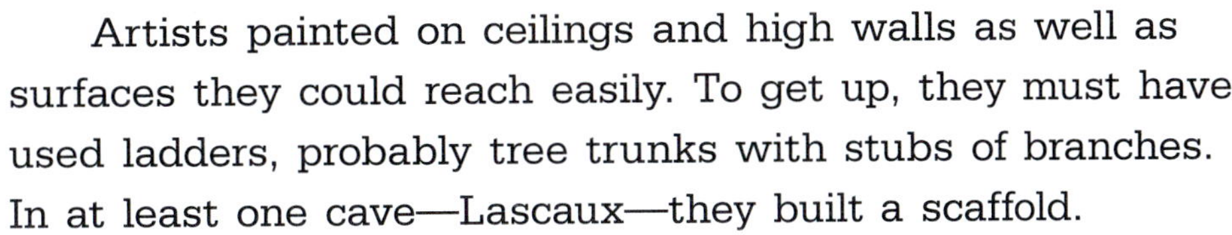

Artists painted on ceilings and high walls as well as surfaces they could reach easily. To get up, they must have used ladders, probably tree trunks with stubs of branches. In at least one cave—Lascaux—they built a scaffold.

The depths of caves are dark. To see, the artists needed light. It came from torches of wood and from lamps that burned animal fat. A few deep caves also have hearths, where fires may have given off a strong light.

There were also places where artists worked outdoors, engraving, and probably painting, on rock-faces. A few of these engravings have been found in sheltered places. Many others must have weathered away. Outdoor art may have been the way a group staked its claim to a certain region.

The world of the modern humans was the world of nature. In it they found food, clothing, and shelter. They observed it closely, so closely that artists working in caves, without models, were able to draw from memory.

The animals they painted most often were horses and bison—the forest-dwelling bison of Europe, which are different from the bison of the American plains. Caves also hold many pictures of wild cattle, deer, goats, and mammoths. Bears and lions appear. Many animals are rare—the rhinoceros, musk-ox, ass, wolf, fox, hyena. There are few fish, birds, or reptiles. Plants are also rare, although they were important foods.

Few human figures appear in cave art, but a number of figures appear to be part human, part animal—or perhaps humans wearing animal masks and skins.

Like the art that could be carried around, cave art also includes markings that are not pictures. There are many, many dots. There are circles, rectangles, zigzags, grids, and other signs, as well as stencils and prints of hands.

No one today knows what the signs mean. No one knows what the paintings mean. But scientists and others who study the art have some ideas.

Story Questions & Activities

1. What did the three explorers find in a cave near Avignon, France?
2. Who were the painters of the caves? Why do you think they made these wall paintings?
3. How do these cave paintings link people of the present to people of the Stone Age?
4. How would you summarize this selection?
5. If Sholo and Banzar in "The Singing Man" were to tell the story of the cave paintings in song, how would their song sound? What would their lyrics be like?

Write About a Discovery

After the amazing discovery of the cave paintings, scientists used information to piece together the remarkable story of the ancient cave artists. Use your research skills to learn about another amazing discovery. It might be the discovery of electricity, penicillin, or King Tut's tomb. In your paper, explain how the discovery was made. List the steps in the process.

Create a Mural

Cave paintings link modern-day people to people of the prehistoric past. Now imagine that you are going to make a paper mural of modern life that people might see 30,000 years from now! What images would you include? Get together with a group of classmates to plan and design a mural of today's world. Then write an exhibit card that explains your mural, including your reasons for choosing certain items.

Write an Encyclopedia Entry

Cave bears, woolly rhinos, mammoths, aurochs—these animals of the Stone Age have all disappeared. What did these ancient animals look like? How were they different from their descendants of today? Choose an extinct animal. Learn about it in an encyclopedia or in a book about prehistoric times. Use the information to write a brief encyclopedia entry about the animal. Include an illustration or a map showing where the animal lived.

Find Out More

Cave art has been found in other parts of the world, including the Americas, Australia, and Africa. Explore the art of cave painting. Begin your search by looking in an encyclopedia, in the *Readers' Guide to Periodical Literature*, or on the Internet. Compare the cave paintings discovered in France with those found in another part of the world.

Read a Map

Cave paintings have been discovered in the Border Cave, located in Zululand at the northeastern tip of South Africa. These paintings have been dated about 10,000 years earlier than the ones near Avignon, France. You can find the exact location of the Border Cave on the map below.

Use the map to answer these questions.

1. How do you think the cave got its name?
2. What country is bordered by South Africa on all sides?
3. What countries border South Africa to the north?
4. What bodies of water lie on either side of Africa?
5. How is the inset of the globe helpful?

TEST POWER

Test Tip

Take your time as you do your work.

DIRECTIONS

Read the sample story. Then read each question about the story.

SAMPLE

Jane Goodall and the Chimpanzees

From the time she was a young girl, Jane Goodall dreamed of spending her life working with animals. When she was twenty-six years old, she traveled into the forests of Africa to watch chimpanzees in the wild.

While in Africa recently, Dr. Goodall discovered a dramatic drop in the chimpanzee population. In parts of Africa, where there had been more than a million chimps only a few years ago, today only about 250,000 are still alive. She found that some chimps had died from the effects of the forests being destroyed. Other chimps were captured and then sold as pets or as subjects in scientific experiments. Some were sold to circuses.

Dr. Goodall hopes that her research and her efforts to educate people will help save the chimps and will result in an increase in the chimp population.

1 Which of these is the best summary of the passage?

- **A** Dr. Goodall set up a research center.
- **B** Many scientists dream of working with animals.
- **C** Dr. Goodall's research and conservation efforts aim to preserve the African chimpanzee.
- **D** Chimpanzees live in the wild.

2 What is one reason the chimpanzee population has decreased?

- **F** They lost their natural habitat.
- **G** They migrated to a colder climate.
- **H** There was too much food.
- **J** They were homesick.

Stories in Art

Think of some real-life objects you could use to create a still life. How would you put these objects together? What would you make your center of interest?

Look at this pastel drawing. What do you see? How does the pattern in the carpet get you to focus your eyes on the center? What do you notice about the clarinet? What steps would you take to put it together? What would you do to play it? How would you take it apart?

Look at the drawing again. Do you think the clarinet player was called away suddenly? Why? What will he or she do to put away the clarinet?

Still Life with Clarinet
by Sandra Lawrence, 1980
Private Collection

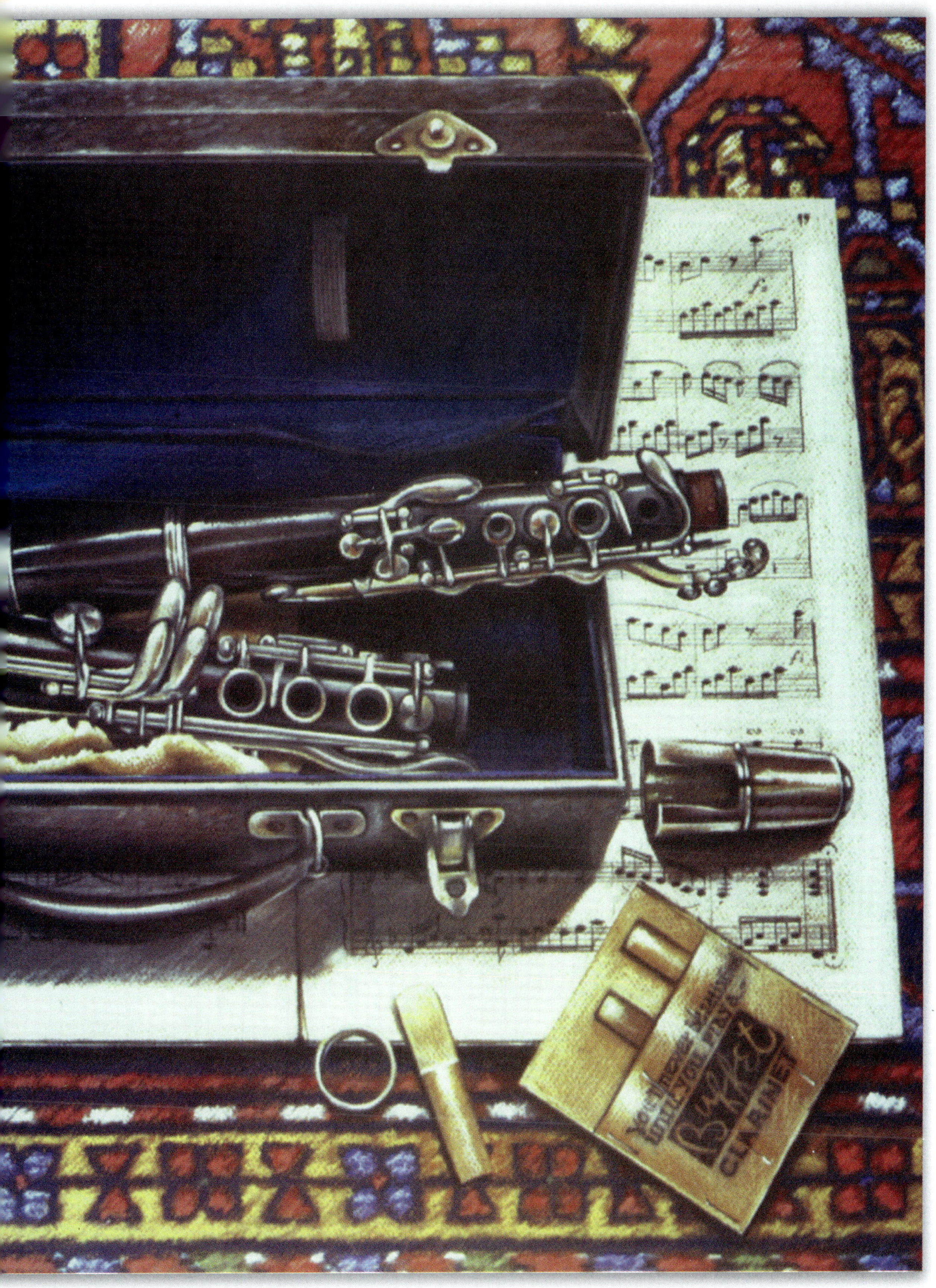
Buffet
CLARINET

TIME FOR KIDS

SPECIAL REPORT

IS THIS ANCIENT BONE THE WORLD'S FIRST FLUTE?

Scientists can't decide.

Let the Music Begin!

High in the mountains, a few lonely musical notes break the silence of the evening. A Neanderthal is playing the flute. The flute's notes float away on the wind and disappear.

For years, this prehistoric scene would have seemed laughable to scientists. Neanderthals were once seen as stocky, brute creatures who grunted and couldn't produce anything as lovely as music.

But the discovery of an unusual bone in Slovenia has changed some scientists' ideas about Neanderthals and what they may have known about music. It has also created a controversy as experts try to figure out just what the bone is.

A NOTEWORTHY DISCOVERY

It all began when paleontologist Ivan Turk made a surprising discovery in 1995 as he dug through a cave thought to be a Neanderthal hunting camp. He found a bone, from a bear cub's leg, with four holes in it. To Turk, the holes didn't look as if they had been made by an animal. They looked as if they had been drilled by someone. Was it a prehistoric flute?

"The holes are well rounded and spaced the right length apart," says scientist Bonnie Blackwell. "The bone is hollow; so this would allow air to pass through."

COVER: IVAN TURK/SLOVENIAN ACADEMY OF SCIENCES; THIS PAGE: AMERICAN MUSEUM OF NATURAL HISTORY

Some scientists think Neanderthals crafted flutes in Slovenia (map) more than 40,000 years ago.

Back in the U.S., Blackwell's research team tried to figure out when the flute was made. On the team was Beverly Lau, then a New York City high school student. She helped date the flute by examining bear teeth found in the same layer of rock.

The researchers announced that the find is at least 43,000 years, and perhaps as much as 82,000 years old. If so, and if it is a flute, it is the oldest musical instrument ever found.

THE SOUND OF MUSIC

Neanderthals stood at about five feet, shorter than today's humans. They had sloping foreheads, large, thick skulls, and chinless jaws. Even though their brains were somewhat larger than those of modern humans, scientists aren't sure of their ability to use complex language. Their lack of speech may have been one reason why Neanderthals became extinct about 35,000 years ago. Meanwhile *Homo sapiens*—modern humans—took over.

FIND OUT MORE
Visit our website:
www.mhschool.com/reading

INSTITUTE OF HUMAN ORIGINS

Jaw Bones Tell a Story

Ethiopia's dry Hadar region is a fossil hunter's heaven. It was there, in 1974, that scientists found the 3 million-year-old bones of an apelike creature known as Lucy. Many scientists believe Lucy is a very distant ancestor of humans.

Twenty years after the discovery of Lucy, scientists announced another important discovery made in Hadar: a 2 million-year-old jaw. Compared to Lucy, the jaw looks more humanlike. It is the oldest fossil ever found belonging to the species known as *Homo* (Latin for "man"). This group includes modern humans (*Homo sapiens*).

Scientists were also surprised to find some stone tools near the upper jaw. The oldest known stone tools date back perhaps 2.5 million years, but they were found without any fossils nearby to indicate who made them. The latest discovery suggests that toolmaking began around the same time the first true humans appeared.

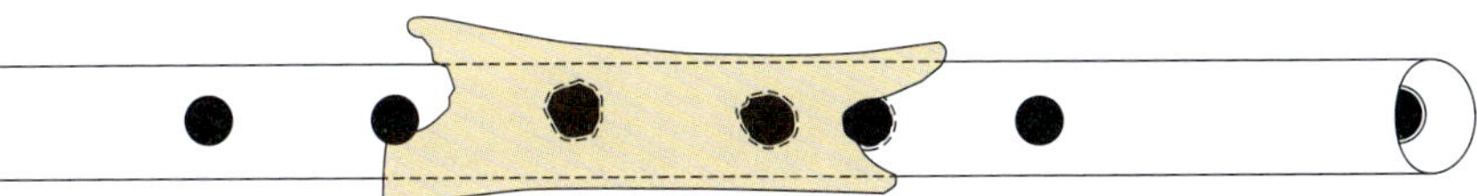

Was the bear bone a part of a flute, as shown in this drawing?

According to Blackwell, who thinks the bone is a flute, the discovery shows that Neanderthals may have been smarter and communicated more than scientists realized. "This changes our perceptions a lot," says Blackwell. "This says to us they actually had complex thought patterns."

"Neanderthals probably first used the flute to signal other hunters without alarming the animals," says Blackwell. "Then it could have been used around the campfire to tell hunting stories." Over time, sweet sounds may have been made just for pleasure. Then, says Blackwell, "you've got music."

A SOUR NOTE?

Not everyone agrees that the bone is a flute, however. And not everyone is certain that the Neanderthals made music. In 1998, two archaeologists, April Nowell and Philip G. Chase, both of the University of Pennsylvania, studied the bone. They believe the bone's holes were made by the teeth of a meat-eating animal—such as a wolf. They say the holes were not drilled by Neanderthals. They think a wolf punctured the bone as it was eating the meat off it.

It is possible, Nowell says, that the Neanderthals blew single notes through the holes chewed by the animals. So it might have made music even if it wasn't made to be a flute.

Is the find a chewed-up bone or a flute? No one knows for certain. Unless other similar finds are made, the answer to whether Neanderthals danced to Stone Age music may never be known.

DID YOU KNOW?
NEANDERTHAL FACTS

- **Neanderthals are named after the Neander Valley, an area in Germany. It was there, in 1856, that the first Neanderthal skull and bones were found. Since then, Neanderthal remains have been found in France, England, Italy, Iraq, and Israel.**
- **Evidence shows that Neanderthals knew about stone tools, used fire, and lived in cave shelters.**

Based on an article in *TIME FOR KIDS.*

Story Questions & Activities

1. What steps did Ivan Turk take to try to discover if the bone is really the world's first flute?
2. Why are scientists arguing over whether or not the bone is a flute?
3. How does this article make you see that science is exciting? Explain.
4. What is the main idea of this selection?
5. Suppose that the bone is the world's first flute. Compare its discovery with that of the cave paintings in "Painters of the Caves." What do these discoveries tell you about the people of the prehistoric past?

Write a How-to Manual

If the unusual bone that Ivan Turk found is really a flute, then it is the oldest musical instrument ever found. Choose a musical instrument you play or would like to learn how to play. Research how to play it. Then write a how-to manual that explains the steps in the process. Include an illustration, a chart, or a diagram with your instructions.

Make a Musical Instrument

Musical instruments are based on simple principles. They are either struck, like drums, blown into, like flutes, or strummed, like guitars. Here is your chance to create your own musical instrument. First, decide how your instrument will be played. Next, decide how it will look. Then draw or make your instrument. Explain how to play it to your group or the class.

Draw a Poster

What people lived in your area in prehistoric times? The answer probably is a Native American group. Read about the people who lived in your region. Who were they? What kinds of homes did they build? Did they farm or hunt? What kind of clothing did they wear? Create a poster of important facts about them. Illustrate it with drawings. Include captions or labels.

Find Out More

The bone Ivan Turk discovered came from the Stone Age. What was the Stone Age? How long did it last? How did people survive? Find out more about the Stone Age by looking in an encyclopedia, a book, or a video about prehistoric times. Discover five interesting facts about the Stone Age. Use them to write an outline for a research report.

Read a Time Line

The "flute" the researchers found is from the Stone Age. The Stone Age lasted for hundreds of thousands of years. Look at the time line below. A **time line** is a diagram of a series of events in time. It shows events in the order in which they took place. When you are reading about a long period of time, making a time line is a good way to organize information.

Early Man The Stone Age

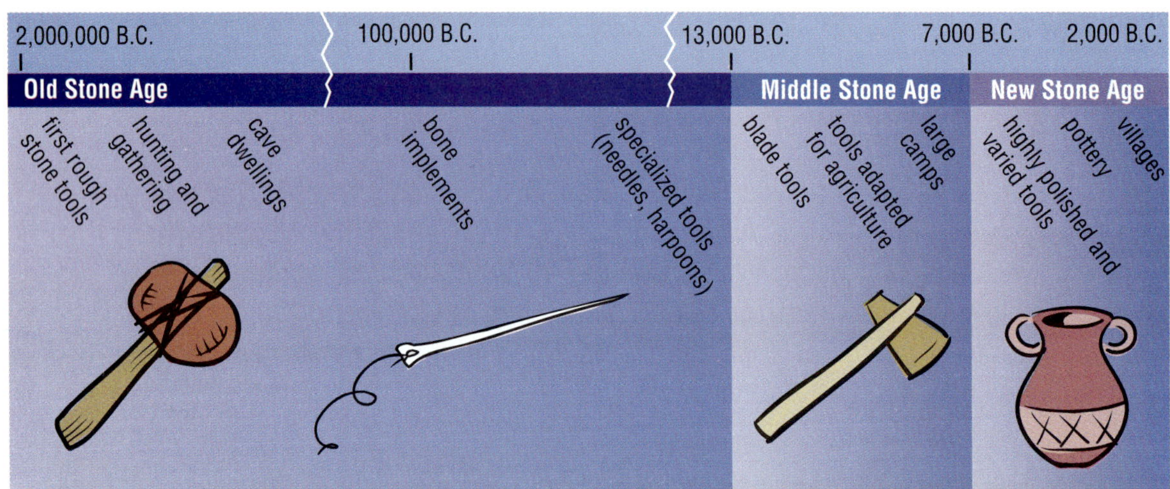

Use the time line to answer these questions.

1. What does the time line show?
2. During which period were the first stone tools made?
3. When did people begin to make tools for farming?
4. When was pottery first made?
5. Why do you think it is useful to know how to read a time line?

TEST POWER

Test Tip

Enjoy what you are reading.

DIRECTIONS

Read the sample story. Then read each question about the story.

SAMPLE

Rosalyn Sussman Yalow

Rosalyn Sussman Yalow was born in New York, in 1921. Because both of her parents had quit school in the eighth grade, they pushed Rosalyn to further her education.

In those days it was uncommon for a woman to get an advanced degree. But because many of the men in the country were fighting in World War II, the universities were empty. Rosalyn was accepted into college. In 1945, she received a degree in nuclear physics.

For many years after that, Rosalyn worked as a researcher. She discovered a process called RIA. RIA allows doctors to find tiny amounts of chemicals in a person's blood. RIA was so useful to doctors that Rosalyn won the Nobel Prize for it in 1977. The Nobel Prize is one of the most admirable awards a scientist can receive. Rosalyn Yalow was the first American woman to win one.

1 The author probably wrote this passage to —

A tell about life during World War II

B explain the importance of the Nobel Prize

C tell about a successful scientist

D show that women are better scientists than men

2 Which of these happened to Rosalyn after she discovered RIA?

F She won the Nobel Prize.

G She graduated from college.

H She worked as a researcher.

J She was encouraged to further her education.

Did you remember to answer both questions?

Purple Snake

"It's in there, sleeping,"
Don Luis says and winks.
He knows I want to feel
the animal asleep in a piece of wood,
like he does
turning it this way and that,
listening.
Slowly he strokes the wood,
rough and wrinkled. Like his hands.
He begins to carve his way.
"Mira. Its head, its scales, its tail."
Don Luis rubs and strokes
the animal before he paints
its eyes open.
When the paint dries,
I place the purple snake
by the green bull and red frog
that Don Luis found asleep
in a piece of wood.

by Pat Mora

Seek and Discover

UNIT 4

To Look at Any Thing

To look at any thing,
If you would know that thing,
You must look at it long:
To look at this green and say
'I have seen spring in these
Woods,' will not do—you must
Be the thing you see:
You must be the dark snakes of
Stems and ferny plumes of leaves,
You must enter in
To the small silences between
The leaves,
You must take your time
And touch the very peace
They issue from.

by John Moffitt

Stories in Art

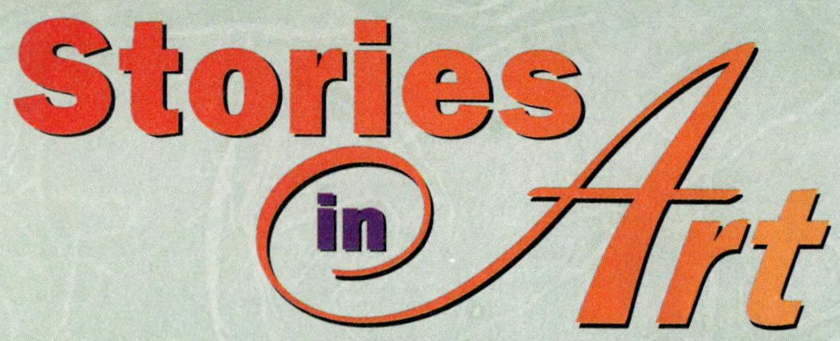

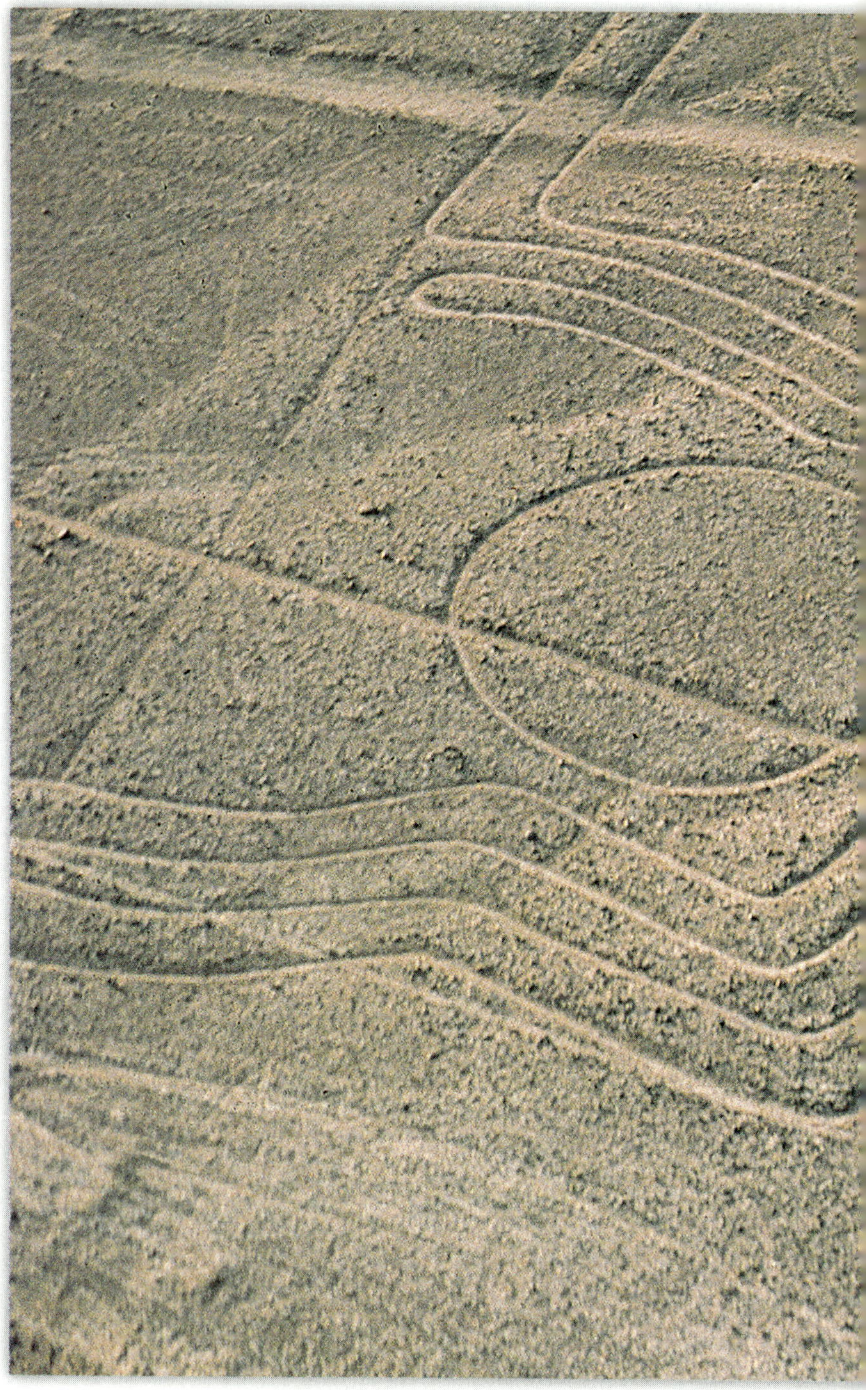

It is a fact that centuries ago some people carved figures into the soil. These figures are called earthworks. Why the people did this is largely unknown.

Look at this earthwork. It is known as the Nazca Lines, drawn on the Nazca Plain in Peru. How would you describe this drawing? Why does it have so many arms and legs? What is factual in this work of art? What is not? What is it a picture of?

Notice the two people in red jackets. What do they tell you about the size of the figure? Why do you think this earthwork was made?

Nazca Lines **by William Allard,**
National Geographic Society
Nazca Plain, Peru

Mummies, Tombs, and Treasure

SECRETS OF ANCIENT EGYPT

by Lila Perl

A night view of the pyramid of King Khafre with the Sphinx in the foreground, lit by floodlights. Insets, clockwise from top: the coffin of a royal official of Thebes, a pendant from King Tutankhamen's tomb, and a statue of King Ramses II

The ancient Egyptians believed that a dead person's spirit could live forever if the body was preserved as a mummy. They developed elaborate burial customs, building magnificent tombs to house the bodies of Egyptian royalty and upper-class citizens. A tomb contained everything the spirit would need for a comfortable life after death—favorite possessions, games, food, and water. Shabtis, *miniature figures of humans, were placed in the tomb to act as servants to the dead. Containers called* canopic jars *held the deceased's preserved internal organs, which would magically rejoin the body in the afterlife. After the funeral, the tomb was sealed, supposedly forever. But often, robbers opened tombs in search of the riches buried within.*

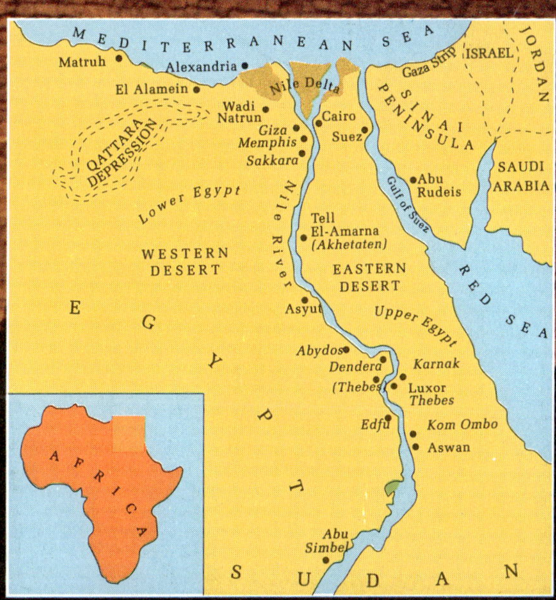

Map of Egypt today. Cities and sites of ancient Egypt are in italics.

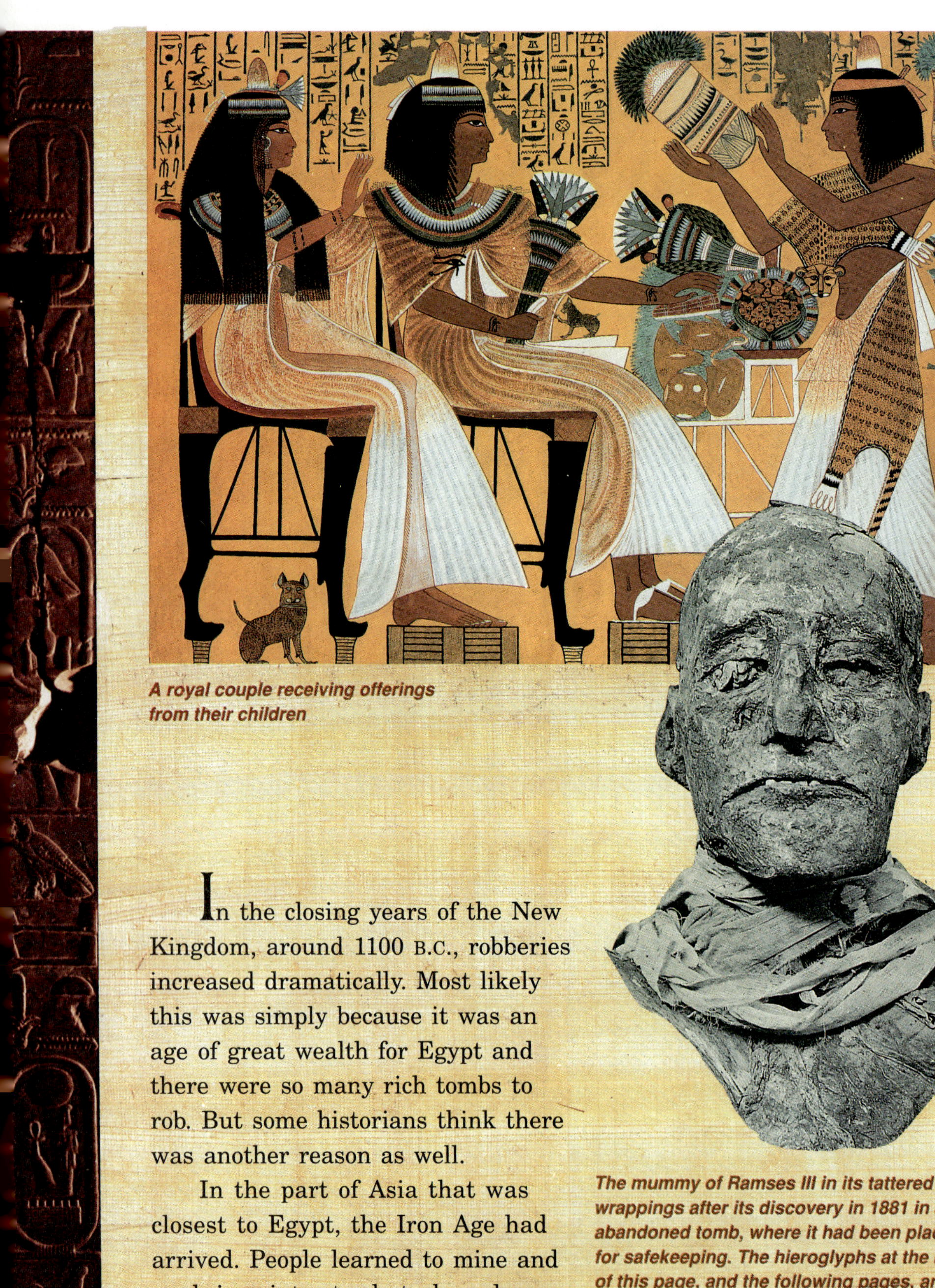

A royal couple receiving offerings from their children

The mummy of Ramses III in its tattered wrappings after its discovery in 1881 in an abandoned tomb, where it had been placed for safekeeping. The hieroglyphs at the border of this page, and the following pages, are taken from a list of ancient Egyptian rulers found at Abydos, in the Temple of Seti I.

In the closing years of the New Kingdom, around 1100 B.C., robberies increased dramatically. Most likely this was simply because it was an age of great wealth for Egypt and there were so many rich tombs to rob. But some historians think there was another reason as well.

In the part of Asia that was closest to Egypt, the Iron Age had arrived. People learned to mine and work iron into sturdy tools and weapons. Egypt, however, did not have large iron deposits. It was still making most of its tools out of bronze, a mixture of copper and tin. Egypt was forced to import iron. This caused such an increase in taxes and in the cost of living that many more people turned to thievery.

Whatever the reason, around 1000 B.C. a group of priests of the Twenty-first Dynasty took steps to rescue the tattered remains of some of the royal mummies whose graves had been looted. They found an abandoned tomb near the temple of Queen Hatshepsut and secretly transferred the mummies to the new hiding place. Many were rebandaged and marked with their names taken from the old wrappings. Even the dates of rewrapping were inscribed on the cloth. Some of the mummies were given new coffins. Also reburied with them were those belongings the thieves had ignored as being of lesser value. Among them were papyrus scrolls, canopic jars, and *shabtis*.

For nearly three thousand years the mummies rested peacefully in their new home. Then, in 1875, unusual objects began to appear for sale in the shops, hotels, and bazaars of Luxor. This new city had sprung to life on the east bank of the Nile, on the site of ancient Thebes. Ever since the early 1800s, when Egypt's past had begun to be revealed through the discovery of the Rosetta Stone, the country had been swarming with foreign visitors. Among them were tourists, souvenir seekers, art collectors, and archaeologists who were studying the monuments and digging for the remains of Egypt's ancient civilization.

The mysterious objects that were coming on the market turned out to be scrolls, *shabtis,* and other articles belonging to various rulers of the New Kingdom and of the Twenty-first Dynasty, which followed it. Finally, in 1881, the Egyptian government tracked down the source of the articles. Sure enough, one of the old tomb-robbing families had been at work again. A pair of brothers had discovered the hiding place of the mummies near the temple of Queen Hatshepsut.

Aside from the items they had stolen, the modern tomb robbers had done little further damage to the mummies. Among them were such famed rulers of the New Kingdom as Ahmose, Amenhotep I, Thutmose I, II, and III, Seti I, and Ramses I, II, and III. With great care, the mummies were transported to Cairo where many can be

seen today in the Mummy Room of the Cairo Museum.

In the case of Thutmose I, however, it was discovered that the priests of the Twenty-first Dynasty had made an error in rebandaging. The mummy labeled Thutmose I turned out to be that of an unknown youth of about eighteen. Thutmose I, who must have been about fifty when he died, has not so far been found.

In 1898, yet another tomb was found in the Valley of the Kings crammed with mummies hidden away for safekeeping by priests. In this group were found Amenhotep II, Thutmose IV, Amenhotep III, Ramses IV, and Ramses V, among others. They, too, were brought to the museum's Mummy Room to be displayed in glass cases.

Little by little the gaps in Egypt's royal history were being filled in. Mummies were being found, and so were the empty, echoing tombs of their onetime owners, magnificent with their painted walls and ceilings but bare of their contents. People wondered if anyone would ever uncover a royal tomb that looked just as it had on the day that the mourners departed and the entrance was sealed, presumably forever.

One such person was a British archaeologist named Howard Carter. He had come to Egypt in 1890 as a very young man and worked there for many years, dreaming constantly of finding an undisturbed tomb in the Valley of the Kings. Digging in the Valley was a costly undertaking, however. So Carter was lucky in having met up with a wealthy British nobleman, Lord Carnarvon, who shared Carter's goal and funded his work.

Because of his health, Lord Carnarvon spent winters in Egypt's warm, dry climate. The months from November to March were also the only time when digging in the Valley was possible. The summers were far too hot.

By 1922, Carter had spent six unsuccessful seasons fine-combing a particular part of the Valley in search of the burial place of a little-known pharaoh named Tutankhamen. Years earlier another archaeologist had discovered some puzzling remains both near and under a large tilted rock in the vicinity. They included a bit of gold leaf and a blue cup marked with Tutankhamen's name. There were also some dried floral collars and some animal bones left behind by the guests of a funeral banquet of long, long ago. Could they have

Two of the four seated sandstone colossi of the Great Temple of Ramses II, Abu Simbel, now located on the plateau above its original site

been the guests at the funeral banquet of Tutankhamen?

In the autumn of 1922 Carter arrived in the Valley for what was to be the very last season of the search for Tutankhamen. He brought with him a tiny companion, a canary, to keep him company in the small, domed house he had built for himself on the Valley road on the west bank of the Nile. The local Egyptians hired to work on the dig were amazed by the "golden bird." No songbirds had ever been seen or heard in the grim, treeless Valley.

Perhaps, as Carter's work team predicted, the little canary brought Carter luck. The site he had chosen for the last season's dig was directly under some ancient grave-workers' huts in front of the tomb of Ramses VI, a pharaoh who had lived about two hundred years later than Tutankhamen. In the past, Carter had hesitated to dig there because the empty tomb of Ramses VI was a heavily visited tourist attraction.

As it turned out, the innocent-appearing workers' huts stood atop none other than the long-forgotten tomb of Tutankhamen. On the very day that the foundations of the first hut were dug away, a step was discovered cut into the rock beneath it. Another step and then another revealed sixteen steps in all. These led down to a sealed passageway filled with broken rocks and then to a second sealed doorway leading into the tomb itself.

Carter sent a historic telegram to Lord Carnarvon who was still in England. It read: "At last have made wonderful discovery in Valley; a magnificent tomb with seals intact; re-covered same for your arrival; congratulations."

On November 26, 1922, with Lord Carnarvon beside him, Carter made an eye-level opening

in the door to the tomb and put a candle through the hole. His own words record the thrill of that moment in which he glimpsed the inside of the tomb.

"At first I could see nothing, the hot air escaping from the chamber causing the candle to flicker, but presently, as my eyes grew accustomed to the light, details of the room within emerged slowly from the mist, strange animals, statues, and gold—everywhere the glint of gold. For the moment. . . . I was struck dumb with amazement, and when Lord Carnarvon, unable to stand the suspense any longer, inquired anxiously, 'Can you see anything?' it was all I could do to get out the words, 'Yes, wonderful things.'"

Carter was looking into the first of four rooms of a surprisingly small royal tomb. The Antechamber, as the first and largest room was called, was only about twelve by twenty-six feet, the measurements of a fair-sized living room. It was heaped with chairs, footstools, and chests of alabaster, ebony, and ivory, and strange couches of gilded wood in the form of animals, including a cow and a lion. Piled beneath the cow-bed were egg-shaped food containers made of clay.

Sealed doorways, one guarded by two gold-encrusted statues of Tutankhamen, led to the other three rooms of the tomb—an Annex that was even more jumbled than the Antechamber, the Burial Chamber in which the mummy lay, and a small room beyond that called the Treasury.

Carter was not surprised at the disarray that met his eyes, for he had already suspected that Tutankhamen's tomb had been broken into in ancient times. But the robbers had had to leave hastily, even dropping some gold rings and other small articles on their way out. Their lost loot had probably included the bit of gold leaf and the blue cup found outside the tomb in Carter's day. The cemetery officials of ancient times had apparently roughly tidied and resealed the tomb. Then, happily, its entrance had been completely covered over by the building of the Ramses VI workers' huts.

The floor plan of the tomb of Tutankhamen

Three anxious and tension-filled years were to pass before the great moment when Carter opened the coffin containing the mummy of Tutankhamen. During that time, while he was carefully cataloging and clearing the contents of the Antechamber, a number of strange events took place.

First, Carter's canary was eaten by a poisonous desert snake. Those who were superstitious took it as a bad omen. Did the snake represent the pharaoh's anger at having had his tomb disturbed? On his death mask, it was later discovered, Tutankhamen wore the cobra and vulture, twin royal symbols of Lower and Upper Egypt.

Next, less than five months after the opening of the tomb, Lord

The jumbled treasure in the first room of Tutankhamen's tomb as first seen by Howard Carter

Carnarvon died of blood poisoning from a mysterious insect bite on his cheek that had become infected. He was never to see the great, carved stone coffin in the Burial Chamber that rested inside a series of four nested wooden cases covered with gold leaf. Nor was he ever to see the three richly gleaming mummy-shaped coffins nested inside the rectangular stone coffin or, of course, the mummy of Tutankhamen.

Lastly, soon after the discovery of the tomb, Carter himself ran up against numerous problems with the Egyptian government. One of the disputes had to do with which officials and their guests were to be permitted to visit the tomb while the delicate work of recording its contents was going on.

For a time the tomb was sealed up, and Carter actually left Egypt in anger and despair.

Did all of these unpleasant happenings have a hidden meaning? Was there such a thing as a "mummy's curse"? Were Carter and Carnarvon being punished for unearthing the resting place of the pharaoh who had slept longer in his treasure-filled tomb than any other yet known?

Many people thought so. They went to great trouble to try to prove that death was stalking and striking all who had worked with Carter, from the humblest laborer to the most distinguished archaeologist. But Carter himself never believed the wild stories that sprang from his discovery. And, in fact, he went on to live for many more years, dying in 1939 at the age of sixty-five.

The first viewing of Tutankhamen's mummy took place at last in the autumn of 1925. Of the three mummy-shaped coffins, the two outer ones were of wood covered with sheets of gold, while the innermost was of solid gold!

Inside the gold innermost coffin lay the bandaged mummy of Tutankhamen, its head and shoulders covered with a solid-gold mask

inlaid with blue lapis lazuli, other semi-precious stones, and colored glass. The mask, serene, youthful, and noble, shows the king wearing the ceremonial false beard and a striped headcloth called a *nemes* (NEM-eez) with the royal cobra and vulture at the brow.

The hasty thieves of ancient times who had invaded Tutankhamen's tomb had been looking only for small objects they could carry away quickly. They had entered the Burial Chamber but had never broken into any of its nested coffins.

On unwrapping the mummy, Carter discovered that there were thirteen layers of linen bandages containing one hundred and forty-three precious gold and bejeweled objects. Among them

The solid-gold mask found on the mummy of Tutankhamen (left)

The outermost gilded wood coffin in which the mummy of King Tutankhamen rests today in the Burial Chamber of his tomb (bottom)

were necklaces, collars, pendants, bracelets, rings, belts, gold-sheathed daggers, gold sandals, and slender golden tubes that encased the mummy's fingernails and toenails.

Beneath all this splendor, however, the mummy itself was a pitiful disappointment. Blackened and shrunken by the careless pouring on of oils and resins, it was one of the poorer examples of the New Kingdom art of mummification.

Who was Tutankhamen? Why was he buried in such a small tomb with such great riches? Why was his mummy so badly prepared?

To Carter's disappointment, no papyrus scrolls telling anything of Tutankhamen's reign or of his family history were found in the tomb. We know only that he is believed to have been either the brother or the illegitimate son of the previous king, Amenhotep IV, who had turned away from the many gods of Thebes to worship the sun as the one and only god. In so doing, Amenhotep IV changed his name to Akhenaten (Ahk-eh-NAH-ten), meaning "pleasing to Aten" (the sun). He also moved his capital from Thebes to a new site known as Akhetaten (Ahk-eh-TAH-ten), or "horizon of the Aten."

As Akhenaten's successor, Tutankhamen is thought to have come to the throne as a child of nine, to have reigned briefly, and to have died as a youth of eighteen. He married a princess who may have been his half-sister. He left no heirs. In the richly stocked Treasury, the room just off the Burial Chamber, Carter found two tiny coffins with the mummified remains of girl infants who had probably been dead at birth. Were they the children of Tutankhamen and his young wife?

As to Tutankhamen himself, we do not know how or why he died. Was his death caused by an accident, an illness, or could he have been murdered? There is a suspicious scar, possibly from an arrow tip, in front of the mummy's ear. Did the priests of Thebes who served the many gods want Tutankhamen dead because of his relationship with Akhenaten, who had turned his back on their religion?

Whatever the reason, Tutankhamen's sudden death may account for the small size of his tomb.

Perhaps it had been meant for someone else but was used for the young pharaoh because his own was not ready. On the other hand, Tutankhamen may simply have been an unimportant king who, through Howard Carter's discovery, became the most famous of all of Egypt's kings.

If Tutankhamen's treasure, however, was that of an "unimportant" king buried in a hastily prepared tomb, can we ever guess at the splendor of the contents of those much larger and grander tombs that the grave robbers of Egypt emptied thousands of years ago!

Meet Lila Perl

Author Lila Perl says that when she was growing up, she "never thought of being a writer." But, as a child, she unknowingly laid the foundation for becoming one. As she says, "I read a lot. Every time I was told to 'go outside and play,' I went off somewhere with a book." She has written more than fifteen books, including cookbooks and fiction and nonfiction books for young adults.

Perl hopes that her joy in creating each story comes across to her readers. Letters from her readers are a source of great satisfaction to her, and she says that "every single letter is answered."

Perl's first book for young adults, *Red-Flannel Hash and Shoo-Fly Pie: American Regional Foods and Festivals,* was an ALA Notable Book.

Gold collar from Tomb of Tutankhamen (left), c. 1342 B.C.; detail from Tomb of Amunherkhopshef, son of Ramses III (below), c. 1160 B.C.

1. What were some burial customs of the ancient Egyptians?
2. Why was Carter's discovery so important?
3. How do you know that "Mummies, Tombs, and Treasure" is a nonfiction selection? Explain.
4. What is the main idea of this selection?
5. Compare the discovery of the cave paintings in "Painters of the Caves" with the discovery of Tutankhamen's tomb. In what ways are the discoveries similar? What are the differences?

Write a News Article

Imagine that it is November 26, 1922. You are an on-the-spot reporter covering the story of Carter's discovery of the tomb of Tutankhamen. Write a brief news article for your newspaper back home. Dazzle your readers by describing the "find." Be sure to answer the questions *Who? What? When? Where?* and *How?*

Create a Travel Brochure

About 100 years ago in Egypt, royal tombs were discovered in the Valley of the Kings. Now it's your turn to discover this area. With a group, design a travel brochure. Include a map of the region, a brief history, a description of the weather and climate, and the magnificent sights that visitors can see.

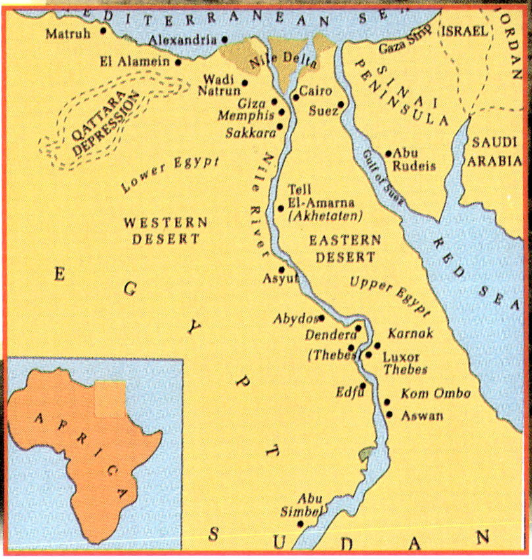

Make a Time Line

How many years ago did Tutankhamen live? What about the rulers known as Amenhotep, Thutmose, and Ramses? Investigate the dates of some of the important Egyptian kings. Then make a time line of the great pharaohs of Egypt.

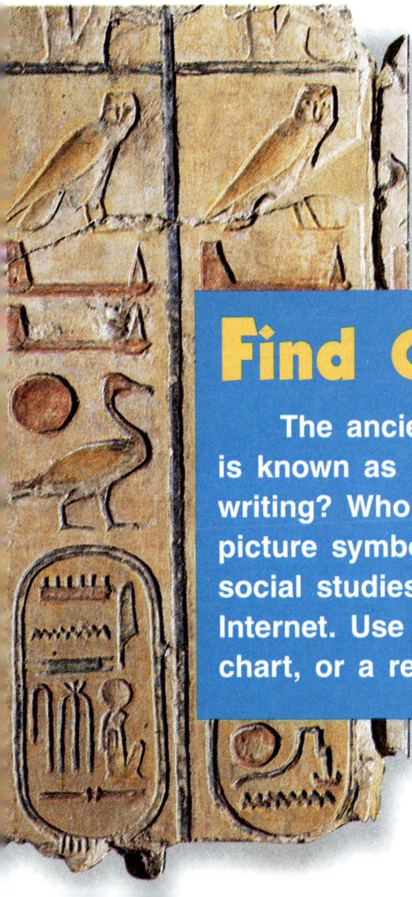

Find Out More

The ancient Egyptian system of picture writing is known as *hieroglyphics.* What is this system of writing? Who used it? What did some of its picture symbols mean? Start by checking your social studies textbook, an encyclopedia, or the Internet. Use your findings to prepare a poster, a chart, or a report on Egyptian hieroglyphics.

Read a Floor Plan

A **floor plan** is a diagram that shows the rooms and hallways on each floor of a building, as seen from above. Here is the floor plan for an art museum. By looking at the label on each gallery, you can tell what exhibit was on display.

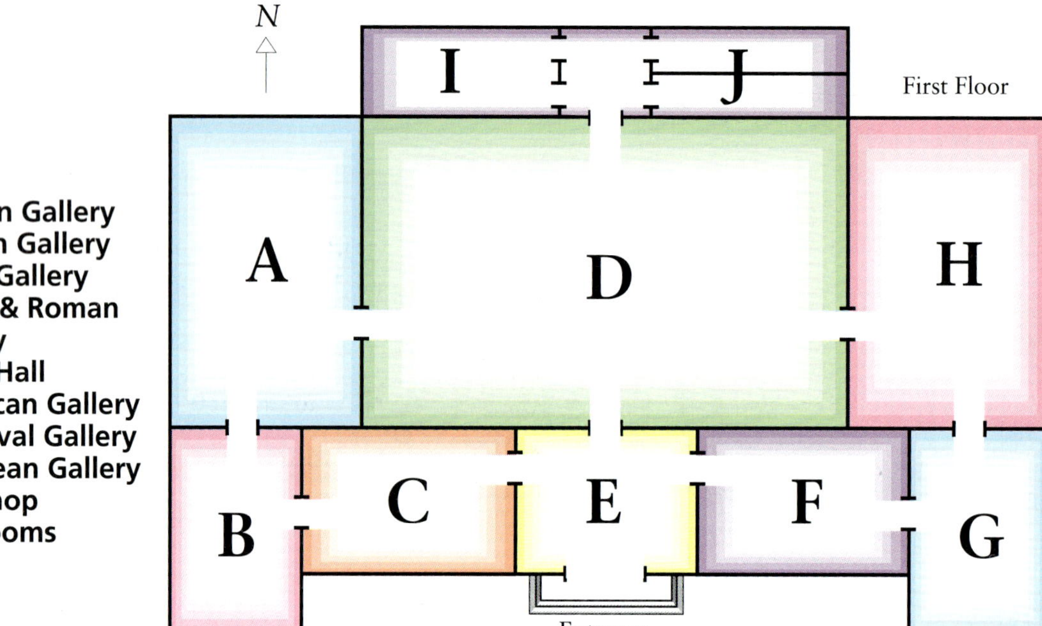

Use the floor plan to answer these questions.

1. After entering the museum, where would you be?
2. If you wanted to see objects that were used by the pharoahs, which gallery would you go to?
3. How would you get there from the Great Hall?
4. Where is the gift shop located?
5. Why is it important to know how to read a floor plan?

TEST POWER

Test Tip

Always read the answer choices carefully.

DIRECTIONS

Read the sample story. Then read each question about the story.

SAMPLE

Gary's Plan for His Neighborhood

Gary was concerned about the number of trees that had to be cut down to make paper. Gary asked his town leaders if he could help to organize a plan for recycling paper. Using recycled paper would allow everyone to use paper over and over again. Here's the plan that Gary devised:

A Plan for Paper Recycling

- Keep paper products separate from other trash. Paper recycling pickup will be on the first and third Saturdays of each month.
- Recyclable paper includes: newspaper, office paper, brown paper bags, envelopes, magazines, paper plates, paper cups, etc.
- Newspaper must be tied in bundles with string or twine and left out by the curb for pick up. Twine may be purchased at the grocery store or the recycling center.
- This program is not mandatory, but strongly encouraged. We can all play a part in protecting the environment!

1 Under Gary's plan, which item will NOT be recycled?

A envelopes

B cardboard

C magazines

D newspapers

2 Twine can be purchased —

F at the recycling center

G at the town hall

H from Gary

J from the trash collector

Westward, the Course of the Empire Takes Its Way **by Emmanuel Leutze,**
National Museum of American Art, Washington, D.C.

Stories in Art

America's pioneers went West to find land and make a better way of life. The goal for some was the Pacific Ocean. Only the most accurate information could get them there.

Look at the painting. What can you tell about it? Notice the many details. Why is the man on top of the rock? Why are the men pointing? Are all the details important to the story being told in the painting? Explain.

Look at the painting again. Are the details in the bottom part important? How? What are the important details in the curled border art? How would it feel to take part in a bold adventure?

MEET WILL STEGER

Will Steger has always loved adventure. As a boy, he and his brother took a boat down the Mississippi River from St. Paul, Minnesota, to New Orleans, Louisiana. Before he was 25, he had climbed mountains in Peru and made long river trips in the Yukon and Alaska. In 1986, Steger led an expedition to the North Pole. Three years later, he led a team nearly 4,000 miles across Antarctica.

In 1995 Steger was awarded a medal by the National Geographic Society for his work as an explorer and a scientist. In receiving this award, he joins such adventurers as Amelia Earhart, Robert Peary, and Jacques Cousteau.

MEET JON BOWERMASTER

No stranger to adventure, Jon Bowermaster is a journalist who writes about the environment. In fact, he has written many articles for magazines such as *National Geographic, The New York Times Magazine, Audubon,* and *Rolling Stone. Over The Top of the World* is not the first book that Bowermaster has written with Will Steger. The two authors have also written *Saving the Earth* and *Crossing Antarctica.* In addition, the same year that Steger won his award from the National Geographic Society, Bowermaster won the Lowell Thomas Award for Environmental Journalism.

OVER THE TOP OF THE WORLD

BY WILL STEGER AND JON BOWERMASTER

PHOTOS BY GORDON WILTSIE

STEGER

In a dangerous expedition across the Arctic Ocean, explorer Will Steger, his teammates, and their sled-dog teams encounter dangerous traveling conditions as they make their way across the North Pole to northern Canada. It is early April when their trip begins. Their goals, as Will says in his journal, are to draw attention to the pollution in the Arctic. It is also to see if it is possible to communicate information on the Internet to schools all over the world.

The journey is both dangerous and exhausting. The five team members must run or ski beside the sleds during the day, often stopping to chop ice or rescue an overturned dogsled. Because of the poor weather conditions and the shifting ice pushing them backward, the explorers are behind schedule. By the end of April, they have only reached the North Pole. It has not been an easy trip, and they still have a long way to go.

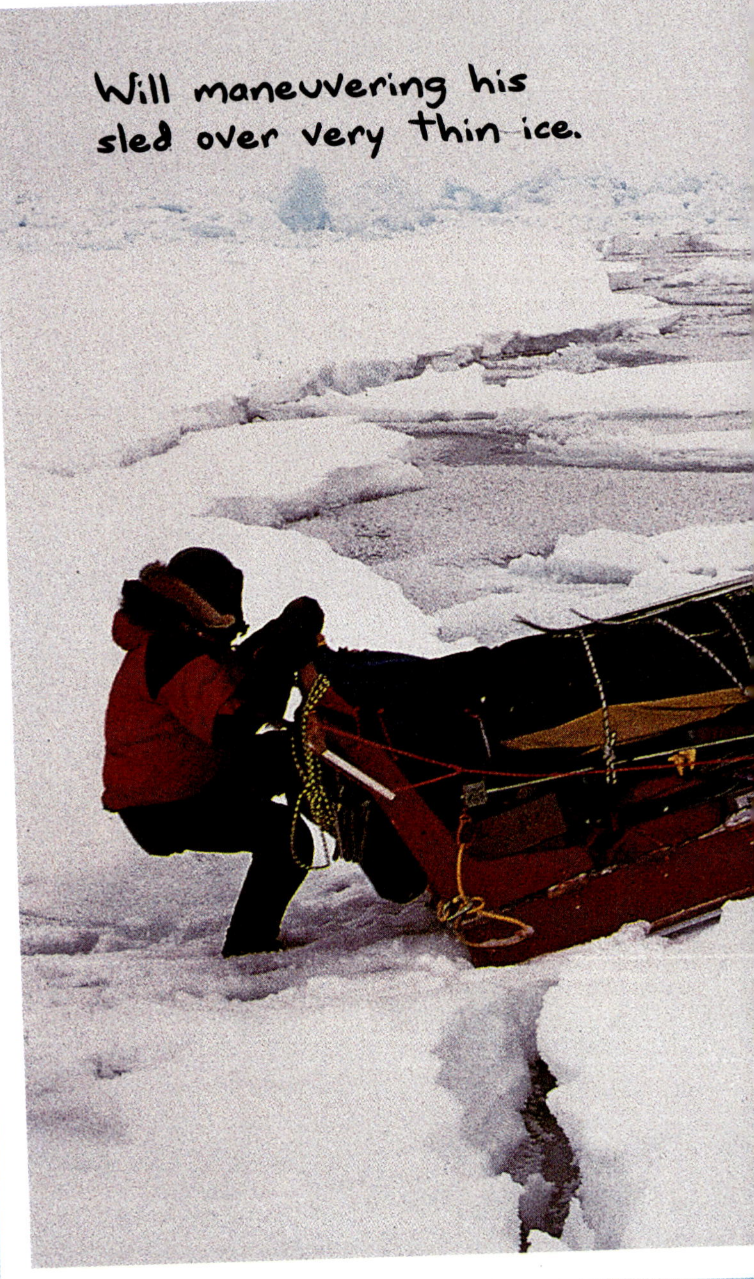

Will maneuvering his sled over very thin ice.

APRIL 27

When we left the North Pole it seemed like a perfect day—sunny and -4. We took our time packing the sleds, enjoying the relative warmth. We sledded along until 11 this morning, when I stopped the sled as the others in front bunched up. I could see Victor ahead poking the ice with a harpoonlike pole that he uses to check its thickness. Martin's sled was just behind; Julie's was next.

I began to notice that the ice beneath our skis was dark, almost black. I could make out in the ice what I call "snow flowers," a flowerlike frost formation that forms on thin ice. I was just about to walk ahead to warn Martin, when his dogs bolted. Almost immediately his sled broke through the ice and tipped onto its side, half in the water, half on thin ice. I left my dogs with Julie, then raced to help, signaling for the help of Takako.

We quickly surveyed the scene. The sled runner in the water was stuck under the lip of the ice. Martin proposed breaking the ice that was already freezing around the runner, and then trying to right the sled. I was afraid this would cause the whole sled to tip and fall into the water. Instead, I suggested knocking the ice out from underneath the other runner, the one on firm ice, and then, as soon as it was level, using the dogs to pull the sled forward.

It was dangerous work. As he chopped at the ice, Martin went into the water a couple of times, up to his waist. After 30 minutes we finally got the sled level, but now it was almost totally submerged underwater.

The team tries to right Martin's sled, which has tipped over into the broken ice. Note the darker color of the ice and the snow flowers.

Takako, Victor, and I stood back as Martin called out commands for the dogs to pull forward, fast and hard. "Hup, hup, dogs. C'mon, Mooch, PULLL!!! PULLL!!!"

As the dogs strained, the front of the sled came out of the water. But our plan wasn't working. While the sled was moving forward, the ice kept breaking beneath it.

Finally, with one last giant pull, the dogs managed to get the sled onto firm ice. We were lucky that the dogs were fresh and excited. They saved the day.

At last, the dogs are able to pull Martin's sled from the water.

APRIL 28

It's 8 o'clock at night and the sun is intense in my tent as I write. It is definitely spring—yesterday we saw fog, a sure sign—and almost too warm. Too much warmth means overheated dogs and more water to cross.

The ice all around us is shattered; it looks as if an earthquake had hit the Arctic Ocean. As a result, sledding is very tricky, very slow. Today we made just two miles. We are now also traveling against the drift—so every night we are pushed backward, back toward the North Pole. It's as if we are traveling on a huge, icy treadmill.

Julie and Takako exchange jokes with children around the world through the computer. Early explorers would never have dreamed of this kind of communication from the Arctic.

One thing that keeps us going is the daily communication with the Internet. Every night, usually in Julie and Takako's tent, messages are prepared and sent around the world by satellite. It's not an easy chore though. After a big, adventurous day we have to compose our thoughts, and then hope that the computers will do their job. One night I walked past their tent as Takako was trying to send a report. I could hear her whispering to the computer we call Charlie, "C'mon, Charlie, c'mon," as if she were talking to a real person.

COMMUNICATING WITH THE WORLD

Our dogs' story

Our mission Search News

As Will Steger and the International Arctic Project team crossed the Arctic Ocean, they wanted to communicate every day on the Internet with schools all over the world. A special system had to be found which would work from the remote Arctic region.

This communication became so important to the team that they felt as if they had another team member with them. They nicknamed the first system "Esmerelda." Every day Julie and Takako would write a brief report, summarizing the day's observations and activities. They would also report on the weather, snow, and ice conditions, samples collected, and sometimes tell a story about one of the dogs.

After writing the report on the computer, the computer would be attached to a transmitter. This transmitter would send the message to one of the very few satellites that orbits the earth around the poles. Each morning, at the International Arctic Project headquarters in St. Paul, Minnesota, the report would be read, and then sent to classrooms, scientists, and friends around the world who were following the team's progress.

When the team reached the North Pole, a new computer was delivered to them. This computer and transmitter could send longer messages and, importantly, could even transmit photographs. In fact, the team made history by transmitting the first photograph ever sent from the pole. The team nicknamed this new system "Charlie."

Most difficult was keeping the computer and batteries warm. The computer had its own "sleeping bag," similar to the team members'. Every morning Julie heated a hot-water bottle and slipped it inside the bag to keep the computer from freezing. The whole unit then traveled in a special case on the sled.

The ability to send information in this manner was one of the main reasons for doing this expedition, and is one of the team's greatest accomplishments. Such communication is the future of education. By using computers and satellite hook-ups, explorers in remote places can connect with students person-to-person, to make subjects like the Arctic come alive.

lews from Will

lews from Jon

lews from Takako

lews from Julie

ews from Victor

ews from Martin

http://www.overthetop.com

e-mail us:travelers.northpole.org

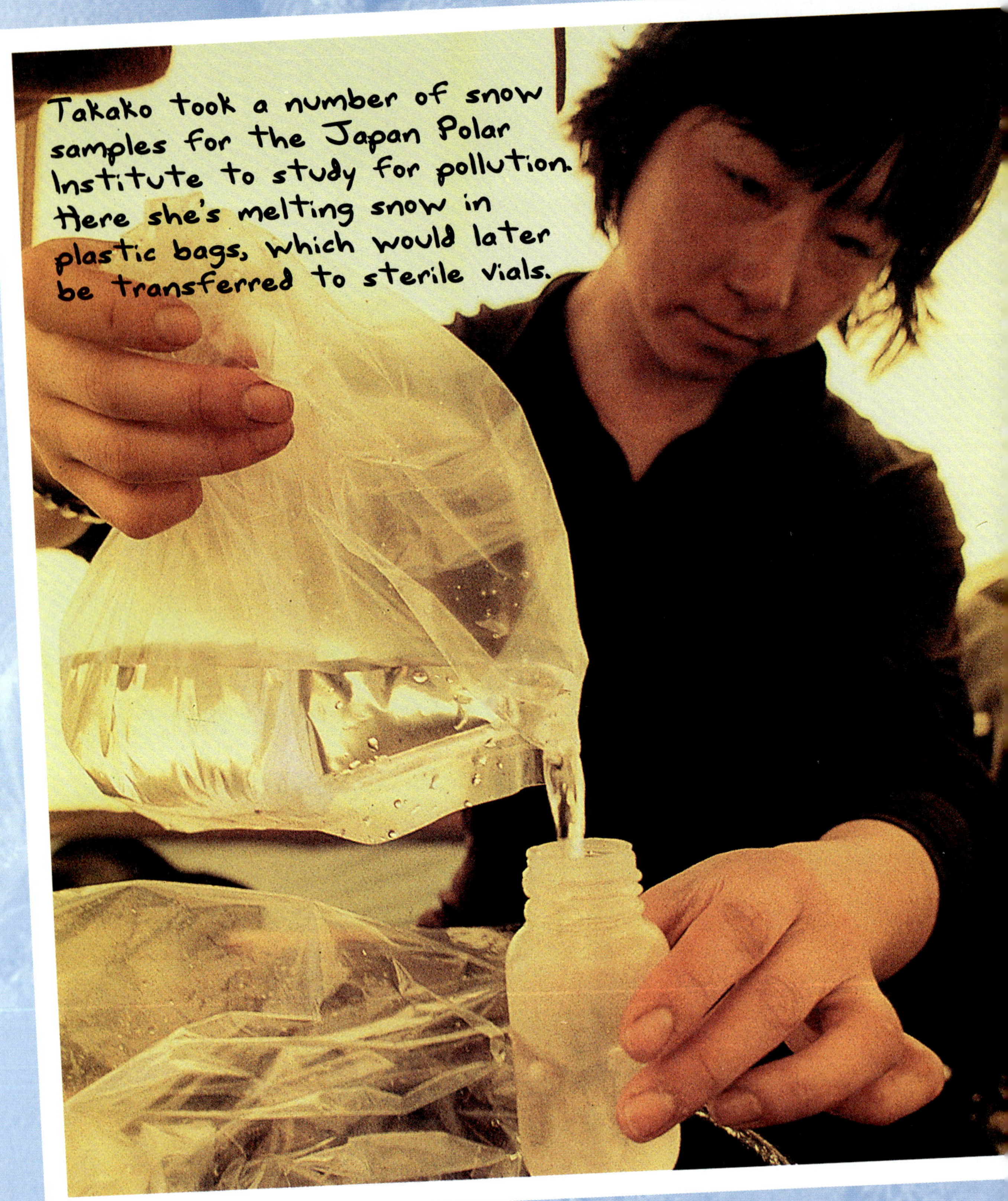

Takako took a number of snow samples for the Japan Polar Institute to study for pollution. Here she's melting snow in plastic bags, which would later be transferred to sterile vials.

MAY 3

Outside this morning it's clear, -20, with a north wind, which is good because it is at our back. I'm looking forward to the days now, as are the dogs, who are strong and excited. It's a very simple existence we lead when we're traveling like this. Most of the days are similar, the food we eat is the same, we don't meet any people. Even though the team has been traveling together for more than two months, we're all still getting along.

As I've said, one of the reasons we're here is to draw attention to the environmental problems that affect the Arctic. We are collecting snow samples along the way for scientists back home to test. On most days it's hard to believe there's pollution out here in the middle of the Arctic Ocean. But there is. In the air, the water, and the ice and, unfortunately, in the wildlife.

The pollution problems that scientists study in the Arctic are created in big industrial cities and on farms, in North America, Asia, and Europe. Pollution travels through the air and water, carried by wind, river, and ocean currents. Once in the Arctic, pollutants "live" longer because of the cold conditions. Studies have shown that man-made pollutants are starting to show up in Arctic animals, like seals and polar bears. So we're not affecting just the air and the water, but the animals, too.

MAY 5

Yesterday we made camp among huge jumbles of ice, some as tall as five-storey buildings. It looks as if a bomb went off in the middle of the Arctic, leaving giant blocks of ice scattered everywhere.

By now, heading south, we thought we would be on smoother ice, trying to get as far as we can before the ice completely melts. Instead, each day seems to lead to another of fighting our way up and over immense, spilled icetrays. At this rate, we may not make it to land until some time in August. And we don't have nearly enough food to last that long.

Dog's-eye view of Totem (left) and Miles (right).

MAY 12

This morning when I woke up I could hear soft snow hitting the tent. The snow was accumulating wet and sticky. It would be a miserable day of travel.

Yesterday we sledded through a whiteout almost all day, and in the late afternoon we ran into some wet snow that was almost like quicksand—you stepped in and it started sucking you down.

At one point my dogs bunched up, waiting to climb a small hill covered with the soft snow. I guess the sight of Canyon just sitting there, patiently waiting, was too much for Rex. He had to jump him. Rex jumped on Canyon, biting at his back legs. Then Totem joined in the frolic and they all balled up in a grand, old-fashioned dogfight. They made a lot of noise, but were not very serious. The problem was that we were not in the best place for fooling around—soft snow surrounded by deep slush and thin ice.

The dogs are almost too well-rested—when they don't get a good workout they have more energy, which means they pull harder, more wildly, and are sometimes difficult to control. Every day I am amazed by my small team. They are 7 in number, but pull like 14.

I was able to separate the dogs as I pushed the sled from behind. It was hard work! We barely made it across one big crack—I thought for sure the sled and the dogs were going for a swim. I was yelling at the dogs so hard that I was sweating. I had to keep the pressure on them, using my voice to let them know how important it was that they pull hard. It was absolutely necessary that they jump when I barked! "Yip, yip, Balzer, c'mon, Canyon and Rex. Dig in! Hep, hep, hep." If you ever heard me talking to my dogs, you'd probably think I'd lost my mind. I use a language all my own. Even my teammates laugh sometimes. I wonder if the dogs do, too?

MAY 13

Early this morning, at 4 o'clock, we were awakened by the sound of dogs howling. All 22 of them in unison. They don't howl for no reason, so I was sure there was a polar bear nearby.

They soon quieted down though and I fell back asleep—only to be awakened again a half-hour later when a gigantic snap in the ice sent a shockwave rolling through camp. A tremor lifted our tents, like an earthquake rolling right beneath our sleeping bags. The air was

The view from the high point on a pressure ridge: Martin and Victor chop a route through with an ax. Takako shovels snow into the big crack to form a bridge for the sleds.

filled with a thundering, grinding, rumbling roar, a very frightening sound, one we had not heard before. I shot out of my bag and quickly unzipped the tent door, ready to jump out in my long underwear to pull the tent to safety.

What I saw amazed me. A wall of ice, 20 feet tall and as long as a football field, was moving our way as if being pushed by the blade of a giant bulldozer. Blocks of ice as big as cars were falling off the top of the moving wall and being crushed beneath it. It moved toward us, threatening to crush us, too.

The dogs were in shock, standing perfectly still and quiet. All five of us were out of our tents, and we, too, were in shock. All we could do was watch, helplessly. Just as suddenly as it began, the wall of ice stopped, only 100 feet from our tents.

Julie has compared traveling on the Arctic Ocean to traveling on a big, floating jigsaw puzzle. This morning we watched as some of the bigger pieces shifted around. It was very powerful, very beautiful, too. And, I admit, quite frightening.

MAY 14

We spent today cutting our way through yet another tall jumble of ice. We would chop through a 20-foot-tall pressure ridge, only to discover a string of ten more beyond. We would travel west, then northwest, due north, then finally the direction we are really trying to go—south.

Due to all the chopping we do every day, our hands and feet are almost always frozen, like blocks of ice. As for the dogs, they are bored, tired of watching us hack away at the ice. They want to run—they didn't come here to sit around and wait! I wonder when will their patience end?

While most days are a lot of hard work, there is also great beauty. This morning a rare sun peeked through a misty fog. Delicate snowflakes parachuted down on us. Black lanes of deep icy water wound through the white snow and blue jumbles of ice. Only a handful of people have ever traveled through such conditions. As Martin and Victor chopped ahead of me, I waited on a floating pan of ice, policing two dog teams. Julie and Takako waited with Julie's team on the other side of a slushy, open lead. The silence was total, except for the distant sound of pickax hitting ice. It was so quiet I could hear individual snowflakes bouncing off the hood of my parka.

MAY 15

This morning when we got out of our tents, we found ourselves on a big slab of ice, completely surrounded by water. The next closest ice was 400 yards away. Victor quickly put on his skis and went searching for any kind of bridge or connection. He called for Martin, and the two of them began chopping at the only bridge they could find, a beautiful blue and green span of ice barely connected to the other side. Swinging their axes in unison, they attempted to smooth it out so that we could run the dogs and sleds across it before it gave way. The rest of us hurried to get the tents down, sleds loaded, and dogs hitched.

As usual, Martin's sled was the first to try to cross. Even as he was crossing, we could see a crack beginning between the bridge and our side of the ice. Julie and her sled quickly followed Martin, hoping to get across before the bridge collapsed. But she didn't make it.

Julie's lead dog, Tex, had just made it across when a big crack opened. Somehow Tex had slipped out of his harness and was on one side of the crack, the sled on the other. Two of her other dogs, Shaklee and Cochise, were dangling in midair, ten feet above the churning water, as big chunks of ice slid down around them. I yelled encouragement as Julie pulled her sled and team back before they fell in. As we watched the crack widen, we quickly realized that we were now truly stranded from Victor and Martin. Julie yelled across to Martin, "See you at Christmas!"—only half-joking.

We had talked many times about what to do if we ever got split up. Now it looked as if it was really happening. Each sled was self-sufficient, packed with a tent and plenty of food for man, woman, and dog. "What if we can never get across?" I said to Victor. "What if we're stuck here?"

On his side, Victor skied up and down the lead, looking for another safe place for us to cross. He found solid ice, but I was concerned that it was too thin. Sure enough, as my team tried to cross they slid into the water several times. At one point Balzer was completely underwater, and Canyon ended up doing a lot of swimming. At last, my team and I were safely across. But we still had to get Julie's team over—and we had to do it without her lead dog, Tex.

Team members are stranded on opposite sides of the ice, looking for a place to cross.
Greenland
North Pole
ARCTIC OCEAN
CANADA
NORTH AMERICA
UNITED STATES

About once a week, on their day off, Will meets with the other team members, usually in Takako and Julie's tent, to review the route. It changes continually because of the varying ice conditions and shifting ice.

As an experiment, Julie put Shaklee in the lead, a position he'd never tried. We had no idea how he'd do. She talked with Shaklee as she slipped the new harness over his shoulders, comforting and encouraging him. Then she walked to the back of her sled, grabbed tightly onto the uprights, and shouted, "Mush, doggies, mush!"

Showing no fear, Shaklee courageously led the team across and pulled Julie's sled powerfully over the thin ice. He was the hero of the day. If he'd chickened out, it would have been a big problem. Julie would have been separated from the rest of the team for who knows how long. As a reward, Julie let Shaklee stay in the lead the rest of the day.

MAY 17

I made an important decision today. It now appears obvious that we will not end the expedition in the town of Resolute, where we had hoped. We are drifting too far east, being pushed backward by moving ice. Every time we try to push west we run into unpassable pressure ridges. All we can do now is go south, and head for the coast of Canada at a point further east.

I have been studying maps at night, searching for a point on land to which we can head. It needs to be near a place of flat ice so that a small airplane can come get us. By that time the dogs will have been flown out and we will be traveling by our specially designed canoe-sleds.

Although we don't talk about it much, we are behind schedule. This travel has been far more difficult than any of us had imagined. It has nothing to do with poor planning—it is just an unusual year in the Arctic. There has been lots of snow, and while the weather is very cold, it is warmer than usual for this region, which means the ice has been unexpectedly thin with lots of open water. Judging by my new plan, we should reach land on July 4, Independence Day.

Story Questions & Activities

1. Why did Will Steger and his team go on this expedition?
2. How was the use of computers a major accomplishment of the trip?
3. Why do you think this selection is presented as a series of journal entries?
4. What is the main idea of this selection?
5. Imagine that Will Steger and his team could join the expedition in the painting on pages 342–343. What important information about exploring could they share with Lewis and Clark?

Write a Journal Entry

Imagine that you are Will Steger. Write a journal entry for July 4, the day that the team probably reached land. Describe how it feels to end the expedition. Then summarize the entire trip in a few sentences. End by explaining the importance of your trek across the Arctic.

Make a Chart

Use an encyclopedia, a geography book, or the Internet to discover the differences between the Arctic and the Antarctic. Make a chart of the major features of each area, including geography, wildlife, plant life, bodies of water, the weather, and early exploration.

Illustrate a Journal Entry

How does this selection show important information? One way is by using photographs and photo captions. Now it's your turn. Illustrate an event from one of the journal entries. Then write a caption for it. Be sure that your picture and the caption help explain the information in the entry.

The team tries to right Martin's sled, which has tipped over into the broken ice.

Find Out More

One of the reasons for the expedition is to draw attention to the problem of pollution in the Arctic. Find out more about pollution in this region. Start by using an encyclopedia, the ***Readers' Guide to Periodical Literature,*** or the Internet. Share your findings in a roundtable discussion with your classmates.

Read a Bar Graph

Like Will Steger, you, too, may have been amazed by the fact that water pollution exists in the Arctic Ocean. During the trip, Will Steger and his team collected many snow samples for scientists back home to test for pollution.

You may know that scientists measure water pollution in parts per million. This is the amount of pollution in a given volume of water. Pollution increases as the parts per million increase.

Look at this bar graph. It shows the changing pollution levels in the Hudson River in New York State. Notice that it measures water pollution in parts per million.

Pollution Level in Hudson River, New York State

Parts per million
800
600
400
200
0
1990 1991 1992 1993 1994 1995 1996 1997

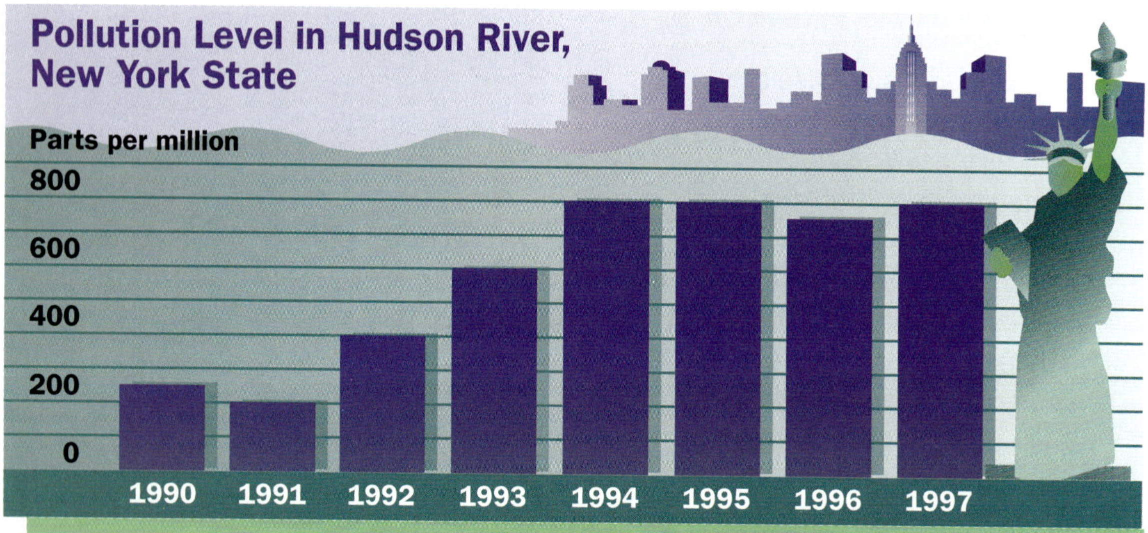

Use the bar graph to answer these questions.

1. What was the level of water pollution in the Hudson River in 1990?
2. What is the highest level of pollution recorded on this graph?
3. What happened to pollution levels between 1994 and 1995?
4. Did water pollution increase or decrease in 1996? By how much?
5. What kind of information can you learn from a bar graph?

TEST POWER

Test Tip

Clues to the meaning of the underlined word can usually be found close to the underlined word.

DIRECTIONS

Read the sample story. Then read each question about the story.

SAMPLE

Benjamin Franklin

When Benjamin Franklin was young, he loved to read. Whenever he could save enough money, he would buy books. Soon, Ben began to write articles and essays for his older brother's newspaper.

By the time Ben was sixteen, his essays had become very popular. Instead of using his own name on his stories, however, he used a <u>pseudonym</u>. He used a made-up name because he wrote things that criticized local politicians and the English government. Those who said negative things about the English were often arrested and put in jail. By using a false name, Benjamin Franklin protected his ability to write freely and honestly.

1 People who use a <u>pseudonym</u> are people who —

A like to buy books

B want everyone to recognize them

C use a name that is not their own

D are proud of their name

2 Benjamin Franklin might best be described as —

F patient

G clever

H snobbish

J unpopular

Stories in Art

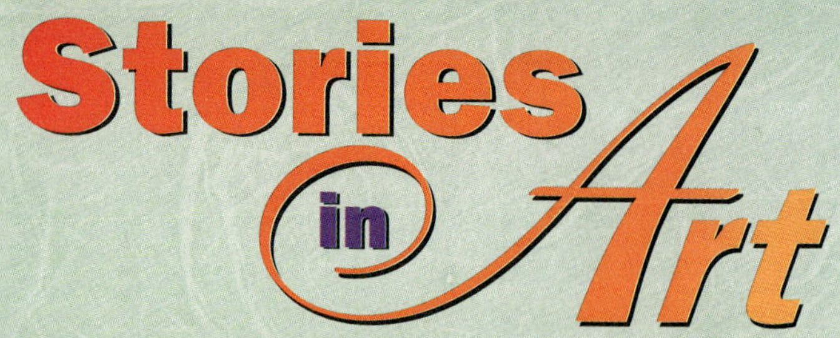

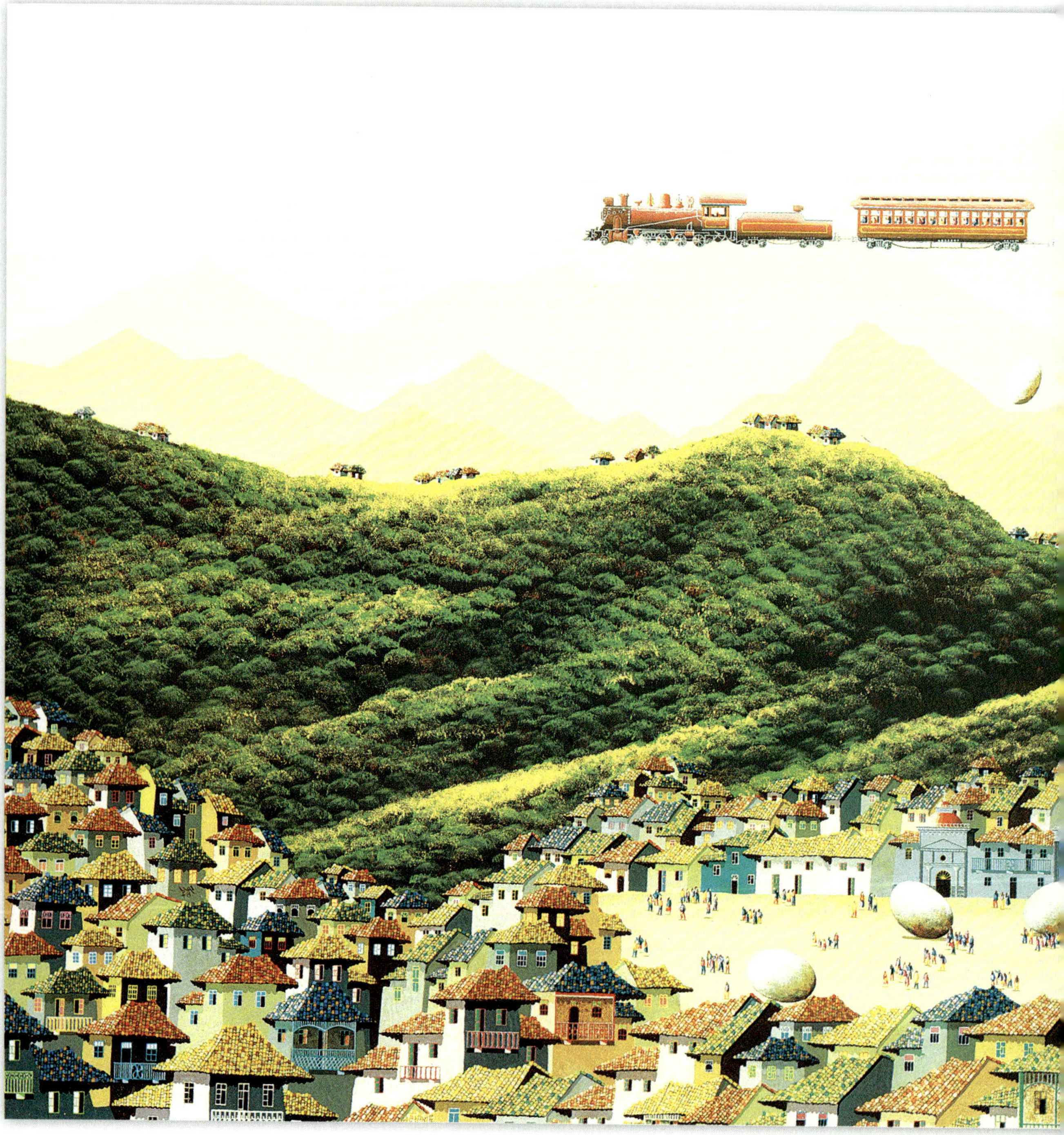

Iban Buscando Los Montes by Gonzalo Endara Crow

Have you used your imagination lately? If not, get ready for a workout!

Look at this painting. What do you notice about the setting? How is the artist using an ordinary hillside village to tell an extraordinary story?

Study the painting. Imagine that you are going to turn this picture into a fantastic story. Who would your characters be? What would be your setting? The problem? The events of your plot?

Meet Matt McElligott

Matthew McElligott has always loved drawing His mother was an art teacher, and he went on to study art in college. "Drawing," McElligott says, "gives me a place to use my imagination." Although much of his early work was with video and computer art, McElligott feels most excited these days working on books for young people. He particularly enjoyed working on *The Phantom Tollbooth.* "I remember reading this story when I was a child," McElligott says, "and I loved the opportunity to invent the strange characters and buildings for this piece."

Meet Susan Nanus

Susan Nanus has won many prizes for her writing, including the Christopher Award in 1988. She currently lives in Los Angeles, where she writes scripts for television and movies. Her skill at writing scripts can be seen in her play version of Norton Juster's *The Phantom Tollbooth.*

Meet Norton Juster

An architect who writes in his spare time, Norton Juster says about *The Phantom Tollbooth*, "I began to write what I thought was a short story—for my own relaxation. Before I knew it, it had created its own life and I was hooked. *The Phantom Tollbooth* was the result."

Juster says, "I am always a little embarrassed to call myself a writer." As he puts it, "The way I see things and think about things is as an architect." However, Juster has written a number of other books in addition to *The Phantom Tollbooth.*

The New York Times listed *The Phantom Tollbooth* as a best-selling children's book in 1962, as well as one of the fifty best books of 1960–1965. The book is the basis for this play and also a movie.

The

To

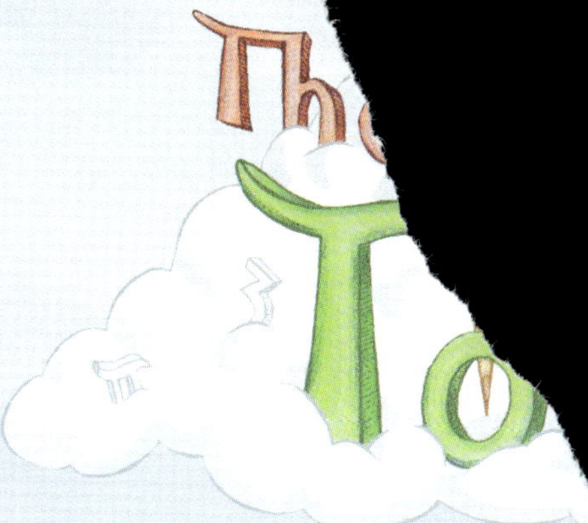

Based on the Boo

Dramatized by
Susan Nanus

Illustrated by
Matt McElligott

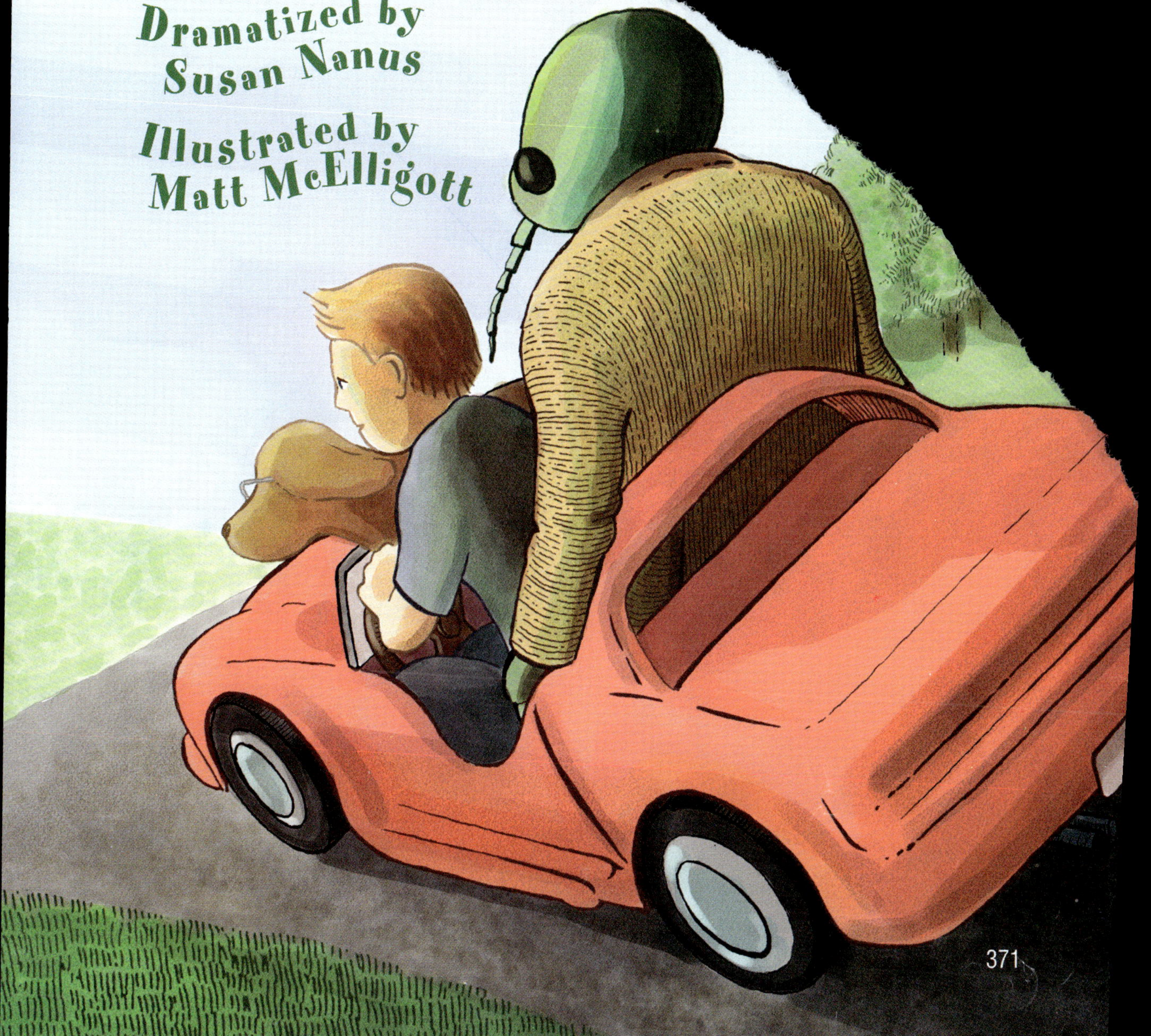

2
3
TER 4
NISTER 5
PAGE
CLOCK

Milo comes home from school one day to discover a mysterious package waiting for him. In it he finds a ready-to-assemble phantom tollbooth, complete with a rule book and map to strange lands that Milo has never heard of before. Milo chooses Dictionopolis as his destination, drives his car up to the tollbooth, deposits a coin, and takes off on his fantastic journey. Along the way, he teams up with the watch dog Tock. Together, they reach Dictionopolis, the land of words, where they meet King Azaz. Azaz has been feuding with his brother the Mathemagician, the king of Digitopolis, the land of numbers. The argument has been over this: Which is more important—words or numbers? It is up to Milo to help solve the kings' argument by rescuing their sisters, the Princesses Rhyme and Reason, who have been banished to the Castle-in-the-Air. In the past, the princesses have been able to settle the kings' differences. With the help of Humbug, who will serve as their guide, Milo and his friends leave for Digitopolis. "Something dreadful is going to happen to us," Humbug fears, as their journey to rescue the princesses begins.

The set of Digitopolis glitters in the background, while upstage right near the road, a small colorful wagon sits, looking quite deserted. On its side in large letters, a sign reads:

KAKAFONOUS A. DISCHORD
DOCTOR OF DISSONANCE

[*Enter* MILO, TOCK *and* HUMBUG, *fearfully. They look at the wagon.*]

TOCK. There's no doubt about it. That's where the noise was coming from.

HUMBUG. [*To Milo.*] Well, go on.

MILO. Go on what?

HUMBUG. Go on and see who's making all that noise in there. We can't just ignore a creature like that.

MILO. Creature? What kind of creature? Do you think he's dangerous?

HUMBUG. Go on, Milo. Knock on the door. We'll be right behind you.

MILO. O.K. Maybe he can tell us how much further it is to Digitopolis.

◀MILO, TOCK and HUMBUG

MILO *tiptoes up to the wagon door and knocks timidly. The moment he knocks, a terrible crash is heard inside the wagon, and* MILO *and the* OTHERS *jump back in fright. At the same time, the door flies open, and from the dark interior, a hoarse* VOICE *inquires.*]

VOICE. Have you ever heard a whole set of dishes dropped from the ceiling onto a hard stone floor? [*The* OTHERS *are speechless with fright.* MILO *shakes his head.* VOICE, *happily.*] Have you ever heard an ant wearing fur slippers walk across a thick wool carpet? [MILO *shakes his head again.*] Have you ever heard a blindfolded octopus unwrap a cellophane-covered bathtub? [MILO *shakes his head a third time.*] Ha! I knew it. [*He hops out, a little* MAN, *wearing a white coat, with a stethoscope around his neck, and a small mirror attached to his forehead, and with very huge ears, and a mortar and pestle in his hands. He stares at* MILO, TOCK, *and* HUMBUG.] None of you looks well at all! Tsk, tsk, not at all. [*He opens the top or side of his wagon, revealing a dusty interior resembling an old apothecary shop, with shelves lined with jars and boxes, a table, books, test tubes and bottles and measuring spoons.*]

MILO. [*Timidly.*] Are you a doctor?

DISCHORD'S VOICE. I am KAKAFONOUS A. DISCHORD, DOCTOR OF DISSONANCE! [*Several small explosions and a grinding crash are heard.*]

HUMBUG. [*Stuttering with fear.*] What does the "A" stand for?

DISCHORD. "AS LOUD AS POSSIBLE!" [*Two screeches and a bump are heard.*] Now, step a little closer and stick out your tongues. [DISCHORD *examines them.*] Just as I expected. [*He opens a large dusty book and thumbs through the pages.*] You're all suffering from a severe lack of noise. [DISCHORD *begins running around, collecting bottles, reading the labels to himself as he goes along.*] "Loud Cries." "Soft Cries." "Bangs," "Bongs," "Swishes," "Swooshes." "Snaps and Crackles." "Whistles and Gongs." "Squeeks," "Squacks," and "Miscellaneous Uproar." [*As he reads them off, he pours a little of each into a large glass beaker and stirs the mixture with a wooden spoon. The concoction smokes and bubbles.*] Be ready in just a moment.

MILO. [*Suspiciously.*] Just what kind of doctor are you?

DISCHORD. Well, you might say, I'm a specialist. I specialize in noises, from the loudest to the softest, and from the slightly annoying to the terribly unpleasant. For instance, have you ever heard a square-wheeled steamroller ride over a street full of hard-boiled eggs? [*Very loud crunching sounds are heard.*]

MILO. [*Holding his ears.*] But who would want all those terrible noises?

DISCHORD. [*Surprised at the question.*] Everybody does. Why, I'm so busy I can hardly fill all the orders for noise pills, racket lotion, clamor salve and hubbub tonic. That's all people seem to want these days. Years ago, everyone wanted pleasant sounds and business was terrible. But then the cities were built and there was a great need for honking horns, screeching trains, clanging bells and all the rest of those wonderfully unpleasant sounds we use so much today. I've been working overtime ever since and my medicine here is in great demand. All you have to do is take one spoonful every day, and you'll never have to hear another beautiful sound again. Here, try some.

HUMBUG. [*Backing away.*] If it's all the same to you, I'd rather not.

MILO. I don't want to be cured of beautiful sounds.

TOCK. Besides, there's no such sickness as a lack of noise.

DISCHORD. How true. That's what makes it so difficult to cure. [*Takes a large glass bottle from the shelf.*] Very well, if you want to go all through life suffering from a noise deficiency, I'll just give this to DYNNE for his lunch. [*Uncorks the bottle and pours the liquid into it. There is a rumbling and then a loud explosion accompanied by smoke, out of which* DYNNE, *a smog-like creature with yellow eyes and a frowning mouth, appears.*]

DYNNE. [*Smacking his lips.*] Ahhh, that was good, Master. I thought you'd never let me out. It was really cramped in there.

DISCHORD. This is my assistant, the Awful Dynne. You must forgive his appearance, for he really doesn't have any.

MILO. What is a Dynne?

DISCHORD. You mean you've never heard of the Awful Dynne? When you're playing in your room and making a great amount of noise, what do they tell you to stop?

MILO. That awful din.

DISCHORD. When the neighbors are playing their radio too loud late at night, what do you wish they'd turn down?

TOCK. That awful din.

DISCHORD. And when the street on your block is being repaired and the drills are working all day, what does everyone complain of?

HUMBUG. [*Brightly.*] The dreadful row.

DYNNE. The Dreadful Rauw was my grandfather. He perished in the great silence epidemic of 1712. I certainly can't understand why you don't like noise. Why, I heard an explosion last week that was so lovely, I groaned with appreciation for two days. [*He gives a loud groan at the memory.*]

DISCHORD. He's right, you know. Noise is the most valuable thing in the world.

MILO. King Azaz says words are.

DISCHORD. NONSENSE! Why, when a baby wants food, how does he ask?

DYNNE. [*Happily.*] He screams!

DISCHORD. And when a racing car wants gas?

DYNNE. [*Jumping for joy.*] It chokes!

DISCHORD. And what happens to the dawn when a new day begins?

DYNNE. [*Delighted.*] It breaks!

DISCHORD. You see how simple it is? [*To* DYNNE.] Isn't it time for us to go?

MILO. Where to? Maybe we're going the same way.

DYNNE. I doubt it. [*Picking up empty sacks from the table.*] We're going on our collection rounds. Once a day, I travel throughout the kingdom and collect all the wonderfully horrible and beautifully unpleasant sounds I can find and bring them back to the doctor to use in his medicine.

DISCHORD. Where are you going?

MILO. To Digitopolis.

DISCHORD. Oh, there are a number of ways to get to Digitopolis, if you know how to follow directions. Just take a look at the sign at the fork in the road. Though why you'd ever want to go there, I'll never know.

MILO. We want to talk to the Mathemagician.

HUMBUG. About the release of the Princesses Rhyme and Reason.

DISCHORD. Rhyme and Reason? I remember them. Very nice girls, but a little too quiet for my taste. In fact, I've been meaning to send them something that Dynne brought home by mistake and which I have absolutely no use for. [*He rummages through the wagon.*] Ah, here it is . . . or maybe you'd like it for yourself. [*Hands* MILO *a package.*]

MILO. What is it?

DISCHORD. The sounds of laughter. They're so unpleasant to hear, it's almost unbearable. All those giggles and snickers and happy shouts of joy, I don't know what Dynne was thinking of when he collected them. Here, take them to the princesses or keep them for yourselves, I don't care. Well, time to move on. Goodbye now and good luck! [*He has shut the wagon by now and gets in. Loud noises begin to erupt as* DYNNE *pulls the wagon offstage.*]

MILO. [*Calling after them.*] But wait! The fork in the road . . . you didn't tell us where it is . . .

TOCK. It's too late. He can't hear a thing.

HUMBUG. I could use a fork of my own, at the moment. And a knife and a spoon to go with it. All of a sudden, I feel very hungry.

MILO. So do I, but it's no use thinking about it. There won't be anything to eat until we reach Digitopolis. [*They get into the car.*]

Humbug. [*Rubbing his stomach.*] Well, the sooner the better is what I say.

[*A sign suddenly appears.*]

Voice. [*A strange voice from nowhere.*] But which way will get you there sooner? That is the question.

Tock. Did you hear something?

Milo. Look! The fork in the road and a signpost to Digitopolis! [*They read the sign.*]

Humbug. Let's travel by miles, it's shorter.

Milo. Let's travel by half inches. It's quicker.

Tock. But which road should we take? It must make a difference.

Milo. Do you think so?

Tock. Well, I'm not sure, but . . .

Humbug. He could be right. On the other hand, he could also be wrong. Does it make a difference or not?

Voice. Yes, indeed, indeed it does, certainly, my yes, it does make a difference.

[*The* Dodecahedron *appears, a 12-sided figure with a different face on each side, and with all the edges labeled with a small letter and all the angles labeled with a large letter. He wears a beret and peers at the others with a serious face. He doffs his cap and recites.*]

Dodecahedron.

My angles are many.
My sides are not few.
I'm the Dodecahedron.
Who are you?

Milo. What's a Dodecahedron?

Dodecahedron. [*Turning around slowly.*] See for yourself. A Dodecahedron is a mathematical shape with 12 faces. [*All his faces appear as he turns, each face with a different expression. He points to them.*] I usually use one at a time. It saves wear and tear. What are you called?

Milo. Milo.

Dodecahedron. That's an odd name. [*Changing his smiling face to a frowning one.*] And you have only one face.

Milo. [*Making sure it is still there.*] Is that bad?

Dodecahedron. You'll soon wear it out using it for everything. Is everyone with one face called Milo?

Milo. Oh, no. Some are called Billy or Jeffrey or Sally or Lisa or lots of other things.

Dodecahedron. How confusing. Here everything is called exactly what it is. The triangles are called triangles, the circles are called circles, and even the same numbers have the same name. Can you imagine what would happen if we named all the twos Billy or Jeffrey or Sally or Lisa or lots of other things? You'd have to say Robert plus John equals four, and if the fours were named Albert, things would be hopeless.

Milo. I never thought of it that way.

Dodecahedron. [*With an admonishing face.*] Then I suggest you begin at once, for in Digitopolis, everything is quite precise.

Milo. Then perhaps you can help us decide which road we should take.

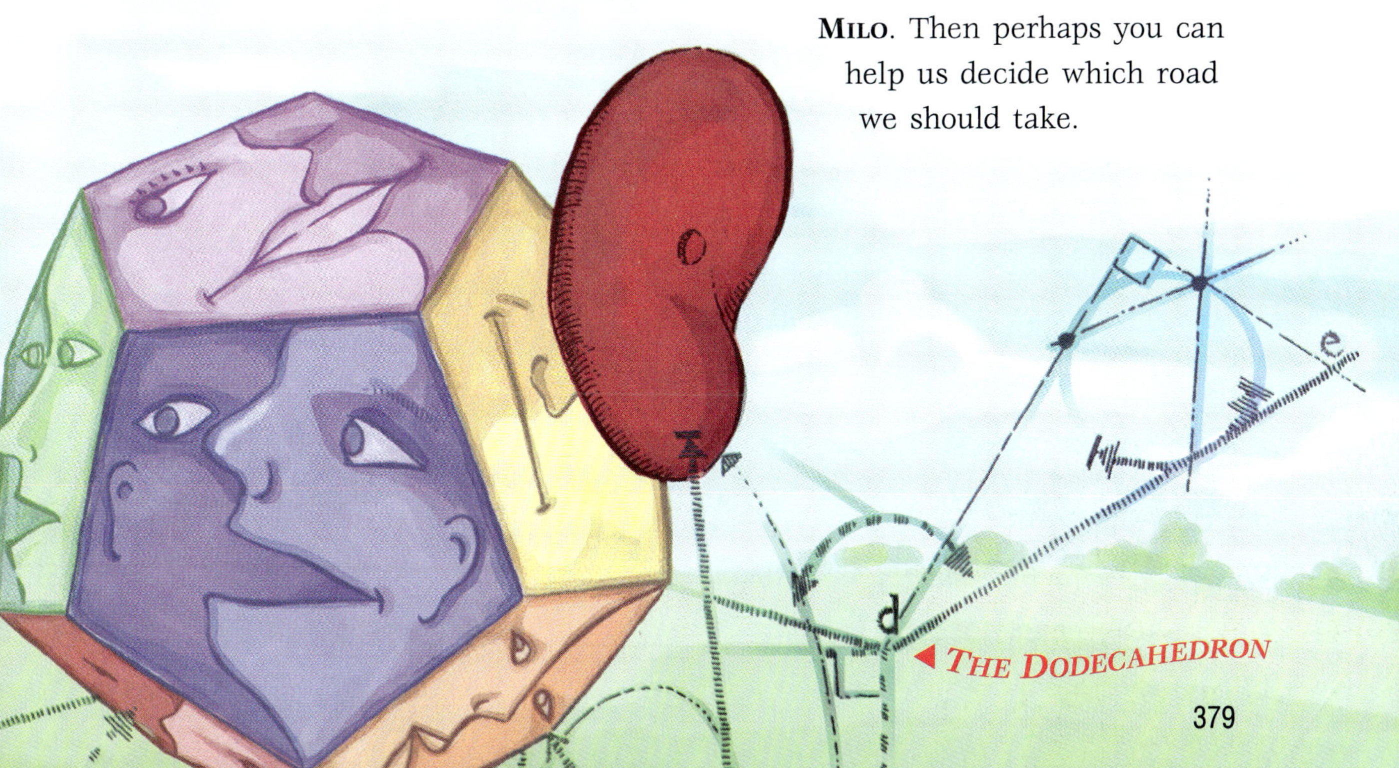

◀ The Dodecahedron

DODECAHEDRON. [*Happily.*] By all means. There's nothing to it. [*As he talks, the* THREE OTHERS *try to solve the problem on a large blackboard that is wheeled on stage for the occasion.*] Now, if a small car carrying 3 people at 30 miles an hour for 10 minutes along a road 5 miles long at 11:35 in the morning starts at the same time as 3 people who have been traveling in a little automobile at 20 miles an hour for 15 minutes on another road exactly twice as long as half the distance of the other, while a dog, a bug, and a boy travel an equal distance in the same time or the same distance in an equal time along a third road in mid-October, then which one arrives first and which is the best way to go?

HUMBUG. Seventeen!

MILO. [*Still figuring frantically.*] I'm not sure, but . . .

DODECAHEDRON. You'll have to do better than that.

MILO. I'm not very good at problems.

DODECAHEDRON. What a shame. They're so very useful. Why, did you know that if a beaver 2 feet long with a tail a foot and a half long can build a dam 12 feet high and 6 feet wide in 2 days, all you would need to build Boulder Dam is a beaver 68 feet long with a 51-foot tail?

HUMBUG. [*Grumbling as his pencil snaps.*] Where would you find a beaver that big?

DODECAHEDRON. I don't know, but if you did, you'd certainly know what to do with him.

MILO. That's crazy.

DODECAHEDRON. That may be true, but it's completely accurate, and as long as the answer is right, who cares if the question is wrong?

TOCK. [*Who has been patiently doing the first problem.*] All three roads arrive at the same place at the same time.

DODECAHEDRON. Correct! And I'll take you there myself. [*The blackboard rolls off, and* ALL FOUR *get into the car and drive off.*] Now you see how important problems are. If you hadn't done this one properly, you might have gone the wrong way.

MILO. But if all the roads arrive at the same place at the same time, then aren't they all the right road?

Dodecahedron. [*Glaring from his upset face.*] Certainly not! They're all the wrong way! Just because you have a choice, it doesn't mean that any of them *has* to be right.

[*Pointing in another direction.*] That's the way to Digitopolis and we'll be there any moment. [*Suddenly the lighting grows dimmer.*] In fact, we're here. Welcome to the Land of Numbers.

Humbug. [*Looking around at the barren landscape.*] It doesn't look very inviting.

Milo. Is this the place where numbers are made?

Dodecahedron. They're not made. You have to dig for them. Don't you know anything at all about numbers?

Milo. Well, I never really thought they were very important.

Dodecahedron. NOT IMPORTANT! Could you have tea for two without the 2? Or three blind mice without the 3? And how would you sail the seven seas without the 7?

Milo. All I meant was . . .

Dodecahedron. [*Continues shouting angrily.*] If you had high hopes, how would you know how high they were? And did you know that narrow escapes come in different widths? Would you travel the whole world wide without ever knowing how wide it was? And how could you do anything at long last without knowing how long the last was? Why numbers are the most beautiful and valuable things in the world. Just follow me and I'll show you. [*He motions to them and pantomimes walking through rocky terrain with the* Others *in tow. A doorway similar to the tollbooth appears and the* Dodecahedron *opens it and motions the* Others *to follow him through.*] Come along, come along. I can't wait for you all day. [*They enter the doorway and the lights are dimmed very low, as to simulate the interior of a cave. The sounds of scrapings and tapping, scuffling and digging are heard all around them. He hands them helmets with flashlights attached.*] Put these on.

Milo. [*Whispering.*] Where are we going?

Dodecahedron. We're here. This is the numbers mine. [*Lights up a little, revealing little* Men *digging and chopping, shoveling and scraping.*] Right this way and watch your step. [*His voice echoes and reverberates. Iridescent and glittery numbers seem to sparkle from everywhere.*]

Milo. [*Awed.*] Whose mine is it?

Voice of Mathemagician. By the four million eight hundred and twenty-seven thousand six hundred and fifty-nine hairs on my head, it's mine, of course! [*Enter the* Mathemagician, *carrying his long staff, which looks like a giant pencil.*]

Humbug. [*Already intimidated.*] It's a lovely mine, really it is.

Mathemagician. [*Proudly.*] The biggest numbers mine in the kingdom.

Milo. [*Excitedly.*] Are there any precious stones in it?

Mathemagician. PRECIOUS STONES! [*Then softly.*] By the eight million two hundred and forty-seven thousand three hundred and twelve threads in my robe, I'll say there are. Look here. [*Reaches in a cart, pulls out a small object, polishes it vigorously and holds it to the light, where it sparkles.*]

Milo. But that's a five.

Mathemagician. Exactly. As valuable a jewel as you'll find anywhere. Look at some of the others. [*Scoops up others and pours them into* Milo's *arms. They include all numbers from 1 to 9 and an assortment of zeros.*]

Dodecahedron. We dig them and polish them right here, and then send them all over the world. Marvelous, aren't they?

Tock. They are beautiful. [*He holds them up to compare them to the numbers on his clock body.*]

Milo. So that's where they come from. [*Looks at them and carefully hands them back, but drops a few, which smash and break in half.*] Oh, I'm sorry!

Mathemagician. [*Scooping them up.*] Oh, don't worry about that. We use the broken ones for fractions. How about some lunch?

[*Takes out a little whistle and blows it.* Two Miners *rush in carrying an immense caldron, which is bubbling and steaming.* The Workers *put down their tools and gather around to eat.*]

Humbug. That looks delicious! [Tock *and* Milo *also look hungrily at the pot.*]

Mathemagician. Perhaps you'd care for something to eat?

Milo. Oh, yes, sir!

Tock. Thank you.

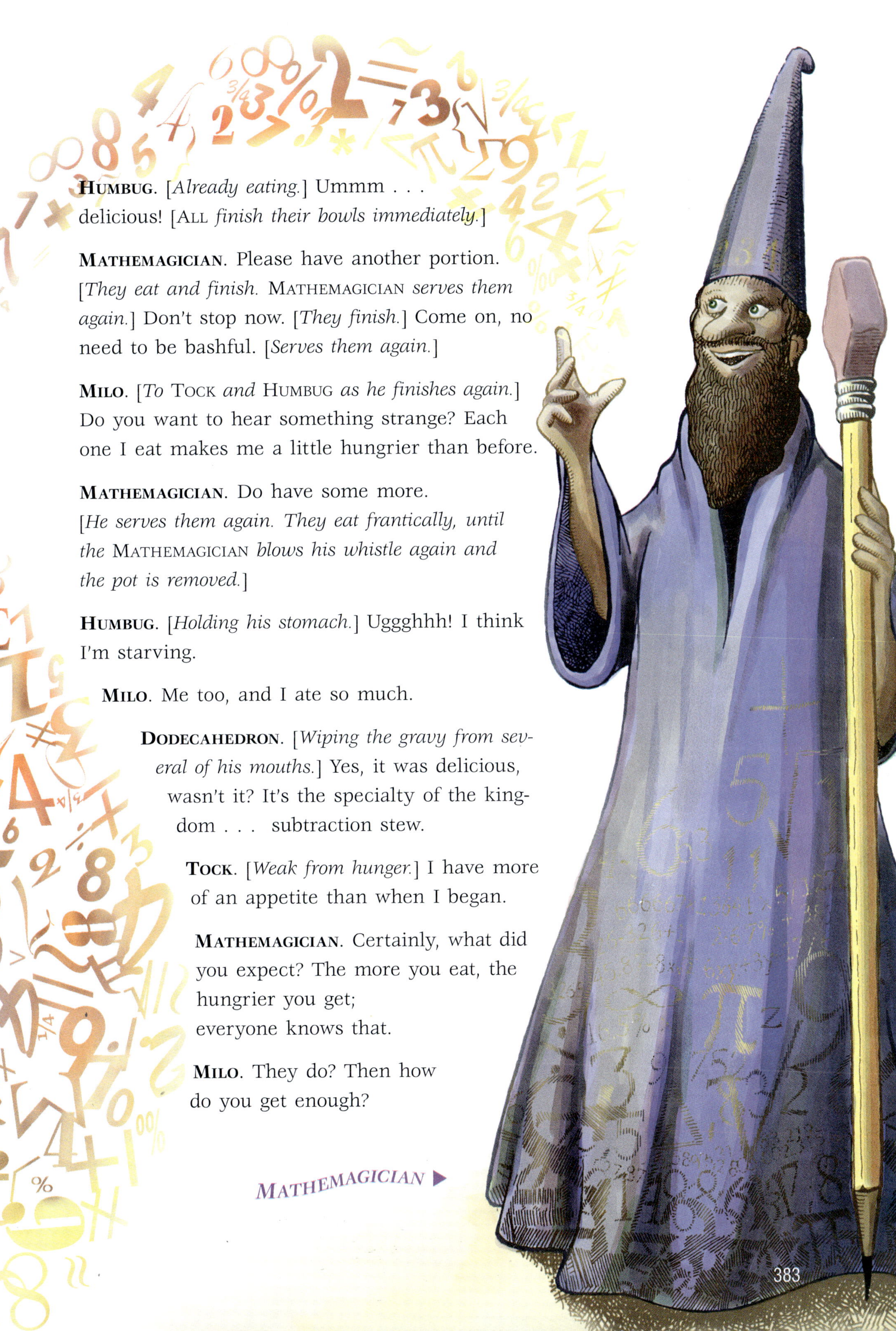

HUMBUG. [*Already eating.*] Ummm . . . delicious! [ALL *finish their bowls immediately.*]

MATHEMAGICIAN. Please have another portion. [*They eat and finish.* MATHEMAGICIAN *serves them again.*] Don't stop now. [*They finish.*] Come on, no need to be bashful. [*Serves them again.*]

MILO. [*To* TOCK *and* HUMBUG *as he finishes again.*] Do you want to hear something strange? Each one I eat makes me a little hungrier than before.

MATHEMAGICIAN. Do have some more. [*He serves them again. They eat frantically, until the* MATHEMAGICIAN *blows his whistle again and the pot is removed.*]

HUMBUG. [*Holding his stomach.*] Uggghhh! I think I'm starving.

MILO. Me too, and I ate so much.

DODECAHEDRON. [*Wiping the gravy from several of his mouths.*] Yes, it was delicious, wasn't it? It's the specialty of the kingdom . . . subtraction stew.

TOCK. [*Weak from hunger.*] I have more of an appetite than when I began.

MATHEMAGICIAN. Certainly, what did you expect? The more you eat, the hungrier you get;
everyone knows that.

MILO. They do? Then how do you get enough?

MATHEMAGICIAN ▶

MATHEMAGICIAN. Enough? Here in Digitopolis, we have our meals when we're full and eat until we're hungry. That way, when you don't have anything at all, you have more than enough. It's a very economical system. You must have been stuffed to have eaten so much.

DODECAHEDRON. It's completely logical. The more you want, the less you get, and the less you get, the more you have. Simple arithmetic, that's all. [TOCK, MILO *and* HUMBUG *look at him blankly.*] Now, look, suppose you had something and added nothing to it. What would you have?

MILO. The same.

DODECAHEDRON. Splendid! And suppose you had something and added less than nothing to it? What would you have then?

HUMBUG. Starvation! Oh, I'm so hungry.

DODECAHEDRON. Now, now, it's not as bad as all that. In a few hours, you'll be nice and full again . . . just in time for dinner.

MILO. But I only eat when I'm hungry.

MATHEMAGICIAN. [*Waving the eraser of his staff.*] What a curious idea. The next thing you'll have us believe is that you only sleep when you're tired.

[*The mine has disappeared as well as the* MINERS. *This may be done by dropping a curtain in front of the mine, through a blackout on the stage, while a single spotlight remains on the* MATHEMAGICIAN *and the* OTHERS, *or through the use of multi-level platforms. The* MINERS *may fall behind the platforms as two-dimensional props, which depict the* MATHEMAGICIAN'S *room, are dropped down or raised up.*]

HUMBUG. Where did everyone go?

MATHEMAGICIAN. Oh, they're still in the mine. I often find that the best way to get from one place to another is to erase everything and start again. Please make yourself at home.

[*They find themselves in a unique room, in which all the walls, tables, chairs, desks, cabinets and blackboards are labeled to show their heights, widths, depths and distances to and from each other. To one side is a gigantic notepad on an artist's easel, and from hooks and strings hang a collection of rulers, measures, weights and tapes, and all other measuring devices.*]

Milo. Do you always travel that way? [*He looks around in wonder.*]

Mathemagician. No, indeed! [*He pulls a plumbline from a hook and walks.*] Most of the time I take the shortest distance between any two points. And of course, when I have to be in several places at once . . . [*He writes "3 × 1 = 3" on the notepad with his staff.*] I simply multiply. [Three Figures *looking like the* Mathemagician *appear on a platform above.*]

Milo. How did you do that?

Mathemagician and the **Three.** There's nothing to it if you have a magic staff. [*The* Three *cancel themselves out and disappear.*]

Humbug. That's nothing but a big pencil.

Mathemagician. True enough, but once you learn to use it, there's no end to what you can do.

Milo. Can you make things disappear?

Mathemagician. Just step a little closer and watch this. [*Shows them that there is nothing up his sleeve or in his hat. He writes.*] "4 + 9 − 2 × 16 + 1 ÷ 3 × 6 − 67 + 8 × 2 − 3 + 26 − 1 − 34 + 3 − 7 + 2 − 5 =" [*He looks up expectantly.*]

Humbug. Seventeen?

Milo. It all comes to zero.

Mathemagician. Precisely. [*Makes a theatrical bow and rips off paper from notepad.*] Now, is there anything else you'd like to see? [*At this point, an appeal to the audience to see if anyone would like a problem solved.*]

Milo. Well . . . can you show me the biggest number there is?

Mathemagician. Why, I'd be delighted. [*Opening a closet door.*] We keep it right here. It took four miners to dig it out. [*He shows them a huge 3 twice as high as the* Mathemagician.]

Milo. No, that's not what I mean. Can you show me the longest number there is?

Mathemagician. Sure. [*Opens another door.*] Here it is. It took three carts to carry it here. [*Door reveals an 8 that is as wide as the 3 was high.*]

Milo. No, no, that's not what I meant either. [*Looks helplessly at* Tock.]

Tock. I think what you would like to see is the number of the greatest possible magnitude.

Mathemagician. Well, why didn't you say so? [*He busily measures them and all other things as he speaks, and marks it down.*] What's the greatest number you can think of? [*Here, an appeal can also be made to the audience or* Milo *may think of his own answers.*]

Milo. Uh . . . nine trillion, nine hundred and ninety-nine billion, nine hundred ninety-nine million, nine-hundred ninety-nine thousand, nine hundred and ninety-nine. [*He puffs.*]

Mathemagician. [*Writes that on the pad.*] Very good. Now add one to it. [Milo *or audience does.*] Now add one again. [Milo *or audience does so.*] Now add one again. Now add one again. Now add . . .

Milo. But when can I stop?

Mathemagician. Never. Because the number you want is always at least one more than the number you have, and it's so large that if you started saying it yesterday, you wouldn't finish tomorrow.

Humbug. Where could you ever find a number so big?

Mathemagician. In the same place they have the smallest number there is, and you know what that is?

Milo. The smallest number . . . let's see . . . one one-millionth?

Mathemagician. Almost. Now all you have to do is divide that in half and then divide that in half and then divide that in half and then divide that . . .

Milo. Doesn't that ever stop either?

Mathemagician. How can it when you can always take half of what you have and divide it in half again? Look. [*Pointing offstage.*] You see that line?

Milo. You mean that long one out there?

Mathemagician. That's it. Now, if you just follow that line forever, and when you reach the end, turn left, you will find the Land of Infinity. That's where the tallest, the shortest, the biggest, the smallest and the most and the least of everything are kept.

Milo. But how can you follow anything forever? You know, I get the feeling that everything in Digitopolis is very difficult.

Mathemagician. But on the other hand, I think you'll find that the only thing you can do easily is be wrong, and that's hardly worth the effort.

Milo. But . . . what bothers me is . . . well, why is it that even when things are correct, they don't really seem to be right?

Mathemagician. [*Grows sad and quiet.*] How true. It's been that way ever since Rhyme and Reason were banished. [*Sadness turns to fury.*] AND ALL BECAUSE OF THAT STUBBORN WRETCH AZAZ! It's all his fault.

Milo. Maybe if you discussed it with him . . .

Mathemagician. He's just too unreasonable! Why, just last month, I sent him a very friendly letter, which he never had the courtesy to answer. See for yourself. [*Puts the letter on the easel. The letter reads:*]

4738 1919,
667 394107 5841 62589
85371 14 39588 7190434 203
27689 57131 481206.
5864 98053,
62179875073

Milo. But maybe he doesn't understand numbers.

Mathemagician. Nonsense! Everybody understands numbers. No matter what language you speak, they always mean the same thing. A 7 is a 7 everywhere in the world.

Milo. [*To* Tock *and* Humbug.] Everyone is so sensitive about what he knows best.

Tock. With your permission, sir, we'd like to rescue Rhyme and Reason.

Mathemagician. Has Azaz agreed to it?

Tock. Yes, sir.

Mathemagician. THEN I DON'T! Ever since they've been banished, we've never agreed on anything, and we never will.

Milo. Never?

Mathemagician. NEVER! And if you can prove otherwise, you have my permission to go.

Milo. Well then, with whatever Azaz agrees, you disagree.

Mathemagician. Correct.

Milo. And with whatever Azaz disagrees, you agree.

Mathemagician. [*Yawning, cleaning his nails.*] Also correct.

Milo. Then, each of you agrees that he will disagree with whatever each of you agrees with, and if you both disagree with the same thing, aren't you really in agreement?

MATHEMAGICIAN. I'VE BEEN TRICKED! [*Figures it over, but comes up with the same answer.*]

TOCK. And now may we go?

MATHEMAGICIAN. [*Nods weakly.*] It's a long and dangerous journey. Long before you find them, the demons will know you're there. Watch out for them, because if you ever come face to face, it will be too late. But there is one other obstacle even more serious than that.

MILO. [*Terrified.*] What is it?

MATHEMAGICIAN. I'm afraid I can't tell you until you return. But maybe I can give you something to help you out. [*Claps hands. Enter the* DODECAHEDRON, *carrying something on a pillow. The* MATHEMAGICIAN *takes it.*] Here is your own magic staff. Use it well and there is nothing it can't do for you. [*Puts a small, gleaming pencil in* MILO'S *breast pocket.*]

HUMBUG. Are you sure you can't tell about that serious obstacle?

MATHEMAGICIAN. Only when you return. And now the Dodecahedron will escort you to the road that leads to the Castle-in-the-Air. Farewell, my friends, and good luck to you. [*They shake hands, say goodbye, and the* DODECAHEDRON *leads them off.*] Good luck to you! [*To himself.*] Because you're sure going to need it. [*He watches them through a telescope and marks down the calculations.*]

DODECAHEDRON. [*He re-enters.*] Well, they're on their way.

MATHEMAGICIAN. So I see. [DODECAHEDRON *stands waiting.*] Well, what is it?

DODECAHEDRON. I was just wondering myself, Your Numbership. What actually is the serious obstacle you were talking about?

MATHEMAGICIAN. [*Looks at him in surprise.*] You mean you really don't know?

Scene 2
The Land of Ignorance

[Lights up on RHYME *and* REASON, *in their castle, looking out two windows.]*

RHYME.
I'm worried sick, I must confess
I wonder if they'll have success
All the others tried in vain,
And were never seen or heard again.

REASON. Now, Rhyme, there's no need to be so pessimistic. Milo, Tock, and Humbug have just as much chance of succeeding as they do of failing.

RHYME.
But the demons are so deadly smart.
They'll stuff your brain and fill your heart
With petty thoughts and selfish dreams
And trap you with their nasty schemes.

REASON. Now, Rhyme, be reasonable, won't you? And calm down: you always talk in couplets when you get nervous. Milo has learned a lot from his journey. I think he's a match for the demons and that he might soon be knocking at our door. Now come on, cheer up, won't you?

RHYME. I'll try.

[Lights fade on the PRINCESSES *and come up on the little car, traveling slowly.]*

MILO. So this is the Land of Ignorance. It's so dark. I can hardly see a thing. Maybe we should wait until morning.

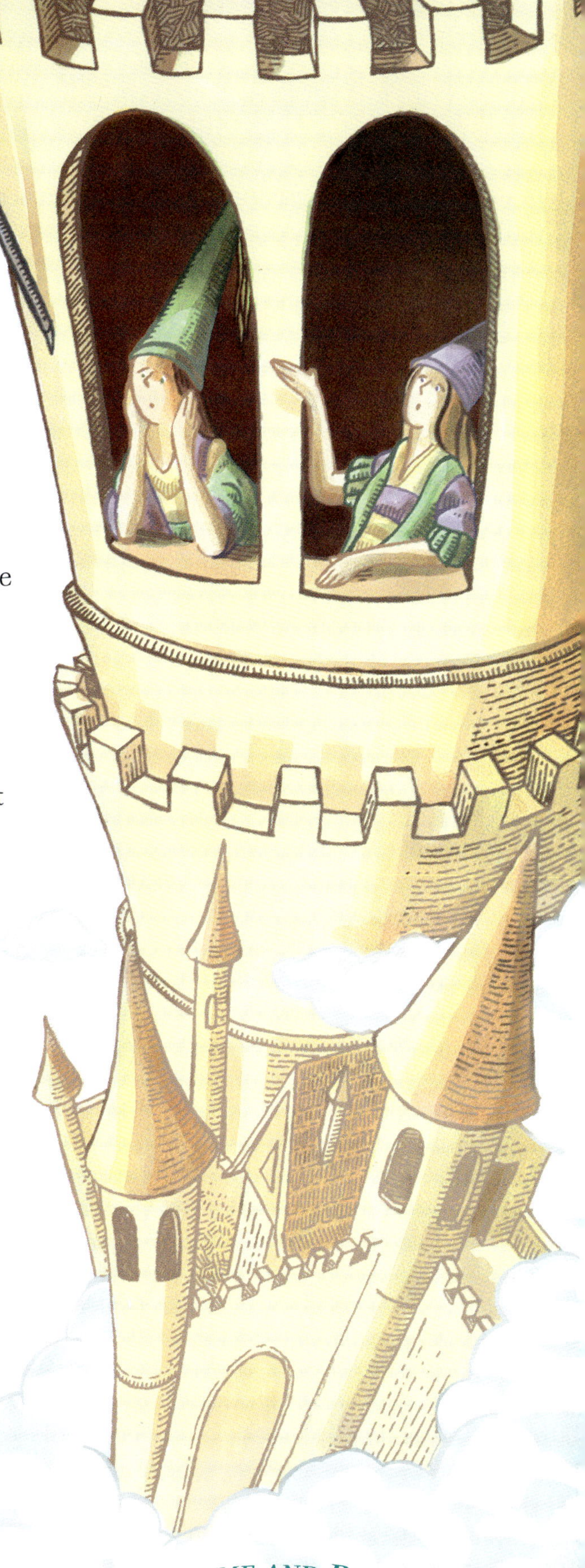

▲ PRINCESSES RHYME AND REASON

◀ BIRD

VOICE. They'll be mourning for you soon enough. [*They look up and see a large, soiled, ugly* BIRD *with a dangerous beak and a malicious expression.*]

MILO. I don't think you understand. We're looking for a place to spend the night.

BIRD. [*Shrieking.*] It's not yours to spend!

MILO. That doesn't make any sense, you see . . .

BIRD. Dollars or cents, it's still not yours to spend.

MILO. But I don't mean . . .

BIRD. Of course you're mean. Anybody who'd spend a night that doesn't belong to him is very mean.

TOCK. Must you interrupt like that?

BIRD. Naturally, it's my job. I take the words right out of your mouth. Haven't we met before? I'm the Everpresent Wordsnatcher.

MILO. Are you a demon?

BIRD. I'm afraid not. I've tried, but the best I can manage to be is a nuisance. [*Suddenly gets nervous as he looks beyond the three.*] And I don't have time to waste with you. [*Starts to leave.*]

TOCK. What is it? What's the matter?

MILO. Hey, don't leave. I wanted to ask you some questions . . . . Wait!

BIRD. Weight? Twenty-seven pounds. Bye-bye. [*Disappears.*]

MILO. Well, he was no help.

MAN. Perhaps I can be of some assistance to you? [*There appears a beautifully-dressed* MAN, *very polished and clean.*] Hello, little boy. [*Shakes* MILO'S *hand.*] And how's the faithful dog? [*Pats* TOCK.] And who is this handsome creature? [*Tips his hat to* HUMBUG.]

HUMBUG. [*To* OTHERS.] What a pleasant surprise to meet someone so nice in a place like this.

MAN. But before I help you out, I wonder if first you could spare me a little of your time, and help me with a few small jobs?

HUMBUG. Why, certainly.

TOCK. Gladly.

MILO. Sure, we'd be happy to.

MAN. Splendid, for there are just three tasks. First, I would like to move this pile of sand from here to there. [*Indicates through pantomime a large pile of sand.*] But I'm afraid that all I have are these tiny tweezers. [*Hands it to* MILO, *who begins moving the sand one grain at a time.*] Second, I would like to empty this well and fill that other, but I have no bucket, so you'll have to use this eyedropper. [*Hands it to* TOCK, *who begins to work.*] And finally, I must have a hole in this cliff, and here is a needle to dig it. [HUMBUG *eagerly begins. The* MAN *leans against a tree and stares vacantly off into space. The lights indicate the passage of time.*]

MILO. You know something? I've been working steadily for a long time now, and I don't feel the least bit tired or hungry. I could go right on the same way forever.

MAN. Maybe you will. [*He yawns.*]

MILO. [*Whispers to* TOCK.] Well, I wish I knew how long it was going to take.

TOCK. Why don't you use your magic staff and find out?

MILO. [*Takes out pencil and calculates. To* **MAN**.] Pardon me, sir, but it's going to take 837 years to finish these jobs.

MAN. Is that so? What a shame. Well then, you'd better get on with them.

MILO. But . . . it hardly seems worthwhile.

MAN. WORTHWHILE! Of course they're not worthwhile. I wouldn't ask you to do anything that was worthwhile.

MAN ▶

◀ INSINCERITY

TOCK. Then why bother?

MAN. Because, my friends, what could be more important than doing unimportant things? If you stop to do enough of them, you'll never get where you are going. [*Laughs villainously.*]

MILO. [*Gasps.*] Oh, no. You must be . . .

MAN. Quite correct! I am the Terrible Trivium, demon of petty tasks and worthless jobs, ogre of wasted effort and monster of habit. [*They start to back away from him.*] Don't try to leave, there's so much to do, and you still have 837 years to go on the first job.

MILO. But why do unimportant things?

MAN. Think of all the trouble it saves. If you spend all your time doing only the easy and useless jobs, you'll never have time to worry about the important ones which are so difficult. [*Walks toward them, whispering.*] Now do come and stay with me. We'll have such fun together. There are things to fill and things to empty, things to take away and things to bring back, things to pick up and things to put down . . . [*They are transfixed by his soothing voice. He is about to embrace them when a* VOICE *screams.*]

VOICE. RUN! RUN! [*They all wake up and run with the* TRIVIUM *behind. As the* VOICE *continues to call out directions, they follow until they lose the* TRIVIUM.] RUN! RUN! This way! This way! Over here! Over here! Up here! Down there! Quick, hurry up!

TOCK. [*Panting.*] I think we lost him.

VOICE. Keep going straight! Keep going straight! Now step up! Now step up!

MILO. Look out! [*They all fall into a trap.*] But he said "up"!

VOICE. Well, I hope you didn't expect to get anywhere by listening to me.

HUMBUG. We're in a deep pit! We'll never get out of here.

VOICE. That is quite an accurate evaluation of the situation.

MILO. [*Shouting angrily.*] Then why did you help us at all?

VOICE. Oh, I'd do as much for anybody. Bad advice is my specialty. [*A little furry* CREATURE *appears.*] I'm the DEMON OF INSINCERITY. I don't mean what I say; I don't mean what I do; and I don't mean what I am.

MILO. Then why don't you go away and leave us alone!

INSINCERITY'S VOICE. Now, there's no need to get angry. You're a very clever boy and I have complete confidence in you. You can certainly climb out of that pit . . . come on, try . . .

MILO. I'm not listening to one word you say! You're just telling me what you think I'd *like* to hear, and not what is important.

INSINCERITY. Well, if that's the way you feel about it . . .

MILO. That's the way I feel about it. We will manage by ourselves without any unnecessary advice from you.

INSINCERITY. [*Stamping his foot.*] Well, all right for you! Most people listen to what I say, but if that's the way you feel, then I'll just go home. [*Exits in a huff.*]

HUMBUG. [*Who has been quivering with fright.*] And don't you ever come back! Well. I guess we showed him, didn't we?

MILO. You know something? This place is a lot more dangerous than I ever imagined.

TOCK. [*Who's been surveying the situation.*] I think I figured a way to get out. Here, hop on my back. [MILO *does so.*] Now you, Humbug, on top of Milo. [*He does so.*] Now hook your umbrella onto that tree and hold on. [*They climb over* HUMBUG, *then pull him up.*]

HUMBUG. [*As they climb.*] Watch it! Watch it, now. Ow, be careful of my back! My back! Easy, easy . . . oh, this is so difficult. Aren't you finished yet?

TOCK. [*As he pulls up* HUMBUG.] There. Now, I'll lead for a while. Follow me, and we'll stay out of trouble. [*They walk and climb higher and higher.*]

HUMBUG. Can't we slow down a little?

TOCK. Something tells me we better reach the Castle-in-the-Air as soon as possible, and not stop to rest for a single moment. [*They speed up.*]

MILO. What is it, Tock? Did you see something?

TOCK. Just keep walking and don't look back.

MILO. You *did see* something!

HUMBUG. What is it? Another demon?

Tock. Not just one, I'm afraid. If you want to see what I'm talking about, then turn around. [*They turn around. The stage darkens and hundreds of yellow gleaming eyes can be seen.*]

Humbug. Good grief! Do you see how many there are? Hundreds! The Overbearing Know-It-All, the Gross Exaggeration, the Horrible Hopping Hindsight . . . and look over there! The Triple Demons of Compromise! Let's get out of here! [*Starts to scurry.*] Hurry up, you two! Must you be so slow about everything?

Milo. Look! There it is, up ahead! The Castle-in-the-Air!
[*They all run.*]

Humbug. They're gaining!

Milo. But there it is!

Humbug. I see it! I see it!

[*They reach the first step and are stopped by a little* Man *in a frock coat, sleeping on a worn ledger. He has a long quill pen and a bottle of ink at his side. He is covered with ink stains over his clothes and wears spectacles.*]

Tock. Shh! Be very careful. [*They try to step over him, but he wakes up.*]

Senses Taker. [*From sleeping position.*] Names? [*He sits up.*]

Humbug. Well, I . . .

Senses Taker. NAMES? [*He opens book and begins to write, splattering himself with ink.*]

Humbug. Uh . . . Humbug, Tock, and this is Milo.

Senses Taker. Splendid, splendid. I haven't had an "M" in ages.

Milo. What do you want our names for? We're sort of in a hurry.

Senses Taker. Oh, this won't take long. I'm the official Senses Taker and I must have some information before I can take your sense. Now if you'll just tell me: [*Handing them a form to fill. Speaking slowly and deliberately.*] when you were born, where you were born, why you were born, how old you are now, how old you were then, how old you'll be in a little while . . .

Milo. I wish he'd hurry up. At this rate, the demons will be here before we know it!

Senses Taker. . . . your mother's name, your father's name, where you live, how long you've lived there, the schools you've attended, the schools you haven't attended . . .

Humbug. I'm getting writer's cramp.

Tock. I smell something very evil and it's getting stronger every second. [*To* Senses Taker.] May we go now?

Senses Taker. Just as soon as you tell me your height, your weight, the number of books you've read this year . . .

Milo. We have to go!

Senses Taker. All right, all right, I'll give you the short form. [*Pulls out a small piece of paper.*] Destination?

Milo. But we have to . . .

Senses Taker. DESTINATION?

Milo, Tock and **Humbug**. The Castle-in-the-Air! [*They throw down their papers and run past him up the first few stairs.*]

Senses Taker. Stop! I'm sure you'd rather see what I have to show you. [*Snaps his fingers; they freeze.*] A circus of your very own. [*Circus music is heard.* Milo *seems to go into a trance.*] And wouldn't you enjoy this most wonderful smell?

[*Tock sniffs and goes into a trance.*] And here's something I know you'll enjoy hearing . . . [*To* Humbug. *The sound of cheers and applause for* Humbug *is heard, and he goes into a trance.*] There we are. And now, I'll just sit back and let the demons catch up with you.

[Milo *accidentally drops his package of gifts. The package of laughter from* Dr. Dischord *opens and the sounds of laughter are heard. After a moment,* Milo, Tock *and* Humbug *join in laughing and the spells are broken.*]

Milo. There was no circus.

Tock. There were no smells.

Humbug. The applause is gone.

Senses Taker. I warned you I was the Senses Taker. I'll steal your sense of Purpose, your sense of Duty, destroy your sense of Proportion—and but for one thing, you'd be helpless yet.

Milo. What's that?

SENSES TAKER. As long as you have the sound of laughter, I cannot take your sense of Humor. Agh! That horrible sense of Humor.

HUMBUG. HERE THEY COME! LET'S GET OUT OF HERE!

[*The* DEMONS *appear in nasty slithering hordes, running through the audience and up onto the stage, trying to attack* TOCK, MILO *and* HUMBUG. *The* THREE HEROES *run past the* SENSES TAKER *up the stairs toward the Castle-in-the-Air with the* DEMONS *snarling behind them.*]

MILO. Don't look back! Just keep going! [*They reach the castle. The* TWO PRINCESSES *appear in the windows.*]

PRINCESSES. *Hurry! Hurry!* We've been expecting you.

MILO. You must be the princesses. We've come to rescue you.

HUMBUG. And the demons are close behind!

TOCK. We should leave right away.

PRINCESSES. We're ready any time you are.

MILO. Good, now if you'll just come out. But wait a minute—there's no door! How can we rescue you from the Castle-in-the-Air if there's no way to get in or out?

HUMBUG. Hurry, Milo! They're gaining on us.

REASON. Take your time, Milo, and think about it.

MILO. Ummm, all right . . . just give me a second or two. [*He thinks hard.*]

HUMBUG. I think I feel sick.

MILO. I've got it! Where's that package of presents? [*Opens the package of letters.*] Ah, here it is. [*Takes out the letters and sticks them on the door, spelling.*] E-N-T-R-A-N-C-E. Entrance. Now, let's see. [*Rummages through and spells in smaller letters.*] P-U-S-H. Push. [*He pushes and a door opens. The* PRINCESSES *come out of the castle. Slowly, the* DEMONS *ascend the stairway.*]

HUMBUG. Oh, it's too late. They're coming up and there's no other way down!

MILO. Unless . . . [*Looks at* TOCK.] Well . . . Time flies, doesn't it?

TOCK. Quite often. Hold on, everyone, and I'll take you down.

HUMBUG. Can you carry us all?

TOCK. We'll soon find out. Ready or not, here we go!

[*His alarm begins to ring. They jump off the platform and disappear. The* DEMONS, *howling with rage, reach the top and find no one there. They see the* PRINCESSES *and the* HEROES *running across the stage and bound down the stairs after them and into the audience. There is a mad chase scene until they reach the stage again.*]

HUMBUG. I'm exhausted! I can't run another step.

MILO. We can't stop now . . .

TOCK. Milo! Look out there! [*The armies of* AZAZ *and* MATHEMAGICIAN *appear at the back of the theater, with the* KINGS *at their heads.*]

AZAZ. [*As they march toward the stage.*] Don't worry, Milo, we'll take over now.

MATHEMAGICIAN. Those demons may not know it, but their days are numbered!

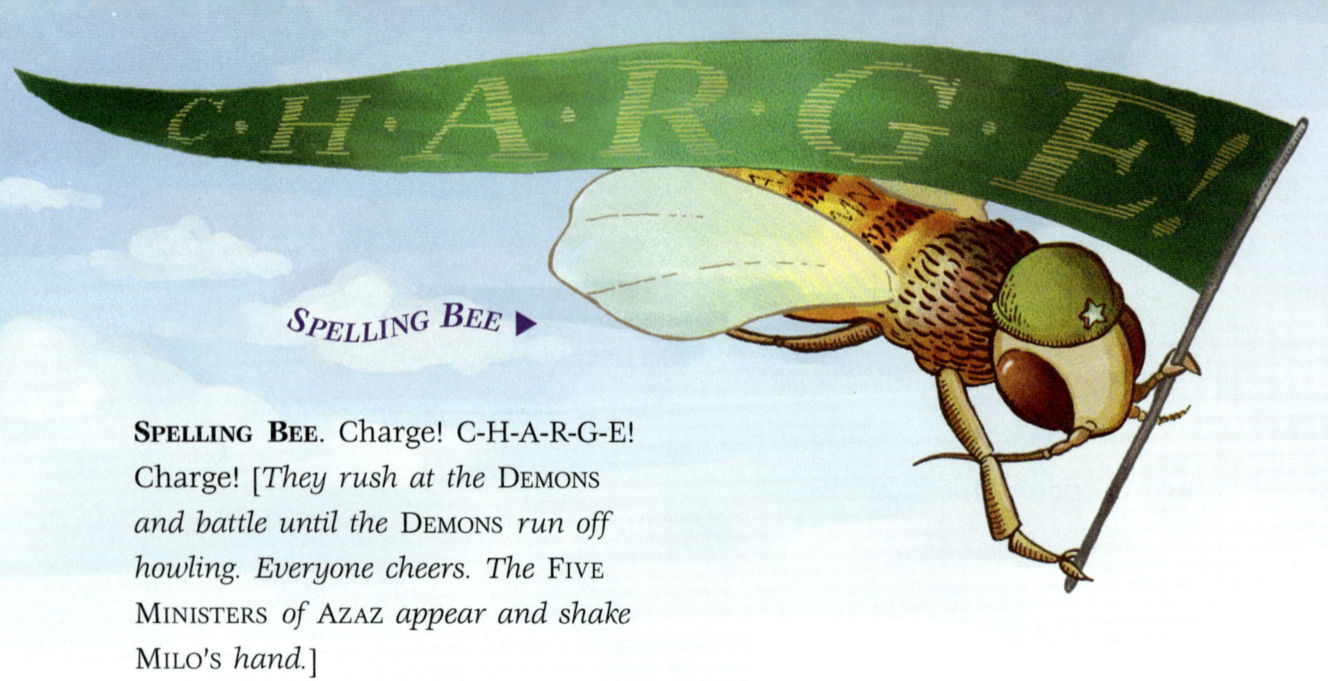

SPELLING BEE. Charge! C-H-A-R-G-E! Charge! [*They rush at the* DEMONS *and battle until the* DEMONS *run off howling. Everyone cheers. The* FIVE MINISTERS *of* AZAZ *appear and shake* MILO'S *hand.*]

MINISTER 1. Well done.

MINISTER 2. Fine job.

MINISTER 3. Good work!

MINISTER 4. Congratulations!

MINISTER 5. CHEERS! [EVERYONE *cheers again. A fanfare interrupts. A* PAGE *steps forward and reads from a large scroll.*]

PAGE.

Henceforth, and forthwith,
Let it be known by one and all,
That Rhyme and Reason
Reign once more in Wisdom.

[*The* PRINCESSES *bow gratefully and kiss their brothers, the Kings.*]

And furthermore,
The boy named Milo,
The dog known as Tock.
And the insect hereinafter
referred to as the Humbug
Are hereby declared to be Heroes
of the Realm.

[ALL *bow and salute the* HEROES.]

MILO. But we never could have done it without a lot of help.

REASON. That may be true, but you had the courage to try, and what you can do is often a matter of what you *will* do.

AZAZ. That's why there was one very important thing about your quest we couldn't discuss until you returned.

MILO. I remember. What was it?

AZAZ. Very simple. It was impossible!

MATHEMAGICIAN. *Completely* impossible!

HUMBUG. Do you mean . . . ? [*Feeling faint.*] Oh . . . I think I need to sit down.

AZAZ. Yes, indeed, but if we'd told you then, you might not have gone.

Mathemagician. And, as you discovered, many things are possible just as long as you don't know they're impossible.

Milo. I think I understand.

Rhyme. I'm afraid it's time to go now.

Reason. And you must say goodbye.

Milo. To everyone? [*Looks around at the* Crowd. *To* Tock *and* Humbug.] Can't you two come with me?

Humbug. I'm afraid not, old man. I'd like to, but I've arranged for a lecture tour which will keep me occupied for years.

Tock. And they do need a watchdog here.

Milo. Well, O.K., then. [Milo *hugs the* Humbug.]

Humbug. [*Sadly.*] Oh, bah.

Milo. [*He hugs* Tock, *and then faces* Everyone.] Well, goodbye. We all spent so much time together, I know I'm going to miss you. [*To the* Princesses.] I guess we would have reached you a lot sooner if I hadn't made so many mistakes.

Reason. You must never feel badly about making mistakes, Milo, as long as you take the trouble to learn from them. Very often you learn more by being wrong for the right reasons than you do by being right for the wrong ones.

Milo. But there's so much to learn.

Rhyme. That's true, but it's not just learning that's important. It's learning what to do with what you learn and learning why you learn things that matters.

Azaz ▶

MILO. I think I know what you mean, Princess. At least, I hope I do. [*The car is rolled forward and* MILO *climbs in.*] Goodbye! Goodbye! I'll be back someday! I will! Anyway, I'll try. [*As* MILO *drives, the set of the Land of Ignorance begins to move offstage.*]

AZAZ. Goodbye! Always remember. Words! Words! Words!

MATHEMAGICIAN. *And* numbers!

AZAZ. Now, don't tell me you think numbers are as important as words?

MATHEMAGICIAN. Is that so? Why, I'll have you know . . . [*The set disappears, and* MILO'*s room is seen onstage.*]

MILO. [*As he drives on.*] Oh, oh, I hope they don't start all over again.

Because I don't think I'll have much time in the near future to help them out. [*The sound of loud ticking is heard.* MILO *finds himself in his room. He gets out of the car and looks around.*]

THE CLOCK. Did someone mention time?

MILO. Boy, I must have been gone for an awful long time. I wonder what time it is. [*Looks at* CLOCK.] Five o'clock. I wonder what day it is. [*Looks at calendar.*] It's still today! I've only been gone for an hour! [*He continues to look at his calendar, and then begins to look at his books and toys and maps and chemistry set with great interest.*]

CLOCK. An hour. Sixty minutes. How long it really lasts depends on what you do with it. For some people, an hour seems to last forever. For others, just a moment, and so full of things to do.

MILO. [*Looks at* CLOCK.] Six o'clock already?

CLOCK. In an instant. In a trice. Before you have time to blink. [*The stage goes black in less than no time at all.*]

Story Questions & Activities

1. Is Digitopolis a real place? How do you know?
2. How is Milo's quest "impossible"?
3. How does this play mix reality and fantasy? Explain.
4. What is this play mostly about?
5. Imagine that this play took place in the land in the painting on pages 368–369. How might the setting, characters, and plot be different?

Write a Play Review

Imagine that you have just seen the play, *The Phantom Tollbooth*. Write a review of the performance for your school newspaper. Explain the stage-set design, the acting, and the action, or plot. End with a recommendation to your readers. Explain why the play is worth seeing—or not.

Design a Costume

Imagine that you are the costume designer for the play. Select one character in *The Phantom Tollbooth* and design a costume for him or her. Use the descriptions given in the play to make your sketches.

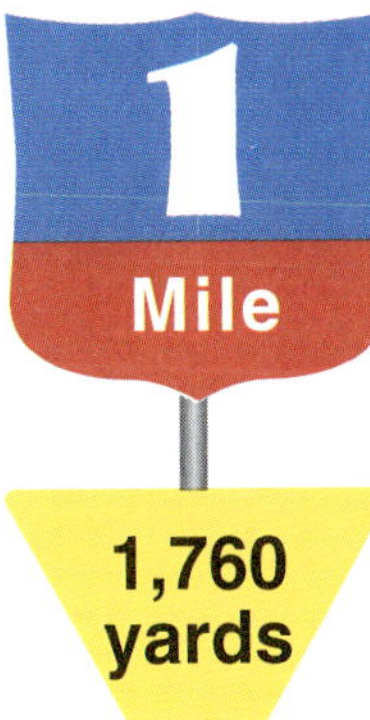

Make Mileage Signs

Milo learns the distance to Digitopolis in miles, yards, feet, inches, and half inches. Find out the distance from your town to three other towns or cities. Make a mileage sign for each place. Give the distance in miles, yards, feet, inches, and half inches.

Dodecahedron Infinity

Find Out More

The Phantom Tollbooth uses several mathematical terms. How many yards are there in a *rod*? How many sides does a *dodecahedron* have? Go through the selection and make a list of math words. Define the words by using a math book or a dictionary. Then use what you learn to prepare a glossary of math terms.

Proportion Rods Fractions

Miles Yards Feet Inches

Use a Map

One of the reasons that Milo's quest is "impossible" is that he doesn't have a map to find his way. If Milo had a map, he would have had less trouble finding the Castle-in-the-Air.

Look at the map below. It is of a typical town anywhere in the U.S.A. As you use the map, think about why maps are such helpful tools.

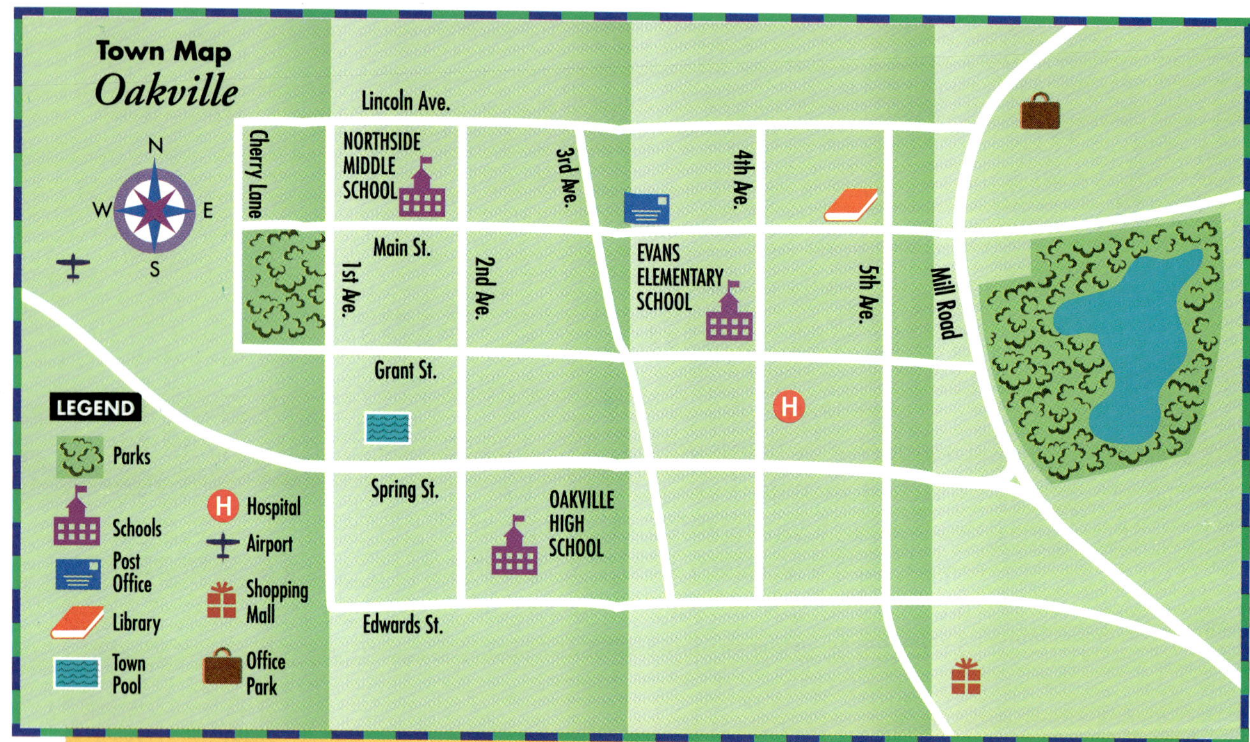

Use the map to answer these questions.

1. What symbol is used to show a park?
2. On what street is the elementary school?
3. How do you get from the post office to the town pool?
4. In which direction is the airport from the office park?
5. Why is it important to know how to read a map of your town?

TEST POWER

Test Tip

Remember that this is an open-book test.

DIRECTIONS

Read the sample story. Then read each question about the story.

SAMPLE

Yoga

Yoga is a combination of exercise, breathing, posture, and meditation. People who practice yoga seek to improve their health and sense of well-being.

No special equipment is needed to perform yoga. The practice uses only the body. When performing yoga, people stretch their bodies into different positions, called poses. These positions are designed to develop flexibility and strength. While the pose is held, it is important to breathe deeply through the nose. This breathing is designed to expand the lungs to their fullest capacity.

This combination of stretching and deep breathing is very healthy for the body. Like most forms of exercise, it takes a great deal of time and practice to become accomplished in yoga.

1 The passage provides evidence that poses are —

A deep breathing exercises

B yoga equipment

C strength builders

D easy

2 Judging by the passage, which of the following is the practice of yoga most likely to do?

F Find a new popularity

G Prepare athletes for swimming

H Cause injuries to joints

J Help muscles stay flexible

Stories in Art

This photograph shows a scene from the famous movie, *Titanic*. What do you notice about the details?

Look at the picture. What is happening to the ship? What information does the rowboat give you? Why is it important to the scene? How does the flare give you more information about the events?

Look at the photograph again. What do you think is the important information in the picture? Why? Do you think this is the most important moment in the movie? Explain.

The sinking *Titanic* from the movie *Titanic*, 1997

EXPLORING THE TITANIC

By Robert D. Ballard

The ocean liner R.M.S. Titanic *was built in 1911 and deemed "virtually unsinkable." However, on its maiden voyage in 1912, the ship struck an iceberg in the North Atlantic and sank, killing 1,500 of the 2,200 passengers aboard. In 1985, Robert D. Ballard and his team discovered the remains of the* Titanic *on the ocean floor. A year later, the team returned to explore the ship in their submarine* Alvin, *with the help of* Jason Jr., *or* JJ, *their robot.*

Rusticles hang from two large bollards.

As *Alvin*'s lights glow from above, *Jason Junior* explores the *Titanic*'s starboard anchor.

Our second view of the *Titanic* was breathtaking. As we glided soundlessly across the ocean bottom, the razor's edge of the bow loomed out of the darkness. The great ship towered above us. Suddenly it seemed to be coming right at us, about to run us over. My first reaction was that we had to get out of the way. But the *Titanic* wasn't going anywhere. As we gently brought our sub closer, we could see the bow more clearly. Both of her huge anchors were still in place. But the bow was buried more than sixty feet in mud, far too deep for anyone to pull her out of the ooze.

It looked as though the metal hull was slowly melting away. What seemed like frozen rivers of rust covered the ship's side and spread out over the ocean bottom. It was almost as if the blood of the great ship lay in pools on the ocean floor.

As *Alvin* rose in slow motion up the ghostly side of the ship, I could see our lights reflecting off the still-unbroken glass of the *Titanic*'s portholes. They made me think of cats' eyes gleaming in the dark. In places the rust formations over the portholes looked like eyelashes with tears, as though

This scale drawing shows the enormous distance between Ballard's search ship *Knorr* and the *Titanic* wreck.

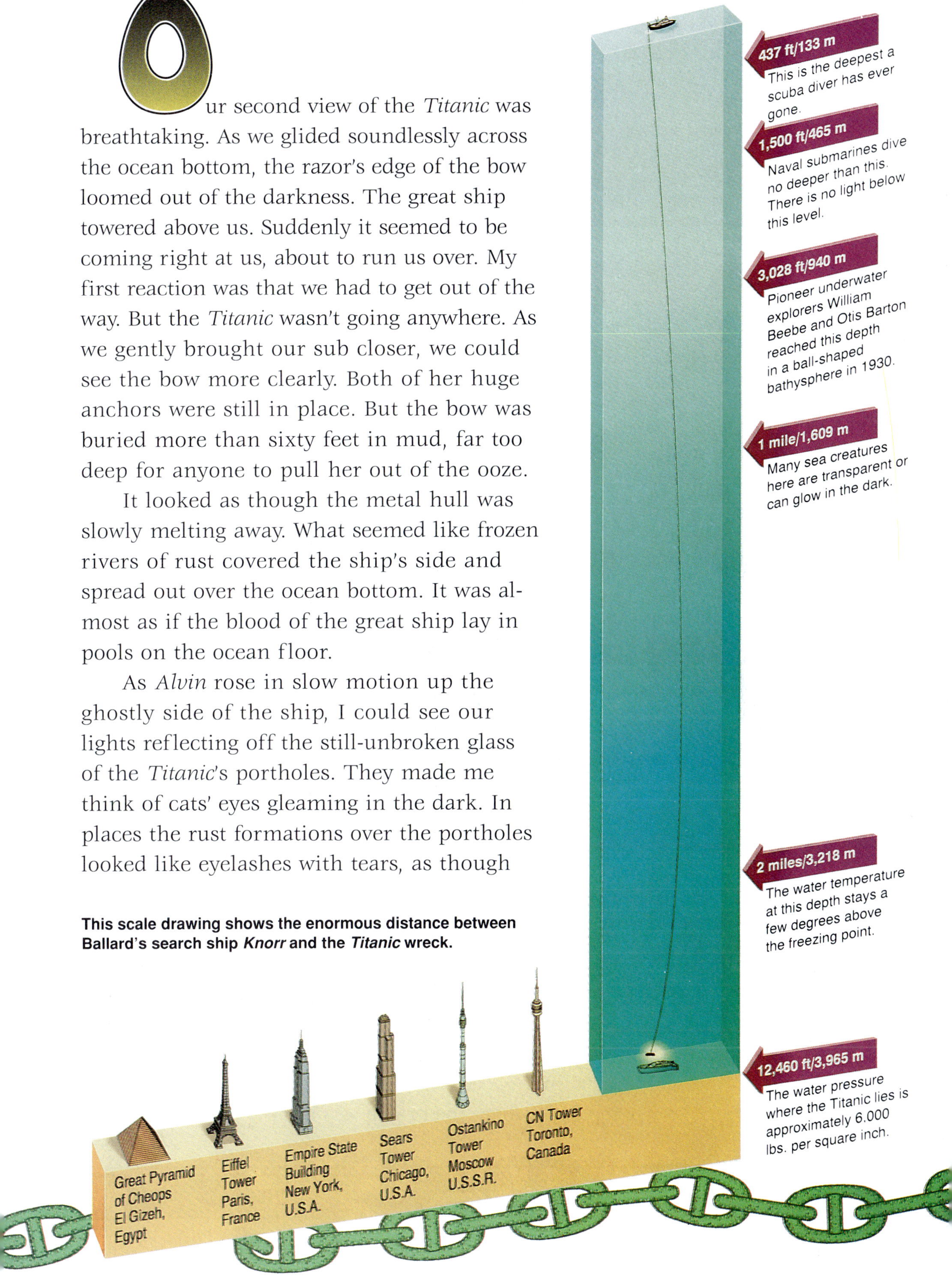

the *Titanic* were crying. I could also see a lot of reddish-brown stalactites of rust over the wreck, like long icicles. I decided to call them "rusticles." This rust turned out to be very fragile. If touched by our sub, it disappeared like a cloud of smoke.

The *Titanic*'s bridge in 1912

The *Titanic*'s bridge in 1986

As we rose further and began to move across the mighty forward deck, I was amazed at the sheer size of everything: giant bollards and shiny bronze capstans that were used for winding ropes and cables; the huge links of the anchor chains. When you were there on the spot, the ship was truly titanic.

I strained to get a good look at the deck's wood planking, just four feet below us. Then my heart dropped to my stomach. "It's gone!" I muttered. Most of the *Titanic*'s wooden deck had been eaten away. Millions of little wood-eating worms had done more damage than the iceberg and the salt water. I began to wonder whether the metal deck below the destroyed wood planking would support our weight when *Alvin* landed.

We would soon find out. Slowly we moved into position to make our first landing test on the forward deck just next to the fallen mast. As we made our approach, our hearts beat quickly. We knew there was a real risk of crashing through the deck. The sub settled down, making a muffled crunching noise. If the deck gave way, we'd be trapped in collapsing wreckage. But it held, and we settled firmly. That meant there was a good chance that the *Titanic*'s decks would support us at other landing sites.

We carefully lifted off and turned toward the stern. The dim outline of the ship's superstructure came into view: first B Deck, then A, finally the Boat Deck—the top deck where the bridge was located. It was here that

The bow section of the *Titanic*

the captain and his officers had guided the ship across the Atlantic. The wooden wheelhouse was gone, probably knocked away in the sinking. But the bronze telemotor control to which the ship's wheel had once been attached stood intact, polished to a shine by the current. We then safely tested this second landing site.

I had an eerie feeling as we glided along exploring the wreck. As I peered through my porthole, I could easily imagine people walking along the deck and looking out the windows of the ship that I was looking into. Here I was at the bottom of the ocean looking at a kind of time capsule from history.

Suddenly, as we rose up the port side of the ship, the sub shuddered and made a clanging noise. A waterfall of rust covered our portholes. "We've hit something!" I exclaimed. "What is it?"

"I don't know," our pilot replied. "I'm backing off." Unseen overhangs are the nightmare of the deep-sub pilot. Carefully, the pilot backed away from the hull and brought us slowly upward. Then, directly in front of our forward porthole, a big lifeboat davit slid by. We had hit one of the metal arms that held the lifeboats as they were lowered. This davit was one of the two that had held boat No. 8, the boat Mrs. Straus had refused to enter that night. She was the wife of the owner of Macy's department store in New York. When she had been offered a chance to save herself in one of the lifeboats, she had turned to her husband and said, "We have been living together for many years. Where you go, I go." Calmly, the two of them had sat down on a pile of deck chairs to wait for the end.

Now, as we peered out our portholes, it seemed as if the Boat Deck were crowded with passengers. I could almost hear the cry, "Women and children first!"

We knew from the previous year's pictures that the stern had broken off the ship, so we continued back to search for the severed end of the intact bow section. Just beyond the gaping hole where the second funnel had been, the deck began to plunge down at a dangerous angle. The graceful lines of the ship disappeared in a twisted mess of torn steel plating, upturned portholes, and jumbled wreckage. We saw enough to know that the decks of the ship had collapsed in on one another like a giant accordion. With an unexpectedly strong current pushing us toward this twisted wreckage, we veered away and headed for the surface.

The Grand Staircase in 1912

The next day we landed on the deck next to the very edge of the Grand Staircase, which had once been covered by an elegant glass dome. The dome hadn't survived the plunge, but the staircase shaft had, and to me it still represented the fabulous luxury of the ship. *Alvin* now rested quietly on the top deck of the R.M.S. *Titanic* directly above the place where three elevators had carried first-class passengers who did not wish to use the splendid Grand Staircase.

We, however, would take the stairs with *JJ* the robot, our R2D2 of the deep. This would be the first deepwater test for our remote-controlled swimming eyeball, and we were very nervous about it. No one knew whether *JJ*'s motors could stand up to the enormous ocean pressure of more than 6,000 pounds per square inch.

Jason Junior **illuminates a pillar still standing in the foyer of the Grand Staircase. *Alvin* has landed on the Boat Deck beside the collapsed roof that once held the glass dome over the staircase. From inside the submarine we guide *JJ* down the staircase shaft as far as B Deck. The illustration (*inset*) shows a cross-section of *JJ*'s descent with an outline of the original staircase.**

Using a control box with a joystick that operated like a video game, the operator cautiously steered *JJ* out of his garage attached to the front of *Alvin.* Slowly *JJ* went inching down into the yawning blackness of the Grand Staircase. More and more cable was let out as he dropped deeper and deeper.

We could see what *JJ* was seeing on our video in the sub. But at first *JJ* could see nothing. Then, as he dropped deeper, a room appeared off the portside foyer on A Deck. *JJ* swung around and our co-pilot saw something in the distance. "Look at that," he said softly. "Look at that chandelier."

Now I could see it, too. "No, it can't be a chandelier," I said. "It couldn't possibly have survived."

I couldn't believe my eyes. The ship had fallen two and a half miles, hitting the bottom with the force of a train running into a mountain, and here was an almost perfectly preserved light fixture! *JJ* left the stairwell and started to enter the room, managing to get within a foot of the fixture. To our astonishment, we saw a feathery piece of coral sprouting from it. We could even see the sockets where the light bulbs had been fitted! "This is fantastic," I exulted.

"Bob, we're running short of time. We have to return to the surface." Our pilot's words cut like a knife through my excitement. Here we were deep inside the *Titanic,* actually going down the Grand Staircase, but we had used up all the time that we had to stay safely on the bottom. I knew our pilot was just following orders, but I still wanted to shout in protest.

Captain Edward J. Smith

Our little robot soldier emerged from the black hole and shone his lights toward us, bathing the interior of the sub in an unearthly glow. For a moment it felt as if an alien spaceship were hovering nearby. But that feeling quickly gave way to one of victory, thanks to our little friend. *JJ* had been a complete success.

On our next day's dive, we crossed over what had once been Captain Smith's cabin. Its outer wall now lay collapsed on the deck, as though a giant had brought his fist down on it. We passed within inches of one of the cabin's windows. Was this, I wondered, a window that Captain Smith had cranked open to let a little fresh air into his cabin before going to bed?

Suddenly a large piece of broken railing loomed out of the darkness. It seemed to be heading right for my viewport. I immediately warned the pilot who quickly turned *Alvin*'s stern around, rotating us free of the obstacle.

Now we began to drop onto the starboard Boat Deck. As we glided along, I felt as though I were visiting a ghost town where suddenly one day everyone had closed up shop and left.

An empty lifeboat davit stood nearby. Ahead I could see where the *Titanic*'s lifeboats had rested. It was on this very deck that the crowds of passengers had stood waiting to get into the boats. They had not known until the last moments that there were not

Wives saying goodbye to their husbands as lifeboats are loaded on the Boat Deck

enough lifeboats for everyone. It was also from this deck that you could have heard the *Titanic*'s brave band playing cheerful music to boost the crowd's spirits as the slope of the deck grew steeper and steeper.

Jason Jr. now went for a stroll along the Boat Deck. As he slowly made his way along, he looked in the windows of several first-class cabins as well as into some passageways, including one that still bore the words, "First-Class Entrance." As *JJ* passed by the gymnasium windows, I could see bits and pieces of equipment amid the rubble, including some metal grillwork that had been part of the electric camel, an old-fashioned exercise machine. We could also see various wheel shapes and a control lever. Much of the gym's

Stern Section

- **A painted metal footboard from a bed (*top left*)**
- **This sink from a second-class stateroom could be tipped to allow the water to drain out (*top middle*)**
- **The white porcelain of this bathtub is almost hidden by rust in contrast (*top right inset*) to the way it appeared when new (*top right*).**
- **The cast-iron frame of one of the benches from the *Titanic's* decks (*bottom right*)**

ceiling was covered with rust. This was where the gym instructor, dressed in white flannel trousers, had urged passengers to try the gym machines. And, on the last night, passengers had gathered here for warmth as the lifeboats were being lowered.

I could see *JJ* far off down the deck, turning this way and that to get a better view inside doorways and various windows. It was almost as though our little robot had a mind of his own.

But now we had to bring him home. We had been on the *Titanic* for hours. Once again it was time to head back to the surface.

The morning of July 18 was lovely and warm, but I felt edgy about the day's mission. We had decided to visit the *Titanic*'s debris field. Along the 1,970 feet that separated the broken-off bow and stern pieces of the wreck, there was a large scattering of all kinds of objects from

The Debris Field
Between the separated sections of the *Titanic* lie thousands of objects that spilled out of the ship when she sank.

Bow Section

the ship. Everything from lumps of coal to wrought-iron deck benches had fallen to the bottom as she broke in two and sank. But I was anxious about what we might find down there among the rubble. I had often been asked about the possibility of finding human bodies. It was a chilling thought. We had not seen any signs of human remains so far, but I knew that if we were to find any, it would most likely be during this dive.

As the first fragments of wreckage began to appear on the bottom, I felt like we were entering a bombed-out museum. Thousands upon thousands of objects littered the rolling fields of ocean bottom, many of them perfectly preserved. The guts of the *Titanic* lay spilled out across the ocean floor. Cups and saucers, silver serving trays, pots and pans, wine bottles, boots, chamber pots, space heaters, bathtubs, suitcases, and more.

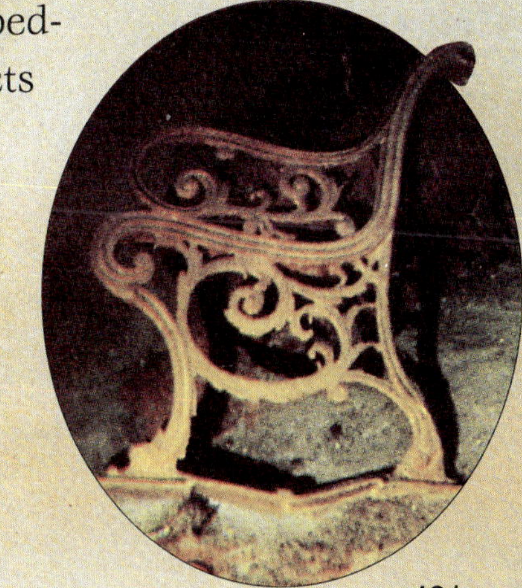

Then, without warning, I found myself looking into the ghostly eyes of a small, white smiling face. For a split second I thought it was a skull—and it really scared me. Then I realized I was looking at a doll's head, its hair and clothes gone.

My shock turned to sadness as I began to wonder who had owned this toy. Had the girl survived in one of the lifeboats? Or had she clutched the doll tightly as she sank in the icy waters?

We moved on through this amazing scenery. There were so many things scattered about that it became difficult to keep track of them. We came across one of the ship's boilers, and there on top of it sat an upright rusty metal cup like the ones the crew had used. It looked as though it had been placed there by a stoker moments before water had burst into the boiler room. It was astonishing to think that in fact this cup had just fluttered down that night to land right on top of a boiler.

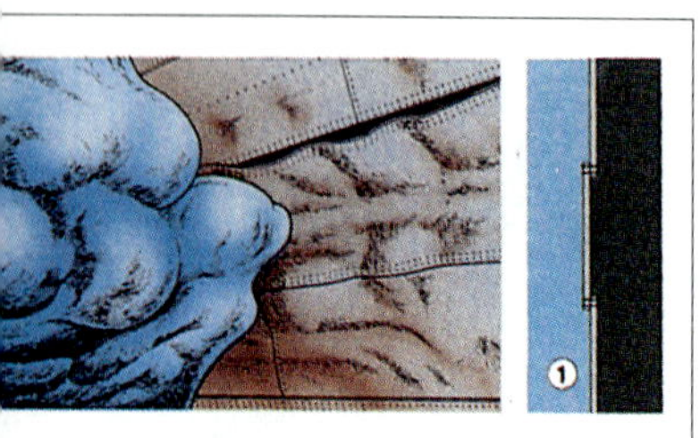

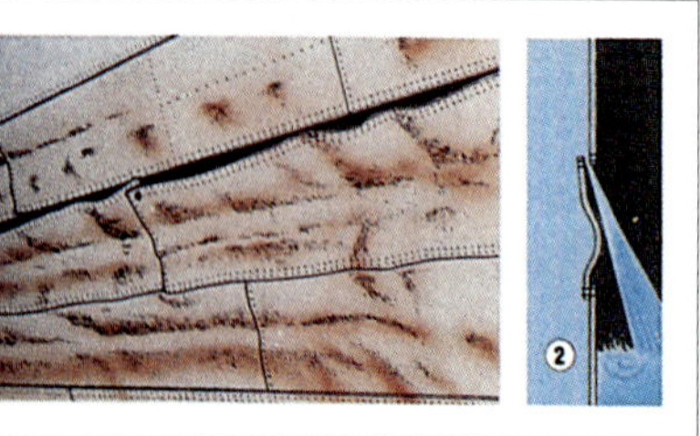

The iceberg scraping against the hull plates of the *Titanic* (*top*) popped many of the steel rivets that held them in place (*top right*). This allowed water to pour in through the seams (*above right*).

Then in the light of *Alvin*'s headlights, we spotted a safe ahead of us. I had heard about the story of fabulous treasure, including a leather-bound book covered with jewels, being locked in the ship's safes when she sank. Here was the chance of a lifetime, and I wanted to get a good look at it.

The safe sat there with its door face up. The handle looked as though it was made of gold, although I knew it had to be brass. Next to it, I could see a small circular gold dial, and above both a nice shiny gold crest.

Why not try to open it? I watched as *Alvin*'s sample-gathering arm locked its metal fingers onto the handle. Its metal wrist began to rotate clockwise. To my surprise, the handle turned easily. Then it stopped. The door just wouldn't budge. It was rusted shut. I felt as if I'd been caught with my hand in the cookie jar.

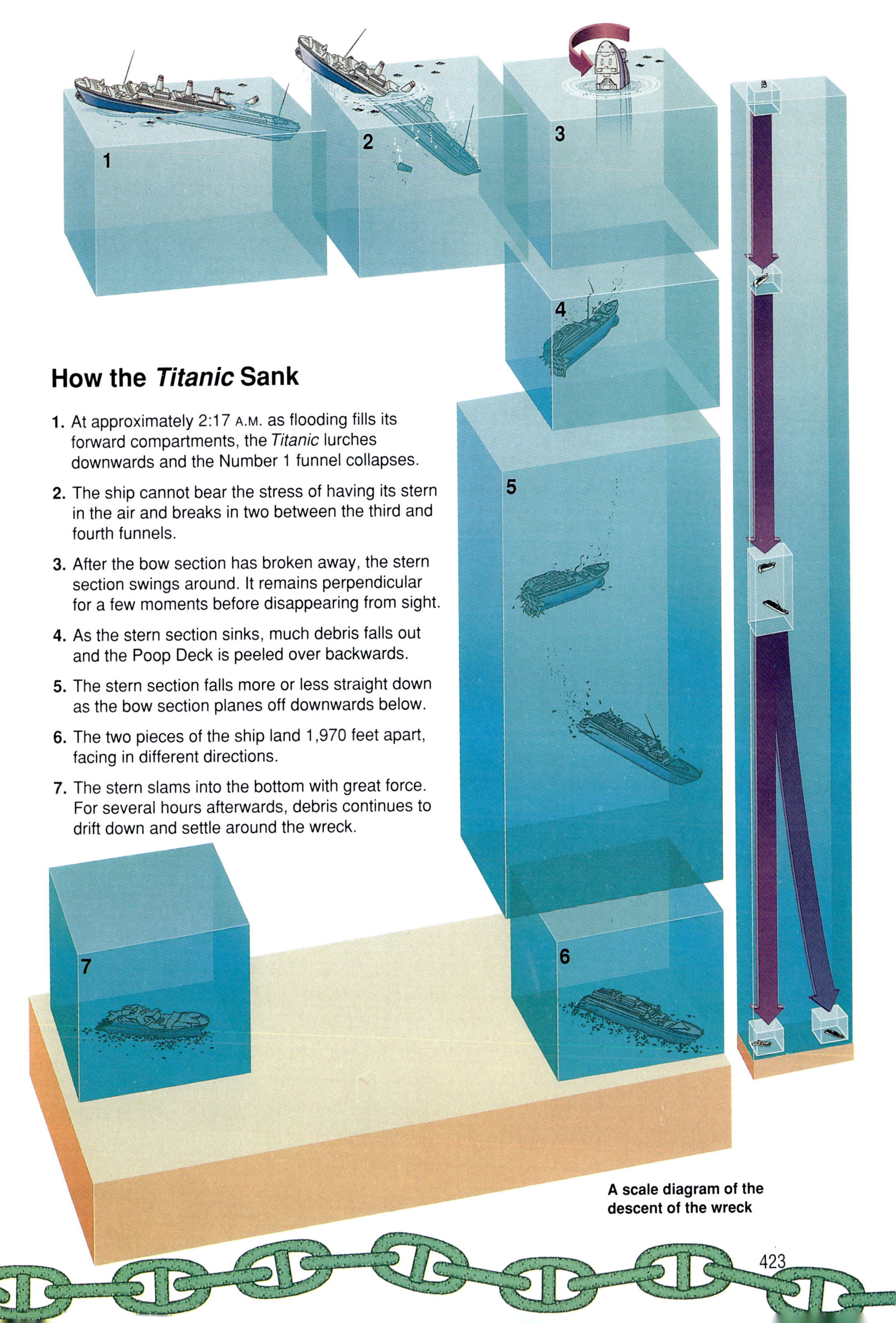

How the *Titanic* Sank

1. At approximately 2:17 A.M. as flooding fills its forward compartments, the *Titanic* lurches downwards and the Number 1 funnel collapses.
2. The ship cannot bear the stress of having its stern in the air and breaks in two between the third and fourth funnels.
3. After the bow section has broken away, the stern section swings around. It remains perpendicular for a few moments before disappearing from sight.
4. As the stern section sinks, much debris falls out and the Poop Deck is peeled over backwards.
5. The stern section falls more or less straight down as the bow section planes off downwards below.
6. The two pieces of the ship land 1,970 feet apart, facing in different directions.
7. The stern slams into the bottom with great force. For several hours afterwards, debris continues to drift down and settle around the wreck.

A scale diagram of the descent of the wreck

The dial and brass crest of this safe are still shiny. We turned the handle with *Alvin*'s mechanical arm.

Oh, well, I thought, it was probably empty, anyway. In fact, when we later looked at the video footage we had taken, we could see that the bottom of the safe had rusted out. Any treasure should have been spread around nearby, but there was none to be seen. Fortunately, my promise to myself not to bring back anything from the *Titanic* was not put to the test.

Two days passed before I went down to the *Titanic* again. After the rest, I was raring to go at it once more. This time we were going to explore the torn-off stern section that lay 1,970 feet away from the bow. It had been very badly damaged during the plunge to the bottom. Now it lay almost unrecognizable amidst badly twisted pieces of wreckage. We planned to land *Alvin* on the bottom directly behind the stern section and then send *JJ* in under the overhanging hull. Unless the *Titanic*'s three huge propellers had fallen off when she sank, I figured they still ought to be there, along with her enormous 101-ton rudder.

We made a soft landing on the bottom and discovered that one of *JJ*'s motors wouldn't work. Our dive looked like a washout. I sat glumly staring out of my viewport at the muddy bottom. Suddenly the mud started to move! Our pilot was slowly inching *Alvin* forward on its single ski right under the dangerous overhanging stern area. He was taking the sub itself to search for the huge propellers. Was he crazy? What if a piece of wreckage came crashing down? But our pilot was a professional, so I figured he must know exactly what he was doing.

I could see an area ahead covered with rusticles that had fallen from the rim of the stern above. Until now we had had ocean above us. Crossing this point was like taking a dangerous dare. Once on the other side, there was no sure way of escaping if disaster struck. None of us spoke. The only sound in the sub was our breathing.

In *Alvin* we explore under the overhanging deck of the *Titanic*'s severed stern section and photograph the buried rudder.

Slowly a massive black surface of steel plating seemed to inch down toward us overhead. The hull seemed to be coming at us from all sides. As we looked closely, we could see that like the bow, the stern section was buried deep in the mud—forty-five feet or so. Both the middle and the starboard propellers were under the mud. Only about sixteen feet of the massive rudder could be seen rising out of the ooze.

"Let's get out of here," I said. Ever so gently, *Alvin* retraced the path left by its ski. As we crossed over from the area covered with rusticles into the clear, we sighed with relief. We were out of danger. All of us were glad that this adventure was over.

Before we left the bottom this time, however, there was one mission that I wanted to complete. I wanted to place a memorial plaque on the twisted and tangled wreckage of the stern, in memory of all those lost on the *Titanic.* Those who had died had gathered on the stern as the ship had tilted bow first. This had been their final haven. So we rose up the wall of steel to the top of the stern. With great care, *Alvin*'s mechanical arm plucked the plaque from where it had been strapped outside the sub, and gently released it. We watched as it sank quietly to the deck of the stern.

As we lifted off and began our climb to the surface, our camera kept the plaque in view as long as possible. As we rose, it grew smaller and smaller, until finally it was swallowed in the gloom.

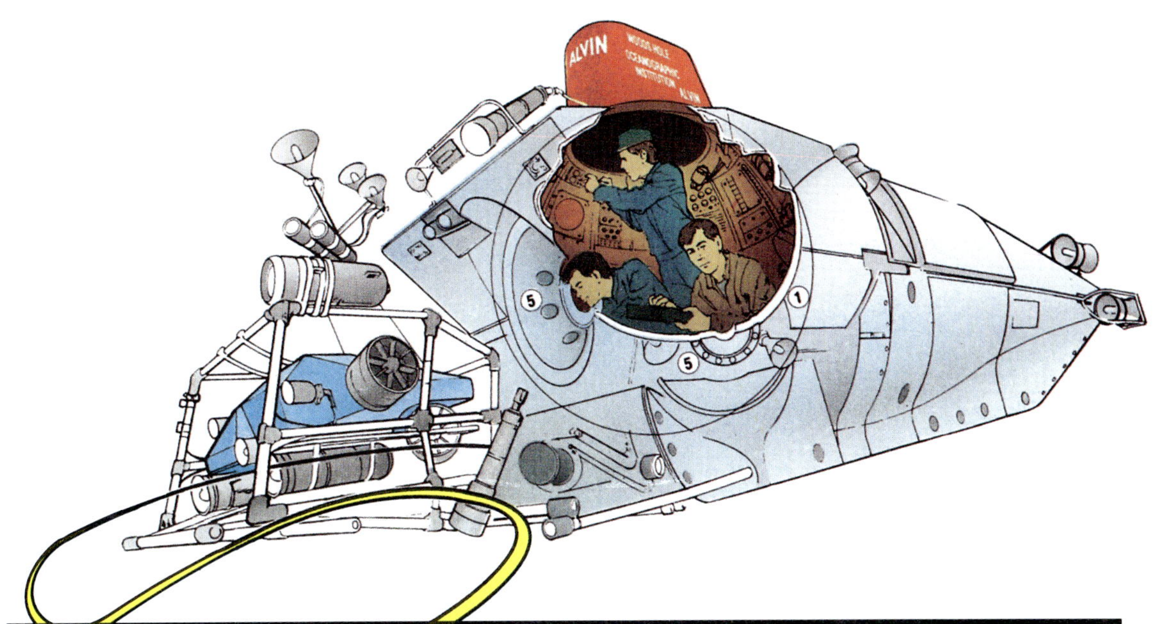

MEET ROBERT D. BALLARD

A doll's head and a man's patent leather shoe are usually not objects of wonder. But they were truly haunting images to explorer and oceanographer Robert Ballard, because of where they were found—among the wreckage of the *Titanic.* Ballard saw these objects through the eyes of a small robot operated from a three-man submarine, both of which he developed. Searching a 150-square-mile area of the ocean floor for the *Titanic* "makes finding a needle in a haystack seem trivial," he says.

Ballard continues to be intrigued by technology and by what lies in the depths of the ocean. His book *The Lost Wreck of the Isis* describes his discovery of a sunken Roman ship.

1. What happened to the *Titanic*?
2. Why do Ballard and his team use a robot to explore the ship?
3. Why do people find the story of the *Titanic* so interesting? Explain.
4. How would you summarize this selection? What important information would you include?
5. Both Robert Ballard and Howard Carter, in "Mummies, Tombs, and Treasure," made important discoveries. Compare their discoveries, and explain why each is important.

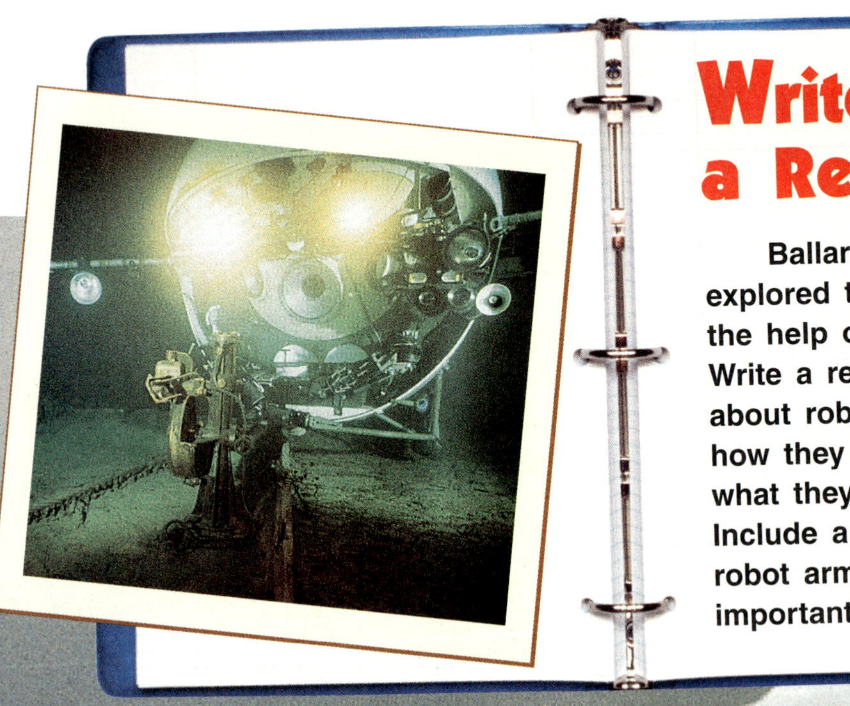

Write a Report

Ballard's team explored the *Titanic* with the help of their robot. Write a research report about robots. Explain how they are made and what they are used for. Include a drawing of a robot arm and other important information.

Draw a Floor Plan

Passengers on the *Titanic* worked out in the ship's gym. If you designed your own luxury liner, what types of activities would you offer your passengers? Draw a floor plan that shows one of the ship's decks. Include separate areas for the different activities.

Broadcast a Message

What happened when the *Titanic* struck an iceberg? How would you report this tragic event? Imagine that you are broadcasting the news to other ships. What would you say in a 60-second report. Be sure to tell *who* was involved, *what* happened, and *when* and *where* it took place.

Find Out More

As you know, the *Titanic* sank when it struck an iceberg. What are icebergs? Where are they found? How do they form? Why do they pose a threat to ships? Look up the entry word *icebergs* in an encyclopedia. Prepare a fact sheet for the information you find.

Read a Schedule

A **schedule** is a kind of table that lists times and events or things to do. Some schedules give a series of places and the times at which a ship, bus, or train is due to arrive at and leave each place. The schedule below shows times and destinations for a cruise ship, the *Caribbean Queen.*

PLACE	ARRIVAL	DEPARTURE
Miami		Saturday, 9 A.M.
St. Thomas	Sunday, 9 A.M.	Monday, 5 P.M.
St. Croix	Monday, 7 P.M.	Wednesday, 11 P.M.
St. Martin	Thursday, 7 A.M.	Friday, 5:30 P.M.
Miami	Saturday, 11:30 A.M.	

Use the schedule to answer these questions.

1. How many islands will passengers on the *Caribbean Queen* be visiting?
2. On what day and at what time does the ship sail for St. Croix?
3. Which of the islands are closest to each other? How do you know?
4. About how much time will the passengers have to see the sights on St. Martin?
5. How many hours longer will the trip back to Miami be than the trip from Miami?

TEST POWER

Test Tip

Look in the passage for clues to answer each question.

DIRECTIONS

Read the sample story. Then read each question about the story.

SAMPLE

Slavery and Spirituals

Almost four million African American people lived in the United States in 1860. In spite of great challenges, enslaved African Americans built a culture of dignity and fellowship.

Since enslaved people were not allowed to go to school, most could not read or write. They passed their traditions from generation to generation through songs. The enslaved people sang these songs, called *spirituals*, as they worked in the fields or in the homes of the plantation owners. The songs also allowed the singers to express their feelings. Today, spirituals are an important part of African American history.

1 According to the passage, how did the enslaved people use the spirituals?

- **A** To pass on tradition
- **B** To keep busy
- **C** To avoid writing
- **D** To learn about farming

2 What is this story mostly about?

- **F** How to free an enslaved person
- **G** What to study in school
- **H** Learning about spirituals
- **J** The feelings of enslaved people

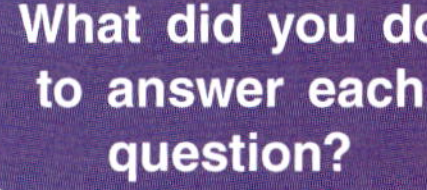

Stories in Art

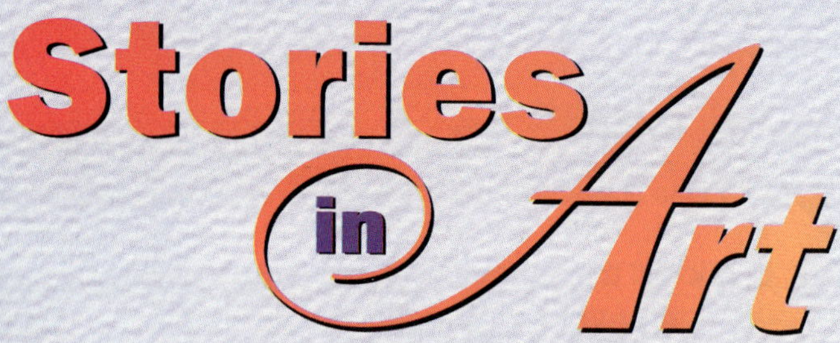

Movies and television programs often blur fact and fiction. Sometimes they make the real seem unreal and the unreal seem real.

Look at this photograph taken from an episode of the original *Star Trek* television series. What can you tell about it? Notice the details. What is flying in the sky? What do you notice about the moon? Could a palace really be built in this setting? Explain.

Look at the picture again. Would you like to live in a city on the moon? Give reasons.

Photo from "A Taste of Armageddon," *Star Trek* original series, 1967

TIME FOR KIDS

SPECIAL REPORT

Back to the Moon!

For the first time ever, a spacecraft mapped every ridge and crater on the moon.

TIME FOR KIDS SPECIAL REPORT

Mission to the Moon!

A tiny spacecraft explores the moon

A half-moon glowed in the night sky in January 1998 as a sleek white rocket blasted off from Cape Canaveral, Florida. A small spacecraft called *Lunar Prospector* was tucked in the rocket's nose. As the rocket rose, people cheered the perfect launch. "We're on our way!" cried one scientist. Soon *Prospector* broke free from the rocket and began to coast toward the shining moon.

For the first time since 1972, NASA, the U.S. space agency, had launched a mission to the moon. *Prospector*, which carried no astronauts, spent one year orbiting the moon. It mapped the deeply cratered surface. It determined what the moon was made of and whether water was present there.

Says program scientist Joseph Boyce, who worked on NASA's 1972 moon trip: "It felt good to be going back."

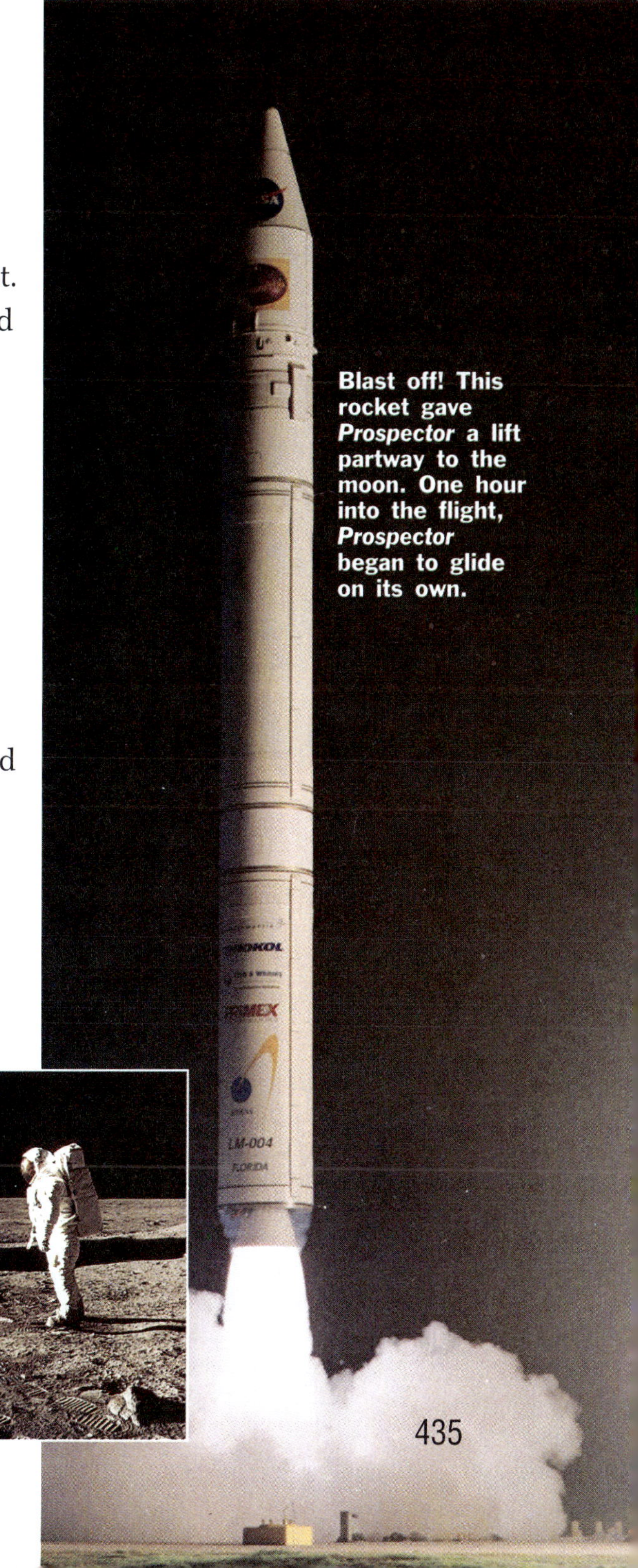

Blast off! This rocket gave *Prospector* a lift partway to the moon. One hour into the flight, *Prospector* began to glide on its own.

SHOOTING FOR THE MOON

Humans have always been fascinated by the moon. For centuries we have tracked the passage of time by watching the moon change shape—from new moon to crescent to full moon and back again. We have marveled at man-in-the-moon shadows that lunar cliffs cast over flat plains.

Neil Armstrong took this photo of fellow *Apollo 11* astronaut Buzz Aldrin on July 20, 1969.

COVER AND RIGHT: NASA; FAR RIGHT: KARL RONSTROM/ARCHIVE

RIGHT AND FAR RIGHT: NASA

DID YOU KNOW? MOON FACTS

- **Most scientists believe the moon was created 4.5 billion years ago after a large object hit the Earth. Gas and dust from the crash formed the moon.**
- **The moon's craters were made when rocky meteors smashed into the moon at high speed.**
- **The moon is about 240,000 miles from Earth, 80 times the distance across the U.S.**
- **The pull of the moon's gravity causes the rising and falling of ocean tides on Earth.**

During the 1950s and '60s, the U.S. and the Soviet Union raced to get to the moon. Soviet rockets got there first, but the U.S. Apollo program landed the first human there: Neil Armstrong in 1969.

Americans were thrilled by the discoveries. By 1972, 12 astronauts had walked on the moon and brought back 850 pounds of moon rocks. But the U.S. could no longer afford NASA's expensive moon missions.

From 1972 to 1998, our only glimpses of the moon were from telescopes or unmanned spacecraft that flew by on their way to other planets. Less than a quarter of the moon had been mapped in detail.

Though *Prospector* didn't land on the moon, scientists compare its mission to *Pathfinder*'s thrilling trip to Mars in 1997. Both ships were built under NASA's new guidelines: "faster, cheaper, better." The missions were, said Boyce, "the start of the next golden age of exploration."

Prospector was less than half the weight of an average car. The spacecraft carried no computer or camera. But it was well equipped for its mission. From 63 miles above the moon, five instruments on the arms and antenna put together the most complete picture ever of the moon.

Eventually, *Prospector* crash-landed on the lunar surface, joining the trash and equipment left behind by astronauts. Scientists will be studying the information from *Prospector* for several years. This will help them learn a lot more about the moon.

WHAT DID *PROSPECTOR* FIND?

The lunar mapping program found quantities of minerals, including titanium, a mineral that is rare on Earth. And *Prospector* confirmed that

Based on an article in *TIME FOR KIDS.*

water ice does exist at the lunar poles, with the most ice at the lunar north pole. Some astronomers believe that the moon holds as much as a billion tons of ice left long ago by crashing comets. Comets are big, dirty snowballs—mixtures of dust and ice.

The water ice is mixed with the lunar soil. "Don't expect to see lunar penguins skating around on a lake!" says Boyce. But ice on the moon may provide water so that astronauts, and maybe ordinary citizens, could live there someday. Scientists would love to set up telescopes on the moon. The views into space would be outstanding.

An air supply would also be needed. But with the right equipment, people can live in strange places. "We have a year-round base in Antarctica," says Boyce. "Today's kids may end up living on the moon."

FIND OUT MORE

Visit our website:

www.mhschool.com/reading

HOW *LUNAR PROSPECTOR* WORKS

After launch, a wide swing around Earth put *Prospector* on the right path to the moon. Once it was in position orbiting the moon, it measured the moon's gravity and magnetism. *Prospector* also looked for minerals, gas, and signs of water.

This instrument determined what the moon is made of.

A sensor in the antenna measured gravity at different points around the moon.

This sensor looked for gas released from the moon's interior. It gave scientists clues about the moon's history.

These solar cells gathered the sun's energy for *Prospector's* instruments.

This instrument looked for hydrogen at the moon's polar areas. Hydrogen is a part of water.

The magnetometer studied the moon's magnetic field.

These arms unfolded when *Prospector* separated from its rocket.

1. What facts about the moon does this article present?
2. How do these "moon facts" help you understand the selection?
3. How do you think *Prospector*'s mission will affect the future? Explain.
4. What is the main idea of this selection?
5. Compare the *Lunar Prospector* with *JJ* the robot in "Exploring the Titanic." How are they both able to explore difficult places? How is exploring space similar to exploring the ocean?

Write a Paragraph

For the first time ever, a spacecraft has mapped the moon. How would you explain *Lunar Prospector* mission to someone who had not read this selection? Write a paragraph that explains or informs. Begin with a strong topic sentence. Use supporting sentences to present your facts and explain your ideas. End with a conclusion that summarizes your information about the *Lunar Prospector* mission.

Create a Mural

The moon goes through many different phases during each lunar month. Refer to the Internet, an encyclopedia, or an astronomy book to find pictures of all the moon's phases. Use a roll of black paper for a background. Then create a mural showing all the phases of the moon. Label each phase, describe it, and tell how long it lasts.

Draw a Moon Colony

Will people live on the moon someday? If so, what do you think a moon colony will look like? How will people get air and water? Draw a picture of a moon colony. Include the gadgets and technology that you think would be found in a high-tech moon settlement.

Find Out More

Prospector is NASA's first mission to the moon since 1972. What other moon missions has NASA launched? Start by checking in an encyclopedia, or use the NASA Web page. Make a chart of three columns that lists every NASA mission to the moon. In the first column list the name of the mission. In the second column list the year of the mission. In the third column list the mission's accomplishments. Use your information to compare missions.

Read a Line Graph

NASA, the United States space agency, has launched many missions into space. Some of these flights have included the space shuttle.

Look at this line graph of space shuttle flights. **Line graphs** are an excellent way to show the changes that take place over time. If you follow the line, you will see whether trends are increasing, getting smaller, or staying the same.

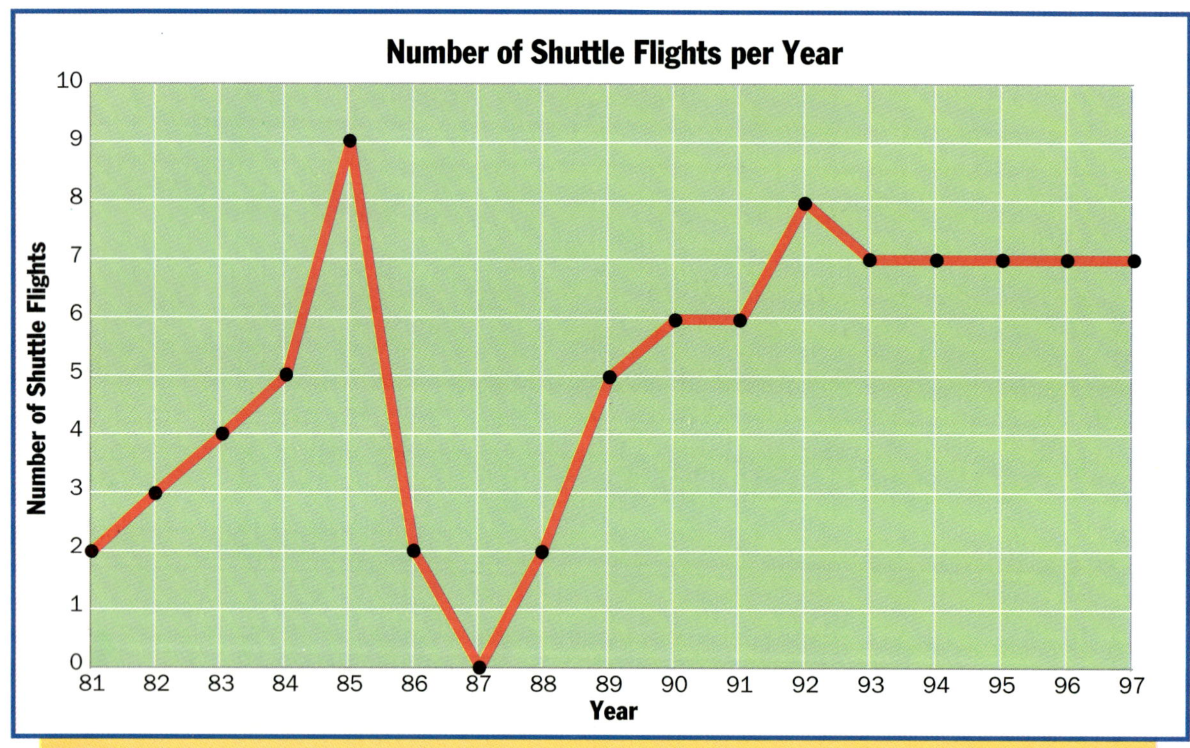

Use the line graph to answer these questions.

1. How many shuttle flights were there from 1981 to 1984?
2. What was the greatest number of flights in any one year?
3. What happened between the years 1985 and 1987?
4. What happened after 1987?
5. What kind of information does a line graph give you?

TEST POWER

Test Tip

There are no extra points for finishing early. Be sure to work slowly and carefully.

DIRECTIONS

Read the sample story. Then read each question about the story.

SAMPLE

The Nene Goose

If you've ever been to Hawaii, you may have seen the rare and beautiful nene goose. The nene is a small land-dwelling bird that lives only on the volcanic islands of Hawaii. In the 1700s, approximately 25,000 nene geese were living on the islands. As the first settlers came to the islands, they brought with them cattle, pigs, sheep, goats, and rats. Unfortunately, these animals unsettled the geese and destroyed their breeding grounds. By 1947, there were only 30 nene geese left alive.

In 1949, a breeding program was begun to help the nene geese <u>repopulate</u> their species. Scientists captured the few remaining birds. The nene geese in the breeding program mated and laid eggs. Today, nearly 2,000 nene geese born in captivity have been released on the islands of Maui and Hawaii.

1 The word <u>repopulate</u> in this passage means —

A reproduce

B research

C encourage

D destroy

2 You can tell from the passage that the nene goose —

F uses its beak to hunt for food

G cannot fly over water

H has been able to increase its population

J does not live in the Hawaiian Islands

THE MICROSCOPE

Anton Leeuwenhoek was Dutch.
He sold pincushions, cloth, and such.
The waiting townsfolk fumed and fussed
As Anton's dry goods gathered dust.

He worked instead of tending store,
At grinding special lenses for
A microscope. Some of the things
He looked at were:
mosquitoes' wings,
the hairs of sheep, the legs of lice,
the skin of people, dogs, and mice;
ox eyes, spiders' spinning gear,
fishes' scales, a little smear
of his own blood,
and best of all
the unknown, busy, very small
bugs that swim and bump and hop
inside a simple water drop.

Impossible! Most Dutchmen said.
This Anton's crazy in the head,
We ought to ship him off to Spain.
He says he's seen a housefly's brain.
He says the water that we drink
Is full of bugs. He's mad, we think!

They called him dumkopf which means
dope.
That's how we got the microscope.

by Maxine Kumin

BRAINSTORMS

UNIT 5

I May, I Might, I Must

If you will tell me why the fen
appears impassable, I then
will tell you why I think that I
can get across it if I try.

by Marianne Moore

Stories in Art

Artists communicate through their work. Some express ideas about their culture, their family, or their feelings. Look at this painting. What is the artist, Diego Rivera, saying to you?

Study this painting. What can you tell about the people in it? How do they feel toward each other? What might the artist be saying about the bond between mother and child? How do these people make you feel?

Look at the painting again. How does the artist control light and shadow? What mood does he create? Was he successful in showing his feelings? Explain why you think so.

Madre y Niña
by Diego Rivera

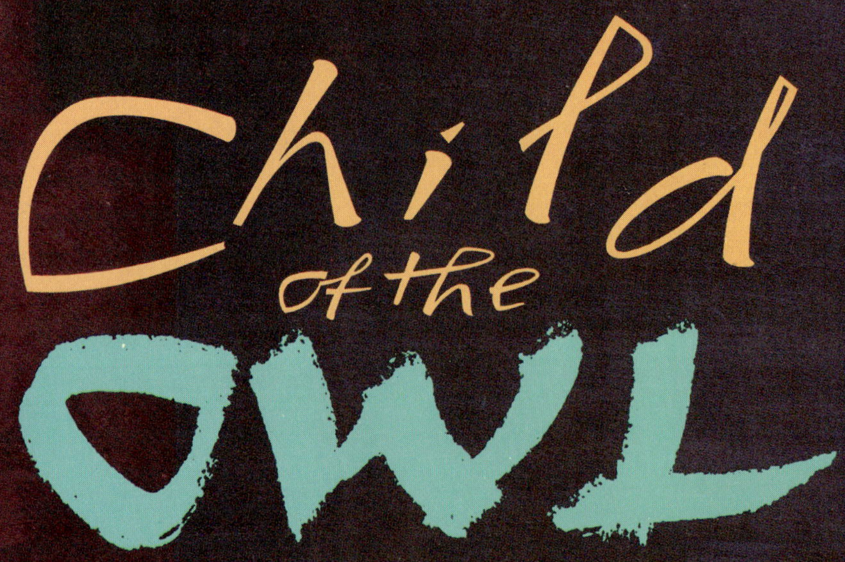

BY LAURENCE YEP

Casey was just a small child when her mother, Jeanie, died. Since then, Casey has been brought up by her father, Barney. When Barney is hospitalized, Casey goes to stay with her uncle Phil and his family. Used to a free-spirited life with her father, Casey is uncomfortable in Phil's strict household. In turn, Phil's family is unwilling to accept Casey's attitudes, ideas, and behavior. The situation is tense for everyone, so Phil decides to take Casey to San Francisco's Chinatown to live with Paw-Paw, her grandmother. On the way, Casey is nervous. She has never met Paw-Paw, and she feels alone and out of place in the unfamiliar setting.

ILLUSTRATED BY WINSON TRANG

Phil headed up Sacramento Street—a steep, slanting street that just zoomed on and on to the top of Nob Hill, where the rich people lived and where they had the swanky hotels. Phil turned suddenly into a little dead-end alley wide enough for only one car. On one side was a one-story Chinese school of brick so old or so dirty that the bricks were practically a purple color. On the other side as we drove by was a small parking lot with only six spaces for cars. Phil stopped the car in the middle of the alley and I could see the rest of it was filled with apartment houses. Somewhere someone had a window open and the radio was blaring out "I Want to Hold Your Hand" by that new group, the Beatles. I couldn't find the place where it was coming from but I did see someone's diapers and shirts hung in the windows and on the fire escape of one apartment.

"Why do they hang their laundry in the windows?" I asked Phil.

"That's what people from Hong Kong use for curtains," Phil grumbled.

The sidewalk in front of Paw-Paw's house was cracked like

someone had taken a sledgehammer to it, and there were iron grates over the lower windows. The steps up to the doorway were old, worn concrete painted red. To the left were the mailboxes, which had Chinese words for the names or had no labels at all. To the right were the doorbells to all the nine apartments. Phil picked out the last and rang. He jabbed his thumb down rhythmically. Three short. Three long. Three short.

"Why are you doing that?" I asked.

"Signaling your Paw-Paw," he grumbled. "She never answers just one buzz like any normal person, or even just three bursts. It's got to be nine buzzes in that way or she doesn't open the door. She says her friends know what she means."

So did I. It was Morse code for SOS. The buzzer on the door sounded like an angry bee. Phil the Pill opened the door, putting his back against it and fighting against the heavy spring that tried to swing it shut. "Go on. Up three flights. Number nine."

I walked into an old, dim hallway and climbed up the wooden steps. As I turned an angle on the stairs, I saw light burning fierce and bright from a window. When I came to it, I looked out at the roof of the Chinese school next door. Someone had thrown some old 45's and a pair of sneakers down there. If I were some kind of kid that felt sorry for herself, I would almost have said that was the way I felt: like some piece of old, ugly junk that was being kicked around on the discard pile while Barney was getting better.

I didn't stay by the window long, though, because Phil was coming up the stairs and I didn't want to act like his kids' stories about Paw-Paw had scared me. Anybody could be better than Phil the Pill and his family . . . I hoped. I stopped by the number-nine room,

afraid to knock. It could not be the right place because I could hear "I Want to Hold Your Hand" coming through the doorway. I scratched my head and checked the numbers on the other doors on the landing. Phil the Pill was still a flight down, huffing and puffing up the steps with my duffel bag—it wasn't that heavy; Phil was just that much out of shape. "Go on. Go on. Knock, you little idiot," he called up the stairwell.

I shrugged. It wasn't any of my business. I knocked at the door. I heard about six bolts and locks being turned. Finally the door swung open and I saw a tiny, pleasant, round-faced woman smiling at me. Her cheeks were a bright red. Her gray hair was all curly and frizzy around her head and a pair of rimless, thick eyeglasses perched on her nose. She was round and plump, wearing a sweater even on a hot day like this, a pair of cotton black slacks, and a pair of open-heeled, flat slippers.

"Paw-Paw?" I asked.

"Hello. Hello." She opened up her arms and gave me a big hug, almost crushing me. It was funny, but even though it was like I said—Barney and me never went in much for that sentimental stuff like hugging and kissing—I suddenly found myself holding on to her. Underneath all the soft layers of clothing I could feel how hard and tough she was. She patted me on the back three times and then left me for a moment to turn down her radio. It really was her old, white, beat-up radio playing rock music.

"Hey, how about a hand?" Phil puffed as he finally got to the landing.

Paw-Paw shuffled out to the landing in her slippered feet and made shooing motions. "You can go home now. We can do all right by ourselves."

Phil heaved his shoulders up and down in a great sigh and set the bag down. "Now, Momma—"

"Go on home," she said firmly. "We need time by ourselves."

I saw that Phil must have had some fine speech all prepared, probably warning Paw-Paw about me and warning me about ingratitude. He was not about to give up such an opportunity to make a speech.

"Now, Momma—"

"Go on. You're still not too old for a swat across the backside."

Phil ran his hand back and forth along the railing. "Really, Momma. You oughtn't—"

"Go on." Paw-Paw raised her hand.

Phil gulped. The thought of having a former district president of the lawyers spanked by his own mother must have been too much for him. He turned around and started down the steps. He still had to get in the last word though. "You mind your Paw-Paw, young lady. You hear me?" he shouted over his shoulder.

I waited till I heard the door slam. "Do you know what those buzzes stand for?"

"Do you?" Her eyes crinkled up.

"It stands for SOS. But where did you learn it?"

"When I worked for the American lady, her boy had a toy . . . what do you call it?" She made a tapping motion with her finger.

"Telegraph?"

"Yes. It's a good joke on such a learned man, no?" Her round red face split into a wide grin and then she began to giggle and when she put her hand over her mouth, the giggle turned into a laugh.

I don't think that I had laughed in all that time since Barney's accident a month ago. It was like all the laughter I hadn't been able to use came bubbling up out of some hidden well—burst out of the locks and just came up. Both of us found ourselves slumping on the landing, leaning our heads against the banister, and laughing.

Finally Paw-Paw tilted up her glasses and wiped her eyes. "Philip always did have too much dignity for one person. Ah." She leaned back against the railing on the landing before the stairwell, twisting her head to look at me. "You'll go far," she nodded. "Yes, you will. Your eyebrows are beautifully curved, like silkworms. That means you'll be clever. And your ears are small and close to your head and shaped a certain way. That means you're adventurous and win much honor."

"Really?"

She nodded solemnly. "Didn't you know? The face is the map of the soul." Then she leaned forward and raised her glasses and pointed to the corners of her eyes where there were two small hollows, just shadows, really. "You see those marks under my eyes?"

"Yes." I added after a moment, "Paw-Paw."

"Those marks, they mean I have a temper."

"Oh." I wondered what was to happen next.

She set her glasses back on her nose. "But I will make a deal with you. I can keep my temper under control if you can do the same with your love of adventure and intelligence. You see, people, including me, don't always understand a love of adventure and intelligence. Sometimes we mistake them for troublemaking."

"I'll try," I grinned.

I went and got my bag then and brought it inside Paw-Paw's place and looked around, trying to figure out where I'd put it. Her place wasn't more than ten by fifteen feet and it was crowded with her stuff. Her bed was pushed lengthwise against the wall next to the doorway leading out to the landing. To the right of the door was another doorway, leading to the small little cubicle of a kitchen, and next to that door was her bureau. The wall opposite the bed had her one window leading out to the fire escape and giving a view of the alley, which was so narrow that it looked like we could have shaken hands with the people in the apartment house across from us. Beneath the window was a stack of newspapers for wrapping up the garbage. Next to the window was a table with a bright red-and-orange-flower tablecloth. Paw-Paw pulled aside her chair and her three-legged stool and told me to put my bag under the table. A metal cabinet and stacks of boxes covered the rest of the wall and the next one had hooks from which coats and other stuff in plastic bags hung.

In the right corner of the old bureau were some statues and an old teacup with some dirt in it and a half-burnt incense stick stuck into it. The rest of the top, though, was covered with old photos in little cardboard covers. They filled the bureau top and the mirror too, being stuck into corners of the mirror or actually taped onto the surface.

Next to the photos were the statues. One was about eight inches high in white porcelain of a pretty lady holding a flower and with the most patient, peaceful expression on her face. To her left was a statue of a man with a giant-sized, bald head. And then there were eight little statues, each only about two inches high. "Who are they?" I asked.

"Statues of some holy people," Paw-Paw said reluctantly.

There was something familiar about the last statue on Paw-Paw's bureau. It was of a fat, balding god with large ears, who had little children crawling over his lap and climbing up his shoulders. "Hey," I said. "Is that the happy god?"

Paw-Paw looked puzzled. "He's not the god of happiness."

"But they call him the happy god. See?" I pulled Barney's little plastic charm out of my pocket and pointed to the letters on the back.

Paw-Paw didn't even try to read the lettering. Maybe Barney had already shown it to her long ago. "He's not the god of happiness. He just looks happy. He's the Buddha—the Buddha who will come in the future. He's smiling because everyone will be saved by that time and he can take a vacation. The children are holy people who become like children again."

"What about the others, Paw-Paw?"

"I don't have the words to explain," Paw-Paw said curtly, like the whole thing was embarrassing her.

I sat down by the table on the stool, which was painted white with red flowers. "Sure you do. I think your English is better than mine."

"You don't want to know any of that stuff." With her index finger Paw-Paw rubbed hard against some spot on the tablecloth. "That stuff's only for old people. If I tell you any more, you'll laugh at it like all other young people do." There was bitter hurt and anger in her voice.

I should have left her alone, I guess; but we had been getting close to one another and suddenly I'd found this door between us—a door that wouldn't open. I wasn't so much curious now as I was desperate: I didn't want Paw-Paw shutting me out like that. "I won't laugh, Paw-Paw. Honest."

"That stuff's only for old people who are too stupid to learn American ways," she insisted stubbornly.

"Well, maybe I'm stupid too."

"No." Paw-Paw pressed her lips together tightly; and I saw that no matter how much I pestered her, I wasn't going to get her to tell me any more about the statues on her bureau. We'd been getting along so great before that I was sorry I'd ever started asking questions.

We both sat, each in our own thoughts, until almost apologetically Paw-Paw picked up a deck of cards from the table. "Do you play cards?"

"Some," I said. "Draw poker. Five-card stud. Things like that."

Paw-Paw shuffled the cards expertly. "Poker is for old men who like to sit and think too much. Now I know a game that's for the young and quick."

"What's that?"

"Slapjack." She explained that each of us took half

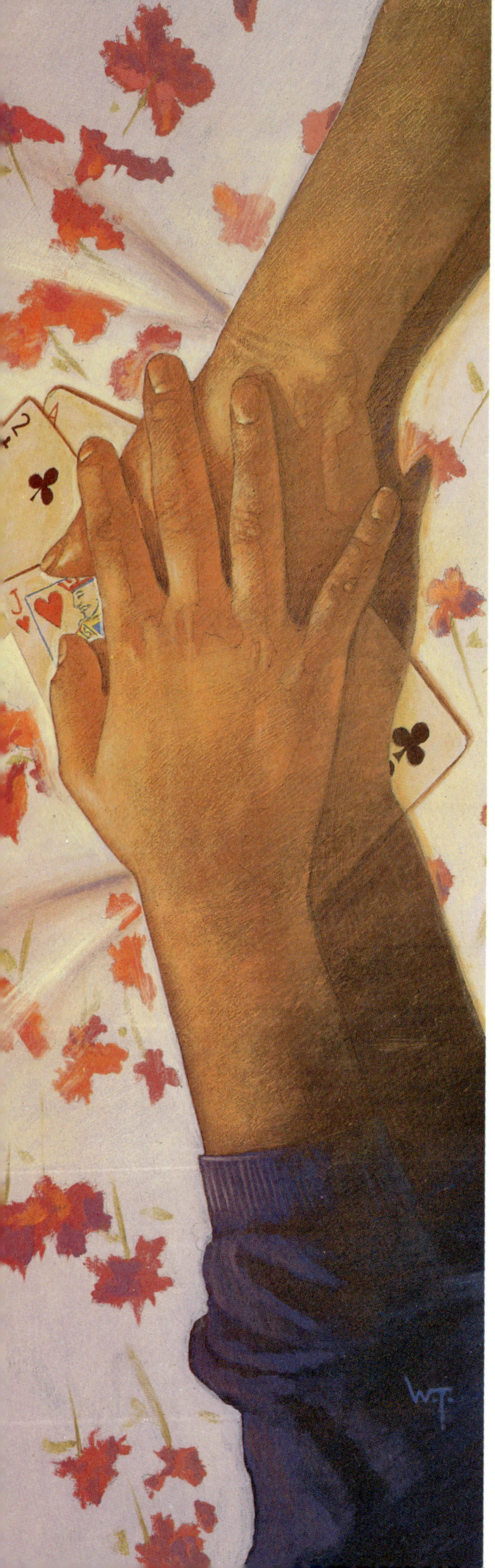

of a deck and stacked it in front without looking at it. Then we would take turns taking the top card off and putting it down in the middle. Whenever a jack appeared, the first one to put her hand over the pile of cards got it. She then mixed the new cards with all the cards she still had in front of her. The first one to get all the cards won the game. It would sound like the advantage was with the person who was putting out the card at that time, but she was supposed to turn up the card away from her so she couldn't see it before the other player.

Paw-Paw had played a lot of card games, since she lived by herself, so she seemed to know when the jacks were going to come up. For a while all you could hear was the *slap-slap-slap*ping of cards and sometimes our hands smacking one another trying to get the pile. And sometimes I'd have more cards and sometimes Paw-Paw would. Eventually, though, she beat me. She shuffled the deck again. "You're a pretty good player," she grudged.

"Not as good as you, though."

Paw-Paw shuffled the cards, tapping them against the table so the cards in the pack were all even. "We used to play all the time. Your mother, Phil, everyone. We'd hold big contests and make plenty of noise. Only when Phil got older, he only wanted to play the games fancy Americans played like—what's that word for a road that goes over water?"

"A bridge? Phil wanted to play bridge."

"Yes." Paw-Paw put the deck on the table. I wandered over to the bed.

The radio was in a little cabinet built into the headboard of the bed. I lay down on the bed and looked at the radio dial. "Do you like rock music, Paw-Paw?"

"It's fun to listen to," Paw-Paw said, "and besides, *Chinese Hour* is on that station every night."

"Chinese Hour?"

"An hour of news and songs all in Chinese." Paw-Paw slipped the cards back carefully into their box. "They used to have some better shows on that station like mystery shows."

"I bet I could find some." I started to reach for the dial.

"Don't lose that station." Paw-Paw seemed afraid suddenly.

"Don't worry, Paw-Paw, I'll be able to get your station back for you." It was playing "Monster Mash" right then. I twisted the dial to the right and the voices and snatches of song slid past and then I turned the dial back to her station, where "Monster Mash" was still playing. "See?"

"As long as you could get it back," Paw-Paw said reluctantly.

I fiddled with the dial some more until I got hold of *Gunsmoke*. It'd gone off the air three years ago but

some station was playing reruns. Paw-Paw liked that, especially the deep voice of the marshal. It was good to sit there in the darkening little room, listening to Marshal Dillon inside your head and picturing him as big and tall and striding down the dusty streets of Dodge City. And I got us some other programs too, shows that Paw-Paw had never been able to listen to before.

Don't get the idea that Paw-Paw was stupid. She just didn't understand American machines that well. She lived with them in a kind of truce where she never asked much of them if they wouldn't ask much of her.

"It's getting near eight," Paw-Paw said anxiously. It was only when I got the station back for her that she began to relax. "I was always so worried that I would not be able to get back the station, I never tried to listen to others. Look what I missed."

"But you have me now, Paw-Paw," I said.

"Yes," Paw-Paw smiled briefly, straightening in her chair. "I guess I do."

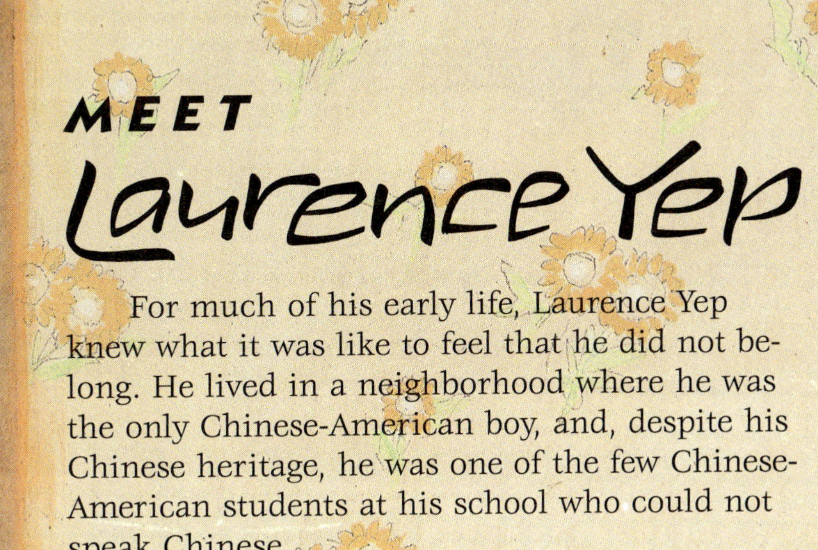

MEET Laurence Yep

For much of his early life, Laurence Yep knew what it was like to feel that he did not belong. He lived in a neighborhood where he was the only Chinese-American boy, and, despite his Chinese heritage, he was one of the few Chinese-American students at his school who could not speak Chinese.

Yep's feeling of being an outsider led him to read science fiction. There, he found characters and situations that seemed familiar, he says, "because in those books children were taken to other lands and other worlds where they had to learn strange customs and languages—and that was something I did every time I got on and off the bus."

Yep sold his first story when he was eighteen and was paid a penny per word. Not surprisingly, that piece was science fiction, as are many of Yep's later works. He also writes realistic novels, often drawing upon his Chinese-American background. One of these is *Dragonwings,* which was a Newbery Honor Book. Another is *Child of the Owl,* which won the Boston Globe–Horn Book Award in 1979.

Story Questions & Activities

1. Who is the main character in the story?
2. How does the author let you know what Casey is thinking and feeling?
3. What makes this story believable? Explain.
4. What do you think is the best part of the story? Why?
5. Look carefully at the people in the painting on pages 446–447. What do they have in common with Casey and Paw-Paw? Do you think Casey and Paw-Paw will develop such a strong bond? Why or why not?

Write a Story

Paw-Paw shows Casey a new game, and Casey shows Paw-Paw how to find new stations on the radio. What other things might older and younger people learn from each other? Write a story about a younger and older person teaching each other something new. Be sure to give good descriptions of each character and tell what they learn.

Paint a Portrait

Casey's grandmother believes that the "face is a map of the soul." What do you think Casey really looks like? Scan the selection for a description of Casey. Pay special attention to what she says and what is said about her. Then use this information and the character description to paint a portrait of Casey.

Make a "Get-well" Card

How would you cheer up Barney in the hospital? Imagine that you are Casey. Make a "get-well" card for your father. Write a poem or a special message on the inside of the card. Then draw a humorous illustration on the front. Include a few words about life with Paw-Paw.

Find Out More

To get into Paw-Paw's apartment, Uncle Phil has to buzz nine times. Casey figures out that nine buzzes is Morse code for SOS. What do you know about Morse code? Who invented it, and why? Look in an encyclopedia, or use the Internet to find out about Morse code. Share your findings with your classmates.

Read a Family Tree

You probably know that a **family tree** is a time map of a family. It is also a diagram. A family tree shows who was married to whom, which children were born to which parents, and often, how distant relatives are related. Family trees can be short or long. If they are long, they can go back many generations.

Look at Casey's family tree. How far does it go back?

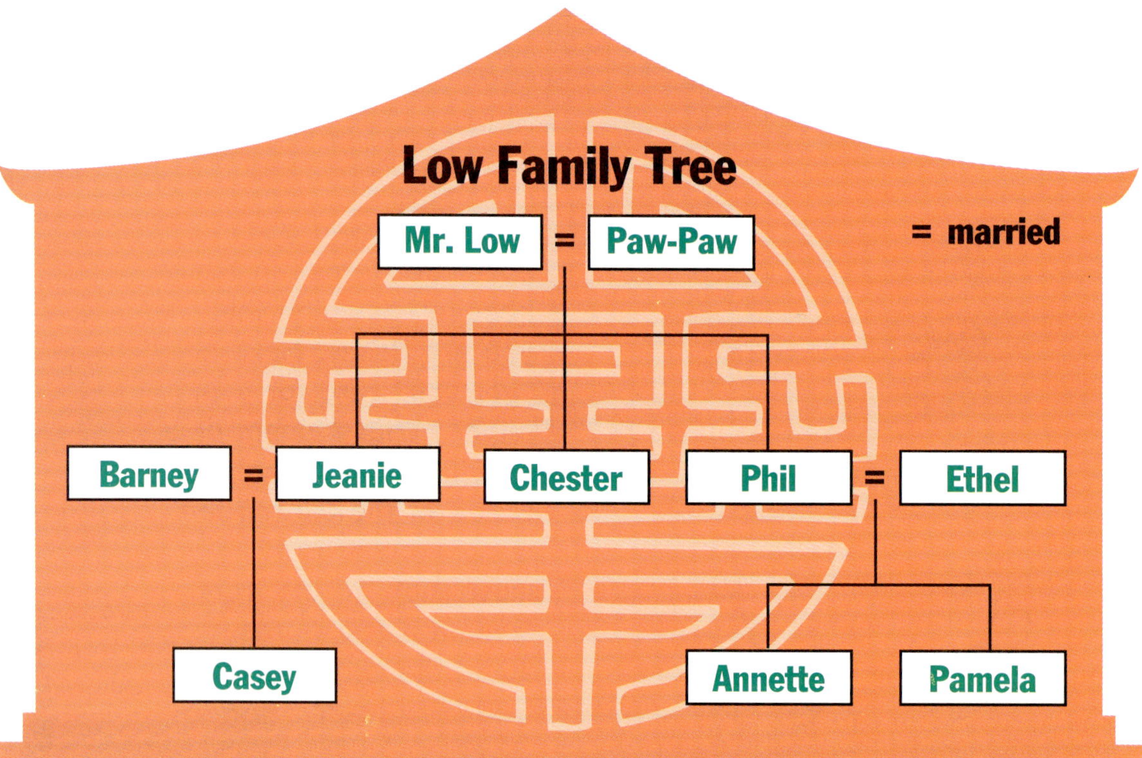

Use the family tree to answer these questions.

1. Who is Phil's wife?
2. How many children does Paw-Paw have?
3. How is Casey related to Annette and Pamela?
4. How is Barney related to Chester?
5. Why do you think people are interested in family trees?

TEST POWER

Test Tip

The summary tells what the passage is mostly about.

DIRECTIONS

Read the sample story. Then read each question about the story.

SAMPLE

Harriet Beecher Stowe

In 1852, a novel was published that exposed the cruelty of slavery to a wide audience. Many people of that day already believed that enslaved people should be freed. But *Uncle Tom's Cabin*, by Harriet Beecher Stowe, broke new ground in educating people about the injustices of slavery.

Uncle Tom's Cabin was first published as a series in an antislavery newsletter. In 1852, after the Fugitive Slave Act was passed, it was published as a book. In its first week, it sold 10,000 copies. The well-received book, based on Stowe's own experiences, portrayed a kind plantation family, a brutal slaveholder, and a benevolent enslaved man, Uncle Tom.

Since then, it has been reprinted in 37 languages, and millions of copies have been sold worldwide.

1 After *Uncle Tom's Cabin* was published, what probably happened next?

A Stowe published her second book.

B Stowe became a teacher.

C Many people wanted to abolish slavery.

D Many people visited plantations.

2 According to the passage, Harriet Beecher Stowe wrote *Uncle Tom's Cabin* to teach people about —

F language

G slavery

H plantations

J fugitives

Stories in Art

Some paintings are almost like a play. The stage is set, the actors are playing their parts, and the events are unfolding. All you need is the audience. But you have it—it's you!

Look at this painting. Notice the many details. What are the builders building? What did they do before laying the bricks? Look at the men in the lower left-hand corner. What are they doing? When will their work be added to the building? What will the builders do last?

Look at the painting again. Who is the man who is bowing? Do you think he is the architect or builder? Why?

Construction of a Chateau,
Early 16th Century Italian,
Bibliotheque Nationale, Paris

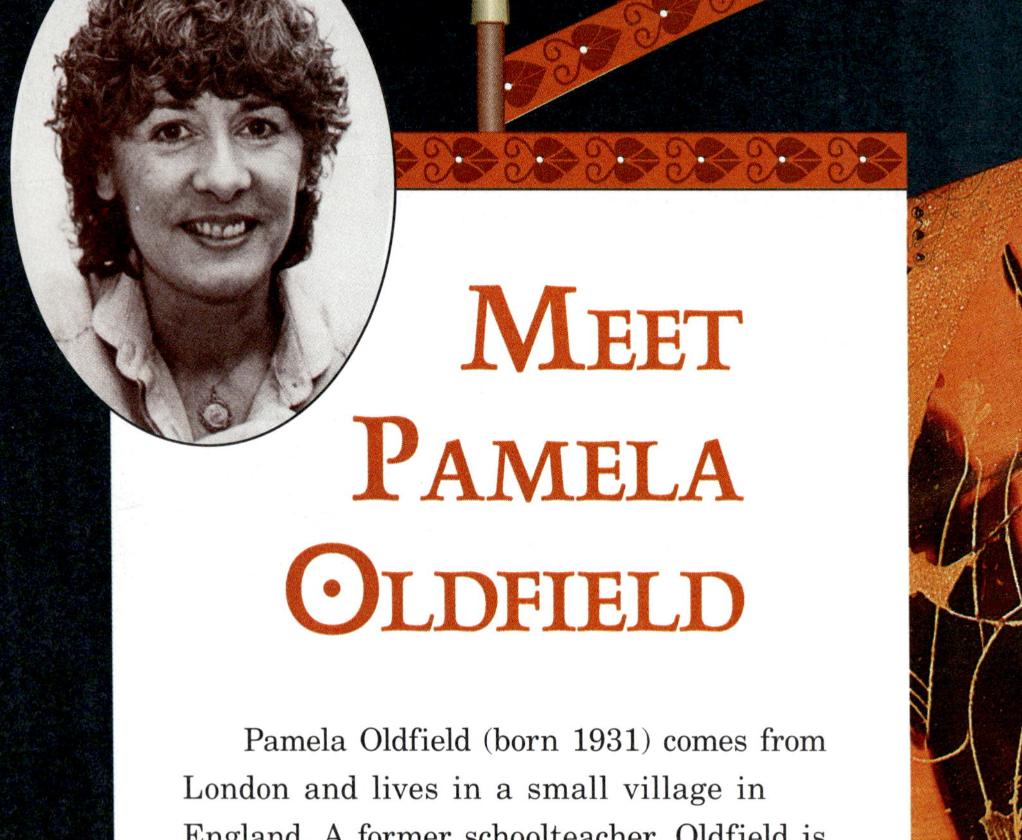

Meet Pamela Oldfield

Pamela Oldfield (born 1931) comes from London and lives in a small village in England. A former schoolteacher, Oldfield is the author of dozens of books for children and adults. Besides retelling Greek myths, she often writes about the supernatural, in books such as *Ghost Stories* and *A Witch in the Summer House.*

BELLEROPHON AND THE FLYING HORSE

Retold by Pamela Oldfield

Bellerophon, riding Pegasus, fights the Chimera *6th century B.C.*
Detail from red-figured cup from Rhodes, Greece The Louvre, Paris

ONCE LONG AGO A YOUNG MAN NAMED BELLEROPHON was staying with the King of Argos. The king's wife was impressed by Bellerophon and said as much to her husband. She talked about him so much that the king grew tired of listening to her.

"All you talk about is Bellerophon," he grumbled. "Try to think about something different for a change. The boy is far too young to be a hero."

His foolish wife took no notice. Day after day she told the king how handsome Bellerophon was, how clever and how brave. At last the king grew so jealous that he decided to get rid of Bellerophon, but without telling his wife. He handed Bellerophon a sealed letter and asked him to deliver it to the King of Lycia.

"This is a most important letter," he told Bellerophon. "Be sure you give it to him."

Bellerophon agreed to deliver the letter and set off at once. He soon reached Lycia and met the king. The two of them got on well right from the start. The king entertained him so lavishly that it was several days before Bellerophon remembered the letter.

"Forgive me, Your Majesty," he said. "I was asked to give you this." The king opened the letter. As he read it he turned quite pale.

"Whatever is the matter?" asked Bellerophon. "Is it bad news?" The king made no answer, but began to mutter to himself.

"This is treachery," he whispered. "I cannot believe it." Then he looked up at Bellerophon. "Never ask me about this letter," he commanded, and he threw it straight on the fire.

That night when Bellerophon went to bed he wondered about what was in the letter, but he was tired and soon fell asleep. The king, however, could not sleep. The letter had given him a terrible shock. It said that Bellerophon was a wicked young man and asked the king to have him killed.

"How could I do such a thing?" murmured the king. "Bellerophon seems such a pleasant young man, and he is a guest in my house. The King of Argos is known for his hot temper and he may soon regret this rash decision."

He paced up and down until at last he had an idea. "I shall send Bellerophon to slay the Chimera," he decided. "He may well die in the attempt, but if he succeeds even the King of Argos will have to admit that he is a true hero."

Chimera *second half of the 6th century* B.C. *Detail from Greek kylix The British Museum, London*

So the next day the king told Bellerophon about the ferocious monster that was causing distress to the people of his kingdom, and begged him to do something about it.

"The Chimera is ruining their lives," said the king. "I implore you to destroy it for me. You will find it over in the hills where the sun rises."

Bellerophon was rather puzzled by all this, but he agreed to go. He walked for many miles without seeing a sign of the monster and eventually stopped to ask an old farmer if he was going in the right direction. When Bellerophon mentioned what he was looking for, the old man's eyes widened in alarm.

"Stay away from the Chimera," he warned Bellerophon. "It's the vilest creature ever born. Plenty of young men have tried to kill it, but they have all died in the attempt."

"Perhaps I will have better luck," said Bellerophon hopefully. The old farmer shook his head.

"Young people today just will not listen to reason," he grumbled, "but if you are determined to get yourself killed, take that path through the woods. It will lead you to the Chimera."

Bellerophon thanked the farmer politely and went on his way, trying not to be alarmed by what he had been told. He was not looking forward to fighting the Chimera, but if he turned back without even trying he would be called a coward.

An hour later he sat down to rest, and to his astonishment a beautiful woman appeared before him.

"I am Athena, goddess of wisdom," she told him. "I know you plan to fight the Chimera and I will help you." She held out a bridle, and as Bellerophon took it from her she smiled at him and vanished.

"How odd," thought Bellerophon, staring at the bridle. "What possible use could a bridle be when I have no horse?" The bridle was of finest white leather studded with gold and decorated with precious jewels. "I shall take it with me," he said, and went on his way, puzzling over the strange gift. What Bellerophon did not notice was that far above him Pegasus, the winged horse of the gods, was wheeling and prancing among the clouds. Suddenly the snow-white horse flew down to earth to drink at a spring of pure water. Bellerophon was overjoyed when he saw the graceful creature before him. Now he knew why Athena had given him the bridle.

He approached the horse slowly, speaking softly to reassure him. "I know you are Pegasus," he said. "You are always ridden by the gods. I am not a god, but Athena has given me this bridle and I must ride you when I go to fight the dreadful Chimera." Pegasus nodded his head as if he understood, but just as Bellerophon reached out to touch him, the horse sprang into the air and out of reach. For a moment Bellerophon thought the horse would fly away, but then he came down again to drink. Eventually Bellerophon gave up his attempt to catch the horse. He put down the bridle and stood by, quietly observing. Pegasus was a fine animal with hoofs and wings of silver and a flowing mane and tail. Suddenly Bellerophon ran forward, jumped onto the horse's back, and clung to its mane. The horse tried every trick he knew to throw off his unwanted rider. He flew up into the air and swooped down again, but somehow Bellerophon managed to stay on its back. At last Pegasus flew down to land beside the spring once more.

Bellerophon guessed that now Pegasus would wear the bridle and he slipped it over the horse's head. Then he sprang once more onto the horse's back. "Take me to the Chimera!" he cried and Pegasus leaped upward, tossing his head with excitement.

They flew for many miles until at last they came to a valley where the grass and trees were trampled and broken. Far below them a village lay in ruins. From the dark hills beyond the valley they heard a thunderous rumbling roar.

Center:
Athena holding a shield with an image of Pegasus *c. 500–490 B.C. Panathenaic amphora The Metropolitan Museum of Art, New York Rogers Fund, 1907 (Accession no. 07.286.79)*

Pallas Athena (bronze)
Archaeological Museum
Piraeus, Greece

"That must be the Chimera," whispered Bellerophon. He leaned forward and reassuringly patted the horse's neck, but his own heart beat faster at the thought of what was to come. Pegasus showed no fear, but flew on toward the rumbling sound. Soon they were confronted by a horrible sight. The Chimera rose up before them . . . this was no ordinary beast—the monster had *three heads*!

One head roared—it was the head of a lion. The second head hissed—it was the head of a giant snake. The third and last head bleated like a goat and had two sharp horns.

Bellerophon was terrified. He almost wished he could turn back, but then he remembered Athena. She had sent Pegasus to help Bellerophon and that made him feel much braver.

"Death to the cruel Chimera!" he shouted, and drew out his sword. The lion's head reached out toward him, its mouth ready to swallow him up, but the winged horse darted sideways and Bellerophon cut off the head with one mighty blow. The Chimera's rage was frightful.

The snake's head lunged at Bellerophon, hissing loudly, but down came the sword again. Chop! And away rolled the snake's head.

"Two heads gone and one to go!" shouted Bellerophon, but the Chimera was not going to be beaten quite so easily. Without warning it reared up on its hind legs and reached out with its fearsome claws. They sank into the winged horse, who whinnied with pain. Silver feathers floated down and the beautiful white mane was suddenly speckled with blood.

The sight of the horse's blood made Bellerophon forget his own fear. Without a thought for his own safety he slashed again and again at the goat's head until that too lay bleeding on the ground. Now the Chimera had lost all three of its heads, and it collapsed in a heap.

Bellerophon waited, his sword at the ready, but the Chimera would rise no more.

A great cry went up as the people ran from their hiding places in the ruined village. "The Chimera is dead!" they cried, cheering and waving as Pegasus and Bellerophon flew skyward once more. They watched the young man and the horse as they rose higher and higher and disappeared at last among the rolling clouds.

The grateful people then set about rebuilding their village and replanting their crops. The memory of the beautiful white horse and its valiant rider would live on in their hearts forever. Bellerophon had escaped death, and no one could now doubt that he was indeed a hero.

Story Questions & Activities

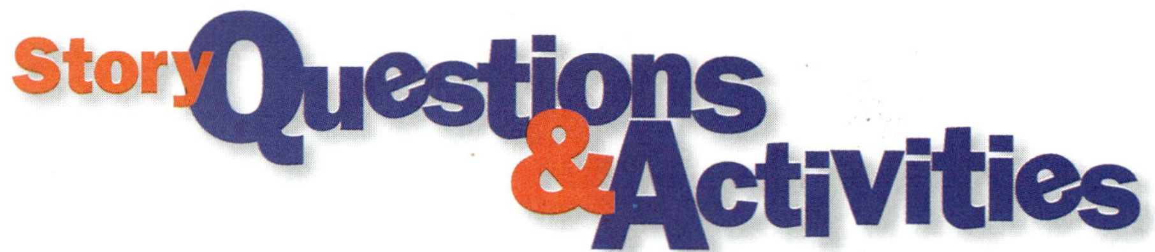

1. What life-or-death challenges does Bellerophon face?
2. How does the delivery of the letter trigger all the events that follow it in the story?
3. What lessons about human nature are taught in this myth?
4. What is this myth mainly about?
5. What traits does Bellerophon share with another superhuman hero you have read about or have seen in movies? What are the differences between the two heroes?

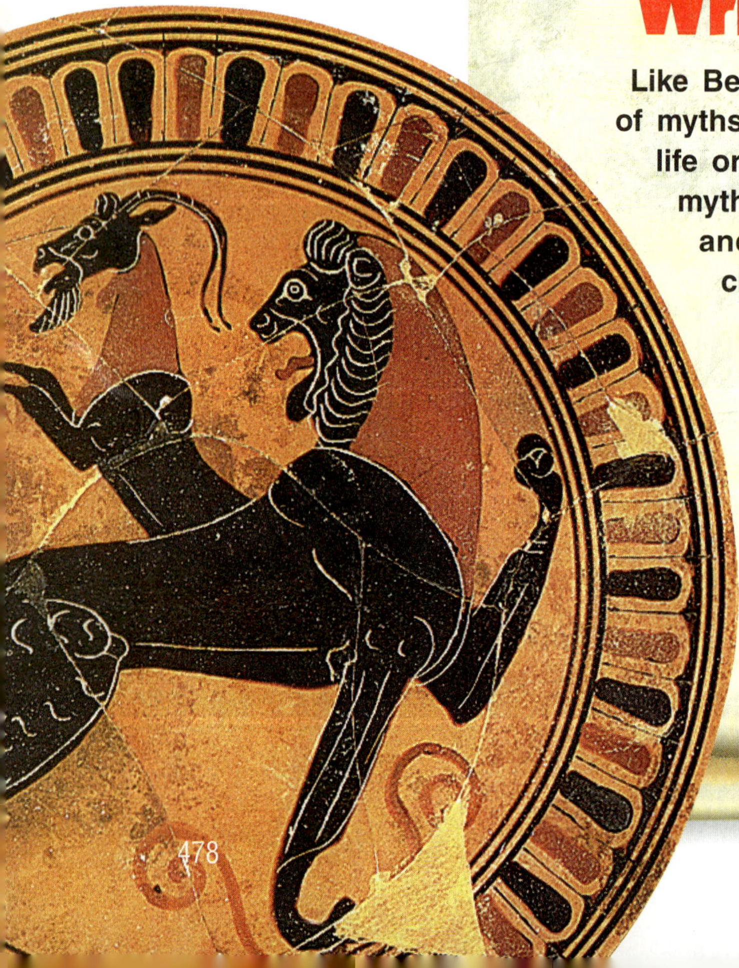

Write A Myth

Like Bellerophon, most heroes of myths face challenges that mean life or death. Now write your own myth. Invent an amazing hero and a larger-than-life challenge. Weave your myth around a strong idea or moral. Be sure to show a clear sequence of events. Explain what happens first, second, third, and so on. Give your myth a title. Then help design a class book of myths.

Decorate a Clay Pot

Greek potters often decorated their jars and other pottery with characters from Greek myths. Now it's your turn. Use clay that dries in the air to make a pot, a bowl, a cup, or a jar. Decorate your work with scenes from the myth you wrote. Use acrylic paints. Then display your handiwork in class.

GREECE

Make a Map

Find out where Greece is. Trace a map of Europe. Label each country and shade in the area that makes up the country of Greece.

Find Out More

Like "Bellerophon and the Flying Horse," myths describe the actions of superhuman heroes. They also tell about fantastic creatures. Find another Greek myth in which a hero slays a monster, such as *Theseus and the Minotaur*. Compare Bellerophon's task with the task of this other Greek hero. Share your findings.

Read a Constellation Map

Some planets, stars, and constellations are named for Greek gods and heroes. When astronomers in ancient Greece began to study the sky, they divided it into regions that had certain groups of stars. They named these constellations after the Greek figures the stars seemed to form. Most of our constellations were devised and named by early civilizations such as the Greeks and Romans.

Look at this constellation map. It shows the sky as it appears from the North Pole, with the North Star directly overhead. To use this map, face south and turn it so that the current month is at the bottom. The stars at the bottom are seen in most of the United States.

SEPTEMBER
OCTOBER
NOVEMBER
DECEMBER
JANUARY
FEBRUARY
MARCH
APRIL
MAY
JUNE
JULY
AUGUST
Aquarius
Pegasus
Pisces
Cetus
Aries
Andromeda
Taurus
Sagitta
Cygnus
Aquila
Cepheus
Cassiopeia
Perseus
Orion
Lyra
Polaris
Draco
Ursa Minor
Gemini
Hercules
Lynx
Ursa Major
Cancer
Boötes
Hydra
Leo
Virgo

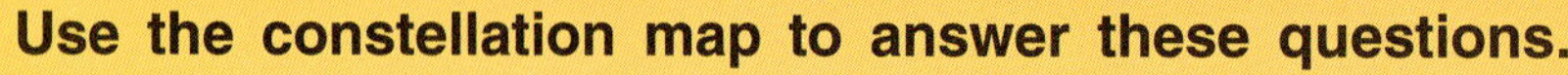

Use the constellation map to answer these questions.

1. How many stars make up Cygnus?
2. How do you think the constellation Pegasus got its name?
3. Why do you think there is a constellation called Hercules?
4. Can every star and constellation be seen during each month of the year? Use the map to explain.
5. Why do you think it is important to know how to read a constellation map?

TEST POWER

Test Tip

If you feel anxious during the test, take a deep breath, relax, and refocus.

DIRECTIONS

Read the sample story. Then read each question about the story.

SAMPLE

The Music of the Bodhran

The bodhran is an ancient frame drum. Pronounced *bow-rawn*, this Irish instrument is played with a double-headed drumstick called a *cipin*.

Although no one knows exactly how old the drum is, or where it was originally developed, it has been played for centuries. Some believe that the drum originated in Africa and was used mostly as a noisemaker in celebrations. Others believe that Celtic people carried the drum from its origins in Central Asia through Europe, and eventually to Ireland.

Today the bodhran is an accompaniment instrument in traditional Irish music. Players follow the rhythm of the music while a fiddle, bagpipe, or flute plays the melody. In fact, the bodhran rarely plays alone. But when the bodhran is played well, there is no sound like it!

1 The word accompaniment in this passage means —

A supporting

B melody

C quiet

D traveling

2 Which is the best summary for this passage?

F The bodhran originated in Africa.

G The bodhran is an accompaniment instrument.

H The bodhran is an ancient instrument that when played well has a beautiful sound.

J The bodhran is played with a double-headed drumstick.

Songs, poems, stories, news articles, and history books have been written about the event in this picture. Yet none is more famous than this painting showing the moment when the last spikes were hammered into the tracks of the transcontinental railroad.

Look at this painting. What can you tell about the setting? Who are the people in the picture? What can you tell about them? Who are the men by the tracks? What are they doing? Why do you think this painting is so famous? Do you like it? Explain your reasons.

Imagine that you are one of the eyewitnesses in the painting. Do you think that this railroad will change the country? In what ways? How will it affect travel in the future?

The Last Spike, May 10, 1869, Union Pacific Railroad, Promontory Point, Utah by Thomas Hill

Adventure

Meet Elaine Scott

"'Curious' is a word that describes me well," says Elaine Scott. Her curiosity has led her to write books on a wide range of topics. Scott has written about what goes on behind the scenes in television shows and movies. She has written about the making of comic strips, the making of oil, and what it is like to be a twin. Besides her nonfiction work, Scott has also written a novel, *Choices*.

Scott's follow-up book to *Adventure in Space* is called *Close Encounters: Exploring the Universe with the Hubble Space Telescope*. It was awarded the 1999 American Institute of Physics Award. Today, Scott makes her home in Houston, Texas.

Meet Margaret Miller

Margaret Miller has worked with Elaine Scott on several successful nonfiction books for young people. Besides her work as a writer, Miller is also a talented photographer. She has created numerous books of photographs, and was awarded a 1992 *New York Times* Best Illustrated Children's Book for her photographs in *Where Does It Go?* Currently, Miller lives in New York City.

in Space

by Elaine Scott and Margaret Miller

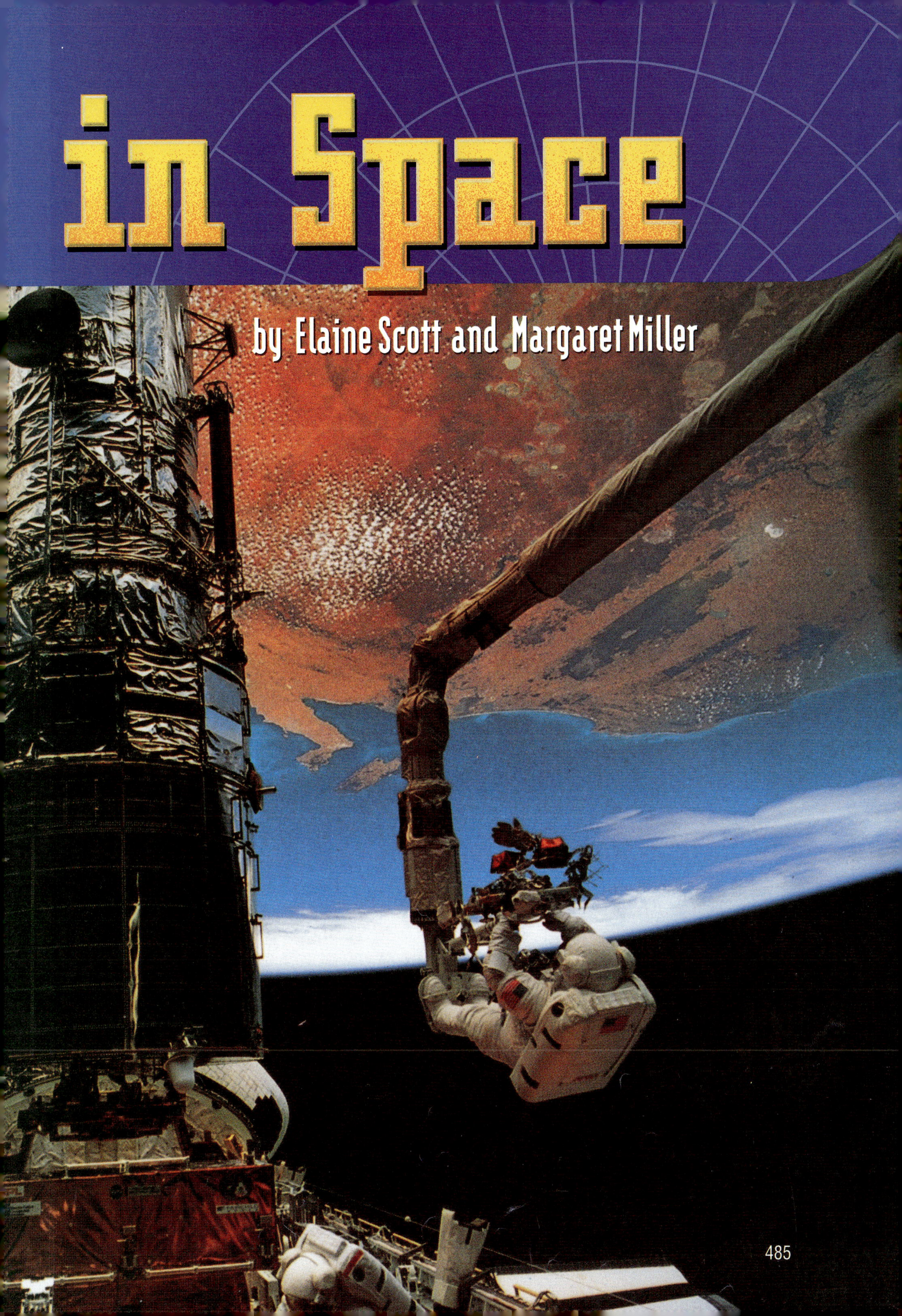

Introduction

For centuries scientists have dreamed of putting a telescope in orbit. With the success of the first space flights, this dream took a giant step closer to becoming a reality. In 1990 NASA, the United States space agency, launched the Hubble Space Telescope. Free from the blur of Earth's atmosphere, this instrument could see farther and more clearly than any telescope on Earth.

Yet two months after the telescope was launched, it ran into problems. Someone had made a mistake. The Hubble's mirror was a little too flat, and the telescope needed new "glasses" to help focus light correctly. The winglike solar arrays, which power the Hubble's cameras and instruments, seemed to be having trouble, too. Their shaking had to be stopped. The gyroscopes were also a problem. Three had already failed. If another one failed, the telescope could not be pointed in the direction that the scientists wanted. The Hubble would be useless.

After much thought, NASA decided to fix the space telescope. By building COSTAR, an instrument with ten tiny mirrors, it would give the Hubble new "glasses." It also decided to give it a new camera, WF/PC II, to study objects at the farthest ends of the universe. Now it just needed to find the right astronauts to do the job.

It found seven. Richard Covey would fly the space shuttle *Endeavour*. His backup would be Kenneth Bowersox, nicknamed "Sox." Story Musgrave, Jeffrey Hoffman, Kathryn Thornton, and Thomas Akers would make the space walks needed to repair the telescope. Claude Nicollier would operate the robot arm that carried the space-walking astronauts. All in all, NASA seemed to have a plan. All the astronauts had to do was make the plan work. That would be the hard part. It would also be one of the greatest adventures in space.

Early on the third day, *Endeavour* was rapidly catching up with the telescope. The crew was excited. Just before sunset, they spotted the Hubble. It was a beautiful sight, glowing blue and silver in the fading light. "Now it's all eyeballs and hands," Sox said, as he and Commander Dick Covey took over from Mission Control and fired small burns from the maneuvering rockets. Slowly and gently, the shuttle approached the forty-three-foot-long telescope looming outside its windows. The rocket burns used fuel, and Ken Bowersox was worried. He knew that there was only one chance to capture the Hubble. If they weren't in the right position, there wouldn't be enough fuel for a second attempt. If they didn't grab the Hubble on their first and only try, the mission would have failed before it began.

Claude was ready at the controls of the robot arm, waiting for the right moment. *Endeavour* glided into place below the telescope. Claude reached out with the mechanical arm and snared it! The telescope was safe, snugly tucked into the payload bay. With relief, Dick Covey radioed Mission Control. "Houston, *Endeavour* has a firm handshake with Mr. Hubble's telescope. It's quite a sight." The first crucial step of the repair mission was over. It was time for the space walks to begin.

The shuttle's robot arm (left) is poised, waiting for the right momentum to capture the Hubble Space Telescope and anchor it in the orbiter's payload bay.

Now the first surprise took its "bite." One of the solar arrays was badly twisted. Would it roll up as planned? Story and Jeff would look more closely the next day, when the "house calls" on Hubble would begin. Commander Dick Covey summed up the spirit of the crew when he said, "We are ready. We are inspired. Let's go fix this thing."

The next day, Kathy and Tom helped Story and Jeff put on their space suits. Their very lives would depend on them. Outer space is just that—space. It is a void. There is nothing in it—no oxygen, no hydrogen, no carbon dioxide—nothing. Human beings without protection would die in that environment in a matter of seconds. The air would rush out of our lungs. Our blood would boil, our skin expand. And as if that weren't a terrible enough picture, we would roast or freeze, depending on whether it was day or night.

While the Hubble Space Telescope was being designed, Story Musgrave suggested that it be fitted with handrails to make it easier for space-walking astronauts to service it. Story uses those handrails on his first space walk.

Going out into space is not like going out your front door. Story and Jeff entered and left the shuttle through its air lock, a small chamber with two hatches, or doors. Before leaving the shuttle, they had to breathe pure oxygen for about forty minutes in order to get rid of the nitrogen in their bloodstream. In outer space, nitrogen can cause a painful and dangerous condition known as the bends. After their "pre-breathe" was over, all of the air was pumped out of the air lock. Now it was a vacuum, just like space. The astronauts could safely open the outer door and float into the payload bay. "It's an exciting moment when you open the air lock and see the entire universe staring you in the face," Jeff said, as he and Story started the first space walk.

For safety, Story and Jeff each attached themselves to the shuttle with a tether, a long metal cable. Moving deliberately and cautiously, Story pulled himself hand over hand along the sixty-foot length of the payload bay to the waiting telescope. His feet secured in foot restraints, Jeff got a ride on Claude's robot arm. All went well as they replaced the faulty gyroscopes—until they tried to close the doors to the instrument compartment. A second surprise took a "bite."

One door sagged slightly below the other, and they would not close. Jeff and Story struggled with the balky doors. Because they no longer matched, the closing bolt would not slide home. The astronauts used their power tools with no results. They talked to Mission Control and even considered leaving the doors slightly ajar. But Story was determined. In a move that was not rehearsed ahead of time, he went to the toolbox and removed a tool called a come-along. The come-along held the two doors together, leaving Story's hands free to push on them and force the closing bolt home. The operation was a success, and Story and Jeff earned a new nickname from NASA—Mr. Goodwrench.

Next, the crew turned their attention to the twisted solar array. The solar arrays were designed to roll up like window shades. The undamaged array rolled up smoothly for storage, but the other would not roll up because it was warped. The Even Couple—Kathy and Tom—would have to throw it overboard the next day, before installing the new arrays.

Story and Jeff put Kathy and Tom in their space suits for the second space walk and sent them off to work. Kathy rode the robot arm while Tom floated. The damaged solar array was still producing electricity from the sun, so Kathy and Tom had to work during the orbiting "night." They had lights on their space helmets, like miners, and from inside the shuttle, Story helped by shining a spotlight on the work area. Still, it was hard for them to see exactly what they were doing. Kathy steadied the large floppy array while Tom unfastened it.

The solar arrays were attached to the telescope with electrical connectors similar to the plugs on the back of a computer. Each connector had many small pins that could be easily bent—especially by someone trying to plug or unplug them wearing bulky space gloves! The connectors and bolts were essential to the telescope's life. If they were damaged during this repair, the new arrays could not be installed. Without solar energy, the Hubble would have no electricity. Without electricity, the Hubble would have no life.

On the fifth space walk, Story Musgrave and Jeff Hoffman performed final repairs. Here they prepare to put new covers on the telescope's magnetometers.

The team worked slowly and deliberately as *Endeavour* fell around the Earth. At last, Kathy, riding on the end of the robot arm, was ready for the crucial and dangerous moment when she alone would hold the array. She had to keep it steady and still. If it flopped around it could hit and damage the telescope. The Hubble had enough trouble; Kathy did not want to "break what isn't broken," as Jeff would say. She waited for Tom's instructions.

"Coming out real smooth," Tom said. "Four inches . . . six inches . . . eight inches out." His voice was calm, a gentle coach.

Kathy said, "OK, Claude, real easy." She truly had her hands full, as the robotic arm pulled her slowly away from the telescope.

"OK, K.T. I'm letting go," said Tom.

"I have it," Kathy answered. The array was perfectly steady and Kathy exclaimed with delight, "Holy moley, a piece of cake!"

But tension mounted again. Everyone was worried about the moment when Kathy would toss the array overboard. It had to be done in daylight, when the entire crew could see clearly. No one wanted the array to hit the top of the Hubble on its way to becoming space junk. Poised on the end of the robot arm, Kathy held it over her head and waited for the sun to rise over Africa.

"I think I see sunrise coming, K.T.," Tom said.

At last, the word came from Story, inside the shuttle. "OK, Tom. Tell K.T. to go for release."

Tom had one request. "Can you just hang on one second, so I can get to where I can watch?" He moved to get a better view, then said, "OK, K.T. You ready?"

"Ready."

"Got a go for release," Tom said. The moment had come. "OK. No hands!" Kathy said as she let go of the 350 pounds of useless metal and fabric.

"There it goes," said Tom. The panel revolved and drifted away. Sox fired a few small burns from the shuttle's rockets to move *Endeavour* and the telescope out of danger. In the void of space, the maneuver caused an artificial wind.

Kathy's voice came over the radio again. "Wonder what it's going to do when it starts flapping in the breeze?"

Suddenly, as she saw the great orange array flexing over the desert, she exclaimed, "It's almost like a bird, Tom. Look at it!" They stared at the incredible sight of a giant "bird" soaring over the African desert below.

Perched on the end of the robot arm, Kathy Thornton steadies the damaged solar array while she waits for dawn and the right moment to release it.

Because COSTAR had to be held directly in front of her face, Kathy Thornton relies on Tom Akers's instructions while guiding it into place.

The results of all the planning and practice were becoming more and more obvious as each team of astronauts completed their space walks successfully. On the third space walk, Story and Jeff installed the new camera, WF/PC II. The critical moment came when Jeff held the camera steady and Story removed the protective cover on the mirror. One slight touch or bump, and the mirror could have been contaminated or knocked out of alignment, a catastrophe that would have crippled the telescope. The astronauts' movements were slow, precise, and delicate. Everyone relaxed a bit when that job was finished, and Jeff said excitedly, "I hope we have a lot of eager astronomers ready to use this beautiful thing."

On the fourth walk, Kathy and Tom became orbiting eye doctors and slid the refrigerator-sized COSTAR into the telescope. Kathy moved the six-hundred-pound instrument with ease, but COSTAR was in front of her face. She knew she had only millimeters of clearance, but she couldn't see what she was doing. Once again, her partner became her eyes, and COSTAR slid into place without a hitch. Tom hummed while he worked. Later, Claude recalled that sound and said, "It was good to hear Tom humming, because we knew when Tom was humming things were going well. And Tom was humming most of the time!"

When the Hubble's "glasses" were in place, Kathy said, "I think everyone can breathe a sigh of relief." Jeff added, "It should be exciting to see what the Hubble can do with a new set of eyeballs."

On the fifth EVA, when Story and Jeff were winding up the repairs, a tiny screw came loose and floated away. On Earth, a dropped screw is not a disaster. In space, it could be. It could contaminate the Hubble. Jeff and Claude spotted it at the same time; Claude noticed it even from his position inside the shuttle. The "famous screw chase," as Story called it, was on. Jeff rode the arm while Claude steered him toward the floating screw, in hot pursuit. Later Jeff said, "When we were chasing it, I actually felt like a kid riding on a merry-go-round, going after the brass ring, holding on with one hand and reaching out." Jeff got the "brass ring," and he and Story finished up their work. They did a final cleanup of the payload bay and reentered the shuttle, knowing that the Hubble was now ready to go. The time had come to send it on its way.

Claude raised the towering observatory from its workbench and released it into orbit once again. As it moved into the blackness of space, its orange solar arrays glowed in the sunset. "It will look far into the cosmos and far into the past," he said. "It is a time machine as well as a space exploration machine."

Looking out the shuttle's window, Tom was wistful. "The payload bay really looks empty."

In a record-breaking five space walks—no mission to space had ever had that many—the heroes of STS-61 had accomplished what many said could not be done. It was time for these space mechanics to return to Earth.

Repaired and ready to observe the universe, the Hubble Space Telescope floats away from *Endeavour's* cargo bay.

(Left) Kathy Thornton works on COSTAR. A checklist containing vital information was attached to the sleeve of each astronaut's space suit.

Story Questions & Activities

1. Why did the *Endeavour* have only one chance to capture the Hubble?
2. How does the crew overcome the obstacles they encounter in space?
3. Why do you think NASA decided to fix the Hubble Space Telescope? Explain.
4. What is the main idea of this selection?
5. In a record-breaking five spacewalks, the space heroes had accomplished what many people thought could not be done. First, decide what makes these astronauts modern heroes. Then compare their mission with the task Bellerophon performs.

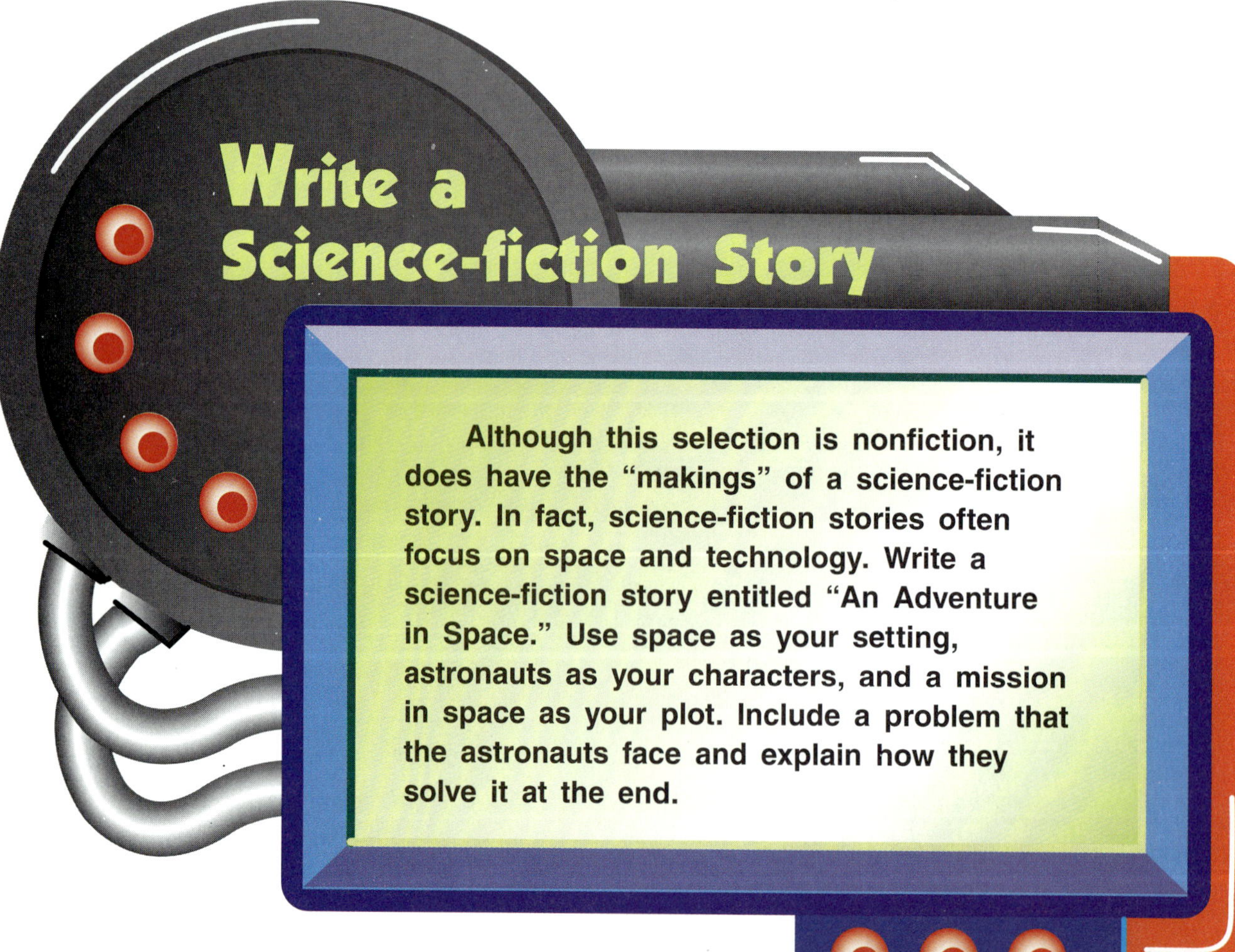

Write a Science-fiction Story

Although this selection is nonfiction, it does have the "makings" of a science-fiction story. In fact, science-fiction stories often focus on space and technology. Write a science-fiction story entitled "An Adventure in Space." Use space as your setting, astronauts as your characters, and a mission in space as your plot. Include a problem that the astronauts face and explain how they solve it at the end.

Create a Mobile

Make a space mobile of planets, stars, constellations, astronauts, and a spacecraft or space station. Cut out pictures from old books or magazines, or use your own colored drawings. Paste them on cardboard and then cut them out. Make a frame for your mobile from one or two metal coat hangers. Then use dental floss, clear fishing line, or yarn to hang the objects from the frame so that they move like real objects in space.

Give a Talk

What would it be like to be part of the crew of the Endeavour? Imagine that you are one of the astronauts. Give a talk to a group about something that happened to you during the mission. Explain a decision that you had to make. Then tell how it felt to be in space. How do you now feel about Earth?

Find Out More

NASA, the United States space agency, worked with 16 other countries to create the Hubble Space Telescope. Find out about some of NASA's other projects. Use an encyclopedia, a book about NASA, or the NASA website on the Internet. Write a short report about one of the projects, stressing its goals and achievements.

Read a Flow Chart

Instead of making lists, NASA might have organized the instructions attached to the astronauts' sleeves into a flow chart. A **flow chart** is a diagram that shows the steps in a process. Some flow charts show different possible steps, depending on outcomes along the way. This flow chart is for a space mission described in a science fiction novel.

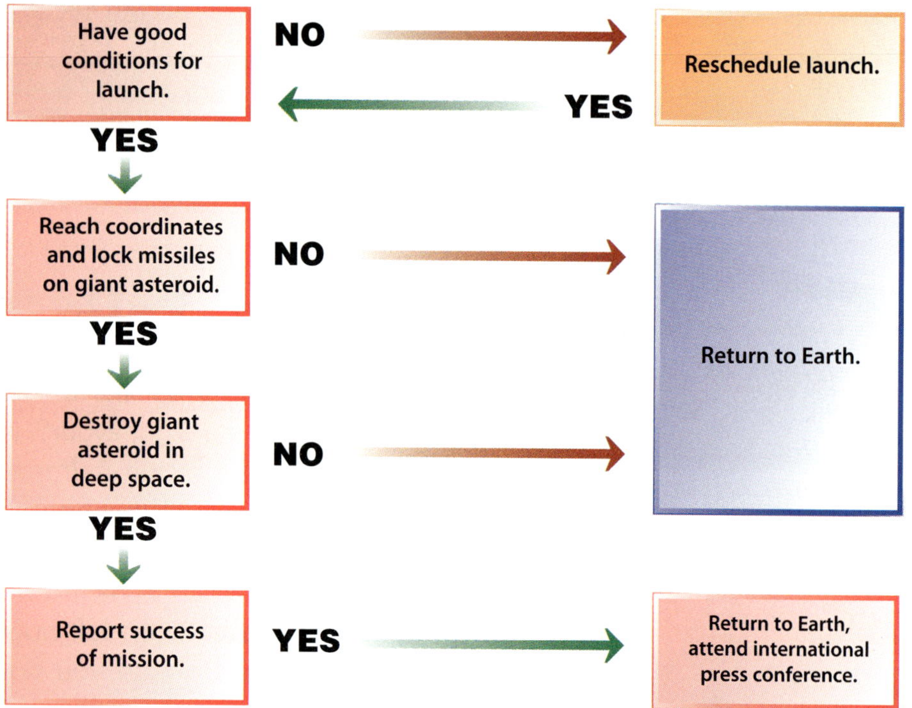

Use the flow chart to answer these questions.

1. What will happen if conditions are not good for the launch?
2. What is the next goal to be achieved after a successul launch?
3. Will there be a press conference if the astronauts fail to destroy the giant asteroid? Why or why not?
4. There are two boxes marked "Return to Earth." How do they reflect the mission's success or failure?
5. How might creating a flow chart help you when you are starting your next big research assignment?

TEST POWER

Test Tip

Tell yourself the story again in your own words.

DIRECTIONS

Read the sample story. Then read each question about the story.

SAMPLE

Ancient Mayan Civilization

The Mayan people were perhaps the most advanced of all ancient cultures. Despite that, this culture remains a mystery.

The Mayans developed a complex writing system and had a keen understanding of natural science. They charted the movements of the sun, the stars, and the planets before the first telescope was ever invented. They were talented artists; they created wonderful pottery, weavings, and paintings. The Mayans were agriculturally advanced. They could harvest crops in even the most difficult conditions.

But as mysteriously as their culture appeared, the Mayan culture disappeared. Some historians think that the Mayans died from famine. They believe that the population had grown so large that it could not support itself. The land could not produce enough food to feed the people.

1 The word famine in this passage means —

A eating bad meat

B poisoning themselves

C a severe food shortage

D growing population

2 The Mayan culture remains a mystery to historians because —

F the Mayan people probably wanted it that way

G the Mayan culture disappeared

H the Mayan leaders were unlike other leaders of the time

J the Mayan artistry was so advanced

Stories in Art

Greasy Spoon Life by John Holcroft, 1996

Look at this painting quickly. What do you see? You probably see a still life of an American breakfast. If you look again, you might just see someone vacuuming under the egg!

What can you tell about this painting? Does it make you laugh? Why? What kind of setting is this? How does the title give you a clue? Notice the tablecloth and other details. How do they help you to figure out who the woman might be?

Look at the painting again. Why is the breakfast larger than the woman? What could the artist be saying about her life? How does he make his point by showing something usual in an unusual way?

Meet Diane Stanley

Diane Stanley never thought she would become a writer and an illustrator of children's books until her own children were born. When she was growing up, she and her mother would create books together. However, her mother would write the stories, and she would draw the pictures to go with them. As an adult, Stanley continued her career as an artist by illustrating medical books.

Today, Stanley has published more than 20 books. Some of these books, like *Rumpelstiltskin's Daughter,* are funny and have a little twist. Stanley has also written illustrated biographies. In fact, her subjects include such famous people from history as Peter the Great, William Shakespeare, and Queen Elizabeth I. In keeping with a family tradition, Stanley wrote several of these books with a family member. This time it was with her husband.

Rumpelstiltskin's Daughter
Diane Stanley

Once there was a miller's daughter who got into a heap of trouble. It was all because her father liked to make up stories and pass them off as truth. Unfortunately, the story he told was that his daughter could spin straw into gold, which, of course, she could not. Even more unfortunately, he told this whopper in the hearing of a palace servant who rushed right off to tell the king. Since the king loved nothing in this world more than gold, he had the miller's daughter hauled up to the palace immediately and made her an offer she couldn't refuse. He put her in a room full of straw and ordered her to spin it into gold by morning, or die.

By one of those unlikely coincidences so common in fairy tales, no sooner had the king closed and bolted the door than a very small gentleman showed up and revealed that he really *could* spin straw into gold. Furthermore, he offered to do it in exchange for her necklace, which was made of gold-tone metal and wasn't worth ten cents. Naturally, she agreed.

The next morning, the king was so overjoyed with his room full of gold that he rewarded the miller's daughter by doubling the amount of straw and repeating his threat. Once again, Rumpelstiltskin (for that was his name) arrived to help her out. This time she gave him her cigar-band pinkie ring.

After this second success, the king was practically apoplectic with greed. He proceeded to empty every barn in the neighborhood of straw and to fill the room with it. This time, he added a little sugar to sweeten the pot: If she turned it all into gold, he would make her his queen. You can just imagine how the miller's daughter was feeling when Rumpelstiltskin popped in for the third time.

"That's quite a pile," he said. "I suppose you want me to spin it into gold."

"Well, the situation has changed just a bit," said the miller's daughter (who also had a name—it was Meredith). "If you *don't*, I will die. If you *do*, I marry the king."

Now *that*, thought Rumpelstiltskin, has possibilities. After all, getting to be the queen was a big step up for a miller's daughter. She would surely pay him anything. And there was only one thing in the world he really wanted—a little child to love and care for.

"Okay, here's the deal," he said. "I will spin the straw into gold, just like before. In return, once you become queen, you must let me adopt your firstborn child. I promise I'll be an excellent father. I know all the lullabies. I'll read to the child every day. I'll even coach Little League."

"You've got to be kidding," Meredith said. "I'd rather marry *you* than that jerk!"

"Really?" said Rumpelstiltskin, and he blushed all the way from the top of his head to the tip of his toes (which admittedly wasn't very far, because he was so short).

"Sure," she said. "I like your ideas on parenting, you'd make a good provider, and I have a weakness for short men."

So Rumpelstiltskin spun a golden ladder, and they escaped out the window. They were married the very next day and lived happily together far, far away from the palace.

Meredith and Rumpelstiltskin lived a quiet country life, raising chickens and growing vegetables. Every now and then, when they needed something they couldn't make or grow, Rumpelstiltskin would spin up a little gold to buy it with.

Now, they had a daughter, and she was just as sunny and clever as you would expect her to be, having such devoted parents. When she was sixteen, they decided she ought to see more of the world, so every now and then they allowed her to take the gold into town to exchange it for coins and to do a little shopping.

The goldsmith grew curious about the pretty country girl who came in with those odd coils of gold. He mentioned it to his friend the baker, who mentioned it to the blacksmith, who mentioned it to the tax collector, who hurried to the palace and told the king.

It may not surprise you to learn that the king hadn't changed a bit. If anything, he was greedier than before. As he listened, his eyes glittered. "I once knew a miller's daughter who could make gold like that," he said. "Unfortunately, she got away. Let's make sure *this* one doesn't."

So the next time Rumpelstiltskin's daughter went to see the goldsmith, two of the king's guards were waiting for her. In a red-hot minute, she was in a carriage and speeding toward the palace. And what she saw on the way broke her heart. Everywhere the fields lay barren. Sickly children stood begging beside the road. Nobody in the kingdom had anything anymore, because the king had it all.

Finally they reached the palace. There were high walls around it and a moat full of crocodiles. Armed guards were everywhere, gnashing their teeth, clutching their swords, and peering about with shifty eyes. As the carriage went over the bridge and under the portcullis, the hungry people shook their fists at them. It was not a pretty sight.

Rumpelstiltskin's daughter was taken at once to the grand chamber where the king sat on his golden throne. He didn't waste time on idle pleasantries.

"Where did you get *this*?" he asked, showing her the gold.

"Uh . . . ," said Rumpelstiltskin's daughter.

"I thought so," said the king. "Guards, take her to the tower and see what she can do with all that straw."

Rumpelstiltskin's daughter looked around. She saw a pile of straw the size of a bus. She saw a locked door and high windows. She gave a big sigh and began to think. She knew her father could get her out of this pickle. But she had heard stories about the king all her life. One room full of gold would never satisfy him. Her father would be stuck here, spinning, until there was not an iota of straw left in the kingdom.

After a while she climbed the pile of straw and thought some more. She thought about the poor farmers and about the hungry children with their thin faces and sad eyes. She put the two thoughts together and cooked up a plan. Then Rumpelstiltskin's daughter curled up and went to sleep.

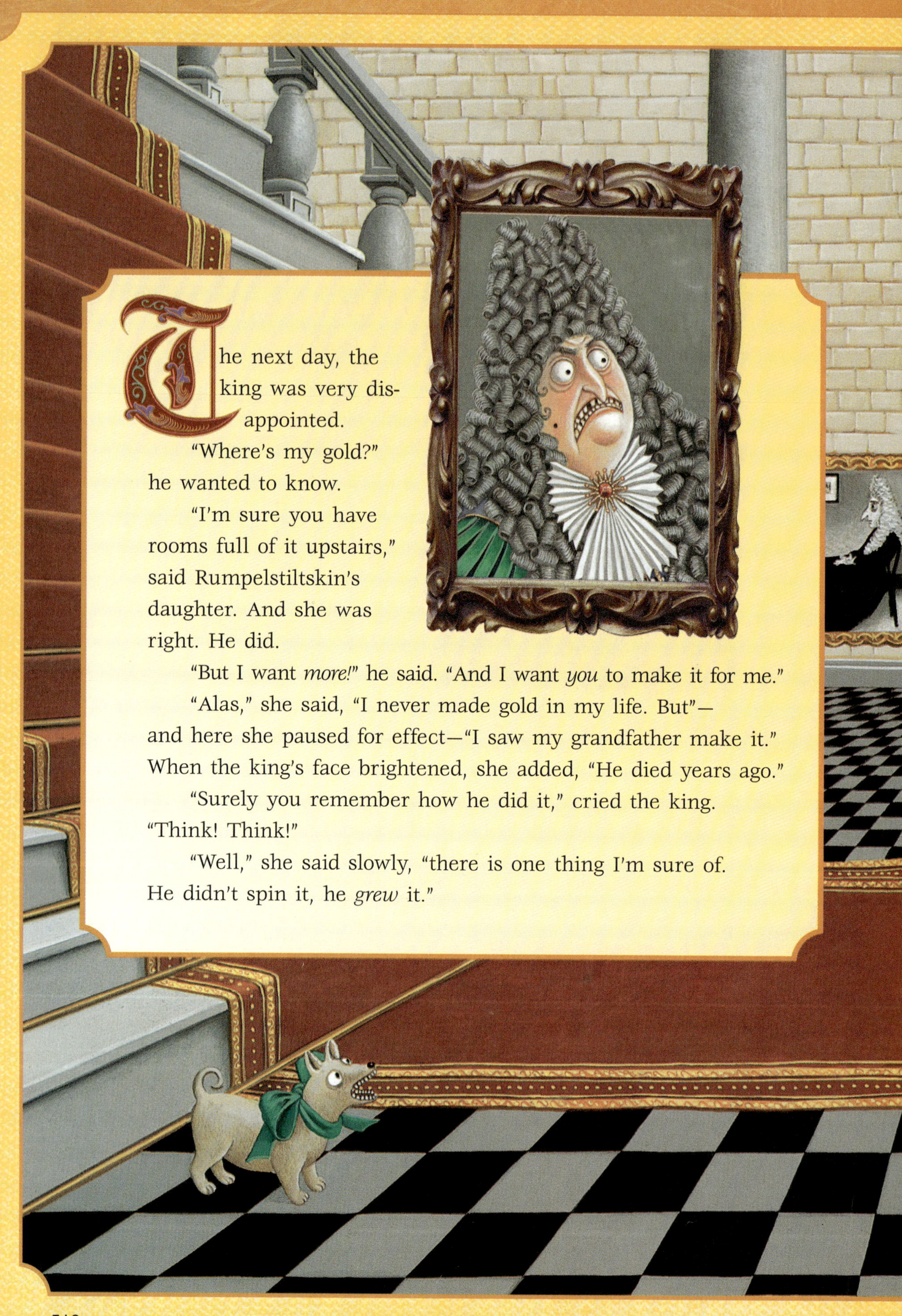

The next day, the king was very disappointed.

"Where's my gold?" he wanted to know.

"I'm sure you have rooms full of it upstairs," said Rumpelstiltskin's daughter. And she was right. He did.

"But I want *more!*" he said. "And I want *you* to make it for me."

"Alas," she said, "I never made gold in my life. But"—and here she paused for effect—"I saw my grandfather make it." When the king's face brightened, she added, "He died years ago."

"Surely you remember how he did it," cried the king. "Think! Think!"

"Well," she said slowly, "there is one thing I'm sure of. He didn't spin it, he *grew* it."

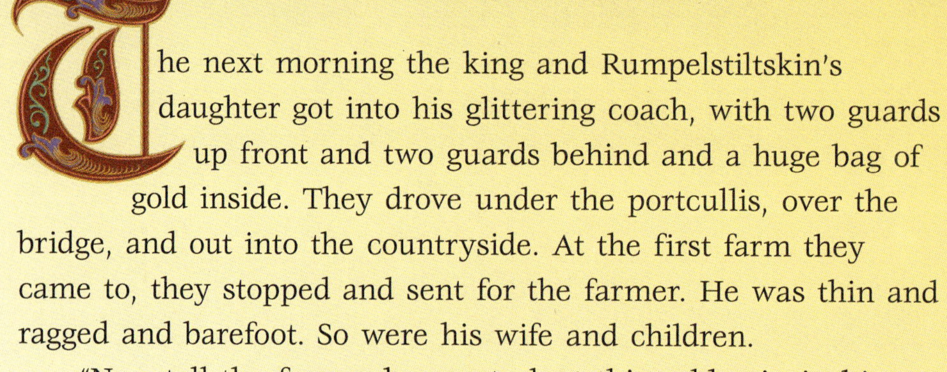

The next morning the king and Rumpelstiltskin's daughter got into his glittering coach, with two guards up front and two guards behind and a huge bag of gold inside. They drove under the portcullis, over the bridge, and out into the countryside. At the first farm they came to, they stopped and sent for the farmer. He was thin and ragged and barefoot. So were his wife and children.

"Now tell the farmer he must plant this gold coin in his field, and you will come back in the fall to collect everything it has grown. Tell him you will give him another gold coin for his pains," she whispered.

"Do I *have* to?" the king whined.

"Well, I don't know," she said. "That's how my grandfather always did it."

"Okay," said the king. "But this better work." He gave the farmer two gold coins, and they hurried on to the next farm. By the end of the week they had covered the entire kingdom.

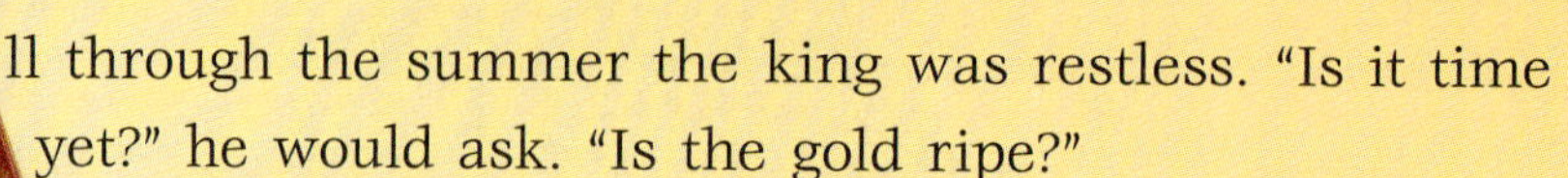

All through the summer the king was restless. "Is it time yet?" he would ask. "Is the gold ripe?"

"Wait," said Rumpelstiltskin's daughter.

Finally August came and went.

"Now," she said. "Now you can go and see what has grown in the fields."

So once again they piled into the glittering coach (with two guards up front and two guards behind) and brought along wagons to carry the gold and a lot more guards to protect it.

As they neared the first farm, the king gasped with joy. The field shone golden in the morning sun.

"Gold!" he cried.

"No," said Rumpelstiltskin's daughter, "something better than gold."

"How can anything be better than gold?" said the king.

"It's wheat," she said. "You can eat it. You can't eat gold."

Before the king could start turning purple, the farmer and his family came running toward the carriage. In their arms they carried baskets of wheat and barley and apples and green beans and pumpkins and corn and I don't know what all. They piled it into the wagon and kissed the king's hand, grinning ear to ear. I can promise you that nothing like that had ever happened to the king before.

"Well," he said sheepishly, "maybe there will be gold at the next place."

But everywhere it was the same. The land prospered, the children looked healthy, and the king was a hero. At the end of the week they returned to the palace with all the food the wagons could carry.

The cook was so overjoyed, he put on a sumptuous feast to celebrate. Unfortunately, there was no one to invite except Rumpelstiltskin's daughter and the guards, who spent the whole meal gnashing their teeth, clutching their swords, and peering about with shifty eyes.

"I wish they'd quit that," said Rumpelstiltskin's daughter.

After dinner, the king spoke. "That was all very nice, my dear," he said, "but you must have been mistaken. That was how your grandfather grew *food*, not how he made gold."

"Right," she said as she pulled her shawl tightly around her shoulders and gazed longingly at the fire. Even in the palace she could feel the chill of autumn. *Time for phase two*, she thought.

"Of course you're right," she said. "I told you it was long ago. But I think I remember now. He didn't grow gold. He *knitted* it with golden knitting needles."

So the next day they loaded the coach with knitting needles, a bag of gold, and lots and lots of yellow wool. Then they headed off under the portcullis, over the bridge (with two guards up front and two guards behind), and out into the countryside.

At the first cottage they came to, they asked to see the granny. She hobbled to the door in her rags and curtsied to the king.

"Now," whispered Rumpelstiltskin's daughter, "give her a bag of wool and a pair of needles. Tell her to knit it all up and you will come back in a month to collect your riches. Give her a gold coin for her pains."

"Do I *have* to?" the king whined.

"My grandfather always did," she said. "I would, if I were you."

And so they went all over the kingdom, hiring every granny they could find.

At the end of the month, the king ordered his coach and wagons, rounded up his guards, and went to see the grannies. As he neared the first cottage, he heard the sound of singing. Looking out the window, the king saw the happy villagers waiting there to greet him, cheering wildly as he passed. And every one of them was warm as toast in yellow woolly clothes.

"Gold!" cried the king.

"Something better than gold," said Rumpelstiltskin's daughter. "Your people will be warm all winter."

Everyone brought presents for the king. By the time he got back to his palace, he had seventeen sweaters, forty-two mufflers, eight vests, one pair of knickers, one hundred and thirty-five pairs of socks, twelve nightcaps, and a tam-o'-shanter. All the color of gold.

Do they suit me?" asked the king as he tried them on.

"Absolutely," said Rumpelstiltskin's daughter.

The guards just stood there, gnashing their teeth, clutching their swords, and peering about with shifty eyes.

"Don't you think it's time you got rid of them?" she suggested. "And the walls and the moat and the crocodiles, too. You don't need them anymore—your people love you now."

She was right, as always, so the king set the guards to work tearing down the walls. And with the stones, they built a zoo for the crocodiles and houses for the poor.

"Are you sure you don't remember how your grandfather made gold?" asked the king one day.

"I'm afraid not," she said.

"It's a terrible pity," he sighed. "But you did try. And as a reward, I have decided to make you my queen."

"Why don't you make me prime minister instead," suggested Rumpelstiltskin's daughter.

And so the king did just that. He built her a nice house near the palace, and once a month she took time off to visit her parents. The people of the kingdom never went cold or hungry again. And whenever the king started worrying about gold, she sent him on a goodwill tour throughout the countryside, which cheered him right up.

Oh, and I forgot to tell you—Rumpelstiltskin's daughter had a name, too. It was Hope.

1. Which character changes the most in the story? How?
2. How do you know that Rumpelstiltskin's daughter is the main character in this version of the fairy tale?
3. Why would Rumpelstiltskin's daughter make a good prime minister? Explain.
4. How would you complete this sentence? This story is a fairy tale because _______.
5. Compare Rumpelstiltskin's daughter with Cinderella or another female character from a fairy tale you know. How are the characters alike? How do they differ?

Write a Fractured Fairy Tale

You may not have expected some of the things that happened in this fairy tale, especially if you knew the original story of Rumpelstiltskin. Such twists in character and plot make this selection a fractured fairy tale. Choose one of your favorite fairy tales and write a funny version of it. For example, the three little pigs might be weightlifters who are not afraid of anyone. Besides differences in character, your story might have a different setting, plot, or ending.

Build a Castle

Even today, most kings and queens live in castles and palaces. Suppose that a royal family asked you to build a castle for them. What would you make the castle look like? Would it be modern? Make a sketch of your castle. Then use your sketch to build a model from cardboard sheets, cardboard tubes from paper towels, construction paper, popsicle sticks, and other art materials.

Draw a Poster

Suppose you were Hope. How much would you charge to meet the king? Why would people want to meet him, anyway? Draw a poster that will make people want to see and hear the king. Illustrate your poster, and give the subject of his "talk." Include the date, time, and place so that people will know when and where to meet the king.

Find Out More

In the story, Rumpelstiltskin's daughter chooses the job of prime minister to that of becoming the queen. What is a prime minister? How is it different from a president? Start by looking in an encyclopedia or a social studies textbook. Gather facts and take notes. Then draw a chart or a Venn diagram to show how the important duties of a prime minister and a president are similar, yet different.

Read a Circle Graph

Rumpelstiltskin's daughter taught the king that wheat is better than gold. The United States is one of the largest wheat-growing countries in the world. Some states grow more wheat than others. A **circle graph** can show how the parts of a whole are related. This circle graph shows how much wheat is produced by different states in the United States.

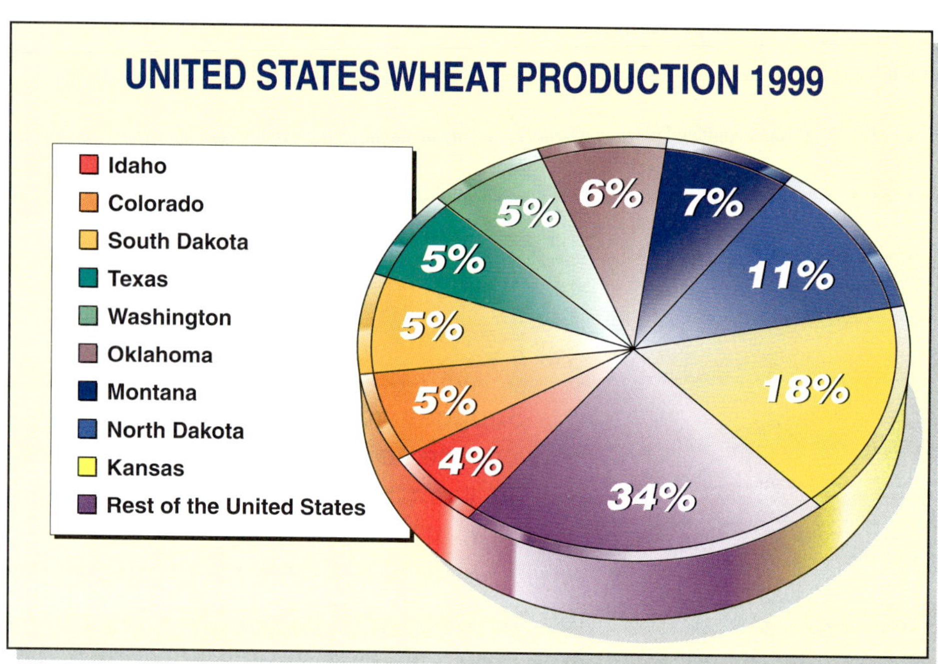

Use the circle graph to answer these questions.

1. What percentage of the wheat is grown in Texas?
2. Which state grows 11% of the wheat?
3. Which state is the largest wheat producer?
4. Which state grows more wheat, North Dakota or South Dakota? How much more?
5. Is the average wheat production of the states not named greater or less than 1%? Explain.

TEST POWER

Test Tip

Always read the directions carefully.

DIRECTIONS

Read the sample story. Then read each question about the story.

SAMPLE

The Great White Shark

One of the scariest and most misunderstood creatures of the ocean is the Great White Shark. Its large triangular dorsal fin and rows of 3-inch, razor-sharp teeth distinguish the Great White. When a shark loses a tooth, another one is ready to replace it.

Great Whites usually live in the warmer waters off the coast of Australia or the Caribbean. The Great White feeds on the remains of dead animals. Its reputation as a "man-eater" comes from the occasional encounter between a swimmer and a wandering, hungry shark. Even though the bite of a Great White can prove fatal, it should be noted that this shark is not inclined to attack humans. Shark attacks are very rare, although the excitement they cause tends to outweigh their infrequency.

1 The Great White Shark can be best described as —

A powerful

B angry

C lonely

D impatient

2 According to the passage, which of these is probably one of the biggest reasons a Great White Shark might attack a human?

F The shark's determination

G The shark's size

H The shark's hunger

J The shark's fear

Which answer choices did you rule out right away? Tell why.

Stories in Art

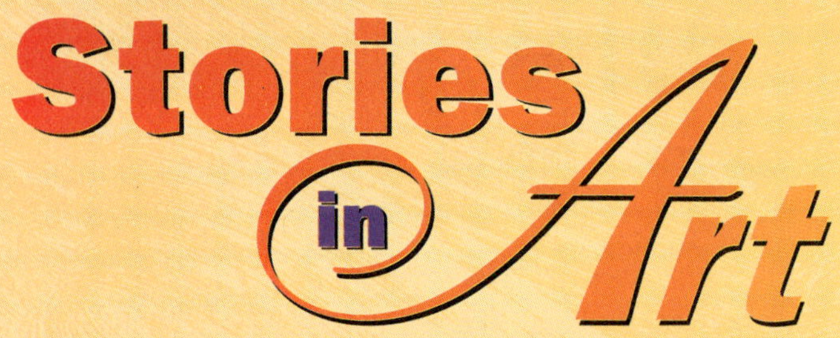

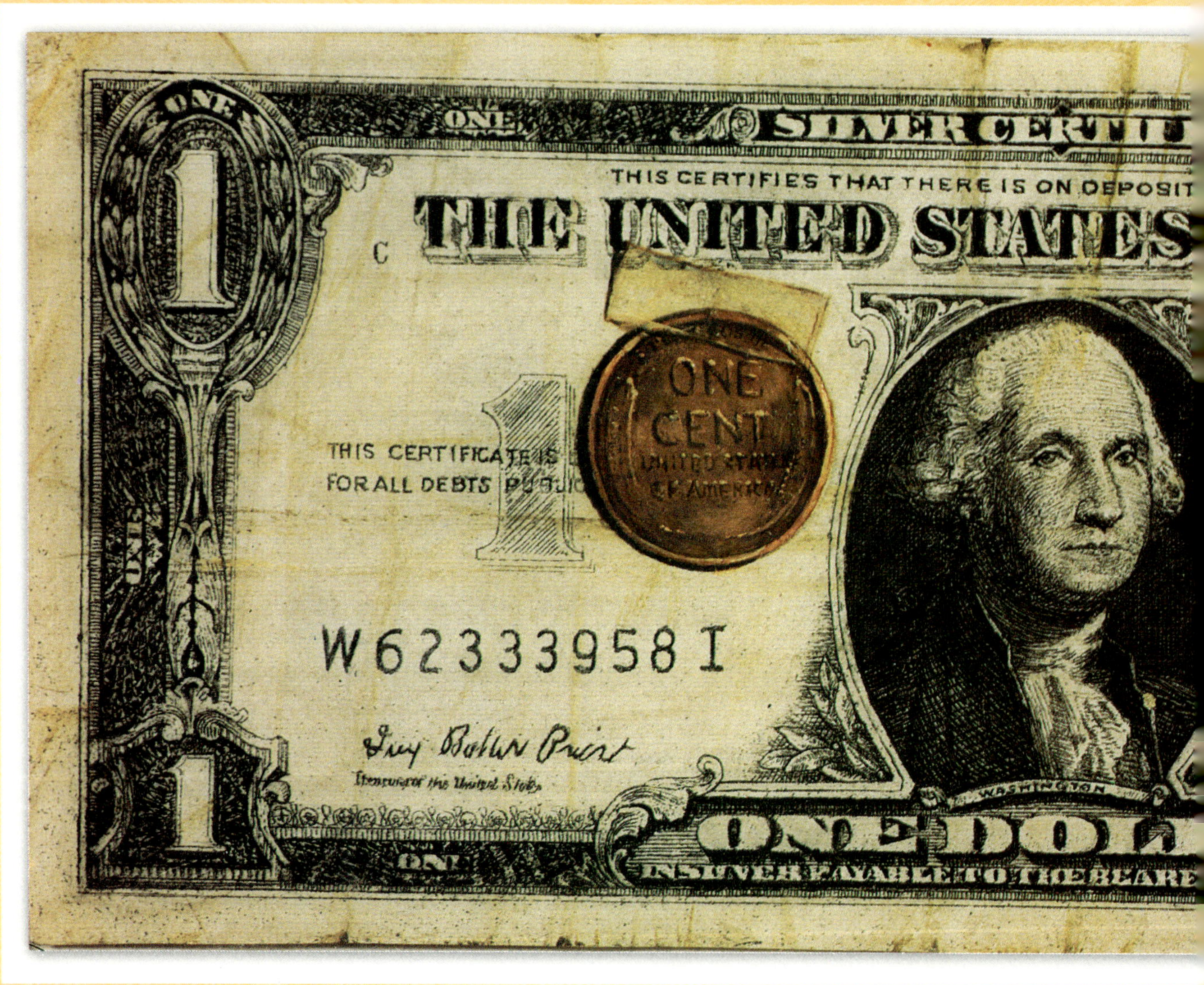

Otis Kaye Dollar Bill **by Carl Rohman, 1989**
Sheldon Memorial Art Gallery

When you first look at this painting, you see a dollar bill. If you look again, you might notice a taped penny and dime. Why do you think the artist has added these coins? When do you think he added them?

What can you tell about this painting? Does it look like a photograph? How? Notice the date on the dollar bill. Notice, too, that it is a silver certificate. What does that mean? Do you think it is worth more than a dollar? Could it have been worth $1.11 when the picture was made? Explain.

Study the painting. Are the coins very old? In the history of money, which do you think came first: coins or paper money? Why?

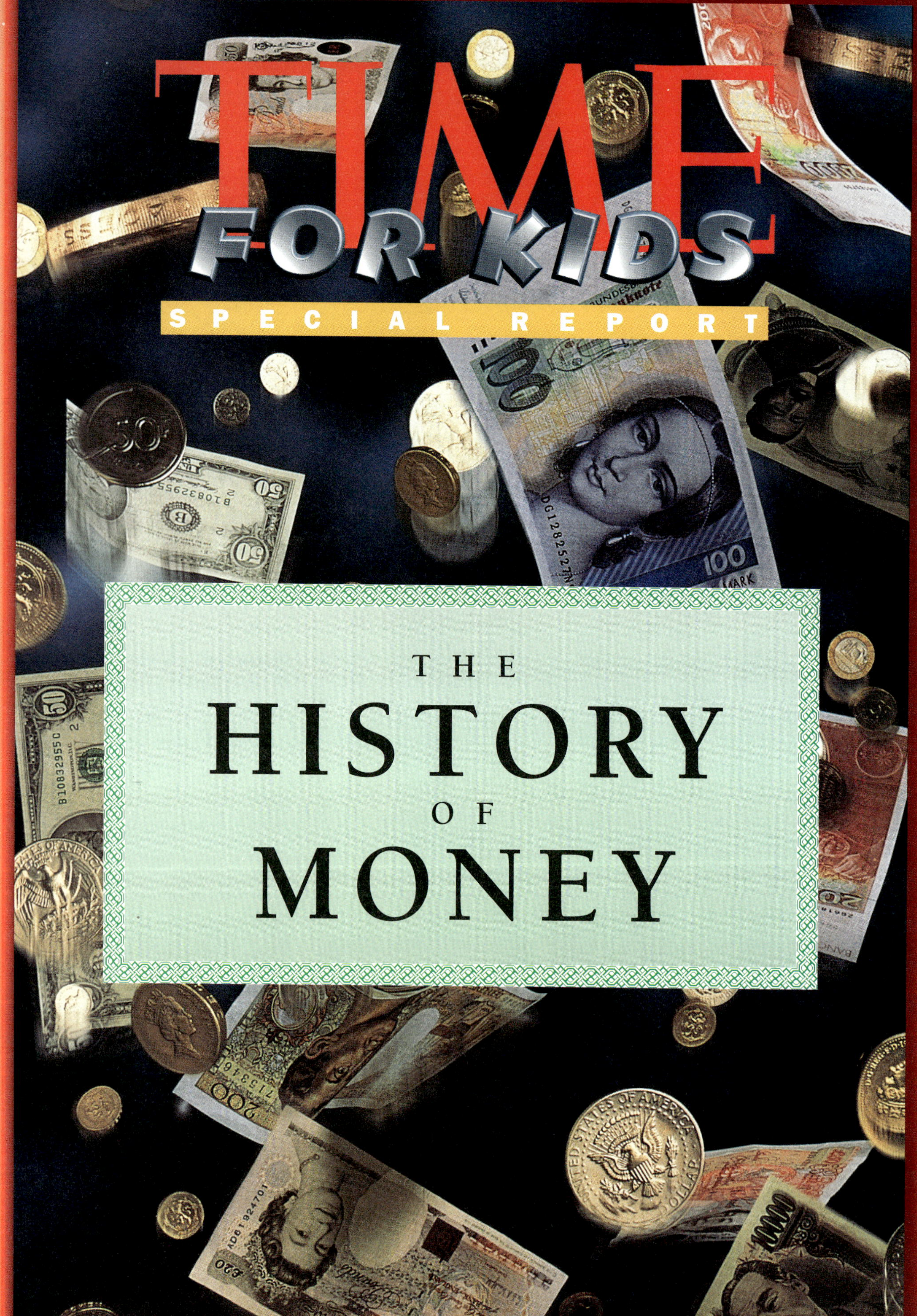
TIME
FOR KIDS
SPECIAL REPORT
THE
HISTORY
OF
MONEY

From Camels to Coins

Thousands of years ago, no one needed money. People traded what they had in order to get what they wanted from others. A person might trade an animal skin for grain, or pottery for food. This is called *bartering*. For bartering to work, each trader must have something the other wants. That didn't always work out. Soon communities invented money—tokens that had the same value to everyone in the marketplace.

Early "money" varied from culture to culture. People traded salt, shells, tea leaves, seeds, camels, or dried fish for the things they needed. The ancient Chinese used cowrie shells. Some Native Americans used *wampum*, small polished shells or beads strung together. But seeds and tea leaves often blew away. And can you imagine taking a couple of camels as cash when you go shopping? To make buying easier, people began using precious metals as money. Gold, silver, and copper were hard to find and therefore valuable.

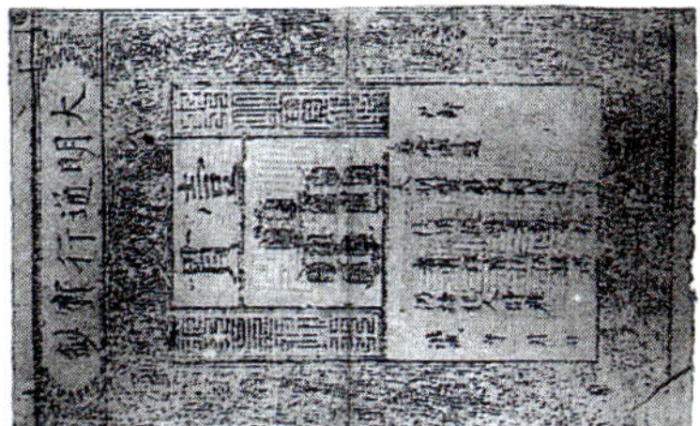

This paper money from China was issued in the 9th century.

Cowrie shells have been used as money in many cultures. These are from Africa.

This beaded belt from the 1600s is an example of *wampum*.

COVER: FPG; WAMPUM: MANSELL/TIME INC; CHINESE PAPER MONEY: TIME LIFE PICTURE COLLECTION; COWRIE SHELLS: BERNHEIM-RAPHO/LIAISON

About 4,500 years ago, in 2500 B.C., precious metals were used to pay for goods and services in Egypt and Asia. Later, metal money began to be used in Europe and the Middle East. When the Chinese invented paper and printing 1,800 years ago, they began using paper money.

Now there are about 140 different kinds of money, or currencies, in use in the world. When you travel in another country and want to buy things, you usually have to exchange your money for the currency of the country you are in.

Today we can also pay for things with credit cards or checks. ATM (automated teller machine) cards allow us to get cash whenever we need it. Money has come a long way. We'll never have to carry change for a camel again!

◀ **A Hebrew coin called a shekel dates from around A.D. 80.**

◀ **This is one of the first coins, made in Persia, from about 400 B.C.**

▲ **A Roman coin from 240–220 B.C., shows the double-faced god Janus.**

◀ **This Egyptian gold coin dates from 170–117 B.C.**

DID YOU KNOW? MONEY FACTS

◆ **The Bank of North America, the first U.S. bank, opened in Philadelphia, Pennsylvania, in 1781.**

◆ **About 63 billion checks are written and cashed in the U.S. each year.**

◆ **The piggy bank got its name from a kind of clay called *pygg*. Long ago, people stored their money in pygg-clay jars. Later, these jars were made in the shape of a pig and were called piggy banks.**

◆ **On Yap Island in the Pacific, money is a stone with a hole in the middle so the stone can be rolled with a long pole. Yap money stones can weigh more than 500 pounds and be 12 feet across.**

HOW BANKS MAKE MONEY

Ancient temples were the first banks. Temples were a safe place to store precious metals. Some temples exchanged foreign coins and made loans to people.

As trade between different cities and countries increased, traveling merchants paid money changers to exchange coins from different cities. Money changers also exchanged coins for gold or silver. They were the first bankers.

Modern banks provide many money-related services. Your money can earn more money in a bank. The bank pays you a fee, called interest, for allowing it to use your money.

Banks make money by lending money. The bank uses your money and other depositors' money to make loans. If you borrow money from a bank, you must pay back the amount you borrowed plus an extra fee. That fee is also called interest. The interest that borrowers pay the bank is more than the interest the bank pays you for letting it use your money. The difference between what borrowers pay in interest and the interest the bank pays out to its depositors is the bank's profit.

TOP RIGHT: JOHN MEYER FOR TIME FOR KIDS; BOTTOM RIGHT: CORBIS; OPPOSITE PAGE: DAVID ARKY

- Arrange 10 pennies in a triangle, as shown above.
- Can you move only three pennies in such a way that the triangle points down instead of up?

FIND OUT MORE

Visit our website:

www.mhschool.com/reading

*inter*NET CONNECTION

A Yap Island rock coin.

Based on an article in *TIME FOR KIDS.*

Story Questions & Activities

1. How did people "buy" things before there was money?
2. Why did early forms of money vary from culture to culture?
3. Why do you think paper money and coins have become so important throughout the years?
4. What different types of payment does this selection describe?
5. What does the picture on pages 532–533 add to this selection? Explain.

Write a Dialogue

Write a dialogue in which you and another person talk about money. Your dialogue can be serious or funny. For example, you could ask a friend to lend you money, or you could ask your parents to raise your allowance. You could even try to explain American money to a person from the Stone Age. Whatever you write, remember to use dialogue form, writing the speaker's name in capital letters followed by a colon.

Design a Coin

One of the first coins was made in Persia, in about 400 B.C. Use modeling clay that dries in the air to make a coin that could be used in a country today. To make your coin interesting, you could use seashells, colored beads, toothpicks, and other small objects. Be sure to include a motto as well as a label that states your coin's value and its country of origin.

Compare Currencies

How many Mexican pesos are there in one U.S. dollar? How many Kenyan shillings? How many Turkish lira? Make a chart to show the exchange rate for five or six countries. Then figure out how much a $100 bicycle would cost in each of these currencies.

Find Out More

Find out more information about one of these topics:

- the history of paper money
- Benjamin Franklin's role in establishing the first U.S. bank
- An unusual type of money used today.

Take notes on the information you find. Use your notes to give an oral report to your group or the class.

Read a Chart

From the Yap money stone to the Italian lira and the U.S. dollar, coins and paper money differ from country to country. Some money has unusual designs, mottoes, or symbols. Other money is plain looking. Some countries change the look of their money every few decades. Others have never redesigned their currency.

Look at the chart below. Notice the style of the ancient and modern coins. What are the similarities and differences?

Use the chart to answer these questions.

1. Is the coin from Rome or Persia older?
2. How are the Persian, Roman, Egyptian, and Hebrew coins alike?
3. Why is there a hole in the Yap Island coin?
4. Why do you think most coins are round?
5. How does this chart help you to understand the history of money?

TEST POWER

Test Tip

Make sure you read charts, graphs, and schedules carefully.

DIRECTIONS

Read the sample story. Then read each question about the story.

SAMPLE

A Saturday at the Community Center

Mark really liked living close to the County Community Center. He enjoyed taking the classes offered at the center on Saturdays. During the last three years, Mark has taken several of the classes at the center, and he is very excited about the watercolor class this coming Saturday.

The new schedule for Saturday classes looks like this:

Time	Room 1	Room 2
3:00	Buying a house	Guitar
3:30		Painting with watercolor
4:00	Movie: Boomtown	
4:30		Piano
5:00		Pottery
5:30		
6:00	Karate	Ballet
6:30	Yoga	

1 According to the schedule, which of these classes will be held first?

A Pottery

B Karate

C Yoga

D Piano

2 According to the schedule, what time will the watercolor class begin?

F 3:30

G 4:00

H 4:30

J 5:00

©
Uncle
Dan
LIONOCERANG-
OUTANGADDER
teeth remover

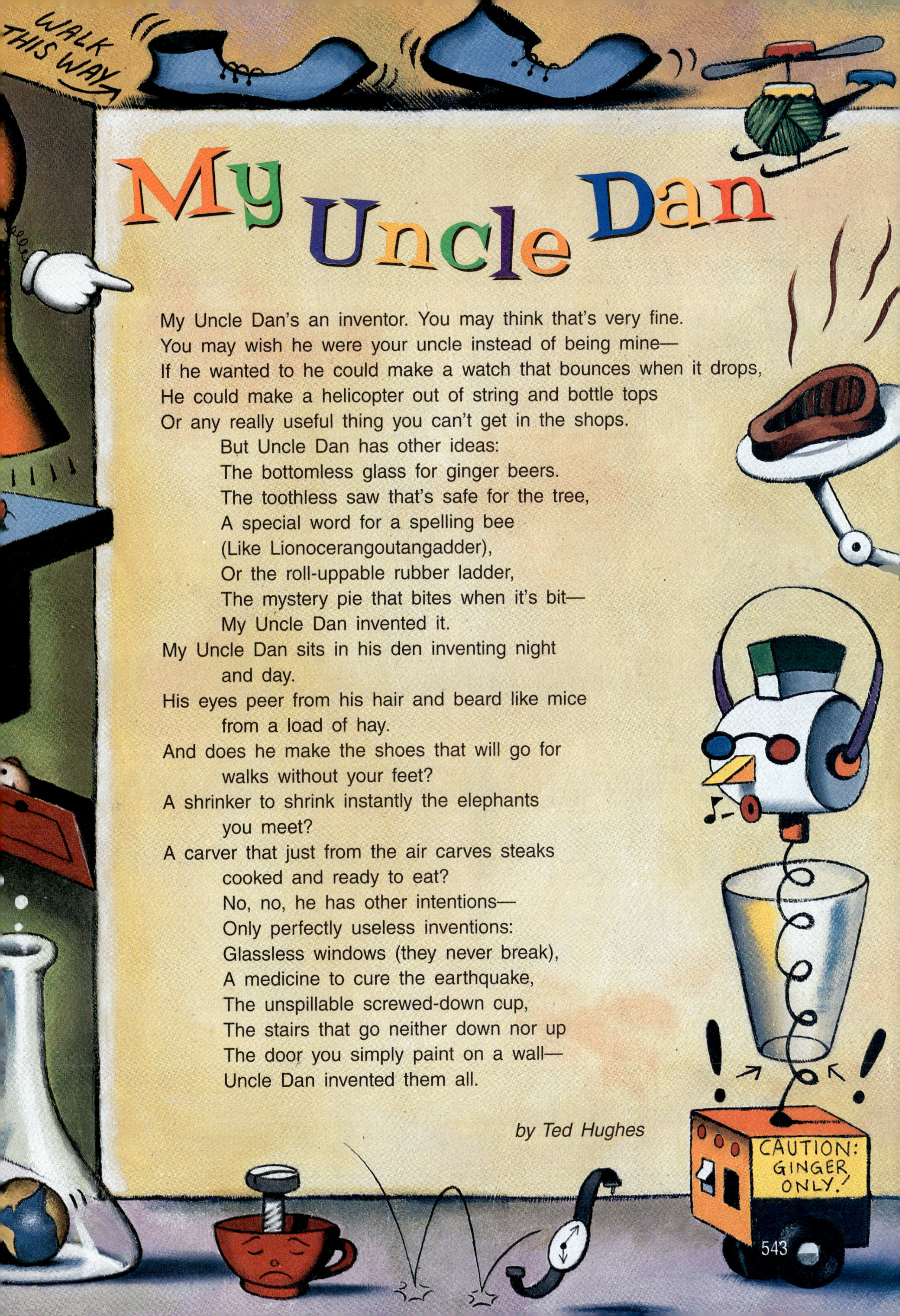

My Uncle Dan

My Uncle Dan's an inventor. You may think that's very fine.
You may wish he were your uncle instead of being mine—
If he wanted to he could make a watch that bounces when it drops,
He could make a helicopter out of string and bottle tops
Or any really useful thing you can't get in the shops.
But Uncle Dan has other ideas:
The bottomless glass for ginger beers.
The toothless saw that's safe for the tree,
A special word for a spelling bee
(Like Lionocerangoutangadder),
Or the roll-uppable rubber ladder,
The mystery pie that bites when it's bit—
My Uncle Dan invented it.
My Uncle Dan sits in his den inventing night
and day.
His eyes peer from his hair and beard like mice
from a load of hay.
And does he make the shoes that will go for
walks without your feet?
A shrinker to shrink instantly the elephants
you meet?
A carver that just from the air carves steaks
cooked and ready to eat?
No, no, he has other intentions—
Only perfectly useless inventions:
Glassless windows (they never break),
A medicine to cure the earthquake,
The unspillable screwed-down cup,
The stairs that go neither down nor up
The door you simply paint on a wall—
Uncle Dan invented them all.

by Ted Hughes

UNIT 6

All Things Considered

I Go Forth to Move About The Earth

I go forth to move about the earth.
I go forth as the owl, wise and knowing.
I go forth as the eagle, powerful and bold.
I go forth as the dove, peaceful and gentle.
I go forth to move about the earth
in wisdom, courage, and peace.

by Alonzo Lopez

Some artists create beautiful objects for people to look at. Others create art to convey a strong message.

Look at this mural. How is it organized like a time line of events in African-American history? Notice the strong figure in the center. To which side of this painting is he pointing? Why? What do you think he is saying about the promise of the future? Who is he trying to persuade with his words?

Study this remarkable painting. What is the meaning of the piece? How do the colors, shapes, balance, and rhythm all work together? Would you like to see this artwork in your school? Why? Would you try to persuade others to see this work? Give three good reasons.

Aspects of Negro Life: From Slavery through Reconstruction,
by Aaron Douglas, 1934 The New York Public Library, New York

MEET FLOYD COOPER

Floyd Cooper studied art at the University of Oklahoma and then moved to New York City to work as an artist. He illustrated his first children's picture book in 1988 and has been working on books for young people ever since. "I feel children are on the front line in improving society," Cooper says. "Illustrating children's books is a very exciting thing to do because it gives you the chance to have an impact on the way the world will be in the future."

Besides doing the illustrations for *Mandela*, Cooper is also the author of the book. Creating both the words and the pictures for a book gives Cooper a chance to share his own ideas. "I believe that affection for other cultures leads to understanding, and I strive to create books that are a bridge between cultures."

MANDELA
FROM THE LIFE OF THE
SOUTH AFRICAN
STATESMAN
Written and
Illustrated by
FLOYD COOPER

He was born on July 18, 1918, at Mvezo, a tiny village on the banks of the Mbashe River in South Africa. His name, Rolihlahla, was the Xhosa way of saying "pulling the branch of a tree," or "troublemaker." But his family called him Buti.

Always, the wind had blown mightily through the valley that cradled his village. Sunsets had forever before kissed the hills, where little boys played and romped and did their chores. Life there was as it always had been.

Buti's ancestors were rulers of the proud Thembu people who had lived in this rich land for generations. His own father, Gadla Hendry Mphakanyiswa of the Mandela family, was chief of the village, a proud chief who ruled with a stubborn sense of fairness and tradition. He was a counselor to kings, as were his father and his grandfather before him.

When it was time, Buti would be told these things about his country and about the wind that blew through the valley that cradled his village. And he too would lead.

Chief Hendry knew this and was happy.

Then one day, when Buti was still a baby, an ox belonging to one of Chief Hendry's subjects wandered into a neighbor's *kraal*. The neighbor, thinking only about his good fortune, ate the ox.

When the chief ordered the man to pay for eating the ox, the neighbor complained to the English magistrate. The magistrate ordered Chief Hendry to appear before him, but he stubbornly refused. A Thembu chief had only to answer to the Thembu king, not any English magistrate.

Because of his refusal, Chief Hendry was dethroned. Standing firm for what he believed cost Buti's father his cattle, his wealth, and his chieftainship. The Mandela family, now poor, had to move to a new village.

The new village, Qunu, was not very different from Mvezo. The wind blew through the valley, and the sunsets had forever kissed the hills. Buti's mother tended the fields of vegetables. His sisters ground the mealies and prepared the pumpkin, beans, and sorghum for dinner. Buti herded the cattle. Although Buti's father was no longer chief, he was respected, and would often be called to settle a dispute or instruct a student in history. And he would storytell about the days of forever before.

Buti grew strong and smart, and when he was seven years old, two old friends of his father recognized how smart he was and told his mother he should be in school. Even Buti's father, who had never gone to school himself, thought this was an excellent idea.

On the first day of school, the English teacher gave all the African children English names. Buti's new name was Nelson.

He wasn't certain if he liked his new English name, but Nelson knew he liked school. He liked the slate tablets used for writing. He liked learning new things and he liked the way his father prepared him for school by telling him always to stand firm for what he believed was fair and right.

One day, when Nelson was nine years old, his father came home early, very ill. He called Nelson, and they talked the words of school-day mornings. He told Nelson always, always to stand firm for what he believed was fair and right. Soon after, his father died.

The wind in the valley that cradled the village blew on, as it always had. But Nelson had gone as far as he could in the school at Qunu. It was time to leave his beloved mother, sisters, and his beloved village for a new school. For this, he must journey to the capital of Thembuland, a neighboring village called Mqhekezweni.

It was a long walk to Mqhekezweni. Nelson and his mother, who took him to the new place, walked on hard, thorny roads, past many villages without stopping. Finally they arrived. The village was like no village Nelson had ever seen before! He saw lush gardens, apple orchards, and maize fields surrounded by peach trees. He saw two rectangular houses, seven round houses ("rondavels," they were called), and a large, honking motorcar. Never would he fit into such a grand place as this!

Nelson was shy and lonely when his mother said good-bye, but as she disappeared over the hill, she knew that the things that awaited Nelson here would prepare him for a bigger, wider world.

Helping Nelson to overcome his shyness was his new family, the family of Chief Jongintaba Dalindyebo.

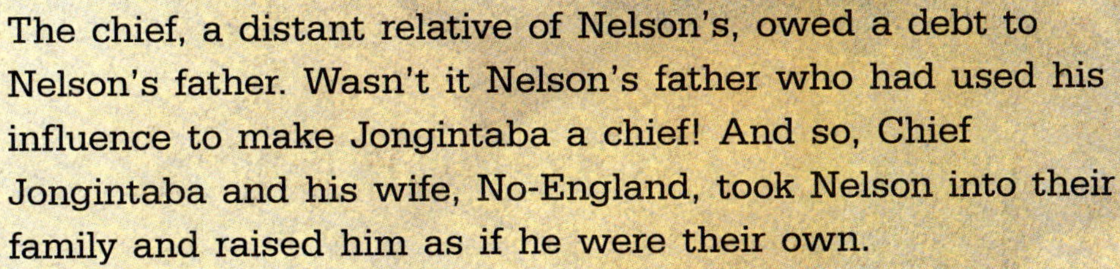

The chief, a distant relative of Nelson's, owed a debt to Nelson's father. Wasn't it Nelson's father who had used his influence to make Jongintaba a chief! And so, Chief Jongintaba and his wife, No-England, took Nelson into their family and raised him as if he were their own.

Nelson shared a rondavel with Justice, the chief's son, who was four years older than Nelson. Together with Justice's sister, Nomafu, they played hard, they studied hard, and they went to Sunday school. The three grew strong and smart.

Nelson thought Mqhekezweni a magnificent place. It was called the Great Place. There, important visitors from all over Thembuland gathered to hold court, to debate, to chat and tell stories. How Nelson listened. And he learned many things at the foot of the chieftains and elders. One very old storyteller was Zwelibhangile Joyi. Old Chief Joyi, with his wrinkled blue-black skin and dry, dusty voice, had lived and seen much from the days of forever before. He entranced the gathered elders, telling ancient tales of great kingdoms like the Zulu and Xhosa, of brave warriors like Ngangelizwe, who fought the British, and of wise kings like Ngubengcuka, who united the Thembu people.

Nelson was most entranced of all. The image of Old Chief Joyi, nimbly stepping like an attacking warrior as the smoky firelight flickered across his moist brow, telling a history not to be found in any book, would remain with Nelson always.

Like a large mimosa tree, Nelson grew sturdy and tall. When he was sixteen, it was time for him to become a man. He journeyed to Tyharlarha, on the banks of the Mbashe River. With the tribal elders guiding them, he and other young men his age rubbed their bodies from head to toe with white clay and put on the traditional grass skirts. They danced. The elders told fables and tales, and finally performed the rites of manhood. Nelson Mandela was now a man.

Nelson had even more responsibilities after this. Not only did he tend the herds and milk the cows, he ran errands for Chief Jongintaba and looked after other matters of business for him. Important work for a young man!

Even so, school stood foremost in Nelson's life. In order to be a counselor to kings, like his father before him, and his grandfather before him, and on forever before, Nelson had to learn more about what Chief Jongintaba called the "wide world." He needed more education. Chief Jongintaba wouldn't have it any other way.

The chief sent both Justice and Nelson to the best African schools in South Africa. Nelson went to Clarkebury Institute, a Thembu college. There Nelson met Thembu people from other villages and cities. And for the first time in his life, he shook hands with a white man, the governor of the college, known as a white Thembu because he loved and understood the Thembu people.

Then Nelson joined Justice at Healdtown, the largest African school below the equator. For the first time, Nelson became friends with people from different tribes—the Sotho, Swazi, and Zulu—and for the first time he saw himself as not just a Thembu or Xhosa, but as an African.

Next Nelson advanced to Fort Hare, a missionary college for African scholars from all over Africa. Here he studied hard, but it wasn't all work! He joined the track team and learned to dance. He became a school leader, too, and in his final year was elected to serve on the student council. When, in a protest for better food, he quit the council, the principal threatened him: come back, or be expelled!

Nelson refused. He stood firm for what he believed was fair and right, and he was expelled.

Nelson returned home, but when Chief Jongintaba learned of his stubbornness, he was furious! He ordered Nelson to return to school, and to rejoin the student council. End of discussion.

Nelson would obey, but until the session began, he enjoyed life as it was always before, herding, looking after matters for the chief. Then one evening, the chief summoned Justice and Nelson to a meeting.

He told them he had selected a bride for each of them. Before he journeyed to the land of his ancestors, he wanted to see his two sons properly married. The dowries had been paid. The marriages would take place immediately!

The chief was merely being a chief—arranging marriages for his children. But Justice and Nelson returned to their rondavel with their heads down. Neither liked the bride that had been picked for him. The two young men decided instead to run away.

Choosing a moment when the chief would be away on business, the lads took two of his prized oxen and sold them for a good price. Then using some of the money to buy passage, they climbed on a train going to Johannesburg, the city of gold.

They arrived just as darkness was settling. Jeweled, flickering lights spread out like spilled treasure. Nelson had heard many stories about Johannesburg. Each year thousands of young men made their way to the gold mines there, seeking fame and fortune. What they found instead was a hard life working long hours in underground darkness for little pay and a dry, wheezing cough as a bonus. Sometimes these people never returned home.

Justice and Nelson were spared such a fate. Because of their royal ancestry, Nelson was made a guard and Justice a clerk. Very soon, however, word of their whereabouts reached Chief Jongintaba. He angrily demanded they return, but this time Nelson, with the winds of all that had come before at his back, stood firm.

Nelson persuaded the chief to let him remain in Johannesburg to continue his schooling at the University of South Africa. But where would he live? How would he pay for school? There is an old Xhosa saying: "People are people through other people." And so Nelson found a place to live with a Xhosa family in Alexandra, one of the few places in Johannesburg where blacks were allowed to live.

This district was overcrowded with small matchbox-type houses that had no plumbing, no electricity, and no heat. Most had tin roofs and dirt floors.

Nelson apprenticed at a law firm during the day, earned a small salary, and went to school at night. These were very poor times for Nelson. For five years straight, he wore a suit given to him by his boss at the law firm. He once said that the suit was patched in so many places it was more patches than suit.

Nelson never imagined the unfairness and inequality that he would find in Johannesburg. He'd known of the attitude most Englishmen had toward anything African (hadn't he had to take an English name on his first day of school?). But he could hardly believe what he saw.

If you were black, you could live only in reserved areas. You could leave only to work in the city, and whenever you left, you had to carry a little book called a "pass book." If you were caught without it, you were thrown into prison. You paid a special tax. You rode "African only" buses, drank from "African only" water taps, and were snubbed and insulted daily. What could possibly happen to any person's pride and self-worth under such terrible conditions?

Nelson couldn't bear to see people treated unjustly. They couldn't better their condition—not because they weren't capable, but because opportunity was taken away from them by laws made to "keep them in their place." This was not the way of Chief Joyi's stories about kings who ruled their subjects with an equal hand! This was not the way it was in the days of forever before.

But nothing stopped Nelson from finishing law school. In fact, he and a partner, Oliver Tambo, opened the doors to the first black law practice in Johannesburg.

At the same time, Nelson began to attend meetings and rallies held by other people who didn't like the unfairness and inequality of the South African government. They wanted change! Their numbers grew and grew, and included not only black people—doctors, lawyers, teachers, artists, writers—not only Indians and other people of color, but many white people.

Yet even as they met, new laws were being created. There were separate doors for blacks and whites in restaurants and stores, separate trains, separate schools, separate restrooms! And the schools, neighborhoods, and restrooms for blacks were far inferior to those for whites. This system of government was called "apartheid," or apart. And these gatherings of people who were against apartheid called themselves the African National Congress or ANC.

Nelson became a strong leader of the African National Congress. He wanted Africans to be able to vote! He wanted apartheid to end! Sometimes now he planned strikes and marches and protests.

Sometimes now demonstrators were rounded up by the police, Nelson among them! Sometimes people were killed. Still Nelson's life was filled with his passion to stand firm in the face of the inequities he saw.

Nelson married Evelyn Mase in 1945, and then, following their divorce, he married Winnie Madikizela in 1958—both women who were not chosen for him by anyone else. In time he had two sons and three daughters.

Thembi was his firstborn. Even as Nelson practiced law, and met and marched, he found time to play with his young son, Thembi, sometimes at the very rocky knoll where protests had been held. One might see them there on an evening, playing and romping as the wind whistled through the great stones, just as it had always done forever before.

Thembi began to know of his father and was proud. But by now, other people in Johannesburg, many white people, began to know about Nelson Mandela and his stand against apartheid, and were angry.

One night, in the still darkness, Thembi was awakened by an awful crash! The door to the Mandela home was smashed in, and four men dressed in khaki rushed in and ransacked everything in the house! Three of the men grabbed Nelson Mandela, and in front of his little boy and wife, dragged him through the door! Like the whoosh of a hurricane, the men came and went. The South African police had taken Nelson Mandela to jail.

Nelson Mandela would be arrested many times over the years and eventually let go. But finally, in 1963, in Rivonia, he was charged with attempting to overthrow the state of South Africa. The only question was: would he be put to death, or sent to prison for the rest of his life?

There was no wind in the courtroom when he stood before this judge. No wind at his back, whispering "Stand firm!" The only wind this day was the wind that blew through the black townships of South Africa: Alexandra, Sophiatown, Sharpeville, and Soweto.

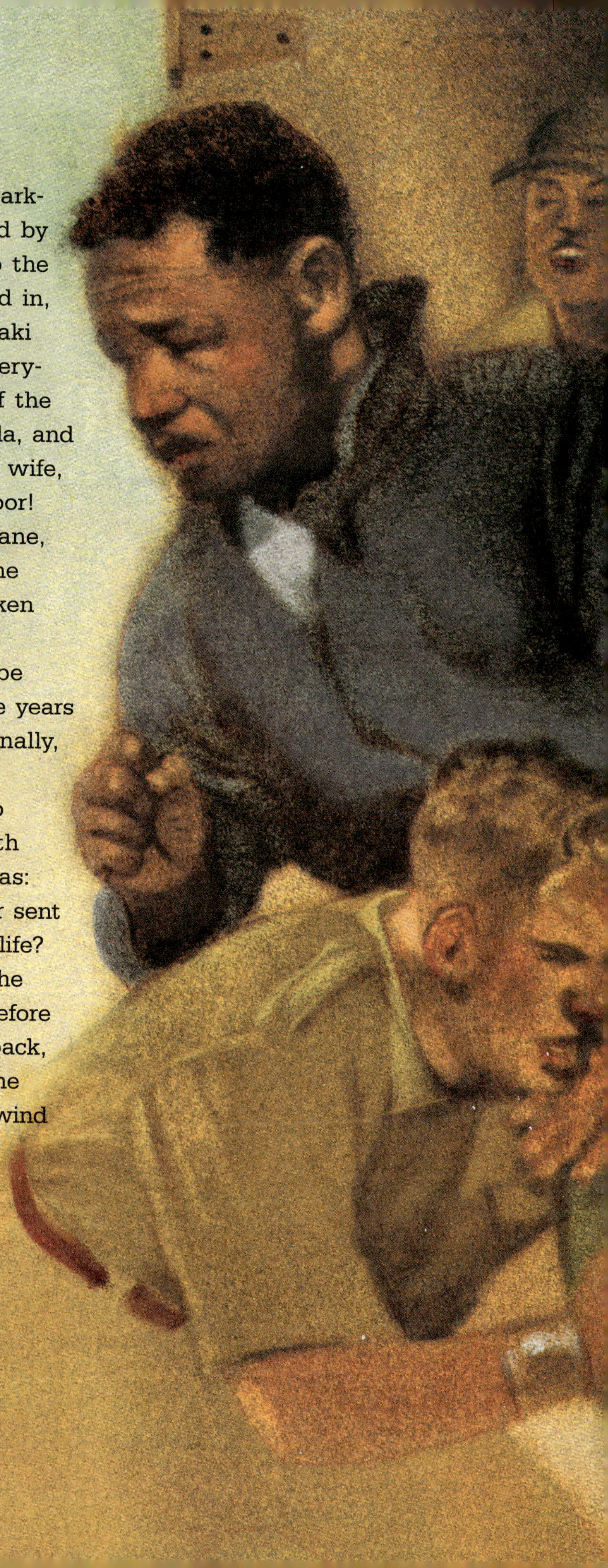

The wind moaned for justice! The wind cried for fairness! Even in the face of losing his own life, Nelson Mandela stood firm that day for what he believed was fair and right, but he was sent to prison.

The prison was called Robben Island. Nelson Mandela remained there for twenty-seven years, stubbornly holding firm for what he believed. But even while he was there, his spirit carried all across South Africa, joined by youthful shouts for freedom: Amandla! Amandla Ngawethu! Power to the people!—until the walls of apartness, apartheid, crashed right down.

Released from prison on February 11, 1990, Nelson Mandela helped create a new constitution for South Africa and became the first president of the new government in an election in which all Africans voted.

Son of chiefs, fighter for equality, he had stood firm.

PRONUNCIATION KEY

Amandla Ngawethu	(ah-MAND-la n-gah-WAY-too)
apartheid	(ah-PAR-tide)
Buti	(BOO-tee)
Jongintaba Danlindyebo	(jong-een-TAH-bah dahl-ind-JAY-boh)
kraal	(KRAWL)
Madikizela	(mah-DEE-kee-zay-lah)
Mbashe	(m-BAH-shay)
Mphakanyiswa	(m-pah-kah-NEE-swah)
Mqhekezweni	(m-kay-KAH-zwee-nee)
Mvezo	(m-VAY-zoh)
Ngangelizwe	(n-gahn-geh-LEE-zway)
Ngubengcuka	(n-goo-BEN-choo-kah)
Qunu	(KOO-noo)
Rolihlahla	(RHOH-lee-hlah-hlah)
rondavel	(ron-DAH-vuhl)
Thembi	(TEM-bee)
Thembu	(TEM-boo)
Xhosa	(KHOH-zah)
Zwelibhangile Joyi	(zway-lee-bahn-GEE-lay JOY-ee)

Note: Buti may also be spelled "Bhuti."

Story Questions & Activities

1. Who is Nelson Mandela?
2. How does Mandela stand firm for what he believes is fair and right?
3. Why do you think it is important for a leader to be able to persuade people to agree with his or her opinion?
4. What is the "message" of this selection?
5. Suppose that Nelson Mandela could speak to the people in the painting on pages 546–547. What do you think he would say? What might he try to persuade them to do?

Write a Persuasive Speech

Throughout his career, Nelson Mandela has made speeches to persuade people to do what is fair and right. Now it's your turn. Write and give a persuasive speech on an issue that is important to you. Try to persuade your classmates to adopt your opinion or point of view. Use these speaking skills to persuade your listeners:

- **Introduce your topic clearly.**
- **Use logical arguments to support your opinion and facts.**
- **Use persuasive words, such as *should* and *must*.**
- **Save your strongest argument for the end of your speech.**

"Tell" Your History

Although Mandela's father was no longer a chief, he "would storytell about the days of forever before." In this way, he would pass on the history of his people. Now it's up to you. Tell the history of your own family, culture, or country. If you prefer, create a dance that expresses your story through movement.

Choose a Role Model

Nelson Mandela saw his father as a role model. Who has been a role model for you? What lessons have you learned from that person? How has that person helped you stand up for what you believe is fair and right? Write your thoughts in your journal.

Find Out More

Many books and articles have been written about Nelson Mandela and other civil rights leaders, such as Martin Luther King, Jr. First, choose one of these civil rights leaders. Then find out as much information as you can about the person by reading and interviewing parents, teachers, and members of your community. Take notes. In a discussion with classmates, talk about the role these leaders have played in the struggle for civil rights.

Conduct an Interview

You know that an **interview** follows a pattern of questions and answers. In order to get the responses you want, you must ask the right questions in the right way.

Suppose that you had the chance to interview Nelson Mandela. How would you prepare for the interview? What questions would you ask? Here is a notecard you could prepare. It has some ideas that will help.

Notes: Interview

1. Purpose: to find out about Nelson Mandela's job as South Africa's first black president.
2. How did your parents and other role models prepare you for the job?
3. How did your schooling prepare you?
4. How did your belief to stand firm for what you believe is fair and right help you?
5. What have you accomplished while in office?
6. What are the benefits and drawbacks to your job?

Use the suggestions below to write five interview questions on a separate sheet of paper.

1. You want to know what Mandela's goals were as a young man.
   My question: ______________________________?
2. You want to learn who helped him believe in himself.
   My question: ______________________________?
3. You want to know what he has accomplished as South Africa's president.
   My question: ______________________________?
4. You want to find out how he feels about his job.
   My question: ______________________________?
5. You want to discover what his dreams are for South Africa today.
   My question: ______________________________?

TEST POWER

Test Tip

Keep your attention turned to your work.

DIRECTIONS

Read the sample story. Then read each question about the story.

SAMPLE

Dragonflies

There are dragonflies just about everywhere there is water. Whether they live in North America, the rain forests of South America, or the North Pole, they always reside somewhere near water.

Dragonflies are usually about two inches long and, including the length of their wings, they are about three inches wide. However, some kinds of dragonflies grow as big as six inches long and eight inches wide!

Dragonflies are very skillful flyers and spend most of their time hunting for insects. A dragonfly is so quick that in 30 minutes it can eat its own body weight in other bugs.

1 The word reside in this passage means —

A swim

B live

C eat

D fly

2 According to the passage, the dragonfly —

F lives in the desert

G mates in the winter

H has difficulty flying for long periods of time

J is wider than it is long

How did you check your answer in the story?

Stories in Art

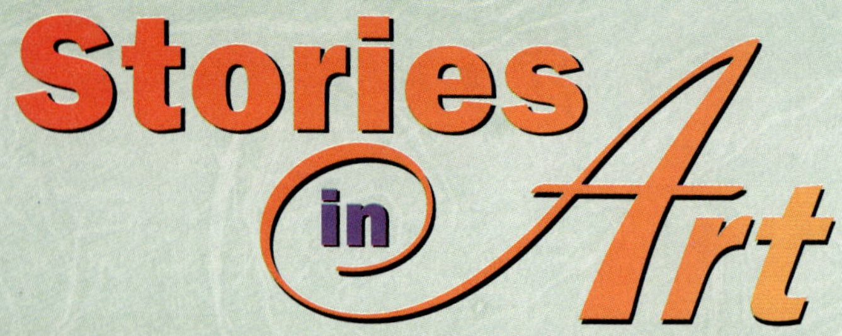

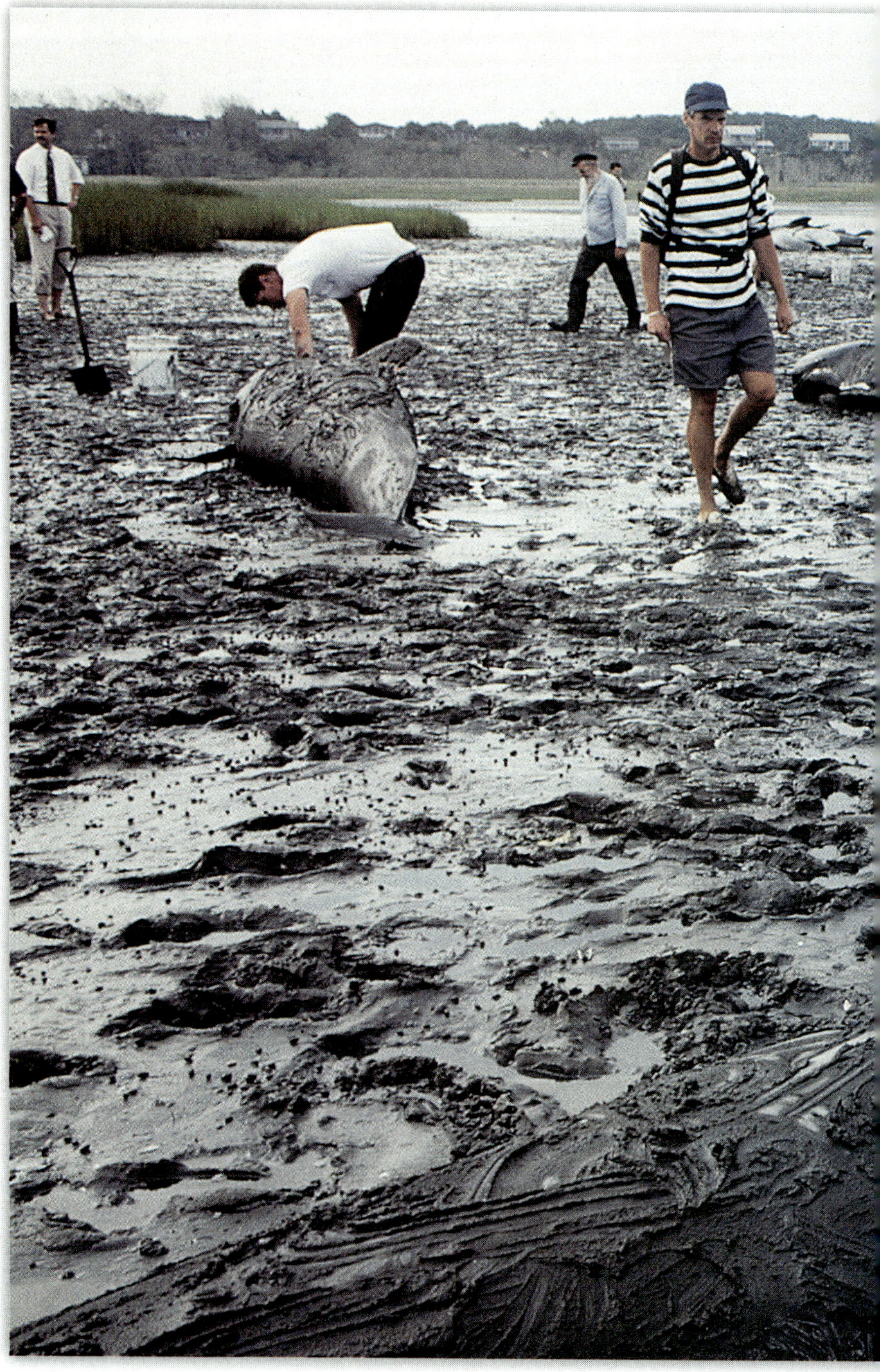

The photographer who took this picture had a very strong message to communicate. He wanted you to see the problem that pollution creates for whales.

Look at the photograph. Can you describe what the people are doing? How are they trying to help save the whales? Do you think they will be successful? Why or why not?

Think about this photograph. Is it more effective than an oil painting? A magazine article? How? What does it say about the bond between people and animals? What are your responsibilities toward animals and pets?

Pilot Whales Mass Stranding
by David Coleman, 1991
Wellfleet, Cape Cod, MA

Meet Mary O'Hara

Mary O'Hara (1885–1980) was a successful screenwriter when she decided to leave Hollywood to move to a ranch in Wyoming. She wrote the story "My Friend Flicka" after a horse on her ranch got sick and died. O'Hara felt that the horse might have recovered if someone had nursed it and kept it company. "My Friend Flicka" was published in January 1941.

A Hollywood editor told her the story would make "tip-top material for the screen"—provided she could first turn it into a popular full-length novel. Amazingly, O'Hara was able to do just that, though she had never before written a book. The novel *My Friend Flicka* was published soon after she finished it. It became a best-seller and has never been out of print since. The classic movie adaptation came out in 1943.

My friend Flicka

by Mary O'Hara

Friends 1995 John Fawcett

Report cards for the second semester were sent out soon after school closed in mid-June.

Kennie's was a shock to the whole family.

"If I could have a colt all for my own," said Kennie, "I might do better."

Rob McLaughlin glared at his son. "Just as a matter of curiosity," he said, "how do you go about it to get a *zero* in an examination? Forty in arithmetic; seventeen in history! But a *zero*? Just as one man to another, what goes on in your head?"

"Yes, tell us how you do it, Ken," chirped Howard.

"Eat your breakfast, Howard," snapped his mother.

Kennie's blond head bent over his plate until his face was almost hidden. His cheeks burned.

McLaughlin finished his coffee and pushed his chair back. "You'll do an hour a day on your lessons all through the summer."

Nell McLaughlin saw Kennie wince as if something had actually hurt him.

Lessons and study in the summertime, when the long winter was just over and there weren't hours enough in the day for all the things he wanted to do!

Kennie took things hard. His eyes turned to the wide-open window with a look almost of despair.

The hill opposite the house, covered with arrow-straight jack pines, was sharply etched in the thin air of the eight-thousand-foot altitude. Where it fell away, vivid green grass ran up to meet it; and over range and upland poured the strong Wyoming sunlight that stung everything into burning color. A big jack rabbit sat under one of the pines, waving his long ears back and forth.

Ken had to look at his plate and blink back tears before he could turn to his father and say carelessly, "Can I help you in the corral with the horses this morning, Dad?"

"You'll do your studying every morning before you do anything else." And McLaughlin's scarred boots and heavy spurs clattered across the kitchen floor. "I'm disgusted with you. Come, Howard."

Howard strode after his father, nobly refraining from looking at Kennie.

"Help me with the dishes, Kennie," said Nell McLaughlin as she rose, tied on a big apron, and began to clear the table.

Kennie looked at her in despair. She poured steaming water into the dishpan and sent him for the soap powder.

"If I could have a colt," he muttered again.

Arizona Cooler *1994 John Fawcett*

"Now get busy with that dish towel, Ken. It's eight o'clock. You can study till nine and then go up to the corral. They'll still be there."

At supper that night, Kennie said, "But Dad, Howard had a colt all of his own when he was only eight. And he trained it and schooled it all himself; and now he's eleven and Highboy is three, and he's riding him. I'm nine now, and even if you did give me a colt now, I couldn't catch up to Howard because I couldn't ride it till it was a three-year-old and then I'd be twelve."

Nell laughed. "Nothing wrong with that arithmetic."

But Rob said, "Howard never gets less than seventy-five average at school; and hasn't disgraced himself and his family by getting more demerits than any other boy in his class."

Kennie didn't answer. He couldn't figure it out. He tried hard, he spent hours poring over his books. That was supposed to get you good marks, but it never did. Everyone said he was bright; why was it that when he studied he didn't learn? He had a vague feeling that perhaps he looked out the window too much; or looked through the walls to see clouds and sky and hills, and wonder what was happening out there. Sometimes it wasn't even a wonder, but just a pleasant drifting feeling of nothing at all, as if nothing mattered, as if there was always plenty of time, as if the lessons would get done of themselves. And then the bell would ring and study period was over.

If he had a colt—

When the boys had gone to bed that night Nell McLaughlin sat down with her overflowing mending basket and glanced at her husband.

He was at his desk as usual, working on account books and inventories.

Nell threaded a darning needle and thought, "It's either that whacking big bill from the vet for the mare that died, or the last half of the tax bill."

It didn't seem just the auspicious moment to plead Kennie's cause. But then, these days, there was always a line between Rob's eyes and a harsh note in his voice.

"Rob," she began.

He flung down his pencil and turned around.

"Hang that law!" he exclaimed.

"What law?"

"The state law that puts high taxes on pedigreed stock. I'll have to do as the rest of 'em do—drop the papers."

"Drop the papers! But you'll never get decent prices if you don't have registered horses."

"I don't get decent prices now."

"But you will someday, if you don't drop the papers."

"Maybe." He bent again over the desk.

Rob, thought Nell, was a lot like Kennie himself. He set his heart. Oh, how stubbornly he set his heart on just some one thing he wanted above everything else. He had set his heart on horses and ranching way back when he had been a crack rider at West Point; and he had resigned and thrown away his army career just for the horses. Well, he'd got what he wanted—

She drew a deep breath, snipped her thread, laid down the sock and again looked across at her husband as she unrolled another length of darning cotton.

To get what you want is one thing, she was thinking. The three-thousand-acre ranch and the hundred head of horses. But to make it pay—for a dozen or more years they had been trying to make it pay. People said ranching hadn't paid since the beef barons ran their herds on public land; people said the only prosperous ranchers in Wyoming were the dude ranchers; people said—

But suddenly she gave her head a little rebellious, gallant shake. Rob would always be fighting and struggling against something, like Kennie; perhaps like herself too. Even those first years when there was no water piped into the house, when every day brought a new difficulty or danger, how she had loved it! How she still loved it!

She ran the darning ball into the toe of a sock, Kennie's sock. The length of it gave her a shock. Yes, the boys were growing up fast, and now Kennie—Kennie and the colt—

After a while, she said, "Give Kennie a colt, Rob."

"He doesn't deserve it." The answer was short. Rob pushed away his papers and took out his pipe.

"Howard's too far ahead of him; older and bigger and quicker and his wits about him, and—"

"Ken doesn't half try; doesn't stick at anything."

She put down her sewing. "He's crazy for a colt of his own. He hasn't had another idea in his head since you gave Highboy to Howard."

"I don't believe in bribing children to do their duty."

"Not a bribe." She hesitated.

"No? What would you call it?"

She tried to think it out. "I just have the feeling Ken isn't going to pull anything off, and—" her eyes sought Rob's, "it's time he did. It isn't the school marks alone, but I just don't want things to go on any longer with Ken never coming out at the right end of anything."

"I'm beginning to think he's just dumb."

"He's not dumb. Maybe a little thing like this—if he had a colt of his own, trained him, rode him—"

Rob interrupted. "But it isn't a little thing, nor an easy thing to break and school a colt the way Howard has schooled Highboy. I'm not going to have a good horse spoiled by Ken's careless ways. He goes wool-gathering. He never knows what he's doing."

"But he'd *love* a colt of his own, Rob. If he could do it, it might make a big difference in him."

"*If* he could do it! But that's a big if."

At breakfast next morning Kennie's father said to him, "When you've done your studying come out to the barn. I'm going in the car up to section twenty-one this morning to look over the brood mares. You can go with me."

"Can I go too, Dad?" cried Howard.

McLaughlin frowned at Howard. "You turned Highboy out last evening with dirty legs."

Howard wriggled. "I groomed him—"

"Yes, down to his knees."

"He kicks."

"And whose fault is that? You don't get on his back again until I see his legs clean."

The two boys eyed each other, Kennie secretly triumphant and

Howard chagrined. McLaughlin turned at the door. "And, Ken, a week from today I'll give you a colt. Between now and then you can decide what one you want."

Kennie shot out of his chair and stared at his father. "A—a—spring colt, Dad, or a yearling?"

McLaughlin was somewhat taken aback, but his wife concealed a smile. If Kennie got a yearling colt, he would be even up with Howard.

"A yearling colt, your father means, Ken," she said smoothly. "Now hurry with your lessons. Howard will wipe."

Kennie found himself the most important personage on the ranch. Prestige lifted his head, gave him an inch more of height and a bold stare, and made him feel different all the way through. Even Gus and Tim Murphy, the ranch hands, were more interested in Kennie's choice of a colt than anything else.

Howard was fidgety with suspense. "Who'll you pick, Ken? Say—pick Doughboy, why don't you? Then when he grows up he'll be sort of twins with mine, in his name anyway. Doughboy, Highboy, see?"

The boys were sitting on the worn wooden step of the door which led from the tack room into the corral, busy with rags and polish, shining their bridles.

Ken looked at his brother with scorn. Doughboy would never have half of Highboy's speed.

"Lassie, then," suggested Howard. "She's black as ink, like mine. And she'll be fast—"

"Dad says Lassie'll never go over fifteen hands."

Nell McLaughlin saw the change in Kennie and her hopes rose. He went to his books in the morning with determination and really studied. A new alertness took the place of the day-dreaming. Examples in arithmetic were neatly written out and, as she passed his door before breakfast, she often heard the monotonous drone of his voice as he read his American history aloud.

Each night, when he kissed her, he flung his arms around her and held her fiercely for a moment, then, with a winsome and blissful smile into her eyes, turned away to bed.

He spent days inspecting the different bands of horses and colts. He sat for hours on the corral fence, very important, chewing straws. He rode off on one of the ponies for half the day, wandering through the mile square pastures that ran down toward the Colorado border.

And when the week was up, he announced his decision. "I'll take that yearling filly of Rocket's. The sorrel with the cream tail and mane."

His father looked at him in surprise. "The one that got tangled in the barbed wire? That's never been named?"

In a second all Kennie's new pride was gone. He hung his head defensively. "Yes."

"You've made a bad choice, son. You couldn't have picked a worse."

"She's fast, Dad. And Rocket's fast—"

"It's the worst line of horses I've got. There's never one amongst them with real sense. The mares are hellions and the stallions outlaws; they're untamable."

"I'll tame her."

Rob guffawed. "Not I, nor anyone, has ever been able to really tame any one of them."

Kennie's chest heaved.

"Better change your mind, Ken. You want a horse that'll be a real friend to you, don't you?"

"Yes—" Kennie's voice was unsteady.

"Well, you'll never make a friend of that filly. She's all cut and scarred up already with tearing through barbed wire after that mother of hers. No fence'll hold 'em—"

"I know," said Kennie, still more faintly.

"Change your mind?" asked Howard briskly.

"No."

Rob was grim and put out. He couldn't go back on his word. The boy had to have a reasonable amount of help in breaking and taming the filly, and he could envision precious hours, whole days, wasted in the struggle.

Nell McLaughlin despaired. Once again Ken seemed to have taken the wrong turn and was back where he had begun; stoical, silent, defensive.

But there was a difference that only Ken could know. The way he felt about his colt. The way his heart sang. The pride and joy that filled him so full that sometimes he hung his head so they wouldn't see it shining out of his eyes.

He had known from the very first that he would choose that particular yearling because he was in love with her.

The year before, he had been out working with Gus, the big Swedish ranch hand, on the irrigation ditch, when they had noticed Rocket standing in a gully on the hillside, quiet for once, and eyeing them cautiously.

"Ay bet she got a colt," said Gus, and they walked carefully up the draw. Rocket gave a wild snort, thrust her feet out, shook her head wickedly, then fled away. And as they reached the spot, they saw standing there the wavering, pinkish colt,

Utah Jingler *1994 John Fawcett*

barely able to keep its feet. It gave a little squeak and started after its mother on crooked, wobbling legs.

"Yee whiz! Luk at de little *flicka!*" said Gus.

"What does *flicka* mean, Gus?"

"Swedish for little gurl, Ken—"

Ken announced at supper, "You said she'd never been named. I've named her. Her name is Flicka."

The first thing to do was to get her in. She was running with a band of yearlings on the saddleback, cut with ravines and gullies, on section twenty.

They all went out after her, Ken, as owner, on old Rob Roy, the wisest horse on the ranch.

Ken was entranced to watch Flicka when the wild band of youngsters discovered that they were being pursued and took off across the mountain. Footing made no difference to her. She floated across the ravines, always two lengths ahead of the others. Her pink mane and tail whipped in the wind. Her long delicate legs had only to aim, it seemed, at a particular spot, for her to reach it and sail on. She seemed to Ken a fairy horse.

He sat motionless, just watching

and holding Rob Roy in, when his father thundered past on Sultan and shouted, "Well, what's the matter? Why didn't you turn 'em?"

Kennie woke up and galloped after.

Rob Roy brought in the whole band. The corral gates were closed, and an hour was spent shunting the ponies in and out and through the chutes, until Flicka was left alone in the small round corral in which the baby colts were branded. Gus drove the others away, out the gate, and up the saddleback.

But Flicka did not intend to be left. She hurled herself against the poles which walled the corral. She tried to jump them. They were seven feet high. She caught her front feet over the top rung, clung, scrambled, while Kennie held his breath for fear the slender legs would be caught between the bars and snapped. Her hold broke, she fell over backward, rolled, screamed, tore around the corral. Kennie had a sick feeling in the pit of his stomach and his father looked disgusted.

One of the bars broke. She hurled herself again. Another went. She saw the opening and as neatly as a dog crawls through a fence, inserted her head and forefeet, scrambled through and fled away, bleeding in a dozen places.

As Gus was coming back, just about to close the gate to the upper range, the sorrel whipped through it, sailed across the road and ditch with her inimitable floating leap, and went up the side of the saddleback like a jack rabbit.

From way up the mountain, Gus heard excited whinnies, as she joined the band he had just driven up, and the last he saw of them they were strung out along the crest running like deer.

"Yee whiz!" said Gus, and stood motionless and staring until the ponies had disappeared over the ridge. Then he closed the gate, remounted Rob Roy, and rode back to the corral.

Rob McLaughlin gave Kennie one more chance to change his mind. "Last chance, son. Better pick a horse that you have some hope of riding one day. I'd have got rid of this whole line of stock if they weren't so fast that I've had the fool idea that some-day there might turn out one gentle one in the lot—and I'd have a race horse. But there's never been one so far, and it's not going to be Flicka."

"It's not going to be Flicka," chanted Howard.

"Perhaps she *might* be gentled," said Kennie; and Nell, watching, saw that although his lips quivered, there was fanatical determination in his eye.

"Ken," said Rob, "it's up to you. If you say you want her, we'll get her. But she wouldn't be the first of that line to die rather than give in. They're beautiful and they're fast, but let me tell you this, young man, they're *loco!*"

Kennie flinched under his father's direct glance.

"If I go after her again, I'll not give up whatever comes, understand what I mean by that?"

"Yes."

"What do you say?"

"I want her."

They brought her in again. They had better luck this time. She jumped over the Dutch half door of the stable and crashed inside. The men slammed the upper half of the door shut and she was caught.

The rest of the band were driven away, and Kennie stood outside of the stable, listening to the wild hoofs beating, the screams, the crashes. His Flicka inside there! He was drenched with perspiration.

"We'll leave her to think it over," said Rob, when dinnertime came. "Afterward, we'll go up and feed and water her."

But when they went up afterward, there was no Flicka in the barn. One of the windows, higher than the mangers, was broken.

The window opened into a pasture an eighth of a mile square, fenced in barbed wire six feet high. Near the stable stood a wagon load of hay. When they went around the back of the stable to see where Flicka had hidden herself, they found her between the stable and the hay wagon, eating.

At their approach she leaped away, then headed east across the pasture.

"If she's like her mother," said Rob, "she'll go right through the wire."

"Ay bet she'll go over," said Gus. "She yumps like a deer."

"No horse can jump that," said McLaughlin.

Kennie said nothing because he could not speak. It was, perhaps, the most terrible moment of his life. He watched Flicka racing toward the eastern wire.

A few yards from it, she swerved, turned and raced diagonally south.

"It turned her! It turned her!" cried Kennie, almost sobbing. It was the first sign of hope for Flicka. "Oh, Dad! She has got sense. She has! She has!"

Flicka turned again as she met the southern boundary of the pasture; again at the northern; she avoided the barn. Without abating anything of her whirlwind speed, following a precise, accurate calculation and turning each time on a dime, she investigated every possibility. Then, seeing that there was no hope, she raced south toward the range where she had spent her life, gathered herself, and shot into the air.

Each of the three men watching had the impulse to cover his eyes, and Kennie gave a sort of a howl of despair.

Twenty yards of fence came down with her as she hurled herself through. Caught on the upper strands, she turned a complete somersault, landing on her back, her four legs dragging the wires down on top of her, and tangling herself in them beyond hope of escape.

"That wire!" cried McLaughlin. "If I could afford decent fences—"

Kennie followed the men miserably as they walked to the filly. They stood in a circle watching, while she kicked and fought and thrashed until the wire was tightly wound and knotted about her, cutting, piercing and tearing great three-cornered pieces of flesh and hide. At last she was unconscious, streams of blood running on her golden coat, and pools of crimson widening and spreading on the grass beneath her.

With the wire cutter which Gus always carried in the hip pocket of his overalls, he cut all the wire away, and they drew her into the pasture, repaired the fence, placed hay, a box of oats and a tub of water near her, and called it a day.

"I don't think she'll pull out of it," said McLaughlin.

Next morning Kennie was up at five, doing his lessons. At six he went out to Flicka.

She had not moved. Food and water were untouched. She was no longer bleeding, but the wounds were swollen and caked over.

Kennie got a bucket of fresh water and poured it over her mouth. Then he leaped away, for Flicka came to life, scrambled up, got her balance, and stood swaying.

Kennie went a few feet away and sat down to watch her. When he went in to breakfast, she had drunk deeply of the water and was mouthing the oats.

There began, then, a sort of recovery. She ate, drank, limped about the pasture; stood for hours with hanging head and weakly splayed out legs, under the clump of cottonwood trees. The swollen wounds scabbed and began to heal.

Kennie lived in the pasture, too. He followed her around, he talked to her. He, too, lay snoozing or sat under the cottonwoods; and often, coaxing her with hand outstretched, he walked very quietly toward her. But she would not let him come near her.

Often she stood with her head at the south fence, looking off to the mountain. It made the tears come to Kennie's eyes to see the way she longed to get away.

Still Rob said she wouldn't pull out of it. There was no use putting a halter on her. She had no strength.

One morning, as Ken came out of the house, Gus met him and said, "De filly's down."

Kennie ran to the pasture, Howard close behind him. The right hind leg which had been badly swollen at the knee joint had opened in a festering wound, and Flicka lay flat and motionless, with staring eyes.

"Don't you wish now you'd chosen Doughboy?" asked Howard.

"Go away!" shouted Ken.

Howard stood watching while Kennie sat down on the ground and took Flicka's head on his lap. Though she was conscious and moved a little, she did not struggle nor seem frightened. Tears rolled down Kennie's cheeks as he talked to her and petted her. After a few moments, Howard walked away.

"Mother, what do you do for an infection when it's a horse?" asked Kennie.

"Just what you'd do if it was a person. Wet dressings. I'll help you, Ken. We mustn't let those wounds close or scab over until they're clean. I'll make a poultice for that hind leg and help you put it on. Now that she'll let us get close to her, we can help her a lot."

"The thing to do is see that she eats," said Rob. "Keep up her strength."

But he himself would not go near her. "She won't pull out of it," he said. "I don't want to see her or think about her."

Kennie and his mother nursed the filly. The big poultice was bandaged on the hind leg. It drew out much poisoned matter and Flicka felt better and was able to stand again.

She watched for Kennie now, and followed him like a dog, hopping on three legs, holding up the right hind leg with its huge knob of a bandage in comical fashion.

"Dad, Flicka's my friend now; she likes me," said Ken.

His father looked at him. "I'm glad of that, son. It's a fine thing to have a horse for a friend."

Kennie found a nicer place for her. In the lower pasture the brook ran over cool stones. There was a grassy bank, the size of a corral, almost on a level with the water. Here she could lie softly, eat grass, drink fresh running water. From the grass, a twenty-foot hill sloped up, crested with overhanging trees. She

Mountain Grown *1994 John Fawcett*

caught sight of him coming and was calling to him!

He placed the box of oats under her nose and she ate while he stood beside her, his hand smoothing the satin-soft skin under her mane. It had a nap as deep as plush. He played with her long, cream-colored tresses; arranged her forelock neatly between her eyes. She was a bit dish-faced, like an Arab, with eyes set far apart. He lightly groomed and brushed her while she stood turning her head to him whichever way he went.

He spoiled her. Soon she would not step to the stream to drink but he must hold a bucket for her. And she would drink, then lift her dripping muzzle, rest it on the shoulder of his blue chambray shirt, her golden eyes dreaming off into the distance; then daintily dip her mouth and drink again.

When she turned her head to the south, and pricked her ears, and

was enclosed, as it were, in a green, open-air nursery.

Kennie carried her oats morning and evening. She would watch for him to come, eyes and ears pointed to the hill. And one evening Ken, still some distance off, came to a stop and a wide grin spread over his face. He had heard her nicker. She had stood tense and listening, Ken knew she heard the other colts galloping on the upland.

"You'll go back there someday, Flicka," he whispered. "You'll be three and I'll be eleven. You'll be so strong you won't know I'm on your back, and we'll fly like the wind. We'll stand on the very top where we can look over the whole world, and smell the snow from the Neversummer Range. Maybe we'll see antelope—"

This was the happiest month of Kennie's life.

With the morning, Flicka always had new strength and would hop three-legged up the hill to stand broadside to the early sun, as horses love to do.

The moment Ken woke, he'd go to the window, and see her there; and when he was dressed and at his table studying, he sat so that he could raise his head and see Flicka.

After breakfast, she would be waiting for him and the box of oats at the gate; and for Nell McLaughlin with fresh bandages and buckets of disinfectant; and all three would go together to the brook, Flicka hopping along ahead of them, as if she was leading the way.

But Rob McLaughlin would not look at her.

One day all the wounds were swollen again. Presently they opened, one by one; and Kennie and his mother made more poultices.

Still the little filly climbed the hill in the early morning and ran about on three legs. Then she began to go down in flesh and almost overnight wasted away to nothing. Every rib showed; the glossy hide was dull and brittle, and was pulled over the skeleton as if she was a dead horse.

Gus said, "It's de fever. It burns up her flesh. If you could stop de fever she might get vell."

McLaughlin was standing in his window one morning and saw the little skeleton hopping about three-legged in the sunshine, and he said, "That's the end. I won't have a thing like that on my place."

Kennie had to understand that Flicka had not been getting well all this time; she had been slowly dying.

"She still eats her oats," he said mechanically.

They were all sorry for Ken. Nell McLaughlin stopped disinfecting and dressing the wounds. "It's no use, Ken," she said gently, "you know Flicka's going to die, don't you?"

"Yes, Mother."

Ken stopped eating. Howard said, "Ken doesn't eat anything any more. Don't he have to eat his dinner, Mother?"

But Nell answered, "Leave him alone."

Because the shooting of wounded animals is all in the day's work on the western plains, and sickening to everyone, Rob's voice, when he gave the order to have Flicka shot, was as flat as if he had been telling Gus to kill a chicken for dinner.

"Here's the Marlin, Gus. Pick out a time when Ken's not around and put the filly out of her misery."

Gus took the rifle. "*Ja*, Boss—"

Ever since Ken had known that Flicka was to be shot, he had kept his eye on the rack which held the firearms. His father allowed no firearms in the bunkhouse. The gun rack was in the dining room of the ranch house; and, going through it to the kitchen three times a day for meals, Ken's eye scanned the weapons to make sure that they were all there.

That night they were not all there. The Marlin rifle was missing.

When Kennie saw that, he stopped walking. He felt dizzy. He kept staring at the gun rack, telling himself that it surely was there—he counted again and again—he couldn't see clearly—

Then he felt an arm across his shoulders and heard his father's voice.

"I know, son. Some things are awful hard to take. We just have to take 'em. I have to, too."

Kennie got hold of his father's hand and held on. It helped steady him.

Finally he looked up. Rob looked down and smiled at him and gave him a little shake and squeeze. Ken managed a smile too.

"All right now?"

"All right, Dad."

They walked in to supper together.

Ken even ate a little. But Nell looked thoughtfully at the ashen color of his face and at the little pulse that was beating in the side of his neck.

After supper he carried Flicka her oats, but he had to coax her and she would only eat a little. She stood with her head hanging, but when he stroked it and talked to her, she pressed her face into his chest and was content. He could feel the burning heat of her body. It didn't seem possible that anything so thin could be alive.

Presently Kennie saw Gus come into the pasture carrying the Marlin. When he saw Ken, he changed his direction and sauntered along as if he was out to shoot some cottontails.

Ken ran to him. "When are you going to do it, Gus?"

"Ay was goin' down soon now, before it got dark—"

"Gus, don't do it tonight. Wait till morning. Just one more night, Gus."

"Vell, in de morning den, but it got to be done, Ken. Yer fader gives de order."

"I know. I won't say anything more."

An hour after the family had gone to bed, Ken got up and put on his clothes. It was a warm moonlit night. He ran down to the brook, calling softly. "Flicka! Flicka!"

But Flicka did not answer with a little nicker; and she was not in the nursery, nor hopping about the pasture. Ken hunted for an hour.

At last he found her down the creek, lying in the water. Her head had been on the bank, but as she lay there, the current of the stream had sucked and pulled at her, and she had had no strength to resist; and little by little her head had slipped down until when Ken got there only the muzzle was resting on the bank, and the body and legs were swinging in the stream.

Kennie slid into the water, sitting on the bank, and he hauled at her head. But she was heavy and the current dragged like a weight; and he began to sob because he had no strength to draw her out.

Then he found a leverage for his heels against some rocks in the bed of the stream, and he braced himself against these, and pulled with all his might; and her head came up onto his knees, and he held it cradled in his arms.

He was glad that she had died of her own accord, in the cool water, under the moon, instead of being shot by Gus. Then, putting his face close to hers, and looking searchingly into her eyes he saw that she was alive and looking back at him.

And then he burst out crying, and hugged her, and said, "Oh, my little Flicka, my little Flicka."

The long night passed.

The moon slid slowly across the heavens.

The water rippled over Kennie's legs, and over Flicka's body. And gradually the heat and fever went out of her. And the cool running water washed and washed her wounds.

When Gus went down in the morning with the rifle, they hadn't moved. There they were, Kennie sitting in water over his thighs and hips, with Flicka's head in his arms.

Gus seized Flicka by the head, and hauled her out on the grassy bank, and then, seeing that Kennie couldn't move, cold and stiff and half-paralyzed as he was, lifted him in his arms and carried him to the house.

"Gus," said Ken through chattering teeth, "don't shoot her, Gus."

"It ain't fur me to say, Ken. You know dat."

"But the fever's left her, Gus."

"Ay wait a little, Ken—"

Rob McLaughlin drove to Laramie to get the doctor, for Ken was in violent chills that would not stop. His mother had him in bed wrapped in hot blankets when they got back.

He looked at his father imploringly as the doctor shook down the thermometer.

"She might get well now, Dad. The fever's left her. It went out of her when the moon went down."

"All right, son. Don't worry. Gus'll feed her, morning and night, as long as she's—"

"As long as I can't do it," finished Kennie happily.

The doctor put the thermometer in his mouth and told him to keep it shut.

All day Gus went about his work, thinking of Flicka. He had not been back to look at her. He had been given no more orders. If she was alive, the order to shoot her was still in effect. But Kennie was ill, McLaughlin making his second trip to town taking the doctor home, and would not be back till long after dark.

After their supper in the bunkhouse, Gus and Tim walked down to the brook. They did not speak as they approached the filly, lying stretched out flat on the grassy bank, but their eyes were straining at her to see if she was dead or alive.

She raised her head as they reached her.

"By the powers!" exclaimed Tim, "there she is!"

She dropped her head, raised it again, and moved her legs and became tense as if struggling to rise. But to do so she must use her right hind leg to brace herself against the earth. That was the damaged leg, and at the first bit of pressure with it, she gave up and fell back.

"We'll swing her on to the other side," said Tim. "Then she can help herself."

"*Ja*—"

Standing behind her, they leaned over, grabbed hold of her left legs, front and back, and gently hauled her over. Flicka was as lax and willing as a puppy. But the moment she found herself lying on her right side, she began to scramble, braced herself with her good left leg and tried to rise.

"Yee whiz!" said Gus. "She got plenty strength yet."

"Hi!" cheered Tim. "She's up!"

But Flicka wavered, slid down again, and lay flat. This time she

Spottin' Strays on Willow Creek *1994 John Fawcett*

gave notice that she would not try again by heaving a deep sigh and closing her eyes. Gus took the pipe out of his mouth and thought it over. Orders or no orders, he would try to save the filly. Ken had gone too far to be let down.

"Ay'm goin' to rig a blanket sling fur her, Tim, and get her on her feet and keep her up."

There was bright moonlight to work by. They brought down the post-hole digger and set two aspen poles deep into the ground either side of the filly, then, with ropes attached to the blanket, hoisted her by a pulley.

Not at all disconcerted, she rested comfortably in the blanket under her belly, touched her feet on the ground, and reached for the bucket of water Gus held for her.

Kennie was sick a long time. He nearly died. But Flicka picked up. Every day Gus passed the word to Nell, who carried it to Ken. "She's cleaning up her oats." "She's out of the sling." "She bears a little weight on the bad leg."

Tim declared it was a real miracle. They argued about it, eating their supper.

"Na," said Gus. "It was de cold water, washin' de fever outa her. And more dan dot—it was Ken—you tink it don't count? All night dot boy sits dere, and says, 'Hold on, Flicka. Ay'm here wid you. Ay'm standin' by, two of us togedder'—"

Tim stared at Gus without answering, while he thought it over. In the silence, a coyote yapped far off on the plains; and the wind made a rushing sound high up in the jack pines on the hill.

Gus filled his pipe.

"Sure," said Tim finally. "Sure. That's it."

Then came the day when Rob McLaughlin stood smiling at the foot of Kennie's bed and said, "Listen! Hear your friend?"

Ken listened and heard Flicka's high, eager whinny.

"She don't spend much time by the brook any more. She's up at the gate of the corral half the time, nickering for you."

"For me!"

Rob wrapped a blanket around the boy and carried him out to the corral gate.

Kennie gazed at Flicka. There was a look of marveling in his eyes. He felt as if he had been living in a world where everything was dreadful and hurting but awfully real; and *this* couldn't be real; this was all soft and happy, nothing to struggle over or worry about or fight for any more. Even his father was proud of him! He could feel it in the way Rob's big arms held him. It was all like a dream and far away. He couldn't, yet, get close to anything.

But Flicka—Flicka—alive, well, pressing up to him, recognizing him, nickering—

Kennie put out a hand—weak and white—and laid it on her face. His thin little fingers straightened her forelock the way he used to do, while Rob looked at the two with a strange expression about his mouth, and a glow in his eyes that was not often there.

"She's still poor, Dad, but she's on four legs now."

"She's picking up."

Ken turned his face up, suddenly remembering. "Dad! She did get gentled, didn't she?"

"Gentle—as—a kitten—"

They put a cot down by the brook for Ken, and boy and filly got well together.

Story Questions & Activities

1. What does Kennie say might solve his problem in school?
2. How are Kennie and Flicka alike?
3. Why do you think this story is one of the most famous in American literature?
4. What is the main problem in this story? How is it solved at the end?
5. Kennie and Bellerophon both have heroic encounters with horses. How are their experiences alike? What are the differences?

Write an Advice Column

Imagine that Kennie wrote a letter asking an advice columnist for ways to persuade his father to give him a colt. Write Kennie's letter. Then write the advice columnist's reply. Give at least three suggestions that will help Kennie persuade his dad.

Design a Stage Set

"My Friend Flicka" has been made into a movie and a television series. Now it's your turn. Build a model of a stage set for a play version of "My Friend Flicka." Choose the most important objects in the story. Use paints, cardboard, sticks, and other art materials to make your model. Do not clutter the set with too many objects. Remember to leave space for the actors to move around on the stage.

Kennie finds out that caring for a wild colt is a great responsibility. What kind of wild pet would you like to have? An elephant? A gorilla? A kangaroo? Make a checklist of all the responsibilities you would have if you owned an unusual pet.

The wide-open spaces of Wyoming are described in detail in this story. Use an encyclopedia, a travel guide, the Internet, or another resource to learn more about this beautiful western state. Describe Wyoming's history, geography, economy, climate, altitude, and national parks. What are some fun places to visit? Use what you learn to create a travel brochure.

Use the Internet

When you need to research a topic, you may want to search for information on the Internet. By typing in *horses,* for example, and clicking the SEARCH button, the **search engine** will explore the Internet and bring up a list of **Web sites**. Clicking on any one of these will bring up a **home page** like the one below.

To find the information you are looking for, you can rely on two skills you already use when you read: **skimming** to give you an overview of the page and **scanning** to find key words. You can also click on underlined words called **links** to go to other sites or other parts of the same site.

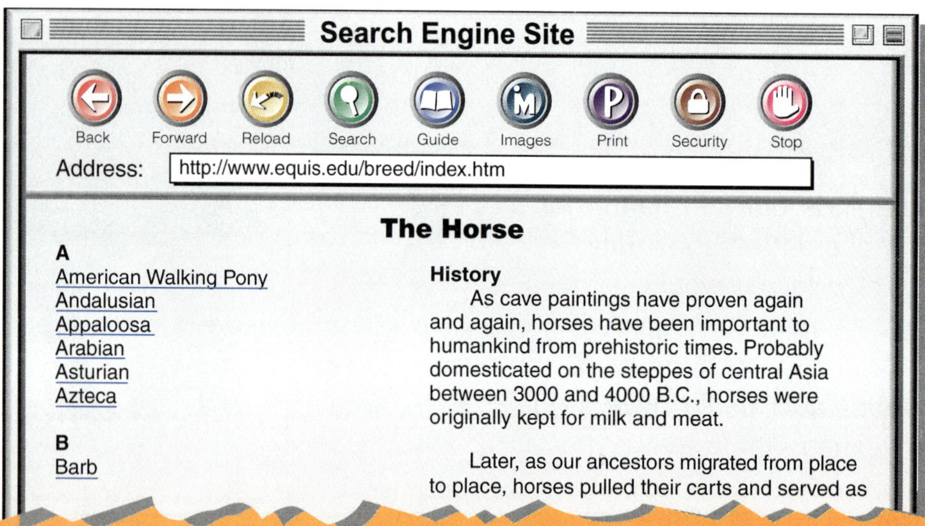

Use the home page above to answer these questions.

1. How many links appear on this screen?
2. According to this Web site, when were horses domesticated?
3. Would this Web site be useful if you wanted to know about rodeos?
4. What would you do if you wanted to compare two breeds of horses, such as Appaloosas and Arabians?
5. Why might it be useful to skim through a Web page?

TEST POWER

Test Tip

Ruling out wrong answers will make it easier to find the best answer.

DIRECTIONS

Read the sample story. Then read each question about the story.

SAMPLE

Badlands National Park

Badlands National Park is one of the most interesting places on Earth! The park is located in the southwestern portion of South Dakota. It covers more than 244,000 acres. Huge stretches of basalt buttes, stony spires, and great gorges tumble and roll their way across the land. Walking through the park makes you feel as if you are walking on the moon.

Modern archaeologists, zoologists, and paleontologists value the Badlands as a living museum. The fossils of many extinct species can be seen embedded in the layers of rock in the Badlands. Scientists have even found the skeletons of three-toed horses, a species that died out thousands of years ago.

Whatever your interest, whether it be fossils, buttes, or rock formations, you will see it in Badlands National Park.

1 The author gives you reason to believe that —

A Badlands National Park is not interesting to scientists

B scientists can find useful information in the park

C Badlands National Park is on the moon

D No one has ever discovered fossils in the park

2 The author probably wrote this passage to —

F persuade people to visit Yellowstone National Park

G encourage people to discover Badlands National Park

H explain how fossils are discovered

J describe how zoologists make a living

The artist painted this picture to illustrate one of the legends of King Arthur and the Knights of the Round Table. What kinds of sources do you think he used to create this painting?

Look closely at the picture. Many historians believe that King Arthur was a real person. Notice the details. Where is Arthur standing at the table? How many knights are around him? What kind of armor are they wearing? Do you think this information is accurate? What might the artist have done to try to add historical facts to his painting?

Notice the words at the bottom of the picture. Do you think this illustration is from a very old book? What makes you think so? What do you think it was like to be a king long ago?

The Knights of the Round Table
from *History of the Holy Grail,*
15th Century French
Bibliotheque Nationale, Paris

COnſiderãt q̃ par les triũphalles et glorieuſes oeuures que les vaillans hommes ⁊ nobles cheualiers anciennement firent en fait de cheualerie acquirent en leurs vies louenges ⁊ gloire de perpetuelle memoire. Je voſtre treſhumble et treſobeiſſãt ſeruiteur a lhõneur ⁊ louẽge de vo⁹ mõ treſredoubte ⁊ ſouuerain ſeigneur chief de toute nobleſſe ⁊ cheualerie. Charles huitieſme de ce nõ treſcreſtiẽ roy de frãce. Affin q̃ voſtre cheualereux couraige ⁊ des ieu

Meet
Olivia Coolidge

A good biography, according to Olivia Coolidge, is "concerned with the effect its hero has on other people, with environment and background, with the nature of the great man's achievements and their value." She says, "Facts are the bricks with which a biographer builds," and stresses that it is important to "distinguish a fact from a judgment."

Coolidge was born in England in 1908. She taught English, Latin, and Greek in Europe and the United States. Her many books include *Greek Myths*, *The Trojan War*, and *Lives of Famous Romans*, as well as biographies of Abraham Lincoln and Gandhi. Several of her books received the American Library Association Notable Book award and were on the *Horn Book* honor list.

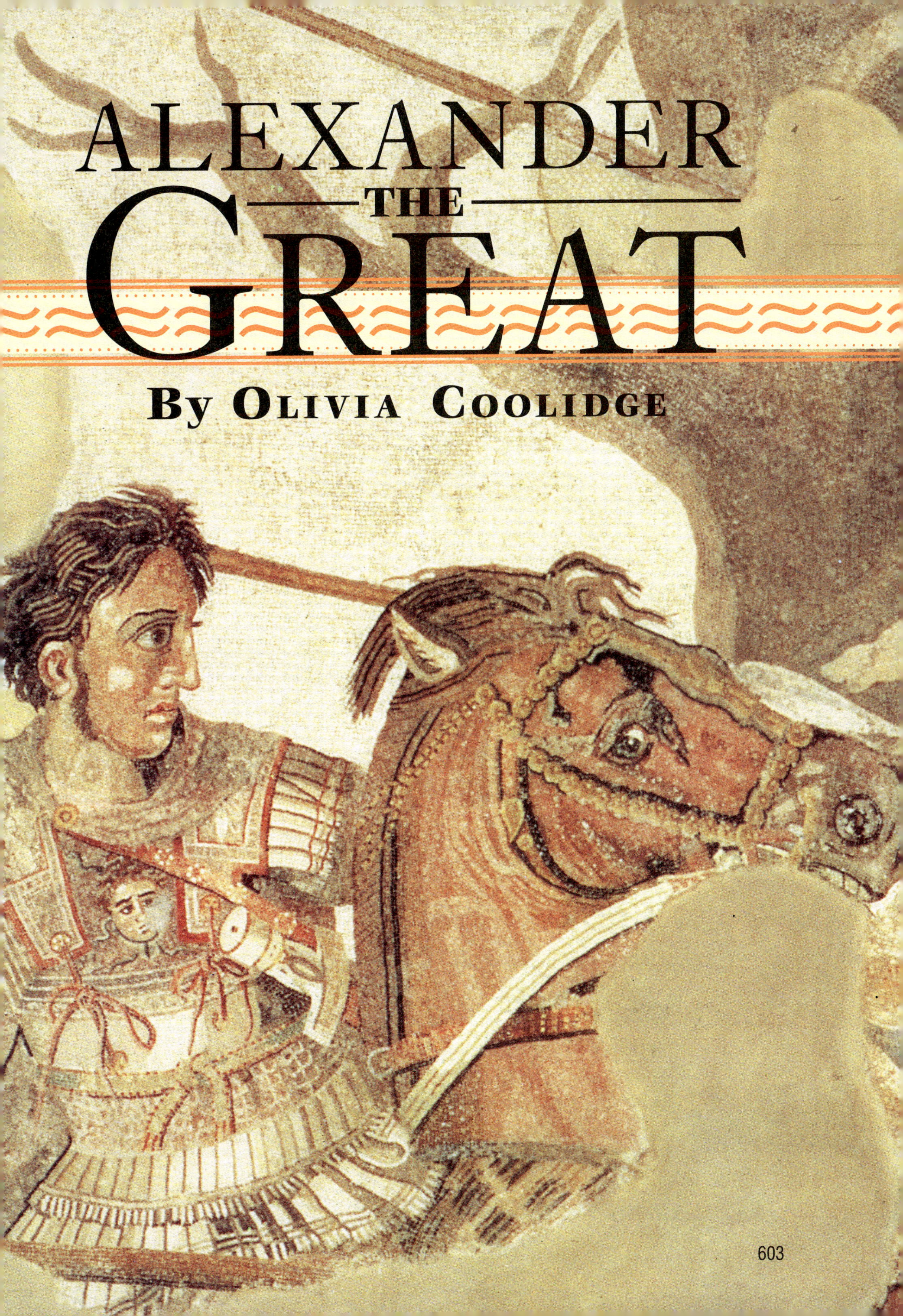

ALEXANDER THE GREAT

By Olivia Coolidge

Alexander (356–323 B.C.) was twenty years old when his father was murdered, the only son of the queen Olympias, who had long ago quarreled with Philip over his custom of taking extra wives like the king of Persia. Partly for this reason, and partly because Philip was busy with his wars, the boy's education was left to his mother, who chose for him a stern tutor. Leonidas would allow no softness in the boy. He used to look through the chest where Alexander kept his clothes and blankets to be sure that the queen had not provided anything costly. He only allowed the plainest food, and he taught the prince that the best "cook" for a good breakfast was an all-night walk, and for a good dinner was a light breakfast. In fact, he gave Alexander the sort of training which Xenophon praised in *The Education of Cyrus*.

When Alexander was about twelve, legend says, an incident attracted Philip's attention. A dealer had a great black horse for sale, which he called Bucephalus, or Bull's-head, because of the shape of a white mark on his forehead. He was indeed a splendid creature, but he would let nobody mount him. Philip told the owner to take him away, but Alexander said it was a shame to lose such an animal because nobody had the skill to ride him.

Philip was angry at his impudence, but the boy offered to bet the price of the horse that he could ride it. He had noticed that Bucephalus was frightened by his own shadow dancing on the ground in front of him. He turned him to face the sun and patted him until he quieted down. Suddenly he sprang on his back, and the horse bolted madly. Philip, who had never thought the boy would mount, was afraid for him now. Alexander, however, clung on until Bucephalus was tired enough to be guided safely home.

We shall never know if the story of how Alexander won his horse is a true one, but it gives a good picture of his cleverness and daring. Philip began to take interest in the boy, and shortly afterward he arranged another tutor for him who was in his own way the most famous man in the Greek world.

Aristotle had come to Plato's Academy when he was seventeen and had proved himself the best pupil Plato had. He had stayed there another seventeen years, learning and teaching, until Plato died. At this point he left the Academy to form a school of his own. Aristotle was a different kind of man from Plato. He did not have as much imagination, but he was more practical. When Plato, for instance, wanted to know what the ideal government might be, he started to consider what the soul of a man was like. When Aristotle asked himself the same question, he collected a hundred and fifty-eight different constitutions which had been set up by the Greek states; and he tried to compare them.

Now Aristotle, as it chanced, had been born in one of the Greek towns on the Macedonian coast. His father had been a doctor and was actually court physician to King Amyntas of Macedonia, Philip's father. Philip and he were about the same age, and shared childhood memories. Since then, Aristotle had learned in the Academy that Plato's purpose was to train the rulers of the future. For both these reasons, Aristotle was willing to tutor Alexander. Thus on top of the education described by Xenophon, Alexander received some of the training of Plato.

Above: Alexander on a horse fighting Poros on an elephant 323 B.C.
Bronze coin from Babylon

He never became a philosopher, but he was clever and eager to learn. Aristotle's position as tutor gave a special interest to the young heir of Macedon, as many remembered Plato saying that the ruler of the future must have this sort of education. Statesmen like Demosthenes who visited the court of King Philip thought it worthwhile to meet the boy.

They were nearly all impressed. Alexander was striking-looking, with blue eyes and golden curls. He was tall for his age, and good at every sport. He loved poetry and music; and he liked to compare himself with his legendary ancestor Achilles, hero of the *Iliad*, who won great glory from his earliest years.

Philip soon gave his son military training. When Alexander commanded a wing in the battle of Chaeronea, he was only eighteen years old; but he had been fighting since he was sixteen, and he had also governed Macedonia while his father was absent.

When Philip died, his son was only twenty. Demosthenes urged the Athenians to regain their freedom. But his plans were upset by the energy of Alexander. The Athenians were forced to receive him as their master. They did not like him. Philip at least, many felt, had been a great man. The Athenians, who were unused to kings, sneered at this untried boy who wanted to be treated like a hero. When Alexander went on to Corinth, everyone laughed at what happened to him there.

There was a philosopher in Corinth called Diogenes who felt that nothing mattered except a man's own soul. To show his contempt for the world, he dressed in rags,

Above: Alexander the Great c. 300 B.C. Silver coin from Thrace

was unshaven and dirty, and had no home but a big tub laid on its side in which he took shelter when the weather forced him to do so. He lost no chance of telling the Corinthians what he thought of them for caring about useless things, and he had become famous for his rude remarks.

Curious, Alexander went to see him. They made a strange contrast as the golden-haired young man in the royal costume stood looking down at the rough philosopher who was squatting in front of his tub. Diogenes took no notice of the king until Alexander asked if he could do anything for him.

There probably was no one in Corinth who would not have been glad to ask a favor of the master of all Greece. Diogenes looked up frowning at the tall young man in front of him and said, "Yes. Stop standing between me and the sun."

The Greeks laughed, but Alexander was not angry. He admired the philosopher's spirit and said to his friends, "If I were not Alexander I should have liked to be Diogenes."

The war which Philip had planned against Persia was only delayed two years by his death. In 334, Alexander invaded Asia Minor with about thirty-five thousand troops. Nearly half were Macedonians, the rest hired soldiers or troops sent by the Greek cities. The army took with it engineers for making bridges or siege towers, well diggers, surveyors to find out about routes and camp grounds, geographers to make maps, botanists and other learned men to collect specimens and find out more about the country they conquered. There was a baggage train, of course, and a military council of high officers trained by Philip. Everything was planned to go like clockwork.

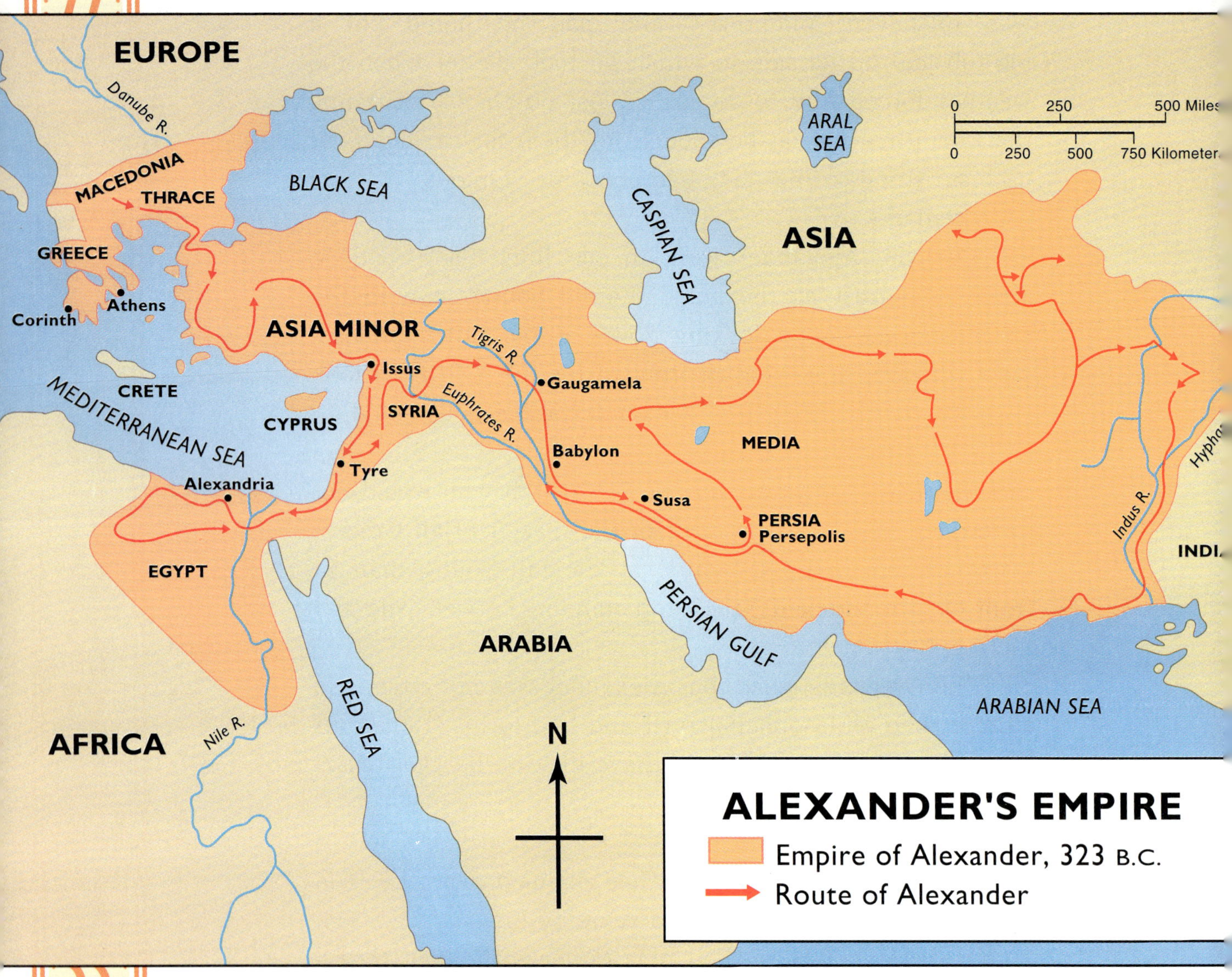

Alexander's empire stretched across three continents. Babylon was its capital.

Philip had merely meant to conquer Asia Minor. The Greek cities on the coast would be easily won over, and they would dry up the stream of hired soldiers on which the Persians relied. The great landowners of the country districts made splendid cavalry in the Persian style; but the peasants, though loyal to their lords and personally warlike, were too poor to afford the armor of Greek infantry. Hard fighting lay ahead of Alexander, but he was victorious.

After a while he found that he could not hold his gains without going further. Control of Asia Minor with its long seacoast depended on a fleet. The fleet of the Persians came from Egypt and the great Phoenician city of Tyre on the Syrian coast. Alexander advanced against Tyre because he had to, descending from mountainous country into the plain where Asia Minor borders on Syria.

Darius III, who had succeeded Artaxerxes, was a weak ruler, but he came of fighting stock and knew that he must battle for his kingdom. He could not, however, get together an army which was larger than the countryside would support. His native infantry was not equal to the Greeks, and his leadership was poor. When he met Alexander at the battle of Issus, the Macedonian charged at the head of his men, while the Persian hovered in a chariot in the rear and speedily fled. Darius's leaderless men were cut to pieces, and Alexander found himself master of Syria.

He hurried to blockade Tyre, but found it difficult. The Tyrians kept his warships off by piling great boulders under water. Alexander sent merchant ships to haul these away, but the Tyrians ventured out in their own warships to attack them. Alexander brought up his fleet to protect his dredgers, but Tyrian divers cut their cables under water. Meanwhile, on the land side his engineers were unable for a long while to make the slightest progress. Tyre held out for seven months, but King Darius did not dare face Alexander again. Unaided, the city fell at last in July, 332. By November, Alexander was in Egypt, where he was received with joy, since the Egyptians had long desired to be free from the Persians. Alexander controlled the whole eastern end of the Mediterranean.

Once more his only defense lay in attack. The true center of the Persian empire lay across the Euphrates, in Media, Babylonia, and Persia. In Susa, long the capital, and in Persepolis, where the kings had built their palaces in the days of their pride, lay uncounted treasure piled up from the tribute of two hundred years. For this even Darius must fight. Eighteen months had gone by since his defeat, and he had by now refitted his forces. The cavalry, which had always been superb, was better armed. For the infantry less could be done, seeing that to make new equipment took much time, and to drill fighters even longer. Darius was relying on chariots whose wheels had long knives sticking out. A few hundred of these might well be able to break up massed infantry if skillfully handled.

Darius gave battle on the flat plain of Gaugamela, since he was anxious to give his chariots a chance. There on the first of October, 331, Alexander found him. The chariots made their charge, but Alexander had screened his infantry by javelin men and slingers. For the sake of speed, the chariots had little armor. Men and horses crashed to the ground, and very few of them reached the infantry. The rest of the battle swayed back and forth. The Persians had the greater numbers, but the Greeks the better army. They had a tradition of victory, too, and a finer commander.

Once more Darius took to flight. He might have spared himself the effort, for he had lost his kingdom by now and even his life. The Persian nobles whom he had twice deserted in battle were finished with him. He was arrested; and as the pursuit of Alexander came close, he was finally murdered.

Above: A detail from the "Alexander Sarcophagus"

There was now no king in the empire but Alexander. The men of Babylon came out to surrender. The satrap of Persia tried to keep him from entering his homeland but was swept aside. Alexander took Susa and Persepolis. He sat on the Great King's throne and seized his treasure. As a sign to the whole East, he set fire to the palace of King Xerxes and burned it to the ground. The miracle had come to pass. Greece had conquered the empire.

We need not follow Alexander farther east across the steppes of Turkestan, through the foothills of the Himalayas, into India. Susa had been only the center of an empire which stretched as far east as it did west. There were adventures ahead for Alexander with tribes, in lands, and on rivers which he had never heard of. But before he pursued his way, he had to face the problem of holding what he had won. It is what Alexander did to found an empire as much as his generalship that made him great.

Greeks generally thought that barbarians, which is what they called non-Greeks, were fit to be plundered or made slaves, rather than to rule. Alexander, however, was half barbarian himself; and he had seen the wonders of Babylonia and Egypt, as well as the splendor of Persian kings. He understood that East and West must be mingled into a greater whole and that he, Alexander, must have a share in both.

The first thing that he did was found many cities through the eastern world where homeless Greek soldiers found a new place to live and build their temples. Those cities acted as market places for country villages or stages on the trade routes which had run far in Persian times and were soon to be thronged with travelers. Alexandria in Egypt has always been the greatest of the towns that Alexander founded, but there were many others, including one called after Bucephalus, his horse. From these cities

Greek ways spread all over the East. When the Romans came to rule two hundred years later they found that Greek had become a second language through the eastern part of their whole empire. They were content to let it remain so and to speak it themselves; for the Romans, like the eastern peoples, had much to learn from the Greeks.

All this Alexander did, but in actually governing the peoples of the East he relied on themselves. He split up the power of the satraps, to be sure; and he left trusty Macedonian generals here and there with troops. All the same, he tried to employ the great Persian nobles, got to know them, dressed in eastern clothes himself, and liked his friends to do so. He married an eastern princess called Roxana and encouraged his friends to follow his example.

He did not want men to think of him as a conqueror, but rather as a godlike hero, born to rule. There is often something of this feeling about kingship. Philip's image had been carried in procession with those of the gods. Egyptian kings were thought divine, and the Persians could claim at least to be God's servants. Alexander had found these ideas in the East and was eager to adopt them because he needed loyalty. They meant something special to him, too. Achilles, his ancestor, was half divine. During the quarrels between his mother and Philip, Queen Olympias made a mystery of his birth, pretending that he was more than Philip's son. It is likely also that his victories had gone to his head. No one had ever done what he had done, and he was not yet thirty. Alexander gave out that he was not really Philip's son, but was born of a god.

It was a wise political stroke, but his Macedonian friends did not like it. They were many years away from home and they may have been tired of adventures. Perhaps they had their ambitions, too; and they did not wish Alexander to show favor to native princes. At all events, there were plots against him.

Alexander was noble and trusting by nature. Early in his campaigns his doctor was mixing a drink of medicine for him when a letter was brought in. He read it. It warned him that the doctor was planning to poison him. Alexander stretched out one hand for the drink, while with the other he offered the letter to his doctor. While the startled man read it, the king drained the medicine down.

After this, it is sad to discover that years later this very doctor took part in an attempt on Alexander's life. Alexander's new position was making him so lofty that he could trust no one.

The strain had begun to tell on him. If he made mistakes, his empire might collapse even more quickly than it had been won. At feasts he began to drink deeply, as his father had once done. His royal rages became terrible to endure. But victory followed him all the same wherever he went.

In 323, he was back from India in Babylon, preparing to conquer Arabia; but his amazing career was over at last. He fell sick of a fever and, weakened by battle wounds, could not throw it off. He died in the palace of the kings of Babylon on June 13, 323 B.C. He was only thirty-two years old and in the thirteenth year of his reign. He had conquered nearly all of the world then known to the Greeks.

Alexander the Great *Bronze statuette from Roman Imperial period British Museum, London*

Story Questions & Activities

1. How old was Alexander when he became the ruler of Macedonia?

2. What did Alexander think of the ragged philosopher, Diogenes?

3. Do you think there is any evidence to prove that Alexander and Diogenes met? What sources could there be to support the story of their meeting?

4. What is the main idea of this selection?

5. Suppose that Alexander the Great could speak to England's legendary King Arthur, shown in the painting on page 601. What questions might Alexander ask him about the Knights of the Round Table? What might Arthur ask Alexander about his victories?

Write a Persuasive Essay

Alexander the Great was a general and a strong leader. Write a persuasive essay that will convince your classmates that Alexander was really "great."

Include

- a strong topic sentence that states your opinion.
- supporting reasons, evidence, and facts.
- persuasive language, such as *should* and *must.*
- a strong conclusion.

Make a Movie Poster

Imagine that you are going to make a remake of the movie, *Alexander the Great*. Which actor will you get to play Alexander? What part of the world will your crew use as a location for the film? Use paints, crayons, colored markers, and oaktag to make a movie poster advertising your new movie of Alexander the Great. Persuade people that the film is worth seeing.

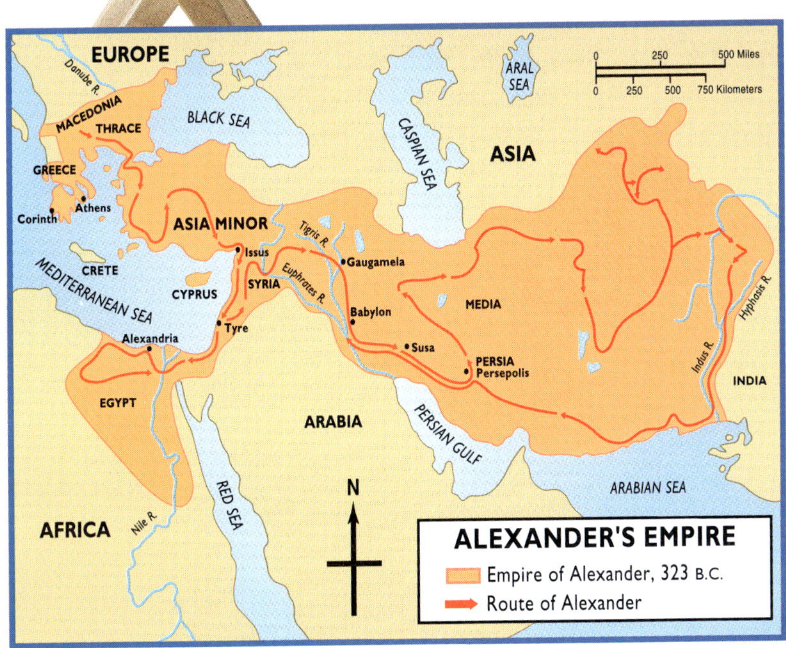

Draw a Time Line

How many countries did Alexander the Great conquer in his short lifetime? What were the dates of his greatest victories? Draw a time line to show the dates and important events in his 12-year reign. Be sure to include his conquest of Tyre in 332 B.C., his greatest military victory.

Find Out More

Alexander was not only a great general and leader. He was also a good student. Find out more about the boy Alexander and his famous teacher Aristotle. Start by looking in an encyclopedia, a book about Alexander or Aristotle, or a social studies textbook. Use two reference sources to check your facts. Then write a brief report about what school must have been like for Alexander.

Use the Card Catalog

Suppose that you were asked to write a research report about Alexander the Great. How would you begin? Your first step might be to check the **card catalog** in the library. The card catalog may be on index cards in drawers, or it may be on computer.

Each library book usually has three cards. These are the **author card**, the **title card**, and the **subject card**. All three cards give the same information about the book, but in a different order. Each card also lists the book's **call number**. The call number tells how the book is classified and where to find it on the library shelf.

You use the author card when you know the author of the book but not the title. You use the title card when you know the title of the book but perhaps not the author. You use the subject card when you know the subject but not the author or the title.

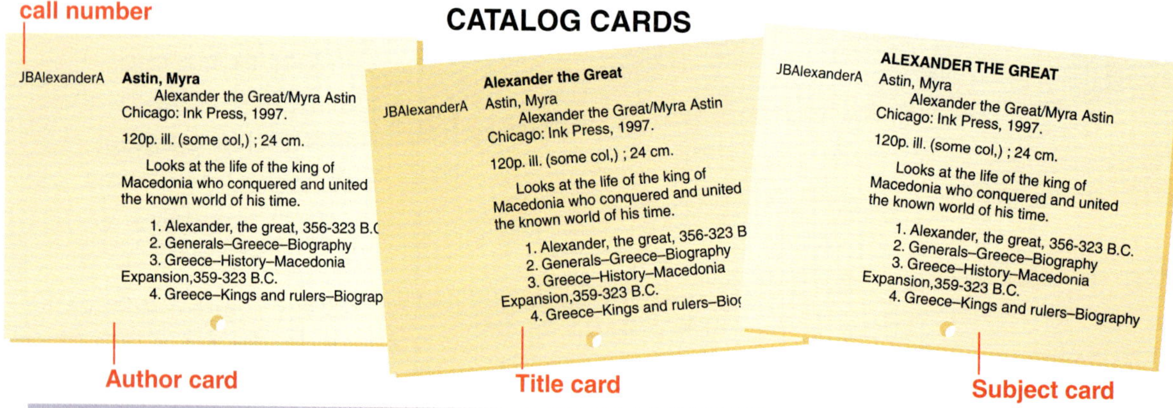

Use the author card, the title card, and the subject card to answer these questions.

1. When would you use the author card?
2. Why would you use the title card instead of the subject card?
3. If the card said *Astin, Myra*, would you classify it as an author card, a title card, or a subject card? Explain.
4. What is the purpose of the call number?
5. How can the card catalog help you write a research report?

TEST POWER

Test Tip

Restate the story in your own words to make sure you understand what you have read.

DIRECTIONS

Read the sample story. Then read each question about the story.

SAMPLE

The Horse of the American Desert

Until the middle 1800s, the regions beyond the Mississippi River to the West had largely gone unexplored. Because it was called the Great American Desert, most people believed the land to be entirely barren. What people didn't know was that the desert was home to many nomadic groups.

Groups like the Sioux traveled the desert to follow their primary source of food: the American bison. Wherever the bison went, the Sioux and other Plains Indians would follow. For centuries they used dogs to carry their possessions from one hunting ground to the next. But at some point in the 1600s, the use of horses was adopted into their culture.

By the middle of the 1700s nearly every group of Plains Indians rode on horseback. Horses became a valuable part of Native American life, both socially and economically.

1 By the middle of the 1700s horses were —

A important

B skilled

C hunted

D hazardous

2 Which of these happened last?

F Sioux followed the American bison.

G Explorers traveled west of the Mississippi River.

H Dogs carried the Plains Indians' possessions.

J Horses became a valuable part of Native American life.

Stories in Art

Near Boulak, Cairo, Egypt
by Charles Theodore Frere

The artist who painted this picture had one big problem. How would he show movement in the heat of the desert?

Look at the painting. Notice how the artist uses the dust kicked up from the sand to show the motion of the caravan. Look at the birds. Why does the artist put them in his picture? Who are the people? Where are they going? Do you think they are about to reach their destination? What makes you think so?

Look at the painting again. How does the caravan give you the feeling of people who are constantly moving? How would you feel if you were always moving to a new place?

MEET FRANCISCO JIMÉNEZ

Sometimes Francisco Jiménez writes in English, and sometimes he writes in Spanish. "The language I use is determined by what period in my life I write about. Since Spanish was the dominant language during my childhood, I generally write about those experiences in Spanish."

Thus, Jiménez first wrote "The Circuit" in Spanish and then translated his work into English. But there was a problem—he could not always find an appropriate translation. Jiménez explains, "Language, especially the spoken word, carries with it an emotion or a feeling." The story's original title was "Cajas de Cartón," or "Cardboard Boxes." Jiménez recalls, "I didn't want to use the same title because 'Cardboard Boxes' didn't sound right to me. 'The Circuit' seemed to be a more appropriate English title."

THE
CIRCUIT
by Francisco Jiménez
illustrated by Robert Rodriguez

It was that time of year again. Ito, the strawberry sharecropper, did not smile. It was natural. The peak of the strawberry season was over and the last few days the workers, most of them braceros, were not picking as many boxes as they had during the months of June and July.

As the last days of August disappeared, so did the number of braceros. Sunday, only one—the best picker—came to work. I liked him. Sometimes we talked during our half-hour lunch break. That is how I found out he was from Jalisco, the same state in Mexico my family was from. That Sunday was the last time I saw him.

When the sun had tired and sunk behind the mountains, Ito signaled us that it was time to go home. "Ya esora," he yelled in his broken Spanish. Those were the words I waited for twelve hours a day, every day, seven days a week, week after week. And the thought of not hearing them again saddened me.

As we drove home Papá did not say a word. With both hands on the wheel, he stared at the dirt road. My older brother, Roberto, was also silent. He leaned his head back and closed his eyes. Once in a while he cleared from his throat the dust that blew in from outside.

Yes, it was that time of year. When I opened the front door to the shack, I stopped. Everything we owned was neatly packed in cardboard boxes. Suddenly I felt even more the weight of hours, days, weeks, and months of work. I sat down on a box. The thought of having to move to Fresno and knowing what was in store for me there brought tears to my eyes.

That night I could not sleep. I lay in bed thinking about how much I hated this move.

A little before five o'clock in the morning, Papá woke everyone up. A few minutes later, the yelling and screaming of my little brothers and sisters, for whom the move was a great adventure, broke the silence of dawn. Shortly, the barking of the dogs accompanied them.

While we packed the breakfast dishes, Papá went outside to start the "Carcanchita." That was the name Papá gave his old '38 black Plymouth. He bought it in a used-car lot in Santa Rosa in the winter of 1949. Papá was very proud of his little jalopy. He had a right to be proud of it. He spent a lot of time looking at other cars before buying this one. When he finally chose the "Carcanchita," he checked it thoroughly before driving it out of the car lot. He examined every inch of the car. He listened to the motor, tilting his head from side to side like a parrot, trying to detect any noises that spelled car trouble. After being satisfied with the looks and sounds of the car, Papá then insisted on knowing who the original owner was. He never did find out from the car salesman, but he bought the car anyway. Papá figured the original owner must have been an important man because behind the rear seat of the car he found a blue necktie.

Papá parked the car out in front and left the motor running. "Listo," he yelled. Without saying a word, Roberto and I began to carry the boxes out to the car. Roberto carried the two big boxes and I carried the two smaller ones. Papá then threw the mattress on top of the car roof and tied it with ropes to the front and rear bumpers.

Everything was packed except Mamá's pot. It was an old large galvanized pot she had picked up at an army surplus store in Santa María the year I was born. The pot had many dents and nicks, and the more dents and nicks it acquired the more Mamá liked it. "Mi olla," she used to say proudly.

I held the front door open as Mamá carefully carried out her pot by both handles, making sure not to spill the cooked beans. When she got to the car, Papá reached out to help her with it. Roberto opened the rear car door and Papá gently placed it on the floor behind the front seat. All of us then climbed in. Papá sighed, wiped the sweat off his forehead with his sleeve, and said wearily: "Es todo."

As we drove away, I felt a lump in my throat. I turned around and looked at our little shack for the last time.

At sunset we drove into a labor camp near Fresno. Since Papá did not speak English, Mamá asked the camp foreman if he needed any more workers. "We don't need no more," said the foreman, scratching his head. "Check with Sullivan down the road. Can't miss him. He lives in a big white house with a fence around it."

When we got there, Mamá walked up to the house. She went through a white gate, past a row of rose bushes, up the stairs to the front door. She rang the doorbell. The porch light went on and a tall husky man came out. They exchanged a few words. After the man went in, Mamá clasped her hands and hurried back to the car. "We have work! Mr. Sullivan said we can stay there the whole season," she said, gasping and pointing to an old garage near the stables.

The garage was worn out by the years. It had no windows. The walls, eaten by termites, strained to support the roof full of holes. The dirt floor, populated by earth worms, looked like a gray road map.

That night, by the light of a kerosene lamp, we unpacked and cleaned our new home. Roberto swept away the loose dirt, leaving the hard ground. Papá plugged the holes in the walls with old newspapers and tin can tops. Mamá fed my little brothers and sisters. Papá and Roberto then brought in the mattress and placed it on the far corner of the garage. "Mamá, you and the little ones sleep on the mattress. Roberto, Panchito, and I will sleep outside under the trees," Papá said.

Early next morning Mr. Sullivan showed us where his crop was, and after breakfast, Papá, Roberto, and I headed for the vineyard to pick.

Around nine o'clock the temperature had risen to almost one hundred degrees. I was completely soaked in sweat and my mouth felt as if I had been chewing on a handkerchief. I walked over to the end of the row, picked up the jug of water

TSI
Grapes

we had brought, and began drinking. "Don't drink too much; you'll get sick," Roberto shouted. No sooner had he said that than I felt sick to my stomach. I dropped to my knees and let the jug roll off my hands. I remained motionless with my eyes glued on the hot sandy ground. All I could hear was the drone of insects. Slowly I began to recover. I poured water over my face and neck and watched the dirty water run down my arms to the ground.

I still felt a little dizzy when we took a break to eat lunch. It was past two o'clock and we sat underneath a large walnut tree that was on the side of the road. While we ate, Papá jotted down the number of boxes we had picked. Roberto drew designs on the ground with a stick. Suddenly I noticed Papá's face turn pale as he looked down the road. "Here comes the school bus," he whispered loudly in alarm. Instinctively, Roberto and I ran and hid in the vineyards. We did not want to get in trouble for not going to school. The neatly dressed boys about my age got off. They carried books under their arms. After they crossed the street, the bus drove away. Roberto and I came out from hiding and joined Papá. "Tienen que tener cuidado," he warned us.

After lunch we went back to work. The sun kept beating down. The buzzing insects, the wet sweat, and the hot dry dust made the afternoon seem to last forever. Finally the mountains around the valley reached out and swallowed the sun. Within an hour it was too dark to continue picking. The vines blanketed the grapes, making it difficult to see the bunches. "Vámonos," said Papá, signaling to us that it was time to quit work. Papá then took out a pencil and began to figure out how much we had earned our first day. He wrote down numbers, crossed some out, wrote down some more. "Quince," he murmured.

When we arrived home, we took a cold shower underneath a waterhose. We then sat down to eat dinner around some wooden crates that served as a table. Mamá had cooked a special meal for us. We had rice and tortillas with "carne con chile," my favorite dish.

The next morning I could hardly move. My body ached all over. I felt little control over my arms and legs. This feeling went on every morning for days until my muscles finally got used to the work.

It was Monday, the first week of November. The grape season was over and I could now go to school. I woke up early that morning and lay in bed, looking at the stars and savoring the thought of not going to work and of starting sixth grade for the first time that year. Since I could not sleep, I decided to get up and join Papá and Roberto at breakfast. I sat at the table across from Roberto, but I kept my head down. I did not want to look up and face him. I knew he was sad. He was not going to school today. He was not going tomorrow, or next week, or next month. He would not go until the cotton season was over, and that was sometime in February. I rubbed my hands together and watched the dry, acid stained skin fall to the floor in little rolls.

When Papá and Roberto left for work, I felt relief. I walked to the top of a small grade next to the shack and watched the "Carcanchita" disappear in the distance in a cloud of dust.

Two hours later, around eight o'clock, I stood by the side of the road waiting for school bus number twenty. When it arrived I climbed in. Everyone was busy either talking or yelling. I sat in an empty seat in the back.

When the bus stopped in front of the school, I felt very nervous. I looked out the bus window and saw boys and girls carrying books under their arms. I put my hands in my pant pockets and walked to the principal's office. When I entered I heard a woman's voice say: "May I help you?" I was startled. I had not heard English for months. For a few seconds I remained speechless. I looked at the lady who waited for an answer. My first instinct was to answer her in Spanish, but I held back. Finally, after struggling for English words, I managed to tell her that I wanted to enroll in the sixth grade. After answering many questions, I was led to the classroom.

Mr. Lema, the sixth grade teacher, greeted me and assigned me a desk. He then introduced me to the class. I was so nervous and scared at that moment when everyone's eyes were on me that I wished I were with Papá and Roberto picking cotton. After taking roll, Mr. Lema gave the class the assignment for the first hour. "The first thing we have to do this morning is finish reading the story we began yesterday," he said enthusiastically. He walked up to me, handed me an English book, and asked me to read. "We are on page 125," he said politely. When I heard this, I felt my blood rush to my head; I felt dizzy. "Would you like to read?" he asked hesitantly. I opened the book to page 125. My mouth was dry. My eyes

began to water. I could not begin. "You can read later," Mr. Lema said understandingly.

For the rest of the reading period I kept getting angrier and angrier with myself. I should have read, I thought to myself.

During recess I went into the restroom and opened my English book to page 125. I began to read in a low voice, pretending I was in class. There were many words I did not know. I closed the book and headed back to the classroom.

Mr. Lema was sitting at his desk correcting papers. When I entered he looked up at me and smiled. I felt better. I walked up to him and asked if he could help me with the new words. "Gladly," he said.

The rest of the month I spent my lunch hours working on English with Mr. Lema, my best friend at school.

One Friday during lunch hour Mr. Lema asked me to take a walk with him to the music room. "Do you like music?" he asked me as we entered the building.

"Yes, I like corridos," I answered. He then picked up a trumpet, blew on it and handed it to me. The sound gave me goose bumps. I knew that sound. I had heard it in many corridos. "How would you like to learn how to play it?" he asked. He must have read my face because before I could answer, he added: "I'll teach you how to play it during our lunch hours."

That day I could hardly wait to get home to tell Papá and Mamá the great news. As I got off the bus, my little brothers and sisters ran up to meet me. They were yelling and screaming. I thought they were happy to see me, but when I opened the door to our shack, I saw that everything we owned was neatly packed in cardboard boxes.

Francisco Jiménez finished his schooling and earned a doctorate from Columbia University in New York. He is now a professor at the University of Santa Clara in California, where he teaches Spanish language and literature.

1. What kind of work do Panchito and his family do?
2. How does Panchito feel when he sees the cardboard boxes at the end of the story?
3. What makes Mr. Lema such a caring teacher?
4. What is the problem in this story? Is it solved at the end? Why or why not?
5. How does the picture on pages 620–621 suggest the life of a migrant worker? How does the caravan express the way Panchito feels each time he sees the cardboard boxes?

Write a Letter

Imagine that you are Mr. Lema. Write a letter to Panchito's parents to persuade them to keep their son in his school. Support your opinion with reasons, including Panchito's improving English skills and his interest in learning to play the trumpet. End your letter by making it clear that education is a good solution to the problems faced by migrant farmworkers.

Create a Dance

Mr. Lema finds out that Panchito likes *corridos*. *Corridos* is a type of Spanish music that has a strong, steady beat good for dancing. Listen to this type of music. Prepare a dance to go with it.

Grapes

CALIFORNIA

Sacramento

San Francisco

Fresno

San Joaquin Valley

Bakersfield

Los Angeles

San Diego

Lettuce

Make a Product Map

One morning, Panchito and his family move to Fresno, where they will start picking grapes. Make a product map of California. Include the products found in Fresno and the San Joaquin Valley, to show why the family is going there to start picking grapes.

Find Out More

Find out more about the life of migrant farmworkers. Look at an encyclopedia, a social studies book, or the Internet for information. Include facts about César Chávez and Dolores Huerta, cofounders of the National Farm Workers Association. How did their efforts help solve some of the problems of migrant farmworkers? Share your information with your classmates, including your list of sources.

Use an Online Library Catalog

Panchito and his family are migrant workers. To find out more about migrant workers, you can look in a library's **online catalog** for books on the subject. You can search for books by author, title, or subject.

Use the online library catalog to answer these questions.

1. What information is listed on the SUBJECT SCREEN?
2. Which key would you press to find the name of the author of *The Farmworkers Movement*?
3. Which book may have information on whether migrant workers get good medical care?
4. What other subject might lead to information on migrant workers?
5. How can doing a subject search help you find a book in the library?

TEST POWER

Test Tip

If you change your answer, make sure you erase completely.

DIRECTIONS

Read the sample story. Then read each question about the story.

SAMPLE

Explorers: Lewis and Clark

At the turn of the nineteenth century, much of the land west of the Mississippi River was unexplored. President Jefferson arranged for Meriwether Lewis and William Clark, who were former army officers, to explore the area completely. Lewis and Clark were joined by Sacagawea, a Shoshone Indian, who served as an interpreter and guide.

The expedition was the first federally funded project in American history. Anything but spontaneous, the goals of the trip were clearly planned. Jefferson ordered Lewis and Clark to find the source of the Missouri River and to find a safe route to the Pacific Ocean. President Jefferson also asked them to record everything they saw, including the customs of the local people they met.

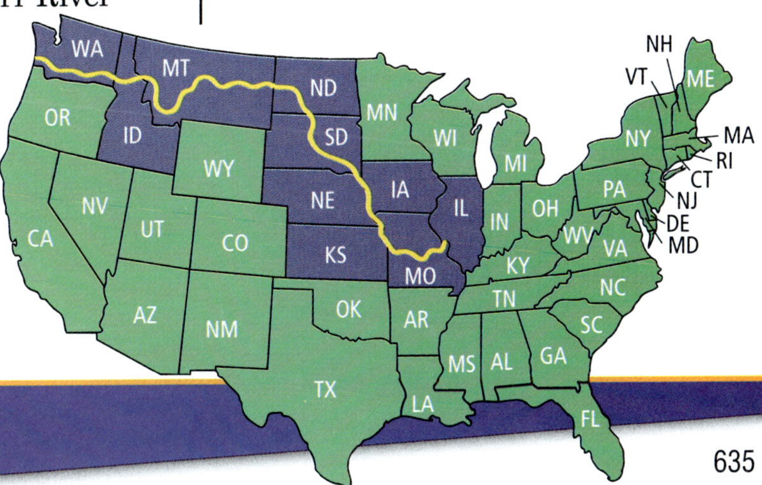

1 The word spontaneous in this passage means —

A unplanned

B quick

C rainy

D quarrelsome

2 According to Figure 1, which of these states did the Lewis-and-Clark expedition cross?

F Ohio

G Idaho

H California

J Nevada

Stories in Art

Construction of the Dam, Mural Study **(detail)**
by William Gropper, 1937
National Museum of American Art, Washington, D.C.

Many people were out of work during the Great Depression of the 1930s. President Franklin D. Roosevelt persuaded Congress to pay unemployed people to build dams such as this one. He also persuaded the government to pay artists to paint murals such as the one in this picture.

Look at this mural. What can you tell about it? How does the artist show the everyday job of workers building a dam? How does he feel toward his subject? What makes you think so?

Study the mural. How do its size, shape, and figures show the conquest of nature? Do you agree with the artist's point of view on the subject? Why or why not?

TIME FOR KIDS

SPECIAL REPORT

A Great Wall?

China's Three Gorges Dam is the world's biggest construction project, but is it a good idea?

Workers build the giant Three Gorges Dam on the Yangtze River.

China's Big Dam

The Three Gorges Dam will control flooding and provide power. It will also destroy towns and animal habitats. Is it worth it?

COVER: BOB SACHA; RIGHT: ROBERT WALLIS/SABA; FAR RIGHT: CHRISTOPHER LIU/CHINASTOCK

Farmer Wang Zuolu grew oranges and peanuts on a hilltop overlooking China's beautiful Yangtze River. His family had lived there for generations in a house that his great-grandfather built. "It's so peaceful here," says Wang.

But the lives of Wang and his wife Zhang Changying have changed forever. Their farm was going to be covered with water. They had to start a new life in a new village farther away from the Yangtze.

Wang and his wife were just two of the 1.2 million Chinese who must move from their homes because of the construction of the world's largest and most powerful dam.

The Three Gorges Dam is named for three gorges, or canyons, in central China. It is the biggest construction job in China since work began on the Great Wall more than 2,500 years ago. When it is completed in 2009, the dam will use water power to create electricity. It will also prevent flooding by the Yangtze. At the same time, the $24 billion dam will change China's natural scenery and the lives of many of its people forever.

A model shows what the Three Gorges Dam will look like when it is completed in 2009.

Dam workers will move more than 3.5 billion cubic feet of stone and earth.

GREAT WALL OF POWER

For hundreds of years, poets and painters have been inspired by the Yangtze, the third longest river in the world. They admire its winding path and the steep cliffs and flat plains bordering it.

But the Yangtze can rise over its banks. In the 1900s alone, some 300,000 people have been killed by Yangtze floods.

In November 1997, China completed a temporary dam to dry up part of the riverbed. Since then, workers have been building a 607-foot-high wall that will stretch across 1.3 miles of the Yangtze. Engineers will install giant generators to create electricity for the area. When river water rushes through the generators, it will move wheels and magnets, producing hydroelectric power. The dam project will provide the same amount of energy as 15 large coal-burning power stations.

Hydroelectric power is better for the environment than power produced

The dam will create a lake so deep that it will cover this bridge.

Families forced to leave the scenic Three Gorges cram all they can onto boats. They will move into homes on higher ground.

LEFT: BOB SACHA; ABOVE: ROBERT WALLIS/SABA; OPPOSITE PAGE: LYNN STONE/THE PICTURE CUBE

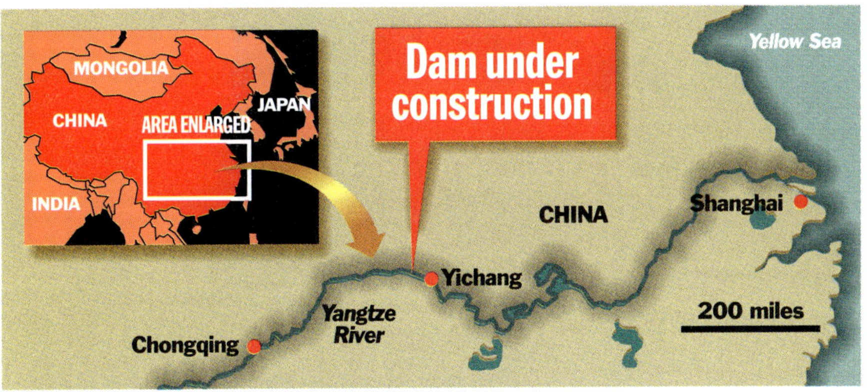

The clouded leopard's habitat is being destroyed to make way for the dam.

by burning coal, which is China's main energy source. But many scientists say the dam will be an ecological disaster. Not only will people be displaced, it will also destroy the natural surroundings and threaten wildlife.

FLOODED HABITATS AND HOMES

By blocking the flow of the Yangtze, the dam will create a 370-mile-long lake, or reservoir, west of the city of Yichang. It will swallow hundreds of towns and villages.

The reservoir will also threaten the habitats of hundreds of fish, plant, and animal species. Among the creatures most at risk: rare river dolphins, clouded leopards, and Siberian white cranes. The government promises to monitor the environment around the dam, and has set aside money to create a protective area for the dolphins.

But scientists warn that blocking the river will create sewage backups and may even cause more floods. Some fear that the dam may collapse.

The Chinese who must leave their homes have no choice but to find new homes and jobs. By 2009, about 200,000 students will have switched to new schools.

Some families are excited about moving to newer, more prosperous towns. While Wang is sad to leave his home, his trip to the market is now much shorter. "In the end, we'll make it work," he says.

FIND OUT MORE
Visit our website:
www.mhschool.com/reading

Based on an article in *TIME FOR KIDS.*

Story Questions & Activities

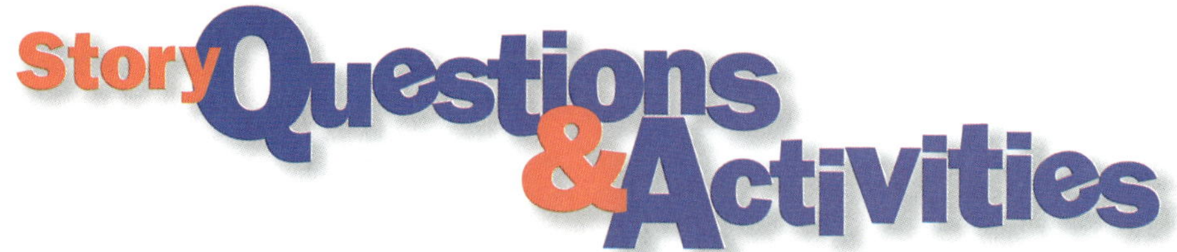

1. How will the Three Gorges Dam help people in the area? How will it hurt them?

2. How has the government tried to persuade the Chinese people to believe that the dam is a good idea?

3. Do you think the Chinese government is telling the people the truth about the dam? Explain.

4. What is the main idea of this selection?

5. Big ideas can lead to great success or huge failure. Compare the construction of this dam to the landing of the first man on the moon. What are the risks and the benefits of each?

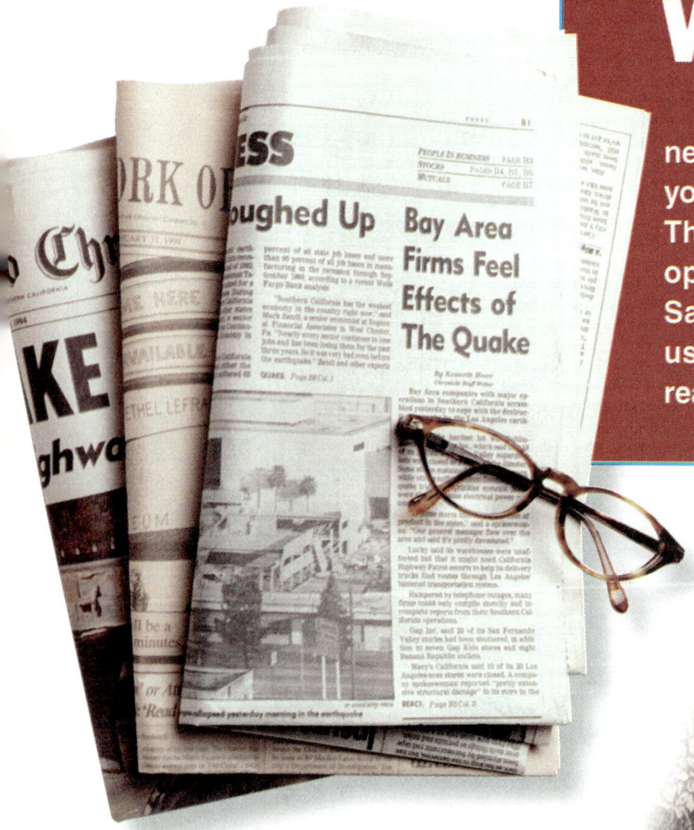

Write an Editorial

Imagine that you are the editor of a newspaper. Write an editorial in which you give your opinion about building the Three Gorges Dam. Support your opinion with facts and strong reasons. Save your best argument for last, and use persuasive language to get your readers to agree with your point of view.

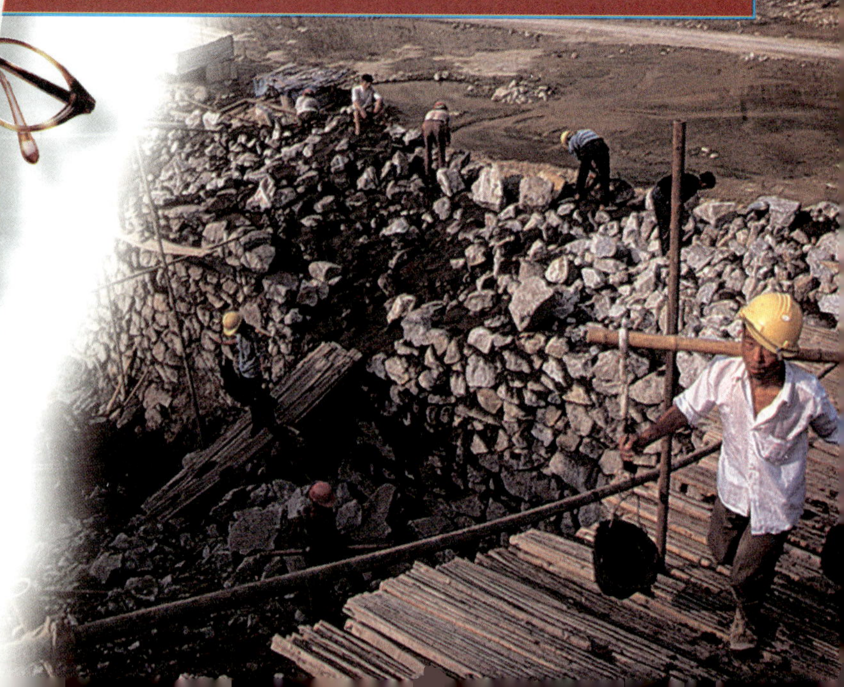

Draw a Picture

Imagine that you are one of the people in China who has no choice but to find a new home and a new school. How would you feel? Would you be happy or sad? Draw or paint a picture that expresses your emotion. What will your main color be?

Write a Letter

The clouded leopard, the rare river dolphins, and the Siberian white cranes may not survive after the dam is built. Find out about other endangered animals. What can you do to help? Write a letter to your senator or congressperson asking how he or she can help protect other endangered creatures and their habitats.

Find Out More

Like the Three Gorges Dam, the Hoover Dam was built to supply hydroelectric power. It was built along the Colorado River. Find out more about the Hoover Dam. How long did it take to build? How did it affect people and wildlife? In an informal debate, argue the pros and cons of building a dam.

Use an Encyclopedia

Your teacher has just given you the assignment of writing a research report about the Hoover Dam. Where would you look for information? You could start by looking in an encyclopedia.

An **encyclopedia** is a set of books that has articles about people, places, things, events, and ideas. The articles are arranged in alphabetical order in volumes. When you use an encyclopedia to find facts about a topic, you must have a **key word** in mind. For example, you would look under *Hoover Dam* to find information about this topic.

You might also look in the encyclopedia index to find your topic quickly. The **index** is the last book in the set of encyclopedias. In it, the volume and page number are given for each topic listed in the encyclopedia.

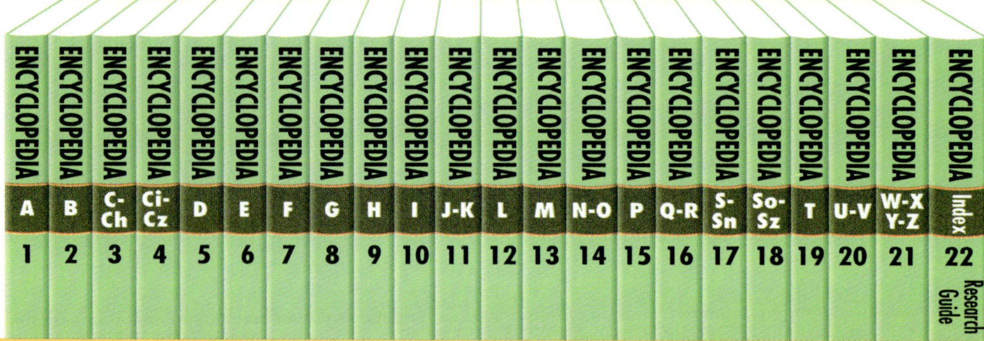

Use the sample set of encyclopedias to answer these questions.

1. What is an encyclopedia?
2. In which volume would you look to find general information about China?
3. What key word would you look under to find general information about dams?
4. How would you use an encyclopedia index?
5. How can an encyclopedia give you general information about a topic?

TEST POWER

Test Tip

Ruling out wrong answers will make it easier to find the best answer.

DIRECTIONS

Read the sample story. Then read each question about the story.

SAMPLE

What is a Tsunami?

The scientists trying to uncover the mysterious nature of Earth's oceans are called oceanographers. They study the physical and biological aspects of the seas.

One natural phenomenon that puzzles oceanographers is the *tsunami*. Tsunamis are powerful waves caused by large undersea disturbances. Although landslides and volcanoes cause some tsunamis, most are the result of earthquakes under the ocean floor. The size of the tsunami is related to the area that moves on the ocean bottom, and how far it moves.

One factor that distinguishes tsunamis from familiar waves is their very long wavelength. Oceanographers call tsunamis "shallow water waves" because the energy of these destructive waves hides under the surface.

1 Which is a FACT in this passage?

A Tsunamis are more dangerous than landslides.

B Scientists will never be able to predict tsunamis.

C Tsunamis are volcanoes.

D Tsunamis are destructive.

2 According to the passage, what is one cause of a tsunami?

F An earthquake

G Warm weather

H A tornado

J A thunderstorm

Did you rule out wrong answers right away? Tell why.

Whose woods these are I think I know.
His house is in the village though;
He will not see me stopping here
To watch his woods fill up with snow.

My little horse must think it queer
To stop without a farmhouse near
Between the woods and frozen lake
The darkest evening of the year.

He gives his harness bells a shake
To ask if there is some mistake.
The only other sound's the sweep
Of easy wind and downy flake.

The woods are lovely, dark and deep
But I have promises to keep,
And miles to go before I sleep,
And miles to go before I sleep.

by Robert Frost

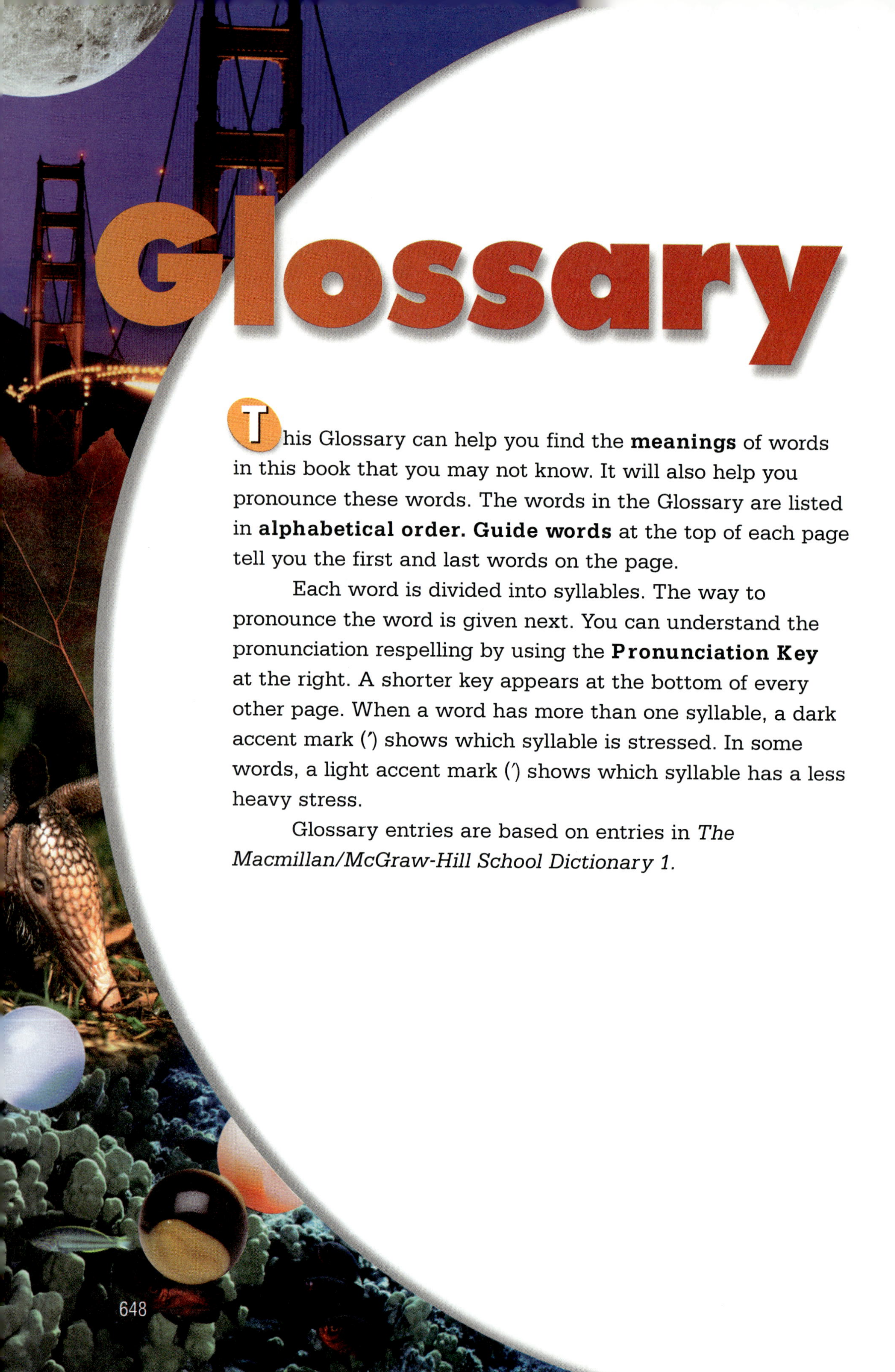

Glossary

This Glossary can help you find the **meanings** of words in this book that you may not know. It will also help you pronounce these words. The words in the Glossary are listed in **alphabetical order. Guide words** at the top of each page tell you the first and last words on the page.

Each word is divided into syllables. The way to pronounce the word is given next. You can understand the pronunciation respelling by using the **Pronunciation Key** at the right. A shorter key appears at the bottom of every other page. When a word has more than one syllable, a dark accent mark (ʹ) shows which syllable is stressed. In some words, a light accent mark (ʹ) shows which syllable has a less heavy stress.

Glossary entries are based on entries in *The Macmillan/McGraw-Hill School Dictionary 1.*

Guide Words

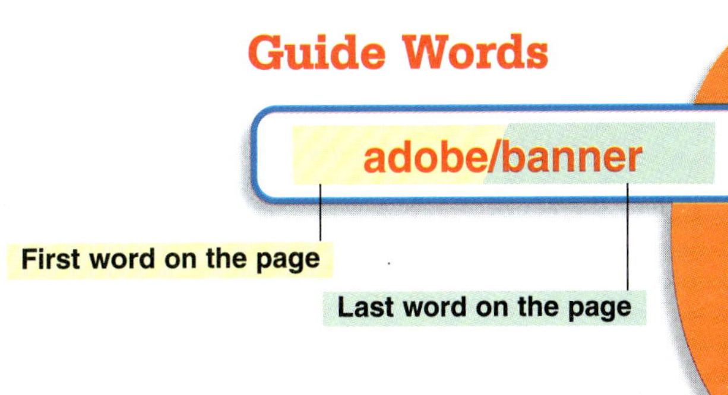

Sample Entry

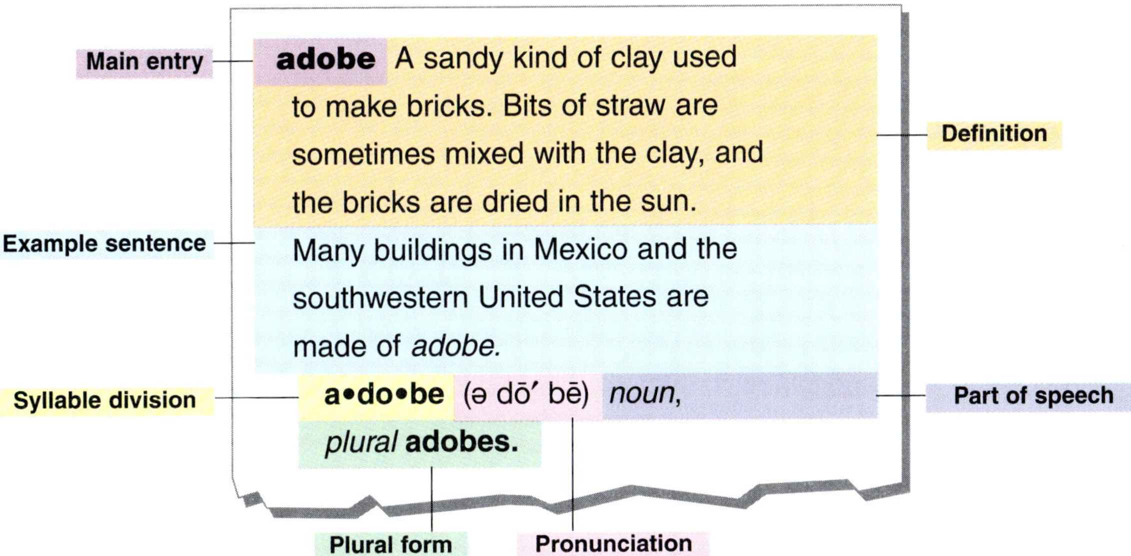

a	**a**t, b**a**d
ā	**a**pe, p**ai**n, d**ay**, br**ea**k
ä	f**a**ther, c**a**r, h**ea**rt
âr	c**are**, p**air**, b**ear**, th**eir**, wh**ere**
e	**e**nd, p**e**t, s**ai**d, h**ea**ven, fri**e**nd
ē	**e**qual, m**e**, f**ee**t, t**ea**m, pi**e**ce, k**ey**
i	**i**t, b**i**g, **E**nglish, h**y**mn
ī	**i**ce, f**i**ne, l**ie**, m**y**
îr	**ear**, d**eer**, h**ere**, p**ier**ce
o	**o**dd, h**o**t, w**a**tch
ō	**o**ld, **oa**t, t**oe**, l**ow**
ô	c**o**ffee, **a**ll, t**au**ght, l**aw**, f**ou**ght
ôr	**or**der, f**or**k, h**or**se, st**or**y, p**our**
oi	**oi**l, t**oy**
ou	**ou**t, n**ow**
u	**u**p, m**u**d, l**o**ve, d**ou**ble
ū	**u**se, m**u**le, c**ue**, f**eu**d, f**ew**
ü	r**u**le, tr**ue**, f**oo**d
u̇	p**u**t, w**oo**d, sh**ou**ld
ûr	b**ur**n, h**ur**ry, t**er**m, b**ir**d, w**or**d, c**our**age
ə	**a**bout, tak**e**n, penc**i**l, lem**o**n, circ**u**s
b	**b**at, a**b**ove, jo**b**
ch	**ch**in, su**ch**, ma**tch**
d	**d**ear, so**d**a, ba**d**
f	**f**ive, de**f**end, lea**f**, o**ff**, cou**gh**, ele**ph**ant.
g	**g**ame, a**g**o, fo**g**, e**gg**
h	**h**at, a**h**ead
hw	**wh**ite, **wh**ether, **wh**ich
j	**j**oke, en**j**oy, **g**em, pa**g**e, e**dge**
k	**k**ite, ba**k**ery, see**k**, ta**ck**, **c**at
l	**l**id, sai**l**or, fee**l**, ba**ll**, a**ll**ow
m	**m**an, fa**m**ily, drea**m**
n	**n**ot, fi**n**al, pa**n**, **kn**ife
ng	lo**ng**, si**ng**er, pi**n**k
p	**p**ail, re**p**air, soa**p**, ha**pp**y
r	**r**ide, pa**r**ent, wea**r**, mo**r**e, ma**rr**y
s	**s**it, a**s**ide, pet**s**, **c**ent, pa**ss**
sh	**sh**oe, wa**sh**er, fi**sh**, mi**ss**ion, na**t**ion
t	**t**ag, pre**t**end, fa**t**, bu**tt**on, dress**ed**
th	**th**in, pan**th**er, bo**th**,
<u>th</u>	**th**is, mo**th**er, smoo**th**
v	**v**ery, fa**v**or, wa**v**e
w	**w**et, **w**eather, re**w**ard
y	**y**es, on**i**on
z	**z**oo, la**z**y, ja**zz**, ro**s**e, dog**s**, hous**es**
zh	vi**s**ion, trea**s**ure, sei**z**ure

abide 1. To put up with; bear; endure. My parents cannot *abide* a messy room. **2.** To accept and obey. A good citizen *abides* by the laws.
a•bide (ə bīd′) *verb,* **abided, abiding.**

acceptable Good enough to be accepted; satisfactory. Our plan for the bazaar was *acceptable* to everyone in the club.
▲**Synonym:** tolerable
ac•cept•a•ble (ak sep′tə bəl) *adjective.*

accompany 1. To go together with. One of my parents always *accompanies* me to the movies. **2.** To happen at the same time as. Wind often *accompanies* rain.
ac•com•pa•ny (ə kum′pə nē) *verb,* **accompanied, accompanying.**

acculturate To acquire the culture of a particular society from infancy. Children of immigrants *acculturate* more easily than their parents because they are raised in a new environment.
ac•cul•tur•ate (ə kul′chə rāt′) *verb,* **acculturated, acculturating.**

accumulate To gather or pile up; collect. My cousin *accumulated* a number of books at college.
ac•cum•u•late (ə kū′myə lāt′) *verb,* **accumulated, accumulating.**

Word History

The word ***accumulate*** comes from the latin verb *accumulare,* meaning "to heap up." If you don't empty the trash, it will *accumulate.*

acquaint To make familiar. On the first day of school most teachers become *acquainted* with their students.
ac•quaint (ə kwānt′) *verb,* **acquainted, acquainting.**

acquire To gain as one's own. I *acquired* a taste for Mexican food after visiting Mexico.
ac•quire (ə kwīr′) *verb*, **acquired**, **acquiring**.

afterlife An existence after death. Some people believe that one's spirit continues to live in an *afterlife.*
af•ter•life (af′tər līf′) *noun.*

appreciation 1. A feeling of being thankful; gratitude. I want to show my *appreciation* for your help. **2.** An understanding of the value of something. After studying carpentry, I had a better *appreciation* of fine woodworking.
ap•pre•ci•a•tion (ə prē′shē ā′shən) *noun.*

archaeologist Someone who studies the way humans lived a long time ago. *Archaeologists* dig up the remains of ancient cities and towns and then study the tools, weapons, pottery, and other things they find.
ar•chae•ol•o•gist (är′kē ol′ə jist) *noun, plural* **archaeologists.**

ashore On or to the shore or land. The children paddled the canoe *ashore.*
a•shore (ə shôr′) *adverb.*

astronaut A person trained to fly in a spacecraft. The *astronauts* landed safely on the moon.
as•tro•naut (as′trə nôt′) *noun, plural* **astronauts.**

attitude 1. A way of thinking, acting, or feeling. Your *attitude* toward school is more enthusiastic than mine. **2.** A position of the body. The body's *attitude* often shows the feelings or thoughts of a person.
at•ti•tude (at′i tüd′ *or* at′i tūd′) *noun, plural* **attitudes.**

automate The process of making something function by itself. Bank teller machines are *automated.*
au•to•mate (ô′ tə māt′) *verb,* **automated, automating.**

badge Something worn to show that a person belongs to a certain group or has received an honor. A policeman's *badge* is his identification.
▲**Synonym:** insignia
badge (baj) *noun, plural* **badges.**

banister 1. A railing along a staircase. When you go down stairs, you should hold onto the *banister.* **2.** The posts that support this railing. She polished the *banister* posts.
ban•is•ter (ban′ə stər) *noun, plural* **banisters.**

at; āpe; fär; câre; end; mē; it; īce; pîerce; hot; ōld; sông; fôrk; oil; out; up; ūse; rüle; pu̇ll; tûrn; chin; sing; shop; thin; <u>th</u>is; hw in white; zh in treasure. The symbol ə stands for the unstressed vowel sound in about, taken, pencil, lemon, and circus.

barley The grain of a plant that is like grass. *Barley* is used as animal feed, in cooking, and to make malt.
bar•ley (bär′lē) *noun.*

barter To trade things for other things without using money. The pioneers *bartered* grain for blankets with the natives. *Verb.* —The trading of goods or services without the use of money. Among early settlers in this country, fabrics were used as *barter. Noun.*
bar•ter (bär′tər) *verb,* **bartered, bartering;** *noun.*

bazaar **1.** A market made up of rows of small shops or stalls. When we visited Cairo, we went to the *bazaar.* **2.** A sale of different things for some special purpose. We baked a carrot cake for the church *bazaar.*
ba•zaar (bə zär′) *noun, plural* **bazaars.**

beckon To make a sign or signal by moving the hand or head. I *beckoned* to my friends to come closer.
beck•on (bek′ən) *verb,* **beckoned, beckoning.**

Word History

The verb ***beckon*** comes from the Middle English word *beknen.* Its origin, however, is the Old English word *beacen,* which means "sign."

behavior The way a person acts; manner of conducting oneself. Please be on your best *behavior* at my wedding.
be•hav•ior (bē hāv′yər) *noun, plural* **behaviors.**

belligerently In a quarrelsome manner.
bel•lig•er•ent•ly (bə lij′ər ənt lē) *adverb.*

blissful Full of, characterized by, or causing great happiness or joy.
▲**Synonym:** delightful
bliss•ful (blis′ fəl) *adjective.*

bloodstream The blood flowing through the body. The *bloodstream* delivers nutrients to the body's cells.
blood•stream (blud′strēm′) *noun, plural* **bloodstreams.**

bolt **1.** To spring or move suddenly. The child *bolted* out the door. **2.** To fasten with a bolt. Before the storm strikes, we will have to *bolt* the doors and windows.
bolt (bōlt) *verb,* **bolted, bolting.**

botanist A person who specializes in botany, the study of plants.
bot•a•nist (bot′ə nist) *noun.*

boyhood The time of being a boy. In my *boyhood* I was very shy.
boy•hood (boi′hůd′) *noun, plural* **boyhoods.**

bribe Money or gifts given to make a person do something wrong or something the person does not want to do. The court accused him of accepting a *bribe. Noun.*—To give a bribe to. I *bribed* the child to stop crying by offering her a toy. *Verb.*
bribe (brīb) *noun, plural* **bribes;** *verb,* **bribed, bribing.**

bridle The part of a horse's harness that fits over the animal's head, used to guide or control the horse. The cowboy slipped the *bridle* over the horse's head. *Noun.*—To put a bridle on. Unless you ride bareback, you will have to *bridle* the horse. *Verb.*
bri•dle (brī′dəl) *noun, plural* **bridles;** *verb,* **bridled, bridling.**

brute 1. A cruel person. I saw that *brute* kick an old dog. **2.** An animal. A *brute* cannot reason or feel the way a human being does.
brute (brüt) *noun, plural* **brutes.**

Word History

Brute first appeared in the English language in the 15th century. It came from the Latin word *brutus,* meaning "heavy."

buffet 1. A piece of furniture having a flat top to serve food from and drawers or shelves for storing dishes, silver, and table linen. **2.** A meal laid out on a buffet or a table so that guests may serve themselves. We helped ourselves to the *buffet* twice because the food was excellent.
buf•fet (bə fā′ *or* bů fā′) *noun, plural* **buffets.**

campsite A place suitable for setting up camp. There is too much litter at this *campsite.*
camp•site (kamp′ sīt′) *noun, plural* **campsites.**

at; āpe; fär; câre; end; mē; it; īce; pîerce; hot; ōld; sông; fôrk; oil; out; up; ūse; rüle; půll; tûrn; chin; sing; shop; thin; this; hw in white; zh in treasure. The symbol ə stands for the unstressed vowel sound in about, taken, pencil, lemon, and circus.

capable Having skill or power; able. A *capable* mechanic can fix many things.
▲**Synonym:** competent
ca•pa•ble (kā′pə bəl) *adjective; adverb,* **capably.**

capsule 1. A small, thin case that encloses something tightly, especially one that contains a small amount of medicine and dissolves in the stomach after it is swallowed. She swallowed the *capsule* and hoped it would cure her cold. **2.** A compartment of a spacecraft that carries astronauts or instruments. The space *capsule* plunged into the Pacific Ocean.
cap•sule (kap′səl) *noun, plural* **capsules.**

carriage 1. A vehicle that moves on wheels. Some *carriages* are pulled by horses and carry people. **2.** A movable part of a machine that carries or holds up some other part. The *carriage* of the baggage car was damaged when the train derailed.
car•riage (kar′ij) *noun, plural* **carriages.**

cavalry A group of soldiers fighting on horseback or from tanks. When the bugle sounded, the *cavalry* charged down the hill.
cav•al•ry (kav′əl rē) *noun, plural* **cavalries.**

cellophane A thin, clear material made from cellulose, used to wrap food and to make clear tape. You can use *cellophane* as wrapping paper.
cel•lo•phane (sel′ə fān′) *noun.*

chariot A two-wheeled vehicle drawn by horses, used in ancient times in warfare, races, and processions. The ancient Romans entertained themselves by going to *chariot* races.
char•i•ot (char′ē ət) *noun, plural* **chariots.**

clockwise In the direction in which the hands of a clock move. Move the dial *clockwise* to turn on the radio.
clock•wise (klok′wīz′) *adverb; adjective.*

cobblestone A round stone, formerly used to pave streets. *Cobblestone* streets are difficult to walk on.
cob•ble•stone (kob′əl stōn′) *noun, plural* **cobblestones.**

coffin A box in which the body of a dead person is buried. Dracula slept in a *coffin.*
▲**Synonym:** casket
cof•fin (kô′fin) *noun, plural* **coffins.**

coincidence The happening of two events at the same time or place. A coincidence seems remarkable because although it looks planned, it really is not. It was just a *coincidence* that the two couples went to the same movie.
co•in•ci•dence (kō in′si dəns) *noun, plural* **coincidences.**

compartment A separate division or section. My desk drawer has *compartments* for pencils, erasers, and paper clips.
com•part•ment (kəm pärt′mənt) *noun, plural* **compartments.**

complex Hard to understand or do. He solved a *complex* arithmetic problem. *Adjective.*—A whole made up of many connected parts. His dormitory was located in a *complex* of university buildings. *Noun.*
com•plex (kəm pleks′ *or* kom′pleks) *adjective*; *noun, plural* **complexes.**

conceal To put or keep out of sight; hide. I *concealed* my anger by smiling.
▲**Synonym:** cover
con•ceal (kən sēl′) *verb,* **concealed, concealing.**

congregation 1. The people present at a religious service. The entire *congregation* left after the service.
2. A gathering or crowd of people or things. A large *congregation* assembled in the square.
con•gre•ga•tion (kong′gri gā′shən) *noun, plural* **congregations.**

consultation A meeting to ask advice or share ideas or opinions.
consultation (kon′səl tā′shən) *noun, plural* **consultations.**

contrast A difference. There's a sharp *contrast* between black and white.
con•trast (kon′trast) *noun, plural* **contrasts.**

controversy A disagreement; dispute. The new tax caused much *controversy.*
▲**Synonym:** quarrel
con•tro•ver•sy (kon′trə vûr′sē) *noun, plural* **controversies.**

at; **ā**pe; f**ä**r; c**â**re; **e**nd; m**ē**; **i**t; **ī**ce; p**î**erce; h**o**t; **ō**ld; s**ô**ng; f**ô**rk; **oi**l; **ou**t; **u**p; **ū**se; r**ü**le; p**u̇**ll; t**û**rn; **ch**in; si**ng**; **sh**op; **th**in; **th**is; **hw** in **wh**ite; **zh** in trea**s**ure. The symbol **ə** stands for the unstressed vowel sound in **a**bout, tak**e**n, penc**i**l, lem**o**n, and circ**u**s.

counselor **1.** A person who helps or gives advice. She spent the summer working as a camp *counselor.* **2.** A lawyer. His *counselor* was familiar with the workings of the court.
coun•se•lor (koun′sə lər) *noun, plural* **counselors.**

cringe To draw back in fear, surprise, or disgust; flinch; shrink. The freezing temperature of the water in the pool made me *cringe.*
cringe (krinj) *verb,* **cringed, cringing.**

cultivate **1.** To prepare and use land for growing vegetables, flowers, or other crops. To *cultivate* land, you plow it and fertilize it before you plant seeds. **2.** To plant and help to grow. That farmer *cultivates* corn.
cul•ti•vate (kul′tə vāt′) *verb,* **cultivated, cultivating.**

currency **1.** The money used in a country. Dollars, quarters, and dimes are part of the *currency* used in the United States. **2.** General use or acceptance. As more people use a new word, they give it *currency.*
cur•ren•cy (kûr′ən sē) *noun, plural* **currencies.**

cut-out Something cut out of or off something else. The cereal box came with a free *cut-out* prize.
cut•out (kut′ out′) *noun, plural* **cut-outs.**

Dd

darn To mend by making stitches back and forth across a hole. You should *darn* that hole in your sock.
darn (därn) *verb,* **darned, darning.**

deep-sea Of, relating to, or occurring in the deeper parts of the sea. *Deep-sea* fishing is a popular sport.
deep•sea (dēp′ sē′) *adjective.*

defect A flaw or weakness. That glass bowl has a chip, a crack, and other *defects.*
▲**Synonym:** fault
de•fect (dē′fekt *or* di fekt′) *noun, plural* **defects.**

deliberately **1.** Carefully and slowly; not hastily or rashly. **2.** Intentionally; on purpose.
de•lib•er•ate•ly (di lib′ər it lē) *adverb.*

dent To make a dent or hollow in. I *dented* the soft clay with my thumb. *Verb.*—A small hollow made in the surface of something by a blow or pressure. The accident put a *dent* in the front fender of my bike. *Noun.*
dent (dent) *verb*, **dented, denting;** *noun, plural* **dents.**

depositor One who puts money in the bank or makes a deposit. *Depositors* trust that their money will be safe in the bank.
de•pos•i•tor (di poz′ə tər) *noun, plural* **depositors.**

desolate 1. Without people; deserted. In the winter, that beach is desolate. **2.** Miserable; cheerless. The lost child was *desolate.*
des•o•late (des′ə lit) *adjective.*

destination A place to which a person is going or a thing is being sent. My *destination* is New York.
des•tin•a•tion (des′tə nā′shən) *noun, plural* **destinations.**

detergent A chemical substance that is used for washing things. It may be a liquid or powder. We use *detergent* to wash the dishes.
de•ter•gent (di tûr′jənt) *noun, plural* **detergents.**

Word History

Detergent comes from the Latin verb *tergere,* meaning "to wipe."

devise To think out; invent; plan. We *devised* a secret code that no one could decipher.
de•vise (di vīz′) *verb,* **devised, devising.**

diagonal Having a slant. The dress had a pattern of *diagonal* stripes. *Adjective.*—A straight line that connects the opposite corners of a square or rectangle. He drew a *diagonal* from one corner to the other. *Noun.*
di•ag•o•nal (dī ag′ ə nəl) *adjective; noun, plural* **diagonals.**

diminish To make or become smaller. The campers' supply of food *diminished* as the days wore on.
di•min•ish (di min′ish) *verb,* **diminished, diminishing.**

at; āpe; fär; câre; end; mē; it; īce; pîerce; hot; ōld; sông; fôrk; oil; out; up; ūse; rüle; pu̇ll; tûrn; chin; sing; shop; thin; this; hw in white; zh in treasure. The symbol ə stands for the unstressed vowel sound in about, taken, pencil, lemon, and circus.

dispense To give out. The town *dispensed* food and clothing to the homeless people.
dis•pense (di spens′) *verb,* **dispensed, dispensing.**

disrupt To break up or apart. By talking together, the two pupils were *disrupting* the whole class.
dis•rupt (dis rupt′) *verb,* **disrupted, disrupting.**

doff To remove an article of clothing from the body; also, to take off a hat in greeting or as a sign of respect. The man *doffed* his hat as he passed the mayor.
doff (dof *or* dôf) *verb,* **doffed, doffing.**

dramatically 1. In a manner having to do with plays or acting. My cousin is *dramatically* talented. **2.** In a manner as exciting and interesting as a good play or story. Our team won *dramatically* by scoring the winning point in the last minute of the game.
dra•mat•ic•al•ly (drə mat′ic lē) *adverb.*

dramatics 1. The art or activity of producing or performing plays. ▲Used with a singular verb. **2.** Exaggerated or theatrical behavior. ▲ Used with a plural verb.
dra•mat•ics (drə mat′iks) *noun.*

dreamer 1. One who dreams. When she went to bed, she became a *dreamer.* **2.** One who lives in a world of fancy and imagination. Artists and writers are often said to be *dreamers.*
dream•er (drē′mər) *noun, plural* **dreamers.**

drone A low, steady humming sound. The *drone* of the car's engine made me sleepy. *Noun.*—To talk in a dull, boring way. The speaker *droned* on and on. *Verb.*
drone (drōn) *noun, plural* **drones;** *verb,* **droned, droning.**

duet A piece of music written for two singers or two musical instruments. The soprano and the pianist finished their *duet* to loud applause.
duet (düet *or* dūet) *noun, plural* **duets.**

eavesdrop To listen to other people talking without letting them know you are listening. I learned about my own surprise party by *eavesdropping* as my friends planned the party.
▲**Synonym:** overhear
eaves•drop (ēvz′drop′) *verb,* **eavesdropped, eavesdropping.**

Word History

The word ***eavesdrop*** once meant the area at the side of a house where rainwater on the roof would drop from the eaves to the ground. A person who stood in this place to listen in secret to people talking inside the house was said to be eavesdropping.

ecological Of or relating to ecology, the science that deals with how plants, animals, and other living things live in relation to each other and to their environment.
ecological (ek′ə loj′i kəl *or* ē′kə loj′i kəl) *adjective.*

edible Fit or safe to eat. Not all kinds of berries are *edible.*
ed•i•ble (ed′ə bəl) *adjective.*

encounter To meet in battle. The soldiers *encountered* and defeated the enemy. *Verb.*—A usually unexpected meeting. Your *encounter* with her is the talk of the school. *Noun.*
en•coun•ter (en koun′tər) *verb,* **encountered, encountering;** *noun, plural* **encounters.**

engrave 1. To cut or carve into a surface. The jeweler *engraved* my name on the back of my watch. **2.** To print from a plate that has been cut with letters, figures, or designs. The printer *engraved* the invitations.
en•grave (en grāv′) *verb,* **engraved, engraving.**

enthusiastically In an excited, eager manner. We *enthusiastically* accepted the invitation to the picnic.
en•thu•si•as•ti•cal•ly (en thü′zē as′tik lē) *adverb.*

at; **ā**pe; f**ä**r; c**â**re; **e**nd; m**ē**; **i**t; **ī**ce; p**î**erce; h**o**t; **ō**ld; s**ô**ng; f**ô**rk; **oi**l; **ou**t; **u**p; **ū**se; r**ü**le; p**u̇**ll; t**û**rn; **ch**in; si**ng**; **sh**op; **th**in; **th**is; **hw** in **wh**ite; **zh** in trea**s**ure. The symbol **ə** stands for the unstressed vowel sound in **a**bout, tak**e**n, penc**i**l, lem**o**n, and circ**u**s.

environment **1.** The air, the water, the soil, and all the other things that surround a person, animal, or plant. The *environment* can affect the growth and health of living things. Zoos try to make each animal's enclosure like its natural *environment.* **2.** Surroundings; atmosphere. I loved summer camp because of the friendly *environment.*
en•vi•ron•ment (en vī′rən mənt *or* en vī′ərn mənt) *noun, plural* **environments.**

environmental Concerning or related to the environment. Recently politicians have become more responsive to *environmental* issues.
en•vi•ron•men•tal (en vī′rən mən′ təl) *adjective.*

equator An imaginary line around the earth. It is halfway between the North and South Poles. The United States and Canada are north of the *equator.*
e•qua•tor (i kwā′tər) *noun, plural* **equators.**

Word History

The word ***equator*** is based on the Medieval Latin word *aequator,* which means "equalizer." The equator divides Earth into northern and southern hemispheres.

equip To provide with whatever is needed. The ship was *equipped* with hoses to be used in case of fire.
▲**Synonym:** outfit
e•quip (i kwip′) *verb,* **equipped, equipping.**

essay A short written composition on a subject. I wrote an *essay* about the need for world peace.
es•say (es′ā) *noun, plural* **essays.**

Word History

The word ***essay*** comes from a French word meaning "to try." The first essays modestly claimed to be only attempts to set down the writer's thoughts.

evoke To bring to mind. Seeing those pictures *evoked* childhood memories.
e•voke (i vōk′) *verb,* **evoked, evoking.**

exaggerate To make something seem larger, greater, or more important than it is. The camper *exaggerated* the size of the fish that had gotten away.
ex•ag•ger•ate (eg zaj′ə rāt′) *verb,* **exaggerated, exaggerating.**

exasperate To annoy greatly; make angry. The constant barking of our neighbor's dog has *exasperated* our family.
ex•as•per•ate (eg zas′pə rāt′) *verb,* **exasperated, exasperating.**

existence 1. The fact of being alive or real. The *existence* of some wild animals is in danger because of pollution. **2.** A way of living; life. The early colonists in America led a dangerous *existence.*
ex•is•tence (eg zis′təns) *noun, plural* **existences.**

expel To drive or force out. They *expelled* the child from school for disobeying everyone.
ex•pel (ek spel′) *verb,* **expelled, expelling.**

explosion 1. The act of bursting or expanding suddenly and noisily. The *explosion* of the bomb broke windows in the buildings nearby. **2.** A sudden outburst. The funny joke caused an *explosion* of laughter.
ex•plo•sion (ek splō′zhən) *noun, plural* **explosions.**

famine A great lack of food in an area or country. Many people died of starvation during the *famine* in Ireland in the 1840s.
fam•ine (fam′in) *noun, plural* **famines.**

fee Money requested or paid for some service or right. The city charges a *fee* of ten dollars for a dog license.
fee (fē) *noun, plural* **fees.**

ferocious Savage; fierce. A lion can be *ferocious.*
fe•ro•cious (fə rō′shəs) *adjective; adverb,* **ferociously.**

fidget To move or act restlessly or nervously. I was so nervous about the performance that I couldn't stop *fidgeting. Verb.*—A nervous or restless movement. I could not control the *fidget* in my leg. *Noun.*
fidg•et (fi′ jət) *verb,* **fidgeted, fidgeting;** *noun, plural* **fidgets.**

at; āpe; fär; câre; end; mē; it; īce; pîerce; hot; ōld; sông; fôrk; oil; out; up; ūse; rüle; pu̇ll; tûrn; chin; sing; shop; thin; this; hw in white; zh in treasure. The symbol ə stands for the unstressed vowel sound in about, taken, pencil, lemon, and circus.

fleck A spot or mark. I have a *fleck* of juice on my shirt. *Noun.*—To color as if by sprinkling with dots. Impressionist paintings are often *flecked* with color. *Verb.*
fleck (flek) *noun, plural* **flecks;** *verb,* **flecked, flecking.**

flurry **1.** A brief, light fall of snow. The weatherman predicted a snow *flurry* for tomorrow. **2.** A sudden outburst. There was a *flurry* of excitement when the movie star got out of the limousine.
flur•ry (flûr′ē) *noun, plural* **flurries.**

foremost First in position or importance. She was considered the *foremost* citizen of the town.
fore•most (fôr′ mōst′) *adjective.*

formation **1.** Something formed or made. The placement of the rocks in the garden made an interesting *formation.* **2.** The process of forming or making. The *formation* of ice from water requires a temperature below 32 degrees Fahrenheit.
for•ma•tion (fôr mā′shən) *noun, plural* **formations.**

foyer A lobby or entranceway. She opened the door and walked into the *foyer.*
foy•er (foi′ ər) *noun, plural* **foyers.**

frightful **1.** Causing sudden fear; alarming. The man's mask was *frightful.* **2.** Disgusting or shocking. There was a *frightful* mess on the sidewalk.
fright•ful (frīt′fəl) *adjective.*

froth A mass of bubbles formed in or on a liquid; foam. A *froth* appeared on the milk as it boiled. *Noun.*—To give out or form froth. The mixture *frothed* as it boiled. *Verb.*
froth (frôth) *noun, plural* **froths;** *verb,* **frothed, frothing;** *adjective,* **frothy.**

generator A machine that produces electricity, steam, or other energy. The hospital had an emergency *generator* in case of a power failure.
gen•er•a•tor (jen′ə rā′tər) *noun, plural* **generators.**

goddess A female god. Gods and *goddesses* ruled the world in ancient Greece.
god•dess (god′is) *noun, plural* **goddesses.**

goldsmith One who makes and deals in articles of gold. The *goldsmith* put the new rings in the showcase.
gold•smith (gōld′smith′) *noun, plural* **goldsmiths.**

gravity The force that pulls things toward the core of the earth, the moon, or other planets. *Gravity* is the force that causes objects to fall when they are dropped.
grav•i•ty (grav′i tē) *noun, plural* **gravities.**

grimace To make a grimace. His mother *grimaced* when she saw his bad grades. *Verb.*—A twisting of the face. People often make a *grimace* when they are uncomfortable. *Noun.*
gri•mace (grim′əs *or* gri mās′) *verb,* **grimaced, grimacing;** *noun, plural* **grimaces.**

Word History

The verb ***grimace*** appeared in the English language in 1651. It comes from the Middle French *grimache* and the Old English *grima,* meaning "mask."

grudge To be unwilling to give or allow. Although they don't like you, they won't *grudge* you first prize if you deserve it. *Verb.*—Dislike or anger that has been felt for a long time. Those two have held a *grudge* against each other ever since kindergarten. *Noun.*
grudge (gruj) *verb,* **grudged, grudging;** *noun, plural* **grudges.**

habitat The place where an animal or plant naturally lives and grows. The natural *habitat* of fish is water.
hab•i•tat (hab′i tat′) *noun, plural* **habitats.**

hamlet A very small village. New York City is much larger than a *hamlet.*
ham•let (ham′lit) *noun, plural* **hamlets.**

handrail A railing that can be gripped by the hand, used on stairways and balconies to support and protect people. The elderly woman gripped the *handrail* as she went down the stairs.
hand•rail (hand′ rāl′) *noun, plural* **handrails.**

at; **ā**pe; f**ä**r; c**â**re; **e**nd; m**ē**; **i**t; **ī**ce; p**î**erce; h**o**t; **ō**ld; s**ô**ng; f**ô**rk; **oi**l; **ou**t; **u**p; **ū**se; r**ü**le; p**u̇**ll; t**û**rn; **ch**in; si**ng**; **sh**op; **th**in; **th**is; **hw** in **wh**ite; **zh** in trea**s**ure. The symbol **ə** stands for the unstressed vowel sound in **a**bout, tak**e**n, penc**i**l, lem**o**n, and circ**u**s.

handshake An act in which two people grip and shake each other's hands. A handshake can be a way of greeting someone, a way of saying good-bye, or a way of marking an agreement. They sealed their bargain with a *handshake.*
hand•shake (hand′shāk′) *noun, plural* **handshakes.**

hard-boiled **1.** Boiled until hard. A *hard-boiled* egg is boiled until its yolk and white are solid. **2.** Tough and not sympathetic. The inspector was a *hard-boiled* police detective.
hard•boiled (härd′boild′) *adjective.*

hesitantly In a manner showing hesitation; unwillingly. I was *hesitant* about jumping into the lake.
▲**Synonym:** uncertainly
hes•i•tant•ly (hez′i tənt lē) *adverb.*

hibernate To spend the winter sleeping. Some bears, woodchucks, frogs, and snakes hibernate. The bear went into the cave to *hibernate.*
hi•ber•nate (hī′bər nāt′) *verb,* **hibernated, hibernating;** *noun,* **hibernation.**

honeycomb To make full of tunnels or cells like a bee's honeycomb. Secret passages *honeycombed* the castle. *Verb.*—A wax structure made by bees to store their eggs and honey. A honeycomb is made up of layers of cells that have six sides. Beekeepers often sell honey that is still in the *honeycomb. Noun.*
hon•ey•comb (hun′ē kōm′) *verb,* **honeycombed, honeycombing;** *noun, plural* **honeycombs.**

honor To show or feel great respect for a person or thing. The city *honored* the astronauts with a parade. *Verb.*
— Something given or done to show great respect or appreciation. The hero received a medal and other *honors. Noun.*
hon•or (on′ər) *verb,* **honored, honoring;** *noun, plural* **honors.**

hospitalize To put a person in a hospital. I was *hospitalized* when I had my tonsils removed.
hos•pi•tal•ize (hos′pi tə līz′) *verb,* **hospitalized, hospitalizing.**

husky **1.** Big and strong. Clint is a *husky* football player. **2.** Rough and deep in sound. The bass has a *husky* voice.
hus•ky (hus′kē) *adjective,* **huskier, huskiest.**

hydroelectric Relating to electricity created by generators run by rapidly flowing water. There is a *hydroelectric* power station at the waterfall.
hy•dro•e•lec•tric (hī′drō i lek′trik) *adjective.*

hydrogen A gas that has no color, taste, or odor and that burns very easily. Hydrogen is a chemical element. It is the lightest and most abundant element in the universe. *Hydrogen* is one of the elements of which water is composed.
hy•dro•gen (hī′drə jən) *noun.*

illegible Very hard or impossible to read. The handwriting on the envelope was *illegible.*
il•leg•i•ble (i lej′ə bəl) *adjective.*

implore To ask earnestly or beg for something. I *implore* you to clear the table, even though it's my turn.
▲**Synonym:** plead
im•plore (im plôr′) *verb,* **implored, imploring;** *adverb,* **imploringly.**

improvement **1.** The act of getting better. **2.** A change or addition that makes something better.
im•prove•ment (im prüv′mənt) *noun, plural* **improvements.**

impudence **1.** The quality of being impudent; rudeness; insolence. **2.** Bold and rude speech or behavior.
im•pu•dence (im′pyə dəns) *noun.*

industrial **1.** Having to do with or produced by industry. Iron smelting, coal mining, and the production of plastics are *industrial* processes. **2.** Having highly developed industries. Canada is an *industrial* country.
in•dus•tri•al (in dus′trē əl) *adjective.*

inevitable Not able to be avoided; bound to happen. An *inevitable* result of closing your eyes is not being able to see.
▲**Synonym:** unavoidable
in•ev•i•ta•ble (i nev′i tə bəl) *adjective; adverb,* **inevitably.**

infantry Soldiers trained and equipped to fight on foot. The *infantry* used to be very important in winning wars.
in•fan•try (in′fən trē) *noun, plural* **infantries.**

at; **ā**pe; f**ä**r; c**â**re; **e**nd; m**ē**; **i**t; **ī**ce; p**î**erce; h**o**t; **ō**ld; s**ô**ng; f**ô**rk; **oi**l; **ou**t; **u**p; **ū**se; r**ü**le; p**u̇**ll; t**û**rn; **ch**in; si**ng**; **sh**op; **th**in; **th**is; **hw** in **wh**ite; **zh** in trea**s**ure. The symbol **ə** stands for the unstressed vowel sound in **a**bout, tak**e**n, penc**i**l, lem**o**n, and circ**u**s.

inflection 1. A change in pitch or loudness of the voice. There was a strange *inflection* in his voice. **2.** The change of form that words undergo to show case, number, tense and the like. In English class we studied the *inflection* of nouns.
in•flec•tion (in flek′ shən) *noun, plural* **inflections.**

initiate 1. To be the first to do; begin; start. The new librarian *initiated* the practice of lending books for a month. 2. To make a person a member of an organization or club. The new members were *initiated* into the club.
in•i•ti•ate (i nish′ē āt′) *verb,* **initiated, initiating.**

inquisitive Eager to know; curious. An *inquisitive* student asks a lot of questions.
in•qui•si•tive (in kwiz′i tiv) *adjective.*

instinctively In a manner having to do with a way of acting or behaving that a person or animal is born with and does not have to learn. Birds build nests *instinctively.*
in•stinc•tive•ly (in stingk′tiv lē) *adverb.*

interior 1. The inner side, surface, or part. The *interior* of the cave was dark. **2.** The part of a country or region that is away from the coast or border. The *interior* of Australia is mostly desert.
in•te•ri•or (in tîr′ē ər) *noun, plural* **interiors.**

interview A meeting in which people talk face to face. I had an *interview* with the store manager for a summer job. *Noun.*—To have an interview with. The mayor was *interviewed* about the growing traffic problem. *Verb.*
in•ter•view (in′tər vū′) *noun, plural* **interviews;** *verb,* **interviewed, interviewing.**

inventory 1. A detailed list of articles on hand. The *inventory* showed all the goods the clothing store had on its shelves. **2.** The articles that are on such a list. The store has a large *inventory* of sports equipment.
in•ven•tor•y (in′vən tôr′ ē) *noun, plural* **inventories.**

iota 1. A very small amount. You don't have an *iota* of evidence against me. **2.** The ninth letter of the Greek alphabet. He learned how to write an *iota.*
i•o•ta (ī ō′ tə) *noun.*

jalopy An old, run-down car. This *jalopy* won't make it all the way to Florida from New York.
ja•lo•py (jə lop′ē) *noun, plural* **jalopies.**

jubilantly In a joyous manner. They celebrated their victory *jubilantly.*
ju•bi•lant•ly (jü′bə lənt lē) *adverb.*

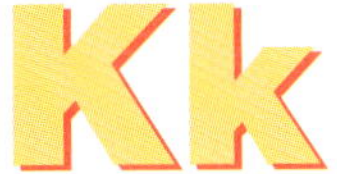

knickers Loose-fitting short pants gathered at the knee. My father wore *knickers* to school.
knick•ers (nik′ərz) *plural noun.*

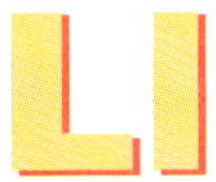

landmark 1. An object that is familiar and serves as a guide. The church steeple is a well-known *landmark* in our town. **2.** An important building, structure, or place. This Civil War battlefield is a national *landmark.*
land•mark (land′märk′) *noun, plural* **landmarks.**

laughable Causing or likely to cause a person to laugh. It was *laughable* to think that all those clowns could fit in one tiny car.
▲**Synonym:** absurd
laugh•a•ble (laf′ə bəl) *adjective.*

lavishly In an extravagant or wasteful manner. We ate *lavishly* at the expensive restaurant.
lav•ish•ly (lav′ish lē) *adverb.*

Word History

The word ***lavish*** comes from two related words in Middle French. *Lavasse* means "downpour of rain" and *laver* means "to wash."

liberation The act or state of being or becoming free.
lib•er•a•tion (lib′ə rā′ shən) *noun.*

lifeboat A boat used for saving lives at sea or along the shore. *Lifeboats* are often carried on larger ships.
life•boat (līf′bōt′) *noun, plural* **lifeboats.**

at; **ā**pe; f**ä**r; c**â**re; **e**nd; m**ē**; **i**t; **ī**ce; p**î**erce; h**o**t; **ō**ld; s**ô**ng; f**ô**rk; **oi**l; **ou**t; **u**p; **ū**se; r**ü**le; p**ù**ll; t**û**rn; **ch**in; si**ng**; **sh**op; **th**in; **th**is; **hw** in **wh**ite; **zh** in trea**s**ure. The symbol **ə** stands for the unstressed vowel sound in **a**bout, tak**e**n, penc**i**l, lem**o**n, and circ**u**s.

loan To lend something to someone. Thank you for *loaning* me your pencil. *Verb.*—Something lent. We received a *loan* of five thousand dollars from the bank. *Noun.*
loan (lōn) *verb,* **loaned, loaning;** *noun, plural* **loans.**

loot To steal valuable things from; plunder. The enemy soldiers *looted* the town. *Verb.*—Things that have been stolen. The thieves hid their *loot* in the barn. *Noun.*
▲ Another word that sounds like this is **lute.**
loot (lüt) *verb,* **looted, looting;** *noun.*

lunar Of or having to do with the moon. The astronauts brought back *lunar* rocks for study.
lu•nar (lü′nər) *adjective.*

Mm

magnetic 1. Acting like a magnet; having to do with magnets or magnetism. The needle of a compass points to the earth's *magnetic* poles. **2.** Able to attract or fascinate people. The actor had a *magnetic* personality.
mag•net•ic (mag net′ik) *adjective; adverb,* **magnetically.**

maiden A girl or young unmarried woman. *Noun.*— First or earliest. The ship's *maiden* voyage was from England to New York. *Adjective.*
maid•en (mā′dən) *noun, plural* **maidens;** *adjective.*

majestic Grand and noble; dignified. The *majestic* mountains rose high above the valley.
ma•jes•tic (mə jes′tik) *adjective; adverb,* **majestically.**

makeshift Used for a time in place of the correct or usual thing. We sometimes use our sofa as a *makeshift* bed. *Adjective.*— Something used for a time in place of the correct or usual thing. When the Venetian blinds broke, we used a sheet as a *makeshift. Noun.*
make•shift (māk′shift′) *adjective; noun, plural* **makeshifts.**

maneuver To move or manage skillfully or cleverly. We *maneuvered* our way to the front of the crowd so we could see the parade. *Verb.*— An organized movement of soldiers or ships. The captain planned the troops' next *maneuver. Noun.*
ma•neu•ver (mə nü′vər) *verb,* **maneuvered, maneuvering;** *noun, plural* **maneuvers.**

manhood **1.** The condition or the time of being an adult male person. The adolescent boy will soon enter *manhood.* **2.** Men as a group. The *manhood* and womanhood of our country always respond well in a national crisis.
man•hood (man′hůd′) *noun.*

marina A small harbor where boats and yachts can be docked and serviced. The *marina* suffered a lot of damage during the hurricane.
ma•ri•na (mə rē′nə) *noun, plural* **marinas.**

melodrama A movie or play that emphasizes plot and action over characterization. The theater group decided to revive an old *melodrama.*
me•lo•dra•ma (me′ lə drä′ mə) *noun, plural* **melodramas.**

mission **1.** A group of people sent somewhere to do a special job. Four rangers formed a rescue *mission* to search for the lost child. **2.** A special job or task. The space agency scheduled another *mission* to the moon.
mis•sion (mish′ən) *noun, plural* **missions.**

mongrel A plant or an animal, especially a dog, that is a mixture of breeds. The dog had a noble face even though he was a *mongrel.*
mon•grel (mung′grəl *or* mong′grəl) *noun, plural* **mongrels.**

monitor To watch over or observe something. Our teacher *monitored* the fire drill. *Verb.*—A student who is given a special duty to do, such as taking attendance. Last year I was the hallway *monitor. Noun.*
mon•i•tor (mon′i tər) *verb,* **monitored, monitoring;** *noun, plural* **monitors.**

at; āpe; fär; câre; end; mē; it; īce; pîerce; hot; ōld; sông; fôrk; oil; out; up; ūse; rüle; půll; tûrn; chin; sing; shop; thin; this; hw in white; zh in treasure. The symbol ə stands for the unstressed vowel sound in about, taken, pencil, lemon, and circus.

monotonous Tiring or uninteresting because it does not change in any way. That job is *monotonous* because you have to do the same thing over and over.
▲**Synonym:** tedious
mo•not•o•nous (mə not′ə nəs) *adjective; adverb,* **monotonously.**

mortar 1. A building material made of sand, water, and lime. The workers mixed *mortar* to build the brick fireplace. **2.** A thick, heavy bowl in which things are crushed or ground by using a pestle. She ground the herbs in a *mortar.*
mor•tar (môr′tər) *noun, plural* **mortars.**

mortify To subject to severe embarrassment. He was *mortified* when she kissed him in front of the other students.
mor•ti•fy (môr′tə fī′) *verb,* **mortified, mortifying.**

mourner A person who is feeling or showing sorrow or grief. The *mourners* walked slowly through the cemetery.
▲**Synonym:** griever
mourner (môr′nər) *noun, plural* **mourners.**

muffler 1. A warm scarf for wrapping around the neck in cold weather. **2.** A device that reduces the noise made by an engine. The noisy car had a damaged *muffler.*
muf•fler (muf′lər) *noun, plural* **mufflers.**

mummy A dead body that has been wrapped in cloth and specially treated to preserve it. Some ancient Egyptian *mummies* are over 3,000 years old.
mum•my (mum′ē) *noun, plural* **mummies.**

murmur A low, soft sound. We heard the *murmur* of the brook. *Noun.*—To make or say with a low, soft sound. I heard you *murmur* in your sleep. *Verb.*
mur•mur (mûr′mər) *noun, plural* **murmurs;** *verb,* **murmured, murmuring.**

mythology A group or collection of myths and legends. All the myths that were told and written in ancient Greece are known as Greek *mythology.*
my•thol•o•gy (mi thol′ə jē) *noun, plural* **mythologies.**

Nn

narrative A story or report on something that happened. The writer gave a long *narrative* of her travels. *Noun.*
—Telling a story. Her favorite poem was a *narrative* poem. *Adjective.*
nar•ra•tive (nar′ə tiv) *noun, plural* **narratives;** *adjective.*

nimbly In a light, quick manner. The cat jumped *nimbly* onto the fence.
nim•bly (nim′blē) *adverb.*

novelty 1. Something new or unusual. **2.** The quality of being new.
nov•el•ty (nov′əl tē) *noun, plural* **novelties.**

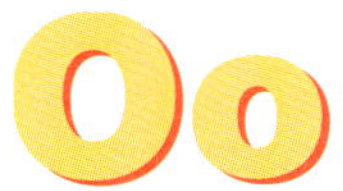

obstacle Something that stands in the way of progress. The roadblock was an *obstacle* to traffic.
▲**Synonym:** obstruction
ob•sta•cle (ob′stə kəl) *noun, plural* **obstacles.**

occupation 1. The work that a person does in order to earn a living; profession. Her *occupation* is teaching. **2.** The act of occupying or the condition of being occupied. The enemy soldiers began their *occupation* of the town.
oc•cu•pa•tion (ok′yə pā′shən) *noun, plural* **occupations.**

ordeal A very hard or painful experience or test. Living through the earthquake was quite an *ordeal.*
or•deal (ôr dēl′ *or* ôr′dēl) *noun, plural* **ordeals.**

painstakingly In a careful manner. She wrote the report *painstakingly,* fretting over every word.
pains•tak•ing•ly (pānz′tāk′ ing lē) *adverb.*

participate To join with others; take part. Everyone *participated* in the rally.
par•ti•ci•pate (pär tis′ə pāt′) *verb,* **participated, participating.**

at; **ā**pe; f**ä**r; c**â**re; **e**nd; m**ē**; **i**t; **ī**ce; p**î**erce; h**o**t; **ō**ld; s**ô**ng; f**ô**rk; **oi**l; **ou**t; **u**p; **ū**se; r**ü**le; p**u̇**ll; t**û**rn; **ch**in; si**ng**; **sh**op; **th**in; **th**is; **hw** in **wh**ite; **zh** in trea**s**ure. The symbol **ə** stands for the unstressed vowel sound in **a**bout, tak**e**n, penc**i**l, lem**o**n, and circ**u**s.

pedestal 1. A base on which a column or statue stands. The sculptor built a *pedestal* for the bronze figure. **2.** The base or other part of something that supports it. The *pedestal* of the lamp was cracked.
ped•es•tal (ped′ə stəl) *noun, plural* **pedestals.**

pep A lively, vital quality; activity; spirit. After the brisk walk outside, I was full of *pep. Noun.*—To make lively or energetic. Whenever I need to be *pepped* up, I do some exercises. *Verb.*
pep (pep) *noun; verb,* **pepped, pepping.**

perception 1. The understanding, comprehension, or knowledge that is the result of perceiving. The astronauts' *perception* of the problems that arose during their flight saved their lives. **2.** The act or power of perceiving. A cat's *perception* of colors is poor.
per•cep•tion (pər sep′shən) *noun, plural* **perceptions.**

pharaoh The title of the kings of ancient Egypt. King Tutankhamen was a *pharaoh.*
phar•aoh (fâr′ō) *noun, plural* **pharaohs.**

pillar A column that supports a building or stands alone as a monument. The roof of the porch is supported by *pillars.*
pil•lar (pil′ər) *noun, plural* **pillars.**

plunder To steal from; rob. Soldiers *plundered* the town. *Verb.*—Something stolen. The outlaws hid their *plunder* in an old shed. *Noun.*
plun•der (plun′dər) *verb,* **plundered, plundering;** *noun.*

populate 1. To live in, inhabit. Nomads *populate* the desert. **2.** To provide with members. The government wants to *populate* the new industrial complex.
pop•u•late (pop′yə lāt′) *verb,* **populated, populating.**

porcelain A kind of hard, fine pottery. It is thin enough to see through when held to the light. Cups, plates, and other dishes are sometimes made of *porcelain.* Antique Chinese *porcelain* objects are very valuable.
por•ce•lain (pôr′sə lin) *noun.*

pore To read or study carefully. I *pored* over my notes the night before the test. *Verb.*—A very small opening in the skin or other surface. Perspiration passes through the *pores* in our skin. *Noun.*

pore (pôr) *verb,* **pored, poring;** *noun, plural* **pores.**

portcullis A grating of iron hung over the gateway of a fortified place and lowered between grooves to prevent passage. Knights in armor stormed the *portcullis.*

port•cul•lis (pôrt kul′ is) *noun.*

porthole A small round window in the side of a boat or ship. It lets in both air and light. She could see the tropical island through the *porthole.*

port•hole (pôrt′hōl′) *noun, plural* **portholes.**

pout To thrust out the lips to show displeasure. The children *pouted* when they were scolded.

▲**Synonym:** scowl

pout (pout) *verb,* **pouted, pouting.**

precise 1. Definite; exact. Your arrival time must be *precise.* **2.** Strict or careful. The teacher speaks in a clear and *precise* way.

pre•cise (pri sīs′) *adjective; adverb,* **precisely.**

prehistoric Belonging to a time before people started writing history. Mammoths and dinosaurs were *prehistoric* animals.

pre•his•tor•ic (prē′his tôr′ik) *adjective.*

prospective Likely to come about in the future. He introduced his *prospective* wife to his parents.

▲**Synonym:** expected

pro•spec•tive (prə spek′tiv) *adjective.*

prosperous Having success, wealth, or good fortune. The *prosperous* family tried to help other less fortunate families.

pros•per•ous (pros′pər əs) *adjective.*

protrude To stick out. Only the tip of an iceberg *protrudes* from the surface of the ocean.

pro•trude (prō trüd′) *verb,* **protruded, protruding.**

at; **ā**pe; f**ä**r; c**â**re; **e**nd; m**ē**; **i**t; **ī**ce; p**î**erce; h**o**t; **ō**ld; s**ô**ng; f**ô**rk; **oi**l; **ou**t; **u**p; **ū**se; r**ü**le; p**u̇**ll; t**û**rn; **ch**in; si**ng**; **sh**op; **th**in; **th**is; **hw** in **wh**ite; **zh** in trea**s**ure. The symbol **ə** stands for the unstressed vowel sound in **a**bout, tak**e**n, penc**i**l, lem**o**n, and circ**u**s.

psychology The study of the mind and of the way people or animals behave. She wants to study *psychology* when she goes to college.
psy•chol•o•gy (sī kol′ə jē) *noun.*

puncture To make a hole in something with a sharp object. I *punctured* the balloon with a pin. *Verb.*— A hole made by a sharp object. They fixed a *puncture* in the tire. *Noun.*
punc•ture (pungk′chər) *verb,* **punctured, puncturing;** *noun, plural* **punctures.**

quantity 1. A number or amount. The recipe calls for a small *quantity* of milk. **2.** A large number or amount. Restaurants buy food in *quantity.*
quan•ti•ty (kwon′ti tē) *noun, plural* **quantities.**

questioningly In an inquiring manner. The judge looked *questioningly* at the witness.
ques•tion•ing•ly (kwes′chən ing lē) *adverb.*

Rr

rash Too hasty; not careful. Unfortunately, he made a *rash* decision. *Adjective.*—A condition in which red spots appear on the skin. Poison ivy causes a *rash. Noun.*
rash (rash) *adjective,* **rasher, rashest;** *noun, plural* **rashes;** *adverb,* **rashly;** *noun,* **rashness.**

ration To limit to fixed portions. The government *rationed* meat during the war. *Verb.*—A fixed portion or share, especially of food. The mountain climbers carried *rations* in their backpacks. *Noun.*
ra•tion (rash′ən *or* rā′shən) *verb,* **rationed, rationing;** *noun, plural* **rations.**

reassure To restore confidence or courage in. Before the curtain rose, the director *reassured* the actors.
▲**Synonym:** comfort
re•as•sure (rē′ ə shůr′) *verb,* **reassured, reassuring;** *noun,* **reassurance.**

rebellious Resisting or refusing to obey authority. The *rebellious* sailors ignored the captain's orders.
re•bel•lious (ri bel′yəs) *adjective.*

recite 1. To repeat something from memory. Can you *recite* the names of all the fifty states? **2.** To tell the story of. I *recited* my adventures at camp to the class.
re•cite (ri sīt′) *verb,* **recited, reciting.**

rectangle A figure with four sides and four right angles. A square is a *rectangle* whose four sides are of equal length.
rec•tan•gle (rek′tang′gəl) *noun, plural* **rectangles;** *adjective,* **rectangular.**

relish 1. A mixture of spices, pickles, olives, and chopped vegetables, used as a side dish and to flavor food. The *relish* tray was passed around the table after the curry was served. **2.** Interest or pleasure; enjoyment. The child opened the presents with *relish.*
rel•ish (rel′ish) *noun, plural* **relishes.**

remote 1. Not near; far away. The explorer traveled to *remote* regions. **2.** Far from cities or towns. The children grew up in a *remote* mountain village.
re•mote (ri mōt′) *adjective,* **remoter, remotest;** *adverb,* **remotely;** *noun,* **remoteness.**

researcher A person who performs investigations to find facts in a particular field of study. The *researcher* observed fifteen different kinds of fish.
re•search•er (ri sûrch′ər *or* rē′sûrch′ər) *noun, plural* **researchers.**

reservoir A place where water is stored. Although there are fish in the *reservoir,* it is prohibited to go fishing there.
res•er•voir (rez′ər vwär′) *noun, plural* **reservoirs.**

residence 1. A place where a person lives. You enter his *residence* from a side door. **2.** A period of time spent living in a place. After ten years' *residence* in the city, my family moved.
res•i•dence (rez′i dəns) *noun, plural* **residences.**

retrieve 1. To get back; recover. The golfer *retrieved* the ball from the pond. **2.** To find and bring back dead or wounded game. Our dog is trained to *retrieve.*
re•trieve (ri trēv′) *verb,* **retrieved, retrieving;** *noun,* **retrieval.**

at; **ā**pe; f**ä**r; c**â**re; **e**nd; m**ē**; **i**t; **ī**ce; p**î**erce; h**o**t; **ō**ld; s**ô**ng; f**ô**rk; **oi**l; **ou**t; **u**p; **ū**se; r**ü**le; p**u̇**ll; t**û**rn; **ch**in; si**ng**; **sh**op; **th**in; **th**is; **hw** in **wh**ite; **zh** in trea**s**ure. The symbol **ə** stands for the unstressed vowel sound in **a**bout, tak**e**n, penc**i**l, lem**o**n, and circ**u**s.

rhythmically In a manner having a steady or consistent beat.
rhyth•mi•cal•ly (rith′mik lē) *adverb.*

riverbank The bank of a river. He sat on the *riverbank* and watched for boats coming downstream.
riv•er•bank (riv′ər bangk′) *noun, plural* **riverbanks.**

romance 1. A love affair. *Sleeping Beauty* is about the *romance* between a prince and a sleeping princess. **2.** A quality of love, excitement, mystery, or adventure. The dim lights gave a sense of *romance* to the room.
ro•mance (rō mans′ *or* rō′mans) *noun, plural* **romances.**

Word History

The word ***romance*** comes from an old French word that meant "something written in a Romance language." In the Middle Ages, stories of love and adventure were usually written in one of these Romance languages instead of in Latin, which was used in more serious writings.

rudder 1. A broad, flat, movable piece of wood or metal attached to the rear of a boat or ship. It is used in steering. Without a *rudder* the captain could not guide his ship. **2.** A similar piece at the tail of an aircraft. The pilot adjusted the *rudder* as he circled the airport.
rud•der (rud′ər) *noun, plural* **rudders.**

rummage To search completely by moving things around. I *rummaged* in the closet for my missing shoe.
▲**Synonym:** ransack
rum•mage (rum′ij) *verb,* **rummaged, rummaging.**

saunter To walk around in a leisurely manner; stroll. The young girl *sauntered* to the candy store.
saun•ter (sôn′tər) *verb,* **sauntered, sauntering.**

savings Money that is saved. It will take all of your *savings* to buy that camera.
sav•ings (sā′vingz) *plural noun.*

scaffold A platform that workers stand on as they work on a building. The construction workers stood on a *scaffold.*
scaf•fold (skaf′əld) *noun, plural* **scaffolds.**

scrawl To write or draw quickly and carelessly. Somebody *scrawled* on my test paper and covered up my grade.
▲**Synonym:** scribble
scrawl (skrôl) *verb,* **scrawled, scrawling.**

scrumptious Delicious; delightful. The chocolate cake we ate for dessert was *scrumptious.*
scrump•tious (skrump′ shəs) *adjective.*

sculpt To shape or give form to. She *sculpted* a bust of Mozart in marble.
sculpt (skulpt) *verb,* **sculpted, sculpting.**

sensor A device that detects changes in heat, sound, or pressure and sends the information to another instrument that controls it. My friend has a motion *sensor* in his car.
sen•sor (sen′sər) *noun, plural* **sensors.**

sentimental Having or showing tender feeling. The couple in the movie sang a *sentimental* song.
sen•ti•men•tal (sen′tə men′təl) *adjective.*

sever To cut or break apart. Our friendship was *severed* when she told everyone my secret.
sev•er (sev′ər) *verb,* **severed, severing.**

sharecropper A farmer, especially in the southern United States, who works the land and receives an agreed share of the crop. The *sharecroppers* had a good harvest.
share•crop•per (shâr′ krop′ər) *noun, plural* **sharecroppers.**

sheepishly In an embarrassed manner.
sheep•ish•ly (shē′ pish lē) *adverb.*

shuttle *See* **space shuttle.**

silhouette To show as a dark outline against a lighter background. The horse standing on the hill was *silhouetted* against the sky. *Verb.*—The outline of a figure or object filled in with black or another solid color. *Noun.*
sil•hou•ette (sil′ü et′) *verb,* **silhouetted, silhouetting;** *noun, plural* **silhouettes.**

Word History

Silhouette comes from the last name of Etienne de Silhouette, who was the French Controller of Finances for a brief time in 1767. The meaning of *silhouette* is based on his very short, almost "invisible" time on the job.

at; **ā**pe; f**ä**r; c**â**re; **e**nd; m**ē**; **i**t; **ī**ce; p**î**erce; h**o**t; **ō**ld; s**ô**ng; f**ô**rk; **oi**l; **ou**t; **u**p; **ū**se; r**ü**le; p**ů**ll; t**û**rn; **ch**in; si**ng**; **sh**op; **th**in; **th**is; **hw** in **wh**ite; **zh** in trea**s**ure. The symbol **ə** stands for the unstressed vowel sound in **a**bout, tak**e**n, penc**i**l, lem**o**n, and circ**u**s.

site The position or location of something. Our house is on a mountain *site* with a beautiful view.
▲ Other words that sound like this are **cite** and **sight.**
site (sīt) *noun, plural* **sites.**

smirk To smile in a self-satisfied or silly manner. My brother *smirked* at me because he got two cookies and I only got one.
smirk (smûrk) *verb,* **smirked, smirking.**

sneer A facial expression or a remark that shows hatred or scorn. The rude child answered with a *sneer. Noun.* —To show or say with a sneer. The thief *sneered* at the police. *Verb.*
sneer (snîr) *noun, plural* **sneers;** *verb,* **sneered, sneering.**

somber Dark or gloomy. The sky became gray and *somber* before the thunderstorm.
som•ber (som′bər) *adjective; adverb,* **somberly;** *noun,* **somberness.**

sophisticated Having or showing much knowledge and experience of the world. I hope to be as *sophisticated* as my mother someday.
so•phis•ti•cat•ed (sə fis′ti kā′tid) *adjective; noun,* **sophistication.**

spacecraft A vehicle used for flight in outer space. Also, **spaceship**. I always wanted to see the inside of a *spacecraft.*
space•craft (spās′kraft′) *noun, plural* **spacecraft.**

space shuttle A spacecraft that carries a crew into space and returns to land on Earth. The same space shuttle can be used again. I would like to fly in a *space shuttle.*
space shut•tle (spās′ shut′əl) *noun, plural* **space shuttles.**

spacious Having a lot of space or room; roomy; large. The apartment was very *spacious.*
▲ **Synonym:** extensive
spa•cious (spā′shəs) *adjective; noun,* **spaciousness.**

spat The past tense and past participle of **spit**. He quickly *spat* out the words of the speech. *Verb.*—A short, unimportant argument or disagreement. The sisters had a *spat* about what to watch on TV. *Noun.*
spat (spat) *verb; noun, plural* **spats.**

sphinx 1. A mythical creature having a human head and a lion's body. In Greek mythology the *sphinx* had a woman's head and killed anyone who couldn't answer its riddle. **2.** The Sphinx; a large statue of this creature in Egypt. The *sphinx* was erected to honor a pharaoh.
sphinx (sfingks) *noun, plural* **sphinxes.**

splendor Magnificence; brilliance. In all its *splendor,* the mansion sits high on a hill.
splen•dor (splen′dər) *noun; adjective,* **splendorous.**

starboard The right side of a boat, ship, or aircraft when a person standing on deck faces forward. We stood on the *starboard* while sailing to sea. *Noun.*— On, of, or relating to the right side of a boat, ship, or aircraft. The tugboat moved toward the *starboard* side of the ship. *Adjective.*
star•board (stär′bərd) *noun; adjective.*

storage 1. The act of storing things or the condition of being stored. The furniture was picked up for *storage* today. **2.** A place for storing things. The chest is used as a *storage* for our toys.
stor•age (stôr′ij) *noun.*

stubbornness Obstinacy; refusal to yield or give up. The horse's *stubbornness* caused the race to be postponed.
stub•born•ness (stub′ərn nəs) *noun.*

subdue 1. To defeat; conquer. The soldiers *subdued* the enemy. **2.** To control or overcome. I *subdued* my anger.
sub•due (səb dü′ *or* səb dū′) *verb,* **subdued, subduing.**

submerge To place under or cover with some liquid, especially water. Add water until the potatoes are completely *submerged.*
sub•merge (səb mûrj′) *verb,* **submerged, submerging.**

at; āpe; fär; câre; end; mē; it; īce; pîerce; hot; ōld; sông; fôrk; oil; out; up; ūse; rüle; pu̇ll; tûrn; chin; sing; shop; thin; th̲is; hw in white; zh in treasure. The symbol ə stands for the unstressed vowel sound in about, taken, pencil, lemon, and circus.

suds Soapy water with foam or bubbles. When you wash the car, spread the *suds* on it first.
suds (sudz) *plural noun.*

support 1. To give strength or comfort to. The family *supported* each other during a difficult time. **2.** To hold up. The columns *support* the roof.
sup•port (sə pôrt′) *verb,* **supported, supporting;** *adjective,* **supportive.**

surprise 1. To cause to feel sudden wonder or amazement. You *surprised* me with all the gifts you brought. **2.** To come upon suddenly and unexpectedly. One morning we *surprised* two deer in our backyard.
sur•prise (sər prīz′) *verb,* **surprised, surprising.**

surprisingly In a manner causing wonder or amazement. I did *surprisingly* well on the pop quiz.
sur•pris•ing•ly (sər prīz′ing lē) *adverb.*

survey 1. A measuring of land. That family had a *survey* made of their property. **2.** A detailed study. The company did a *survey* to find out who used its products. *Noun.*—To view, examine, or measure as a whole. *Verb.*
sur•vey (sər vā′ *for verb;* sûr′vā *or* sər vā′ *for noun*) *noun, plural* **surveys;** *verb,* **surveyed, surveying.**

surveyor A person who takes measurements to determine the shape, area, and boundaries of a piece of land.
sur•vey•or (sər vā′ər) *noun, plural* **surveyors.**

sweeten To make or become sweet or sweeter. The cook *sweetened* the lemonade with sugar.
sweet•en (swē′tən) *verb,* **sweetened, sweetening;** *noun,* **sweetener.**

synagogue A building used by Jews for worship and religious instruction. My friend went to *synagogue* for Yom Kippur.
syn•a•gogue (sin′ə gog′) *noun, plural* **synagogues.**

tattoo A colored figure or design made on the skin with needles that have been dipped in colors. The sailor had *tattoos* of ships on each arm. *Noun.*—To mark with tattoos. I *tattooed* a butterfly on my arm. *Verb.*
tat•too (ta tü′) *noun, plural* **tattoos;** *verb,* **tattooed, tattooing.**

technology 1. The use of science for practical purposes, especially in engineering and industry. Space exploration contributed important changes in *technology.* **2.** Methods, machines, and devices that are used in doing things in a science or profession. X rays were an important advance in medical *technology.*
tech•nol•o•gy (tek nol′ə jē) *noun, plural* **technologies.**

teller 1. A person who works in a bank giving out and receiving money. The bank *teller* counted the deposits for the day. **2.** A person who tells or relates. He is a *teller* of tall tales.
tell•er (tel′ər) *noun, plural* **tellers.**

temporary Lasting or used for a short time only. Some students try to find *temporary* jobs for the summer.
▲**Synonym:** makeshift
tem•po•rar•y (tem′pə rer′ē) *adjective.*

terminal 1. A station at either end of a railroad, bus, air, or other transportation line. We waited at the bus *terminal* for my sister to arrive. **2.** A keyboard and a monitor that can be connected to a computer. Before we could work, we had to connect the *terminal* to a CPU and a printer.
ter•mi•nal (tûr′mə nəl) *noun, plural* **terminals.**

thunderous Making or accompanied by a noise like thunder. The audience gave the solo violinist *thunderous* applause.
thun•der•ous (thun′dər əs) *adjective; adverb,* **thunderously.**

token 1. A piece of metal that looks like a coin and is used in place of money. **2.** A sign of something else; symbol. Please accept this gift as a *token* of our appreciation.
to•ken (tō′kən) *noun, plural* **tokens.**

at; **ā**pe; f**ä**r; c**â**re; **e**nd; m**ē**; **i**t; **ī**ce; p**î**erce; h**o**t; **ō**ld; s**ô**ng; f**ô**rk; **oi**l; **ou**t; **u**p; **ū**se; r**ü**le; p**ů**ll; t**û**rn; **ch**in; si**ng**; **sh**op; **th**in; **th**is; **hw** in **wh**ite; **zh** in trea**s**ure. The symbol **ə** stands for the unstressed vowel sound in **a**bout, tak**e**n, penc**i**l, lem**o**n, and circ**u**s.

tollbooth A stall where fees are paid, usually found at the entrance to a bridge or highway. The traffic at the *tollbooth* moved very slowly.
toll•booth (tōl′ büth′) *noun, plural* **tollbooths.**

tomb A grave or building in which a dead body is placed. The king's body was placed in an elaborate *tomb.*
tomb (tüm) *noun, plural* **tombs.**

transmitter A device that sends out radio or television signals. The *transmitter* had to be upgraded to send digital signals.
trans•mit•ter (trans mit′ər) *noun, plural* **transmitters.**

treason The betraying of one's country by helping an enemy. Giving the army's battle plans to the enemy was an act of *treason.*
trea•son (trē′zən) *noun.*

Word History

The word ***treason*** comes from the Latin word *traditio,* which means "the act of handing over," as in handing over information or secrets. *Treason* first appeared in the English language in the 13th century.

tremor A shaking or trembling. Earthquakes cause *tremors* in the earth.
tre•mor (trem′ər) *noun, plural* **tremors.**

triangle **1.** A figure or object with three sides and three angles. The architect designed a building that was shaped like a *triangle.* **2.** A musical instrument made of a metal bar bent in the shape of a triangle. A *triangle* sounds like a bell when it is struck.
tri•an•gle (trī′ang′gəl) *noun, plural* **triangles.**

triangle *(def. 2)*

trill The rapid vibration of a musical tone. There were many *trills* in the Beethoven sonata. *Noun.*—To vibrate a musical note on an instrument or with the voice. The singer *trilled* the note with great ease. *Verb.*
trill (tril) *noun, plural* **trills;** *verb,* **trilled, trilling.**

troublemaking Willful disruption. Her *troublemaking* always upsets the teacher.
trou•ble•mak•ing (trub′ əl māk′ ing) *noun.*

truce A short stop in fighting. A *truce* is agreed to by both sides, who then try to reach a peace agreement. The enemies agreed to a *truce.*
truce (trüs) *noun, plural* **truces.**

Word History

Truce comes from a Middle English word meaning "agreement."

tutor A teacher who gives private lessons to a pupil. When I was sick for three months, I had a tutor at home. Noun.—To teach privately; act as a tutor. The college student made money by tutoring French. Verb.
tu•tor (tü′tər *or* tū′tər) *noun, plural* **tutors;** *verb,* **tutored, tutoring.**

Word History

Tutor comes from a Latin word meaning "defender" or "guardian." In some English universities, the word *tutor* was used for a graduate responsible for a younger student. From this meaning came the sense of "private teacher."

unconsciously Not intentionally; not on purpose.
un•con•scious•ly (un kon′shəs lē) *adverb.*

undersea Lying, done, or used below the surface of the sea. There have been several *undersea* explorations to photograph the remains of the *Titanic.*
un•der•sea (un′dər sē′ *or* un′dər sē′) *adjective.*

unison The making of the same sounds or movements at the same time. We recited the poem in *unison.*
u•ni•son (ū′nə sən) *noun.*

universe Everything that exists, including the Earth and all of space. It is difficult to imagine the size of the *universe.*
u•ni•verse (ū′nə vûrs′) *noun, plural* **universes.**

Word History

Universe comes from a Latin word that means "the whole world."

at; āpe; fär; câre; end; mē; it; īce; pîerce; hot; ōld; sông; fôrk; oil; out; up; ūse; rüle; pu̇ll; tûrn; chin; sing; shop; thin; <u>th</u>is; hw in white; zh in treasure. The symbol ə stands for the unstressed vowel sound in about, taken, pencil, lemon, and circus.

Vv

valiant Brave; courageous; heroic. The *valiant* knight saved the princess from danger.
▲**Synonym:** stouthearted
val•iant (val′ yənt) *adjective.*

victorious Having won a victory. The *victorious* army was welcomed home.
vic•to•ri•ous (vik tôr′ē əs) *adjective.*

vilest Most repulsive; most foul. It was the *vilest* smell I had ever encountered.
▲**Synonym:** nastiest
vilest (vīl′ əst) *adjective.*

visual **1.** Relating to or used in seeing. Eyeglasses are used to correct *visual* defects. **2.** Able to be seen; visible. The teacher used charts, slides, and other *visual* aids to help explain how the heart works.
vis•u•al (vizh′ü əl) *adjective.*

void An empty space. The whole group fell silent, leaving an awkward *void. Noun.*—Having no legal force; not valid. After the investigation, the election results were declared *void. Adjective.*
void (void) *noun, plural* **voids;** *adjective.*

voyage **1.** A journey by water or through space. Christopher Columbus made *voyages* to the New World in 1492 and 1493. **2.** A long journey. A *voyage* around the Earth in a sailing ship takes many months.
voy•age (voi′ij) *noun, plural* **voyages.**

Ww

ware **1.** Things for sale. The street vendors put their *wares* on display in the public square. **2.** Dishes, pots, and other things used for cooking or eating. We bought a new piece of ceramic *ware* at the fair.
▲ Another word that sounds like this is **wear.**
ware (wâr) *noun, plural* **wares.**

wave To move freely back and forth or up and down; move with a swaying motion. The stalks of wheat *waved* in the wind. *Verb.* —A long, moving ridge of water on the surface of a body of water. The ship rode gently over the *waves. Noun.*
wave (wāv) *verb,* **waved, waving;** *noun, plural* **waves.**

whopper 1. A monstrous lie. I told my teacher a *whopper* because I hadn't done my homework. **2.** Something unusually large. The fish I caught this weekend was a *whopper!*
whop•per (hwop′ər *or* wop′ər) *noun, plural* **whoppers.**

whopper *(def. 2)*

wide-open Opened to a large or to the full extent. Our dog escaped through the *wide-open* gate.
wide•o•pen (wīd′ ō′ pən) *adjective.*

worthwhile Good enough or important enough to spend time, effort, or money on. Doing volunteer work at the hospital is a *worthwhile* activity.
worth•while (wûrth′hwīl′ *or* wûrth′wīl′) *adjective.*

at; **ā**pe; f**ä**r; c**â**re; **e**nd; m**ē**; **i**t; **ī**ce; p**î**erce; h**o**t; **ō**ld; s**ô**ng; f**ô**rk; **oi**l; **ou**t; **u**p; **ū**se; r**ü**le; p**u̇**ll; t**û**rn; **ch**in; si**ng**; **sh**op; **th**in; **th**is; **hw** in **wh**ite; **zh** in trea**s**ure. The symbol **ə** stands for the unstressed vowel sound in **a**bout, tak**e**n, penc**i**l, lem**o**n, and circ**u**s.

ACKNOWLEDGMENTS

The publisher gratefully acknowledges permission to reprint the following copyrighted material.

ADVENTURE IN SPACE: THE FLIGHT TO FIX THE HUBBLE by Elaine Scott, photographs by Margaret Miller. Text copyright © 1995 by Elaine Scott. Photographs copyright © 1995 by Margaret Miller. Used by permission of Hyperion Books for Children.

"Alexander the Great" from THE GOLDEN DAYS OF GREECE by Olivia Coolidge. Copyright © 1968 by Olivia Coolidge. Used by permission of Russell and Volkening, Inc.

"The All-American Slurp" by Lensey Namioka from VISIONS, edited by Donald R. Gallo. Copyright © 1987 by Lensey Namioka. Reprinted by permission of Lensey Namioka. All rights reserved by the Author.

"Bellerophon and the Flying Horse" from TALES FROM ANCIENT GREECE by Pamela Oldfield. Copyright © 1988 by Grisewood and Dempsey, Ltd. Used by permission of Doubleday, a division of Random House, Inc.

"A Boy of Unusual Vision" by Alice Steinbach. Article courtesy of The Baltimore Sun. Used by permission.

"Child of the Owl" from CHILD OF THE OWL by Laurence Yep. Copyright © 1977 by Laurence Yep. Published by HarperCollins Publishers, Inc. Reprinted by permission of the Author and Curtis Brown, Ltd.

"The Circuit" by Francisco Jiménez first published in the Arizona Quarterly Autumn, 1973. Copyright © 1973 by Francisco Jiménez. Reprinted by permission of the author.

"Daydreamers" by Eloise Greenfield. Text copyright © 1981 by Eloise Greenfield. Reprinted by permission of the publisher, Dial Books for Young Readers, a division of Penguin Putnam, Inc.

"Exploring the Titanic" from EXPLORING THE TITANIC by Robert D. Ballard. A Scholastic/Madison Press book copyright © 1988. Reprinted by permission of the publisher.

"I Go Forth to Move About the Earth" by Alonzo Lopez from WHISPERING WIND by Terry Allen. Copyright © 1972 by the Institute of American Indian Arts. Used by permission of Doubleday, a division of Random House, Inc.

"I May, I Might, I Must" copyright © 1959 by Marianne Moore, © renewed 1987 by Lawrence E. Brinn and Louise Crane, Executors of the Estate of Marianne Moore from THE COMPLETE POEMS OF MARIANNE MOORE by Marianne Moore. Used by permission of Viking Penguin, a division of Penguin Putnam, Inc.

"Last Summer with Maizon" excerpts from LAST SUMMER WITH MAIZON by Jacqueline Woodson. Copyright © 1990 by Jacqueline Woodson. Used by permission of Random House, Inc.

MANDELA written and illustrated by Floyd Cooper. Copyright © 1996 by Floyd Cooper. Used by permission of Philomel Books, a division of Penguin Putnam, Inc.

"The Microscope" by Maxine W. Kumin. Originally published in The Atlantic Monthly. Copyright © 1963 by Maxine W. Kumin. Used by permission of WW Norton and Company.

Excerpt from MUMMIES, TOMBS, AND TREASURE. Text copyright © 1987 by Lila Perl. Reprinted by permission of Clarion Books/Houghton Mifflin Company. All rights reserved.

"My Friend Flicka" by Mary O'Hara. Copyright © 1941 by Mary O'Hara. Used by permission of HarperCollins Publishers, Inc.

"My Uncle Dan" from POETRY IS by Ted Hughes. Copyright © 1967 by Ted Hughes. Used by permission of Doubleday, a division of Random House, Inc.

"Number the Stars" from NUMBER THE STARS by Lois Lowry. Copyright © 1989 by Lois Lowry. Reprinted by permission of Houghton Mifflin Company. All rights reserved.

"Opera, Karate and Bandits" from THE LAND I LOST: ADVENTURES OF A BOY IN VIETNAM by Huynh Quang Nhuong. Copyright © 1982 by Huynh Quang Nhuong. Reprinted by permission of HarperCollins Publishers.

OVER THE TOP OF THE WORLD by Will Stegner and Jon Bowermaster. Published by Scholastic Press, a division of Scholastic, Inc. Copyright © 1997 by Expeditions Unlimited, Inc. Used by permission of Scholastic, Inc.

PAINTERS OF THE CAVES by Patricia Lauber. Copyright © 1998 by Patricia Lauber. Used by permission of National Geographic Society.

"People" from ALL THAT SUNLIGHT by Charlotte Zolotow. Text copyright © 1967, renewed copyright © 1995 by Charlotte Zolotow. Reprinted by permission of Scott Treimel New York.

"The Phantom Tollbooth" by Susan Nanus, based on the book by Norton Juster. Copyright ©1977 by Susan Nanus and Norton Juster. Reprinted by permission of Samuel French, Inc.

"Purple Snake" text copyright © 1996 by Pat Mora. From the book CONFETTI: POEMS FOR CHILDREN by Pat Mora. Permission granted by Lee and Low Books, Inc., 95 Madison Avenue, New York, NY 10016.

"Rain, Rain, Go Away" copyright © 1959 by King Size Publications, Inc. from BUY JUPITER AND OTHER STORIES by Isaac Asimov. Used by permission of Doubleday, a division of Random House, Inc.

RUMPLESTILTSKIN'S DAUGHTER by Diane Stanley. Copyright © 1997 by Diane Stanley. Used by permission of Morrow Junior Books, a division of William Morrow & Company, Inc.

"The School Play" from LOCAL NEWS by Gary Soto. Copyright © 1993 by Gary Soto. Used by permission of Harcourt, Inc.

THE SINGING MAN: Adapted from a West African Folktale by Angela Shelf Medearis, illustrated by Terea Shaffer. Text copyright © 1994 by Angela Shelf Medearis. Illustrations copyright © 1994 by Terea Shaffer. Reprinted by permission of Holiday House, Inc.

"A Song of Greatness" from THE CHILDREN SING IN THE FAR WEST by Mary Austin. Copyright 1928 by Mary Austin. Copyright © renewed 1956 by Kenneth M. Chapman and Mary C. Wheelwright. Reprinted by permission of Houghton Mifflin Co. All rights reserved.

S.O.R. LOSERS reprinted with the permission of Simon & Schuster Books for Young Readers, an imprint of Simon & Schuster Children's Publishing Division from S.O.R. LOSERS by Avi. Copyright © 1984 by Avi Wortis.

"Stopping by Woods on a Snowy Evening" from THE POETRY OF ROBERT FROST, edited by Edward Connery Lathem. Copyright © 1951 by Robert Frost. Copyright ©1923, 1969 by Henry Holt and Co., Inc. Reprinted by permission of Henry Holt and Co., Inc.

TA-NA-E-KA by Mary Whitebird, published in SCHOLASTIC VOICE, December 13, 1973. Copyright © 1973 by Scholastic, Inc. Used by permission.

"To Look at Any Thing" from THE LIVING SEED by John Moffitt. Copyright © 1962 by John Moffitt and renewed 1989 by Henry Moffit. Reprinted by permission of Harcourt Brace & Company.

"To You" from COLLECTED POEMS by Langston Hughes. Copyright © 1994 by the Estate of Langston Hughes. Reprinted by permission of Alfred A. Knopf, Inc.

"Travellers" by Arthur St. John Adcock from THE BOOK OF A THOUSAND POEMS. Reprinted by permission.

"Viva New Jersey" by Gloria Gonzalez. Copyright © 1993 by Gloria Gonzalez. From JOIN IN: MULTIETHNIC SHORT STORIES edited by Donald R. Gallo. Used by permission of Delacorte Press, a division of Random House, Inc.

Cover Illustration
Kinuko Y. Craft

Illustration
Larry McEntire, 16; Annie Bissett, 38; Tuko Fujisaki, 39; Carl Mazer, 43; Yoshi Miyake, 42-59; Rose Zgodzinski, 62; Annie Bissett, 82; Annie Bissett, 83; David Bamundo, 83; Joe LeMonnier, 98; Stanford Kay, 108; Tom Feelings, 110-111; Linda Frichtel, 112; Annie Bissett, 136; David Bamundo, 137; Shonto Begay, 140-154; Rose Zgodzinski, 158; Stanford Kay, 186; Annie Bissett, 206; Annie Bissett, 216; Chuck Gonzales, 217; Shane Warren Evans, 220; Stanford Kay, 238; Jack E. Davis, 242-255; Rose Zgodzinski, 258; David Bamundo, 259; Stanford Kay, 286; Chris Lensch, 287; Joe LeMonnier, 293; Annie Bissett, 306; Stanford Kay, 316; David Bamundo, 317; Phillip Dvorak, 318-319; Linda Montgomery, 320; Annie Bissett, 340; Annie Bissett, 341; Chuck Gonzales, 341; 344-345: Corel; insets:Gordon Wiltsie/International Arctic Project 346-347, t. & b.: Corel; inset: Gordon Wiltsie/International Arctic Project 346, t.l.: Corel 348-49 t. & b.: Corel; inset: Gordon Wiltsie/International Arctic Project 348 b.l.: Corel 350-351 t. & b.: Corel 350 t.: Gordon Wiltsie/International Arctic Project 351 b.: Gordon Wiltsie/International Arctic Project 352: Gordon Wiltsie/International Arctic Project 354: Corel; inset: Gordon Wiltsie/International Arctic Project 355 t. & b.: Corel 356: Corel 357 t. & b.: Gordon Wiltsie/International Arctic Project 358-359 t. & b.: Corel 358 inset: Gordon Wiltsie/International Arctic Project 360: Corel 361: Corel; t.l.: Gordon Wiltsie/International Arctic Project; b.r.: Corel 362: Corel; inset: Gordon Wiltsie/International Arctic Project 363: Corel; b.: Corel Peter Neumann, 353; Rose Zgodzinski, 366; Matt McElligott, 370-401; Annie Bissett, 404; Chuck Gonzales, 405; Rose Zgodzinski, 430; Chuck Gonzales, 431; Stanford Kay, 440; Bob Dombrowski, 444; Stanford Kay, 466; Joe LeMonnier, 480; Rose Zgodzinski, 530; Chris Lensch, 531; Annie Bissett, 540; Rose Zgodzinski, 541; David Bamundo, 541; Gary Taxali, 542-543; Stefano Vitale, 544; Joe LeMonnier, 548; Rose Zgodzinski, 572; Chris Lensch, 573; Stanford Kay, 598; Rose Zgodzinski, 618; Rose Zgodzinski, 634; David Bamundo, 635; Stanford Kay, 644; Tuko Fujisaki, 645; Chuck Gonzales, 656, 680, 685; John Carrozza, 660, 675; Katie Lee, 664, 671.

Photography
18-19: Dale Kennington/Superstock. 40-41: Jane Wooster pScott/Superstock. 61: Dave Bartruff. 64-65: Christian Pierrre/Private Collection/Superstock. 66-67: Estate of Ralph Fasanella. 84-85: Menil Foundation, Houston, TX/Lauros-Giraudon, Paris/Superstock. 100-101: David David Gallery, Philadelphia/Superstock. 107: David Lomax/Robert harding Picture Library. 107: Werner Forman Archive/Statens Historiska Museum, Stockholm/Art Resource, NY. 114-115: National Museum of American Art, Washington, DC/Art Resource, NY. 138-139: Buffalo Bill Historical Center, Cody, WY. 157: B. Seitz/Photo Researchers, Inc. 160-161: National Museum of American Art, Washington, DC/Art Resource, NY. 185: Vanessa Vick/Photo Researchers, Inc. 205: Keren Su/Pacific Stock. 208-209: Museum of Fine Arts, Springfield, MA. 215: Archaeological Museum, Jerash, Jordan/Erich Lessing/Art Resource, NY. 215: Kenneth Garrett/National Geographic Society Image Collection. 218-219: Peter Van Rhijn/Superstock. 223: Tate Gallery, London/Art Resource, NY. 237: Will and Deni McIntyre/Photo Researchers, Inc. 257: David Frazier/The Image Works. 240-241: The Whitney Museum of American Art, NY. 260-261: Manya Igel Fine Arts Ltd., London/The Bridgeman Art Library International. 284: W. Robert Moore/National Geographic Society Image Collection. 288-289: The Freer Gallery of Art, Washington, DC. 306: Erwin and Peggy Bauer. 308-309: The Bridgeman Art Library International. 322-323: William Allard/National Geographic Society Image Collection. 338: Michael Holford. 342-343: National Museum of American Art, Washington, DC/Art Resource, NY. 344-345: Corel; insets: Gordon Wiltsie/International Arctic Project. 346-347: t.&b.: Corel; inset: Gordon Wiltsie/International Arctic Project. 346: t.l: Corel. 348-349 t.&b.: Corel; inset: Gordon Wiltsie/International Arctic Project. 348 b.l.: Corel. 348: b. l. WorldSat International Inc., Mississauga, Ontario, Canada. 350-351: t.&b.: Corel. 350: t.: Gordon Wiltsie/International Arctic Project. 351 b.: Gordon Wiltsie/International Arctic Project. 352: Gordon Wiltsie/International Arctic Project. 354: Corel; inset: Gordon Wiltsie/International Arctic Project. 355 t.&b.: Corel. 356: Corel. 357 t.&b.: Gordon Wiltsie/International Arctic Project. 358-359 t.&b.: Corel. 358 inset: Gordon Wiltsie/International Arctic Project. 360: Corel. 361: Corel; t.l.: Gordon Wiltsie/International Arctic Project; b.r.: Corel 362: Corel; inset: Gordon Wiltsie/International Arctic Project. 363: Corel; b.: Corel. 368-369: Christie's Images. 406-407: Motion Picture and Television Photo Archive. 428: Emory Kristof/National Geographic Society Image Collection. 432-433: Motion Picture and Television Photo Archive. 439: Science Photo Library, London/Photo Researchers, Inc. 442: t.r. Biophoto Associates/Science Source. 442-443: c. Science VU/Visuals Unlimited. 447: Christie's Images. 468-469: Bibliotheque Nationale Paris/E.T. Archive. 482-483: Superstock. 499: Mehau Kulyk/Science Photo Library, London/Photo Researchers, Inc. 502-503: John Holcroft/Superstock. 532-533: Sheldon Memorial Art Gallery, Nebraska Art Association, Gift of Carl Rohman. 546-547: Schomburg Center, The New York Public Library/Art Resource, NY. 574-575: David Coleman/Stock Boston. 596-597: Buddy Mays Travel Stock. 601: Bibliotheque Nationale Paris/E.T. Archive. 620-621: Sotheby's Picture Library. 633: Corbis Images. 636-637: National Museum of American Art, Washington, DC/Art Resource, NY. 643: David Parker/Science Photo Library, London/Photo Researchers, Inc. 643: Christie's Images. 646-647: c. Jack Jeffers/Superstock.